The
Minister's
Wife

The Minister's Wife

Her Role in Nineteenth-Century American Evangelicalism

Leonard I. Sweet

Temple University Press • Philadelphia

To

• Winthrop S. Hudson •

Who taught me what it means
to be a historian and a human being

Temple University Press
© 1983 by Temple University. All rights reserved
Published 1983
Printed in the United States of America

Library of Congress Cataloging in Publication Data

Sweet, Leonard I.
    The minister's wife.

    Includes bibliographical references and index.
    1. Clergymen's wives—United States—History—
19th century.   2. Evangelicalism—United States—
History—19th century.   3. United States—Church
history—19th century.   I. Title.
BV4395.S94   1982   280'.4   82-10738
ISBN 0-87722-283-5

Contents

Acknowledgments

The Devil is once said to have been asked, "Why did you leave paradise?" "I wanted to be an author," he replied. It is a sad day when a person sets out to write a book. From then on one's thoughts are no longer one's own; the mind drifts away from conversations with friends; blank stares greet family importunities; peace is vanished; tranquility departs; and restlessness becomes a constant companion. If writing a book is a special torture, it behooves an author to thank those who endured the pain.

My wife Joan and sons Leonard Jr. and Justin have put up with a typewriter at the beach, papers on the dining room table, books in the bathroom, and research expenses in the family budget. Scholarship requires many hermit tasks, and their good humor about the writer's unwilling vow of "poverty, chastity and obedience" brightened many a lonely day.

The support system of friends sustained my research and writing at various points of need. Craig Brown generously allowed me the use of his Toronto home for writing one summer month, and thanks to Edith and Philip Ditzel a cottage at Conesus Lake was always available for short writing stints. Myrtle Merritt, after spending a small fortune fixing up the pastor's study at the Geneseo United Methodist Church, gracefully took in stride my scarring of the new office with mountains of files and deserts of notepaper. Connie Johnston typed the manuscript for an author who can never resist defacing a neatly typed page. Michelle Mahoney Matison's sunny disposition and winning smile accompanied many trespasses on her patience. One of my students, Susan Tew, proofread the page proofs with dispatch and rigor. My sincere apologies also go to copy editor Jane Barry for testing her skills so severely. A copy editor, I have discovered, can be a writer's best friend.

The staffs of the two libraries with which I am associated, Colgate Rochester Divinity School/Bexly Hall/Crozer and the University of Rochester, have nurtured my research in knowledgeable and kind ways. Ann Finger and Carol Cavanaugh from the university and Peter VandenBerge, Patricia Keller and Connie Reed from the seminary have kept me out of mischief fighting interlibrary loan deadlines and tracking their leads. Thanks to them no one can grouse at the absence of enough footnotes. During my stay at Oberlin College, archivist W. E. Bigglestone demonstrated over and over again his professionalism and mastery of Finney bibliographies. Except for an absolutely horrid restaurant tip, all his suggestions proved unerring and invaluable. Margaret Clune of the Chemung County Historical Society, and Hazel Bird of the First Presbyterian Church in Batavia guided me through their collections with skill and dispatch. I also want to thank the Maryland Historical Society, Moorland-Spingarn Research Center, the Oberlin College Archives, and the Vermont Historical Society for permission to quote from manuscript collections.

My thinking about the traditions of women in the ministry has been steered along the way by various conversations with scholars. Timothy L. Smith and Nancy Hardesty first helped me to see how the holiness movement helped to thrust the pastor's wife into positions of public eminence alongside her husband. Faith Burgess provided insightful criticism on an early draft of Chapter seven, delivered at the 1979 American Society of Church History meeting. Dorothy Sterling directed me down trails to black ministers' wives, William R. Phinney gave some helpful ideas on where to locate material on John Wesley's position on women preachers, and Garth Rosell allowed me an advance look at the unexpurgated memoirs of Finney he is editing with Richard Dupuis. I am convinced, after numerous transatlantic communications with Dupuis, that this London psychotherapist knows more about Finney than any person alive.

It never ceases to amaze me how gracious and unselfish scholars can be about reading and reviewing other people's manuscripts. The book has been immeasurably enriched by critical readings from Winthrop S. Hudson, Ralph E. Luker, Martin E. Marty, John M. Mulder and Richard Dupuis. They kept me from many unguarded statements and underdeveloped ideas.

Finally, I dedicate this book to my mentor, Winthrop S. Hudson, a lover of history and a hater of uncivility. Win has taught generations of American religious historians what it means to be a true scholar. We are all proud to be his students.

The
Minister's
Wife

Introduction

> Of the Ecclesiastical Historian we can complain, as we did of his Political fellow-craftsman, that his inquiries turn rather on the outward mechanism, the mere hulls and superficial accidents of the object, than on the object itself: as if the Church lay in Bishops' Chapter-houses and Ecumenic Council-halls, and Cardinals' Conclaves, and not far more in the hearts of Believing Men. . . . The History of the Church is a History of Invisible as well as of the Visible Church; which latter, if disjointed from the former, is but a vacant edifice.
>
> Thomas Carlyle

The majority of pew occupants throughout the history of American religion have been women, and scholars are now furiously studying their attitudes and activities. The nineteenth century saw the minister's wife emerge from the crowd to become the institutional leader of church women and to occupy one of the most coveted careers available to American women. If we are to fully understand the history of women in American religion, a pursuit that has already turned so much of our historiography upside down, the place of ministers' wives deserves protracted discussion. This study is a modest first step in the exciting direction of restoring the missing words "minister's wife" to the lexicon of American religious history and reconstructing the diverse and complex historical experiences of this remarkable group of nineteenth-century women.[1]

Four models illustrate the images and roles available to ministers' wives from the sixteenth to the nineteenth centuries: the Companion, a ministering angel who held up her husband's hands in his sacred calling; the Sacrificer, who clasped her hands in pious resignation, asked little from her husband, financially or emotionally, and "hindered him not in his work" by staying out of his way and raising the family on her own; the Assistant, who became her husband's right-arm, sharing many pastoral responsibilities and functioning as an extension of his ministry; and the Partner, who ministered with both her own hands, developed a ministry alongside her husband, and often served as the pastor's pastor. The models also embody the four major types of spirituality available to women and promoted in the Sunday school libraries of the nineteenth century. I have selected certain women to exemplify the possibilities, the perils, and some of the peculiarities of these four models of women in ministry: Katherine Luther and Sarah Edwards (Companion), Peggy Dow (Sacrificer), Lydia Finney (Assistant), and Elizabeth Atkinson Finney (Partner).

These models are used with some trepidation. First, every minister's wife no doubt developed her own unique strategy. The underused William B. Sprague collection at Princeton Theological Seminary, for example, contains numerous funeral sermons for ministers' wives. Many of these reveal styles of ministry that fit nicely into the four models outlined in this book. Some, however, do not. In 1821 Elizabeth Lathrop, a Presbyterian, was portrayed as "unusually domestic in her feelings" for a minister's wife. With the frankness characteristic of the day, little was found to memorialize about her years as the wife of a minister: "As there was little in the *life* of Mrs. Lathrop, to distinguish her greatly from other excellent women moving in the same sphere, so also her *character* was of a cast that was not likely to attract extensively the observation of the world."[2] Similarly, the 1863 funeral sermon for the Lutheran Susan C. Pohlman described her as a minister's wife who shunned the noise of pious assemblies, seldom ventured out of her home, harbored a consuming fear of death, distrusted the solidness of her spiritual state, and was jealous of other women's religious experiences.[3] While not wishing to minimize women's wide range of responses to their husband's vocation, however, my four models depict the options most often pursued by the wives of Evangelical ministers.[4]

The problem of representativeness is the second difficulty in using such a limited number of models. The necessary background sections on the Reformation era and the colonial period are regrettably sketchy and are thus the ones that raise the issue of representativeness most acutely. Because the heart of this book is in the nineteenth-century period, final judgments about the prevalence of the Companion model in the colonial period must await further studies of the wives of less celebrated, more typical ministers, not only in New England, but also in the Middle Colonies and the South. Peggy Dow, Lydia Finney, and Elizabeth Atkinson Finney are lifted out from among the other women studied because their activities, visibility, or publications placed them in positions of influence within the Evangelical sisterhood. These models are not meant to be in any way "ideal types," which do great damage to the integrity of the past because every typology is in some way an intellectual stereotype and thus an assassination of reality. Rather, they are historical reconstructions of reality that must be shaded with the gradations and variations of other experiences. There is no such thing as "women's past" or "the history of the minister's wife." There are only a multiplicity of histories, pasts that are never really past. These four models of women in the ministry, it is hoped, allow faith to be kept with the many pasts of ministers' wives in American religion.

The third difficulty centers on the movement through the chapters of this book from one model to another, a passage through time that should not be interpreted as suggesting any kind of cultural "paradigm shift" in styles of ministry. Wives of ministers kept inventing new roles as they resisted or modified forms of subordination and adjusted to changing historical realities. They did not always throw the old roles away. There can be found in any period of American history a coexistence and intermingling of many models, although at times one model seems to predominate. Indeed, none of these models are obsolete even today. Nor is the career of the minister's wife. Some denominational periodicals and journals, for example, continue to perpetuate the early nineteenth-century custom of printing necrologies for both ministers and their spouses.

The patterns set by the first ministers' wives, Katherine Luther and Idelette Calvin, are explored in Chapter one, as the Companion model is interpreted within the context of Continental and New England influences and precedents. These women in ministry were obedient, subservient companions, or "yoke fellows," to their husbands. They had no public involvement or visibility, and their assistance seldom went beyond the domestic horizon. Here in the background ministers' wives like Margarete Cranmer, Margaret Baxter, Mary Williams, Katharine Mather, and Maria Cotton and Abigail Phillips Mather established warm, financially secure environments hospitable to ministry and developed marital relationships of great tenderness and affection. The image of "yokefellow" was replaced by that of "helpmeet" in the eighteenth century, and Sarah Pierrepont Edwards and her daughter Esther Edwards Burr were transitional figures who tentatively began using their own hands in ministry through visitation and women's prayer meetings, as well as doing all in their power to prop up their husbands' arms.

Chapter two examines the forces that began to crack the Companion model. How did ministers come to require religiously active wives? How did women come from the background of companionship to the forefront of assistantship and partnership? How did women come to dominate the Second Great Awakening? Donald Mathews has written that "women made southern Evangelicalism possible." They also made possible the tradition of American Evangelicalism, called by another of its students "one of the more dynamic and expansive social forces of the early-nineteenth-century era."[5] The stereotype of women as chosen to be and men as chosen to do was shrugged off by Evangelical women. The paradox that "home," "mother," and "heaven" were both America's most sacred words and American women's most liberating words is traced here to the economic consequences of the birth of the modern family, the development of the sphere doctrine (the dominant social myth of the nineteenth century), the emerging notion of a distinct and superior female identity, and the specialization in and professionalization of motherhood. The expansion of women's place to include public forums and the increased authority of women in many realms of life was justified by the perception of woman as guardian of morality, custodian of conversion, and cornerstone of society. The responsibility for the socialization of children and the moralization of men issued from the first role. This self-image also promoted women from agents of moral transmission to agents of cultural transformation as well. The Evangelical religious gestalt, which in some ways supported the erosion of male authority and the conception of women as innately more spiritual than men, defined women as responsible for conversion and permitted them to operate the machinery of evangelism. This trend was magnified by the millennial hopes and thrusts of the Great Awakening. Millennial ideology not only provided theological endorsement for the sexual egalitarianism of the few Shakers and Oneidians, but extricated Evangelicalism from the philosophy that women were private beings without public importance of a social or political nature. Women's millennial vocation as cornerstone of society resolved the contradiction of the sphere doctrine in favor of a more public role for women. In an age of kingdom building, women became the chief brick layers. Fittingly, they believed, the one who brought the Savior into the world was the one who would now bring the kingdom into the world.

Peggy Dow represents in Chapter three the dark side of the sphere doctrine: the thoroughly self-effacing, domesticated figure of the Sacrificer who became a hero because she bore her husband's name and burdens and became a martyr to his ministry. She gave up her dreams and submerged her needs and desires to his calling. Although Peggy did this willingly, other minister's wives were forced into the Sacrificer role by social and economic circumstances. As a foil against which the other models are discussed, Dow represents the redemptive model of spirituality that was reflected in countless memoirs of women sufferers and invalids whose piety brightened the dark, sickly rooms where they spent their short lives.

Charles G. Finney's first wife, Lydia, represents the liberating side of spherical ideology, the active Assistant whose physical landscape was open and expansive and who refused to hide her candle under a broom, mop, or dustpan. Her duties were as much kingdom building as homemaking. The antecedents of the Assistant role are traced in Chapter four to the eighteenth-century Evangelical Revival, where women were given unprecedented positions of leadership. Charles Finney was made from the same clay as John Wesley. Early Methodist women, whose lives were widely publicized through tracts and biographies that did not tone down Wesley's belief that obedience to God sometimes necessitated rebellion against social convention, served as role models for ministers' wives stirred by the doctrine of "usefulness," the Evangelical equivalent of the Puritan concept of "calling." Lydia Finney lived a life of social, religious, and even political influence. For her, the role of the minister's wife became an occupation, a profession, a ministerial vocation.

Chapter five explores, within the framework of revivalism's debt to women, how the ambition to become a minister's wife both reflected and raised female aspirations. Frances Trollope contended that the clergy were the most eligible group of males in America,[6] and never more so than after a Finney revival. While a teacher at a Rochester seminary, Elizabeth Atkinson (the future Elizabeth Finney) observed the effect of Finney's 1830–1831 Rochester revival on one school. Over forty of the male students would become "ministers and missionaries."[7] At Oberlin College, a millennial community inspired by an evangelist whose theology, it was believed, would "be the theology of the Millennium," women were trained to "take up their cross" and become the heartbeat of new measures revivalism.[8] Forty-three Oberlin women students were asked their vocational ambitions in 1836, and twenty-seven confessed to aspiring to labor either as a missionary (i.e., a missionary wife, since almost all of Oberlin's women graduates married) or in "some sphere of Christian usefulness," code words, as we shall see, for marriage to a minister.

Between 1837 and 1846, 65 percent of Oberlin's women graduates married Oberlin men, while many others found minister husbands trained in other theological schools.[9] The ministers Finney trained did not pick the shy, retiring types for their wives. They looked for women with the domestic skills of a Martha (Luke 10:40), the commitment to motherhood of a Hannah (1 Samuel 1:20–2:19), the humility of an Elizabeth (Luke 1:43), the ambition of a Miriam (Numbers 12:1, 2), the public courage and leadership of a Deborah (Judges 4:4), the mental alertness of a Mary (Luke 10:39), the business sense of a Lydia (Acts 16:14, 15), the sure-footed hospitality of a Shunammite (2 Kings 4:8–10), the talent for public speaking of a Priscilla (Romans 16:3), and the pious zeal and benevolent engagement of a Dorcas (Acts 9:36). A New York Baptist minister asked the daring abolitionist schoolteacher Prudence Crandall to marry him at the peak of her troubles in Canterbury, Connecticut. Such clergymen's wives as Prudence Crandall Philleo were some of the least likely women in antebellum society to be blank sheets on which men projected their desires and definitions.[10]

Marrying a minister was more than a blessed alternative to domestic humdrum and the humbug of social formulas, and more than the right to pick up the crumbs and bones of religious opportunity that dropped from the table of a husband's ministry. It was a passport to influence, deference, and power. Women were rarely allowed to participate actively in nineteenth-century culture; of the few exceptions to this rule, the most important was the church. Here they created and inhabited a world that was remarkably permissive. Here the Baptist and Methodist encouragement to tell conversion stories and spark revivals led to such forms of public speaking as prayer, testimony, and exhortation. It was here, in prayer meetings and class meetings, not in antislavery societies, that women first learned to speak in public and men first learned to respond to female public proclamations ("I felt very happy under her wholesome admonitions").[11] Wives of preachers were even further exempted from the restrictions on public speaking imposed on the rest of their sex. They benefited both from the ice-cutting examples of female preachers, a prominent feature of antebellum popular religion slighted, if not skipped entirely, by American religious historians, and from the threefold rationale for their labors: pragmatism, millennialism, and perfectionism. Energetic evangelists all, ministers' wives became professional guides through the dark places of the soul. They labored actively on the Damascus Road and did patrol duty on the Jericho Road as well. They made up, with other Evangelical women what Joan Jacobs Brumberg felicitously calls "the apostolate of women."[12] In short, as Whitney Cross pointed out long ago, women dominate the history of revivalism.[13]

The institutional history of women in American religion is the subject of Chapter Six, which explores Lydia Finney's religious and social life in the antebellum period. What absorbed the Assistant's attention and energies; what excited her ambitions; what mobilized her talents? Ministers' wives founded many of the women's organizations that burst upon the scene around 1800, stirred up by economic and social conditions and most particularly by revivalism, and they managed them so well that women became the major force to be reckoned with in America's voluntary system. Like Dickens's Mrs. Pardiggle ("I am a School lady, I am a Visiting lady, I am a Reading lady, I am a Distributing lady; I am on the local Linen Box Committee, and many general Committees; and my canvassing alone is very extensive"), women's societies were humming beehives of activity and energy, and their communication networks honeycombs of sororal solidarity. Ministers' wives became the heart and soul of religious organizations in America's churches and towns.

If industry was women's forte, excess was their foible. Some never learned that Christians must agree not to oppress one another with their piety. But in spite of, or perhaps because of, this merciless exuberance, women wound themselves around every artery of Evangelicalism's heart. To appropriate a *mot* by the celebrated nineteenth-century preacher Phillips Brooks, women often became the pillars of religion in the sense of the Pillars of Hercules, beyond whom no one might sail. When Evangelical women stood up, men often sat down. The charge that women clutched at the symbols of power, missing the substance for the shadows but patronized for their big hearts, bottomless pocketbooks, and nimble fingers, are addressed in this chapter both by appeals to social science theories about power and by an examination of the ecclesiastical, psychological, and economic hold women had over the clergy. Special attention is paid to ministerial dependence on women for bankrolling the building of the millennium. "If the fifteenth century discovered America to the Old World," Frances Harper observed at the World Congress of 1893, "the nineteenth is discovering woman to herself."[14] Evangelical women and the Lydia Finneys who ministered with them did not simply squirm in the nets of definition cast over them by society; with remarkable strength and resourcefulness, they grappled with constraints and contradictions. We owe these women of the Second Great Awakening our greatest tribute. They improved situations by living in them.

Elizabeth Atkinson Finney, the revivalist's second wife, represents the Partner of ministry: she did not remain in the background of her husband's career like Peggy Dow or roam independently behind him like Finney's first wife, Lydia, but stood beside him. After Finney's marriage to Elizabeth, it is no longer appropriate to speak of "Finney's revivals"; one must speak of "the Finneys' revivals." While strongly supporting Finney, Elizabeth was also true to herself, drawing upon her own unique personality to carry out her special ministry. Charles's third wife, Rebecca Rayl, like Elizabeth, found restrictive notions of "woman's place" a daily grief and grind and kicked against cramping cultural expectations. Her story is not featured in Chapter seven, among other reasons because one plays fast and loose with fragmentary evidence if more is said than that she lobbied for the hiring of female clerks in the nation's capital, floated free of sexual stereotypes, and assisted Finney in his feminist-oriented anti-Masonic crusade. The career of the fiercely independent Julia Jones Beecher, wife of the Elmira, New York, pastor Thomas Kennicut Beecher, illustrates that the Partner model encompassed cases where the wife's ministry eclipsed that of her husband.

The final chapter takes some tentative steps into the last third of the nineteenth century, and the early part of the twentieth to see what happened to the tradition of women in the ministry. The title of Mary Schauffler Platt's handbook for missionary wives, *The Home with the Open Door* (1920), summarizes how far many had come from defining ministers' wives vocationally.[15] The wife of a minister or missionary was increasingly roped off within the realm of homemaker. A minister's wife did not help her husband *in* ministry so much as help him prepare *for* ministry; that is, her assets were primarily psychological. The reasons for the fraying of the Assistant and Partner models include sociosexual developments, the professionalization of the ministry, the diversionary effect of the Civil War, the wedding of Protestantism to capitalist culture, the secularization of the feminist movement, industrialization and immigration, the reassertion of male authority with the end of itinerancy, and the emergence of the constitutional issues that dominated women's religious history in this period. Although the tradition of ministers' wives as women in the ministry lost much of its vitality in the twentieth century, men like Robert Semple, a missionary evangelist to China, could still be found searching for wives who could face and outface the challenge of ministry. He discovered such a person in a woman who would go on after his death to establish a ministry that far eclipsed his: Aimee Semple McPherson. But for the most part the status of the minister's wife became less and less functionally relevant to the profession of ministry; and more and more women married ministers, not because of, but either in spite of or in indifference to, their husbands' calling. In the first half of the twentieth century, more women chafed under the classification "the minister's wife," and women increasingly talked of being companions to their husbands as they walked together through life, not of being helpers to their husbands' calling as they performed the sacred duties of God's service.[16] A position that once had advanced opportunities and creativity for women was now seen as potentially hazardous to these same developments.

• Chapter One •

"She Held Up His Hands"

The Protestant Parsonage and the Companion Model

I love her with all my heart. For she has been created to keep up
your hearth so that you may serve the church born under you,
that is, all that hope in Christ.

> Wolfgang Capito (to Martin Luther
> about Luther's wife, Katherine)

The minister's wife is not the child of the Reformation. She is
the child of the early church, when married men were regularly
ordained. Not until the fourth century did Pope Siricius (384–398)
ban sex for both married and unmarried clergy, thereby paving the
way for the twelfth-century requirement of universal clerical
celibacy.[1] When Martin Luther dropped a bombshell on heaven and
earth, making, in his words, "the angels laugh and the devils weep"
by his 1525 marriage to the courageous Nimpschen nun, Katherine
von Bora, he was neither a traitor to tradition nor a foe of the future.
He had but wended his way back to a more ancient, more apostolic
past—a past, however, that had been suppressed and forgotten by
the people of his day. That is why news of this marriage was a great
scandal. Surely the fruit of this union, some said, must be Antichrist.

The importance of this brazen act does not lie in its challenge to
clerical celibacy, although John K. Yost is correct in writing that
"legalized marriage was the greatest single change which the Protestant Reformation made in the status of the clergy and its relation to
the laity."[2] Rather, it created the Protestant parsonage, which would
have so great an influence upon western attitudes toward family life,
and, as Kenneth Scott Latourette suggested, give new prominence
and esteem to woman's role as wife.[3] A brief look at this first Protestant minister's wife, this "priestes woman" from whom some shrank
as a defiler of the cloth and corrupter of the church, reveals the
originator of the Companion style of clerical marriage that would
dominate Protestant parsonages for the next three hundred years.

Born on 29 January 1499, Katherine von Bora was sent to a
Benedictine convent's boarding school at the age of three, after her
mother's death. At ten she entered a Cistercian cloister at Nimp-

schen for economic reasons and at sixteen became a pious, industrious nun who devoted her time to mass, prayer, embroidery, service in the choir, and reading. The last of these was the cause of her transfer of faith: she was persuaded by Luther's theology as outlined in pamphlets smuggled into the convent. She and eight other renegade nuns pleaded with Luther for assistance in plotting their escape. On Easter eve in 1523, a covered wagon arrived at the Nimpschen convent and left transporting a cargo of nine fish barrels. Such was Luther's scheme for resurrecting nuns from the monastic tomb.

The question now was what to do with them. Luther at first pleaded with their relatives to accept them. When none would, he resolved to marry them off. Katherine had several suitors, but either they summarily left town or they were not to her liking. Frustrated, heartbroken, hounded, she went to Luther's visiting friend and colleague Nicholas von Amsdorf and poured out her troubles. Then, with that dash of daring that would so often spice the personalities of future ministers' wives, she offered, "If I were asked by you or Dr. Luther, I would not say no."

Word of her remark reached Luther, and the seed of an idea began to grow. Katherine was without natural beauty, and Luther's first impression of her was not very positive. He found her reserved and somewhat arrogant. More intimate contact ripened his respect for her, until in May of 1525 he wrote: "If I can manage it, I will take Kate to wife before I die, to spite the devil." On 13 June 1525 he went to her residence, accompanied by four of his friends, and without prior courtship asked for her consent. That same day the forty-two-year-old Martin and the twenty-six-year-old Katherine were married. It was a marriage rooted in esteem that blossomed into love.

On her wedding night Katherine learned that one of her major duties as mistress of a Protestant parsonage was to offer, at whatever hour, welcome and hospitality. Late in the evening Andreas Karlstadt rapped at the door, seeking refuge. She welcomed him with open-handed generosity. She also immediately took on another responsibility that companion-helpmates would come to fulfill, managing the finances, intervening and stopping Luther's careless generosity with the wedding presents, which were going in one hand and out the other. The Black Cloister, a wedding gift from the elector of Saxony, Katherine turned into a parsonage, orphanage, almshouse, and hospital. Her son, Paul, later a distinguished physician himself, called her "half a doctor." Luther called her by more endearing and teasing names: "my lord Moses," "my rib," "my Kind and dear lord and master, Katy, Lutheress, doctoress, and priestess, of Wittenberg." He paid tribute to her ability to manage marvels on a shoestring ("You can strike fire out of flint"), and confessed, "In domestic affairs I defer to Katie. Otherwise I am led by the Holy Ghost." For twenty-one years of married life she was a loving companion, caring for Luther's physical needs, nudging him out of depressions, freeing his mind from domestic concerns, advising him on strategy, raising his six children as well as thirteen orphans, entertaining the students, visiting clergy, and dignitaries who increased her average table setting to twenty-five, nursing Wittenberg's sick and poor, and superintending one three-story house with forty rooms on the first floor, two gardens, one farm, one orchard, one brewery, one fishpond, one dog, and one Wolfgang Sieberger (a luckless theologian who served as one of her domestics). Luther said of her in 1535: "My lord Kate drives a team, farms, pastures, and sells cows . . . and between times reads the Bible." (Reading, according to Luther, made women better wives and Christians.) Because she was a *Hausfrau* ("homer") and not an *Ausfrau* ("roamer"), her unsociability jangled the nerves of Wittenberg's women. They called her proud and imperious. In short, Katherine was subjected to the criticism and gossip that would become familiar to subsequent ministers' wives. But she shared with Luther an intense, earthy, emotional, and sometimes rapturous relationship that put to flight, at least in Luther's mind, Augustine's and Anselm's grim assessment of the married state. Katherine's greatest joy in life was to make Luther happy and useful. She sought to be a faithful companion in marriage and an industrious helpmeet in mothering and managing. She was proud to be the wife of a minister, and proud that she was the one who, like Aaron and Hur with Moses, "held up his hands" (Exodus 17:12) and strengthened them for ministry.[4]

Calvin's wife, Idelette de Bure, carved out a similar role for herself. After making up his mind to marry in 1539, partly to take a stand against celibacy and partly to oblige his friends, John Calvin engaged those friends in the quest for a suitable candidate, giving Guillaume Farel explicit guidelines for this fearsome business: "Remember well what I am looking for in her. I am not of that crazy breed of lovers, who, stricken by the beauty of a woman, love even her faults. The only beauty which captivates me is that of a chaste, kind, modest, thrifty, patient woman, who I might finally hope would be attentive to my health."[5] After some false starts and fumbled arrangements, the Strasbourg pastor married around 10 August 1540. Martin Bucer, himself married to a woman of ample girth whose nickname translates as "Fatso," appears to have come up with the best choice, an older widow of an exiled Anabaptist without form or fortune, but possessed of dignity, equanimity, devotion, and two children. Like Luther's wife, she managed a brood of boarders, helped to lift her husband out of his frequent states of depression, and provided a stable, comfortable home where he could write and think. On her death after nine years of marriage, Calvin was genuinely grieved at the loss of his "companion": "While she lived she was a true help to me in the duties of my office. I have never experienced any hindrances from her, even the smallest."[6]

It was this combination of companionship and assistance—defined in private, not public, terms—that came to characterize the English Protestant parsonage. The parson's wife arrived in England in 1532 after the illegal marriage in Nuremberg of Thomas Cranmer and Margarete, whose surname may have been Hosmer. This was Cranmer's second marriage but the first marriage to break Tudor civil and canon law, since his brief 1515 (or 1516) union with "Black Joan of the Dolphin" occurred before he took holy orders. The most famous of the illegally married priests during the reign of Henry VIII (who feared that if the clergy were allowed to marry their fertility might endanger England's food supply), Thomas Cranmer found himself elevated to the primacy four months after his marriage upon Archibishop William Warham's death. We know very little about Margarete Cranmer except that she was the niece of Andreas Osiander's wife and that she entered England furtively, endured a secret marriage for sixteen years, and, if legend is to believed, traveled with her husband in a tub or trunk with air holes bored in it when she was not contenting herself with a mistress's existence at Manor of Ford, near Canterbury. During the reign of Edward VI, when clerical marriages were briefly legalized and many clerics, including John Knox, rushed to find wives, she was openly acknowledged as Cranmer's wife; after his death in 1556, she lived long enough to enjoy two more husbands. Matthew Parker, later to be Queen Elizabeth's archibishop (1509–1525), was another prominent member of the clergy to marry shortly after Edward's accession in 1547. He had been affianced for seven years to Margaret Harlston but could not formalize the union because Henry VIII had decreed death by hanging for priests and their wives who persisted in cohabitation. Like those that followed them, Margarete Cranmer and Margaret Parker appear in history as faint, silent figures, but they were a courageous lot who endured the peril of marriage to a clergyman. Under Mary Tudor their husbands who wished to remain priests were told to divorce them and disown their children. Yet somehow relationships survived. The deep feeling that characterized these precarious marriages was evident in Archibishop Parker's request that upon his burial his entrails be enclosed in an urn and set on his deceased wife's coffin. Although many of Elizabeth's priests took wives, as English Protestants came to affirm the arguments of Robert Burns, George Joye, and John Ponet for a universal right to marriage, because of a whim of Elizabeth's the status of clerical wives was uncertain and they were treated shabbily on social occasions. Not until 1604, under James I, did the wives of the English clergy obtain secure state recognition.[7]

George Herbert, younger brother of Lord Herbert of Cherbury, in 1652 published a description of the role of the minister's wife in his *Country Parson*. Little had changed in the hundred years since Katherine Luther pioneered this hazardous experiment. Three things Herbert required, one medical, one economic, and one, the most important, spiritual: "His wife is either religious or night and day he is winning her to it."

> First, a training up of her children and maids in the fear of God, with prayers, and catechizing, and all religious duties. Secondly, a curing, and healing of all wounds and sores with her own hands; which skill either she brought with her, or he takes care she will learn it of some religious neighbor. Thirdly, a providing for her family in such sort, as that neither they want a competent sustenation, nor her husband be brought in debt.[8]

George Herbert was said to have chosen Jane Danvers for his wife more by his ears than his eyes, his reason rather than his emotions.

Similarly, the conservative Puritan theologian Richard Baxter, pursued at forty-five by the wealthy, witty, attractive, tempestuous Margaret Charlton, agreed to compromise his well-published opposition to clerical unions and marry her in 1662. But he did so only upon certain conditions. First, she must divest herself of much of her wealth, which she grudgingly did, although she retained enough to build chapels for her husband and schools for the poor. Second, there had to be a clear understanding "that she should expect none of my time which my ministerial work should require." This appears to have been the hardest part of the agreement for her to live up to, for Baxter admits that she felt that he could have written less and spent more time with her. In fact, friction with his wife over whether to neglect his flock or his family and guilt about omitting "secret prayer with my wife when she desired it, for want of time, not daring to omit far greater work," may help explain why Baxter's memorial tribute to her included the recommendation that the marriage of ministers is "to be avoided as far as lawfully we may." Third, he needed her assurance that sex was not the inspiration of her pursuit. The heavenly-minded Margaret, who kept a human skull in her closet to mortify her mind, solemnly explained her motives:

> Dear Mr. Baxter, I protest, with a sincere and real heart, I do not make a tender of myself to you, upon any worldly or carnal account; but to have a more perfect converse with so holy and prudent a yoke-fellow, to assist me in the way to Heaven, and to keep me steadfast in my perseverance; which I design for God' glory, and my own soul's good.[9]

Although Richard called her "the meetest helper that I could have had" and confessed, "I am not ashamed to have been much ruled by her prudent love in many things," Margaret understood, as did all seventeenth-century wives of clergy, that being a "yoke-fellow" involved subservience. Contemporaries may have criticized her because she "worried her head so much about churches, and works of charity, and was not content to live privately and quietly," but Margaret Baxter ever remained faithful to wifely submission and obedience.[10]

George Fox was one of the few seventeenth-century figures whose definition of "helpmeet" did not imply subordination. He argued that before the Fall man and woman had been "helpsmeet," but God had punished the daughters of Eve by giving the sons of Adam rule over them. After Christ restored the primal state by destroying original sin in the believer, man and woman became helpsmeet once again. The congruity between Fox's theology and praxis shines through in his relationship to his wife, Margaret Fell, portrayed by her biographer as a virtual cofounder of Quakerism and a determinative force in directing the experience of inner light toward outer living.[11]

I

The mainstream Companion tradition of the Old World was continued in the New. "One of the most striking phenomena about the New England Puritans is that their greatest ministers," Amanda Porterfield had written, ". . . loved their wives beyond measure."[12]

The mistress of the New England parsonage, like other wives, defined her role totally in relation to her husband's home life. Unblessed with the agony of option, she felt no special calling to be the wife of the minister, although she enjoyed the honor of being married to one of the most spiritual, educated, and prominent people in town and thereby conceded a high social position herself. In a New England meeting house, the best seat in the house, and one that symbolized her role—a high, isolated, solitary pew beside the pulpit and facing the congregation—was reserved for the minister's wife and the widow of his predecessor.[13] By and large fathers deemed it an honor if colonial clergymen courted their daughters, and parsons married into the best families. The wife of a New England parson knew that nothing she could do could make him in the ministry, but she lived in dread of doing anything to unmake him. Indeed, the wife of a colonial minister was less likely to be involved in her husband's vocation than other preindustrial wives, who often worked as unpaid assistants in their husbands' businesses, setting type, ordering supplies and maintaining the financial records, waiting on customers, or shoeing horses. The closest the minister's wife came to colaboring with her husband was in doctoring: many felt the weight of George Herbert's advice: "if there be any of his flock sick, he is their physician or at least his wife."[14] Clerical wives routinely performed duties later entrusted to nurses, midwives, doctors, and surgeons.

The bountiful hospitality of the ministers' wives of the seventeenth century is exemplified by Mary Williams, wife of Roger Williams, whose home became an inn where visitors to Providence (including American Indians) ate, were entertained, and conducted business. The harmony and devotion that united Roger and Mary can be seen in his *Experiments of Spiritual Life and Health* (1652), cited by H. Richard Niebuhr as one of America's most beautiful devotional books.[15] Like Williams's fellow Baptist Obadiah Holmes, who wrote to his wife, Catherine, a touching letter of reassurance and comfort, the Rhode Island pioneer composed while sitting "in the thickets of the naked Indians of America, in their very wild houses, and by their barbarous fires" a devotional tract full of attachment and yearning regard for his wife and concern about the recent illness that had so gravely strained her physical and spiritual state. He tenderly called the *florilegium* his "handful of flowers," a belated get-well present, "a little posy fit and easy for thy meditation and refreshing."[16]

The wives of Richard Mather, Increase Mather, and Cotton Mather advanced their husbands' ministries by making them happy, complementing their dispositions, supplying their needs, working the distaff and the loom, pailing the cows, and raising their children in the fear and admonition of the Lord. Richard Mather's wife, Katharine, described by her son Increase as a "very Holy praying woman," had so freed her husband from all domestic worries that the effect of her death on him was "the more grievous, in that she being a Woman of singular Prudence for the Management of Affairs, had taken off from her husband all Secular Cares so that he wholly devoted himself to his Study, and to Sacred Imployments."[17] Puritan women were taught to read so that they could study the Bible and keep account books, and Increase Mather's articulate, literate first wife, Maria Cotton Mather, retired six times a day for secret prayer and Bible study, besides observing special fast days for the conversion of her children. Her great fear in life was having too many children, "one more child than Jesus would accept of."[18] After deciding in 1685 that God had called him to marry, Cotton Mather resolved to choose his love and then, as Puritans insisted, love his choice. With emotions that would never imperil his good sense, he selected fifteen-year-old Abigail Phillips. Their sixteen years of marriage were marked by "extravagant fondness." In Mather's writings, in David Levin's words, "Abigail Mather appears briefly as a silent companion, a cooperative assistant, 'my dear consort,' when summoned to the study for prayer on a special occasion or when mentioned as a participant in the family's daily worship."[19]

A similar pattern obtained in the eighteenth century, when the helpmeet replaced the yokefellow as the ideal wife.[20] We can see the notion of being married to a husband who happened to be a minister rather than a minister who happened to be a husband in the 1749 marriage of Isaac Backus to the frugal, devout Susanna Mason. They were "companions and helpers, meet for each other," joined in a wedding at which the groom preached his own wedding sermon.[21] When he was eighty years old, Backus called her "the greatest temporal blessing which God ever gave me."[22] We can see the domestic value of the minister's wife in Henry Melchior Muhlenberg's marriage in the 1750s to a "pure of heart, pious, simple-hearted, meek and industrious" girl named Anna Maria. Muhlenberg, who prized the unwed state over marriage, succumbed for two pressing reasons. He hoped by marriage to maintain his good reputation, since he often found himself helping in indelicate situations like childbirth, and he wanted a housekeeper. "I commanded nothing but sincere piety, such as might be convenable both for myself and my work."[23] The Presbyterian clergyman John Wilson, pastor of the Presbyterian Church in Chester, New Hampshire, from 1734 to 1779, erected a tombstone in Chester's Congregational Cemetery to celebrate this latter indispensable function of the minister's wife:

> Here lies the body of
> Mrs. Jean Wilson
> Spouse of the Revd. John Wilson
> who departed this life April 1st AD
> 1752 Aged 36 years.
> She was a Gentlewoman of Piety
> A good Oeconamist[24]

We can see the great affection and companionship that characterized such marriages in the soft, respectful letters John Newton wrote to his wife and the warm, solicitude expressed by Hezekiah Smith, chaplain in the Continental army, for his unconverted but "loving companion," Hephzibah.[25] But we can most clearly see all the aspects of the Companion model, along with some portentous variations, in the lives of Sarah Pierrepont Edwards and her daughter Esther Edwards Burr. In fact, Sarah Edwards was touted in the nineteenth century by a marriage manual that advised women to find, like the exemplary wife of Edwards, her "true greatness . . . in rendering others useful, rather than in being directly useful herself."[26]

The daughter of the New Haven minister James Pierrepont and great-granddaughter of Thomas Hooker, Sarah was a bright, vivacious, beautiful thirteen-year-old with a superior education when the shy, serious, twenty-year-old Jonathan Edwards took notice of her. Perhaps Edwards saw in Sarah some of the qualities of his mother, Esther, remembered by her friends as "tall, dignified and commanding in her appearance" and yet "affable and gentle with her manner." As might be expected of the daughter of the famed minister Solomon Stoddard, Esther had a mind of her own. Although the wife of a minister, she did not join her husband's church until Jonathan was twelve years old. She loved theological disputation and was thought to possess a "native vigor of understanding" that surpassed her husband's.[27] For whatever reason, the greatest theologian America has produced did something lesser minds before him had managed to avoid: he fell in love. Unable to concentrate on his studies, his spiritual state erratic, his mind wandering from his Greek grammar book, in its blank leaf the scholar penned in his spidery handwriting this famous portrait of the woman he would doggedly court and finally persuade to marry him four years later:

> They say there is a young lady in [New Haven], who is beloved of that Great Being who made and rules the world; and that there are certain seasons, in which this Great Being, in some way or other, invisible, comes to her and fills her mind with exceeding sweet delight, and that she hardly cares for any thing, except to meditate on him; —that she expects after a while to be received up where he is; to be raised up out of the world, and caught up into heaven; being assured that he loves her too well to let her remain at a distance from him always. Therefore she is to dwell with him, and to be ravished with his love and delight for ever.
>
> Therefore, if you present all the world before her, with the richest of its treasures, she disregards it and cares not for it, and is unmindful of any pain or affliction. She has a strange sweetness in her mind, and singular purity in her affections; is most just and conscientious in all her conduct; and you could not persuade her to do any thing wrong or sinful, if you would give her all the world, lest she should offend this Great Being. She is of a wonderful sweetness, calmness, and universal benevolence of mind; especially after this Great Being has manifested himself to her mind.
>
> She will sometimes go about from place to place, singing sweetly, and seems to be always full of joy and pleasure, and no one knows for what. She loves to be alone, walking in the fields and groves, and seems to have some one invisible always conversing with her.[28]

On his deathbed Jonathan called their thirty-one-year marriage an "uncommon union," and that it was. Sarah gave birth to eleven children, all of whom miraculously lived through infancy. She managed the property, relieved her husband of household duties and remained poised throughout Edwards's turbulent years at North-ampton, even taking in good spirits the humiliation of being required by a church committee to keep an itemized statement of parsonage expenses as proof that her husband needed a higher salary. Jonathan discussed points of theology with Sarah, who was well versed enough in the nuances of Edwards' stand on who should be admitted to the Lord's Table to write a remarkable letter dated 17 June 1750 to the Northampton council pleading her husband's case and demonstrat-ing the continuity of his position with earlier statements and pub-lished writings.[29] Some said that Sarah was Jonathan's only source of information about what was going on in his parish, so absorbed was he in study and prayer. Her latchstring was always out, signifying to visitors that they were welcome. "She knew the heart of a stranger," Samuel Hopkins recalled.[30] Perhaps the downy, died-in-the-wool bachelor George Whitefield paid her the highest compliment. After visiting in their home in 1740, he resolved to go wife hunting and find himself a helpmeet like her: "A sweeter Couple I have not yet seen. . . . She . . . talked feelingly and solidly of the Things of God, and seemed to be such a Help meet for her Husband that she caused me to . . . [pray] God, that he would be pleased to send me a Daughter of Abraham to be my wife."[31]

Sarah Edwards accepted as part of her family numerous divin-ity students who served their apprenticeship with Edwards, includ-ing Samuel Hopkins and Joseph Bellamy. "The good man does not appear to have been consulted," Roland Bainton informs us. "The candidate reined up at the door of the parsonage and was taken in."[32] These students, who became more numerous in direct proportion to the increase in Edwards's fame and his daughters' beauty, adored Sarah, looking to her for encouragement and advice. In fact, Samuel Hopkins was not merely Jonathan Edwards' closest friend and disci-ple. He was also a student of Sarah Edwards. Hopkins learned from Jonathan Edwards that true virtue consists in "disinterested benevo-lence." But he learned from Sarah Edwards something that became a distinctive contribution of the New Divinity theology to American doctrinal interpretation: holy love requires total selflessness, even the willingness to be damned for the greater glory of God. Or as Sarah first phrased it, "I should be willing to die in darkness and horror, if it was most for the glory of God."[33]

According to the popularized but sensitive portrait by Sarah's biographer, Elisabeth D. Dodds, it was Sarah who stabilized and strengthened Edwards rather than the reverse. In Hopkins's words, "She was unmindful of any pain or affliction. . . . As he was of a weakly, infirm constitution . . . she was a tender nurse to him, cheerfully attending upon him at all times, and in all things ministering to his comfort."[34] But in 1742, an excessive concern over her likeability quotient, her driving need to be admired by everyone, caused her unraveling. Perhaps it had contributed in the past to her emotional "unsteadiness" and "ups and downs," as Edwards described them. While Edwards was away preaching in other towns at the height of the Great Awakening, Sarah lodged her husband's pulpit replacement, Samuel Buell, and watched nervously as he became more successful with the Spirit and popular with the people than her husband. Soon she began hallucinating, fainting, jabbering uncontrollably. Today it would be said that she suffered a nervous breakdown. She transformed the experience into a spiritual breakthrough thanks to the spiritual help of Buell and the psychological intuition of her husband, who instinctively prescribed for her a remarkably modern therapeutic regimen. Sarah began to promote the revival through her attendance at meetings and her influence among women and youth, but more importantly through the magnetic pull of her religious experiences on her husband. It was Sarah's cathartic awakening that Edwards would use, without acknowledging its source, as a paradigm of the mighty acts of God during the Great Awakening. Succeeding generations of Calvinists would test the authenticity of revivals within the context of Sarah's experience that, in Amanda Porterfield's words, "she was not obliged to meet other people's standards for a virtuous wife of a minister of God."[35] For many years, Sarah testified, God had given her a "willingness to die." Now God had made her "willing to live."[36]

II

Esther Edwards was ten when her mother endured this wrenching experience. There is little evidence to suggest its effect on her. Perhaps her reference to her husband as the "head" and herself as the "heart" of their family signified an internalizing of her mother's emotional discovery of religion; one cannot be sure. In other ways mother and daughter were very much alike: beautiful, charming, intelligent and desirous of respect. The difference between them— marking an important alteration in the position of the minister's wife in American religion—was that Esther broke away from the definition of her role exclusively in terms of holding up her husband's hands and began, albeit tentatively and ultimately unsuccessfully, to utilize her own hands in ministry. Esther Edwards Burr may have been known as the daughter of Jonathan Edwards, the wife of Aaron Burr, and the mother of Aaron Burr, Jr., but she was well known in her own right.

Esther Edwards Burr lived in a period, thanks to her father, that embraced greater psychological activism in the process of spiritual transformation and encouraged unbelievers to participate more actively in their conversions.[37] Her age also demanded more lay activism in the promotion of revivals. Esther, who would follow her father to the grave a few weeks after his death, dying of the same smallpox inoculation, also followed him in life. Rather than supporting her husband's usefulness, she experimented with being useful herself. Her mother's public role had been to set an example. She would do that, and spread the gospel as well. She was one of the first American ministers' wives to explore an identity other than that of the bearer of her husband's name, nature, children and career. The power of her witness was carried to its conclusion by her son, Aaron Burr, Jr., who campaigned for the equal rights of women.

In 1752, as the wife of Princeton's debonair president, Aaron Burr, Esther performed functions similar to her mother's. One of her mother's former student-boarders reminded her what they were:

> Madam: I congratulate your late happy marriage to the Rev. President Burr. . . . O, think what God and the world will now expect from you, a professor of religion, and the daughter of such pious parents, and now standing in such a place! O that you might have wisdom and grace to act a noble and pious part; to live above the world; to maintain communion with God; to set a good example; to prepare for unforseen calamities![38]

Esther Burr ran a daily open house. "I expect company every minit," she wrote in 1754. A gregarious hostess and witty conversationalist, Esther surprised many of her guests with her acute interest in political developments. She delighted in entertaining her "visitants," as she called them, notably New Jersey's Governor Belcher and his wife, Mary, the revivalists William and Gilbert Tennent, the controversial itinerant James Davenport, and a legion of visiting trustees, students, parents—even a whole presbytery. She once wrote home that on Wednesday she served eight ministers at dinner and on

Thursday ten, followed by a supper for thirty-one guests. "I do love to entertain good ministers," she wrote, though she could be quite testy with ministers who disparaged women. She complained far more than her mother would have deemed proper about the hardships of being a minister's wife: of the "widowhood" caused by her husband's frequent travels, of never having a spare moment for herself, of her lack of a proper number of servants for someone of her station.[39] But these were a lover's quarrels with the ministry.

Women's prayer groups and house visits she regarded highly, as we learn from her epistolary journal, cited by scholars as "the earliest detailed record of an American woman's life."[40] Laurie Crumpacker, who has edited the journal, has traced the collision of religious and economic forces that sparked women's interest in writing, itself of profound historical importance: first, the Great Awakening's stress on religious sensibilities and the utility of written recitations (originally encouraged by Cotton Mather) in promoting conversions; and second, the changing economic conditions that allowed women more leisure for literary pursuits.[41] There are references throughout Burr's journal to visiting "the Widow, the fatherless, and the sick," and she resented interruptions that prevented these adventures. When she was depressed, she went visiting. When her husband was away, she went visiting. But mostly when members of the parish were suffering or in need, she hastened to their hearth.[42]

After entertaining and visiting, Esther Burr's third love was women's prayer meetings. Identification with members of their sex for religious purposes was being discovered by Evangelical women. The awakening of religious impulses among women during this period was documented by George Whitefield, Joshua Huntington, and women themselves.[43] But the religious aspirations of the women of the First Great Awakening quickly dissipated, and they never transformed America's religious ecology as their sisters of the Second Great Awakening did. The entrepreneurial ecclesiology of voluntarism, and the public activism implicit therein, had not been sufficiently formulated, leaving women without the possibility of a public vocation, even within the realm of religion. Aaron Burr talked of a "vital piety." Charles G. Finney would talk of "vital religion." The absense of a theological rationale for public activism, something which Jonathan Edwards had provided but which was only dimly perceived by his contemporaries, helps to explain the difference between the First Great Awakening and the Second where women were concerned. It also helps to explain why Esther Burr never broke free of the rigidly domestic orientation of the Companion model and why her beloved Sarah Prince's description of her departed friend made no mention of her role as a minister's wife: she was "a Dutifull, affectionate, respectful, obedient Tender Daughter and Wife . . . a tender and wise mother and mistress—a loving and lovely Sister and friend . . . a humble self-denied lively Christian—dead to this world, she panted for a better.[44] Esther's identity was to be found in the roots of her parentage, the trunk of her marriage, and the branch of her offspring, not in the fruits of her labor.

Chapter Two

"Mother—Home—Heaven"

Nineteenth-Century America's Most Sacred Words

Woman, next to God, makes the living world of humanity. She makes man what he is in this world, and very frequently makes him what he shall hereafter be in the world to come.

Alexander Campbell

If womanhood has gone down, woe be to us, but if woman has gone up in intelligence, in virtue and religion, then the country is safe though its fleets were sunk and its cities were buried.

Henry Ward Beecher

The history of women in American religion poses one demanding question after another. This chapter attempts to address only two of them. First, what were the intellectual, social, economic, and religious forces that allowed the wives of clergy to advance from serving their husbands as companions or sacrificers to working with them as assistants or professional partners? Second, how did women come to dominate the Second Great Awakening in numbers and influence? It is important that we confront these questions at the beginning: our understanding of the minister's wife in American religion will depend on how these questions are answered.

I

The sixteenth-century Protestant perception of woman was ambivalent. On the one hand, popular urban opinion held that the Eve bite continued to plague this creature who was always devising new ways to seduce, suborn, or dominate man. She was ridiculed as a "malformed man" and her nature compared to that of a dog. Hans Sachs, a Protestant Nuremberg shoemaker who lived from 1494 to 1576, turned to a tale of rabbinic origin to portray the creation of Eve.

> After God had created the heavens and the earth, day and night, the seas and the mountains, the fish and the animals, He decided that His newest creation needed a helpmate. So God put Adam to sleep and removed a rib. While God was closing Adam's wound with earth, a dog stole the rib. God pursued the dog, grabbed the dog's tail and cut it off with a knife. The dog,

however, escaped with Adam's rib. God, left standing with a dog's tail instead of Adam's rib, used the tail to create the first woman, Eve.[1]

But woman was simultaneously seen as a helper to man, an economic necessity and a spiritual companion in the Christian pilgrimage. It was this image of the "good woman" that eventually triumphed over the "bad woman" as the stereotype of femininity for Protestants. This was due partly to the abolition of the monastic ideal of the religious life, which enabled the home to compete with the monastery as a spiritual icon, and partly to the decline in the veneration of the Virgin Mary, who had always been for women a hard act to follow.[2] The Reformation did not change the place of women in society, but the forces it unleashed gave new dignity to the images of wife, mother, and home.

Puritan contributions to the advancement of women have been seriously questioned ever since the publication in 1980 of Lyle Koehler's *A Search for Power*.[3] Nevertheless, Puritans of the sixteenth and seventeenth centuries saw women as part of the priesthood of believers[4] and ultimately accorded them new measures of respect, reciprocity, and rationality. "Houses where no women bee," the saying went, "are like desarts on untilled land."[5] Some have argued that American Puritan women enjoyed higher economic, social, legal, and religious status than their British counterparts, but recent research has disclosed women's elevated educational status in Tudor England among the merchants, gentry, and nobility.[6] Although recent research has argued that colonial gender roles were more narrowly defined than hitherto realized, women were still judged by the same standards as men.[7] Personality traits were not believed to be distinctly female or male, although one historian of colonial women, Julia Cherry Spruill, has found a colonial ladies' book, *The Ladies' Calling* (1673), which probed the uniqueness (whether intrinsic or accidental is unclear) of feminine virtues.[8] A man was expected to be the master and minister of his house, but Puritan theology chipped away at the familial authority of the father, undermining it to the mother's advantage. The celebrated trial of Anne Hutchinson reveals that Puritans did not object to women's praying and edifying each other, but only to one woman's presiding in a "prophetical way" over large assembles.[9] As we shall see, they were not the last Americans to discover that the line from female prayer to female preaching was disconcertingly straight.

The eighteenth century wrought enormous changes in the religious and social landscape for women by introducing the image of the "two spheres", which would become the established dogma of the nineteenth century. In the 1740s, at the same time that Evangelical religion was beginning to appeal to the affections, to the heart, to "experimental piety," women came to be seen for the first time as more emotional and more religious than men. Scholars have only begun to fuss about whether the ideology or the religious appeal came first, but the equation of femininity with religiosity was a momentous event in the history of American religion.

The doctrine of the spheres defined women's roles in religious, emotional terms and men's in economic, worldly ones. Women's bargain with men was to trade earth for heaven, and they sincerely thought that they got the best of the deal. A man's sphere was deemed different from his wife's but not superior; broader, certainly, but not higher. One's weakness was the other's strength, and women's strengths were seen as the nurturing, affective, intuitive facilities. Although this notion was present in the poetry of courtly love,[10] only in the eighteenth century did the dawning awareness that female "strengths" spelled in some areas female "superiority" quicken the imagination of masses of women and turn their psychological universe upside down. A wife went from being the mistress of a home to being the minister of a home, where, despite some initial male misgivings, she ruled by divine right. Woman was now the expert on something consequential, the home and the church were her passion and preserve, and she occupied an exposed position as a model of morality and piety.[11] In short, with the first stage of American revivalism known as the First Great Awakening, women became conscious of themselves as a special group in church and society and a higher form of being than men.

These developments, as the fascinating and important studies by Carl Degler and Mary Beth Norton have demonstrated, were brought to a head during the period between 1770 and 1820, a watershed period for American middle-class women.[12] The modern family had been born. There was the decline of patriarchy and the conquest of "spherism," not merely an "adhesion" of new views of womanhood on already existing ones, to appropriate Arthur Darby Nock's distinction,[13] but a complete turning, a true conversion, from one mental construct to another. Spherism was an ordered, compact social myth that dovetailed neatly with antebellum romanticism and provided comfort and security to a nation in the birth pangs of an industrial order. There was the development of joint-role relationships between spouses and a trend toward spontaneity in love and marriage. Parents were showing greater sensitivity to the educational needs of their children, and a greater equality in educational opportunity for boys and girls emerged. There was increasing experimentation with methods of birth control and a consequent reduction in fertility. In religion women flaunted their moral superiority and began engaging in public activity. For the next hundred years, America's most sacred words, and paradoxically American women's most liberating words,[14] would be "home," "mother," and "heaven."

The dominant nineteenth-century social fiction engendered by the metaphysical dualism of the spheres doctrine has been variously called the "myth of motherhood," the "cult of true womanhood," or the "cult of domesticity." These prescriptive stereotypes of women, mainly addressed to middle-class and native-born white women, revolved around two ideas: women were the guardians of morality, and women were the custodians of conversion. The first phrase was initially suggested by Rousseau's description of the women of Geneva as "the chaste guardians of our morals, and the surest security for our peace."[15] When the nineteenth century thought of virtue and morality, it thought of woman: chaste, pure, humble, superior in moral values to man, who was increasingly caricatured as the moral deformity attended by woman the moral doctor. "Men are moulded, in mind, in affection, in character, by woman's hand."[16] The exaltation of motherhood, a profound innovation in the history of western civilization, was a logical consequence of the belief in women's moral superiority. As moral preceptor, woman was most fit to instruct the youth of the republic, a belief upheld by Pestalozzian principles, and she began transforming the religious and educational life of youth and adolescents from a casual to a controlled environment. Women thus became responsible for the socialization of children and the moralization of men.

Woman's role as a custodian of conversion was also based on her presumed nature. Christianity's diamonds of discipleship, women either glistened in the light of religion as dazzling paradigms of religiosity (Henry Ward Beecher complimented his father by calling him "two-thirds woman—a woman with man's enamel on") or appeared, without religion, as new, menacing paradigms of apostasy ("Of all the moral monsters, which abound on earth, women without religion are the most disgusting").[17] There developed almost a mystical, if not a sacramental, notion of woman's gravitational pull on males. Either she elevates and converts them, or she debases and debauches them.

One of revivalism's contributions to the history of conversion, in sharp contradistinction to the Puritan practice, was its vigorous jacking up of the role of the laity. For Evangelicals, ministers received their credentials not through the offices of the church, but through the outpouring of the Holy Spirit in conversion.[18] Conversion became the laity's ordination. Saved souls were expected to become soul-savers. And women did. A nineteenth-century clerical autobiography that does not testify to the role of women in religious quickening and training is rare enough to be a collector's item. A marvelous story from the first noon prayer meeting of the "Businessmen's Revival" of 1857–1858 in Kalamazoo, Michigan, provides one example among many. During this service a prayer request from a pious, praying wife who wanted the group to pray for her unconverted husband was announced. For the next hour men popped up all over the hall, vying for the distinction of being the unconverted husband in question because the plea sounded as if it came from each man's own pious, praying wife.[19] As conservators of piety, women transformed the home into a church, preferred houses built in the Gothic style (commonly called "the architecture of Christianity"), erected family altars and guarded their observance, and urged conversions from children at an earlier and earlier age.[20] Jonathan Edwards retained the responsibility for his children's spiritual welfare. Charles G. Finney relinquished his children's spiritual tuition to his wife, Lydia.

The influence of women began in the home, but it did not end there. Invoking the authority of custodians of conversion, they expanded feminine space until it engulfed the church and community as forums for soul winning. "The connection in the popular mind between women and morality," Carl N. Degler has written, "provided strong justification for women's participation in organizations and activities outside the kitchen or the nursery."[21] Here in the public arena, she came to dominate the machinery of evangelism. She visited the sick and sinful, staffed Sunday schools, organized prayer meetings and other women's groups, distributed tracts and pamphlets, interrogated those on death beds about their spiritual state, and insisted that her community found academies and female seminaries. Since conversion had begun with Wesley, Whitefield, and Finney to take place in public, she often testified to her conversion in public. She did everything but preach, and she sponsored preaching through her societies. It is understandable, then, that the roles of mother and minister came to be compared and that the only vocation Evangelicals deemed closer to God than motherhood was ministry. Herein lies the central paradox of antebellum revivalism: at the same time that Evangelicals idealized the feminine attributes of self-denial, humility, submission, purity, and meekness, their commitment to the notion of "women's sphere" led to their endorsement of female involvement in public activities that were not very submissive, humble, meek, self-denying, or even pure.

A probing study of the relationship between sex and revivalism in the burned-over district has led Mary Ryan to the most extreme hypothesis about "maternal evangelism." Since wives, mothers, and sisters led the male converts into Troy's churches, she argues, and since it was "women who orchestrated the domestic revivals, . . . then women were more than the majority of the converts, more even than the private guardians of America's souls. The combination and consequence of all these roles left the imprint of a women's awakening on American society as well as on American religion."[22] An absorbing study remains to be done of the techniques used in shepherding men to the "glory pen." The wife of Oberlin's founder, John Keep, undertook the challenge of corraling and converting the town rowdies in her husband's first parish at Blandford, Massachusetts, by luring them with a reading society formed of the town's "most prominent young ladies." The society successfully drew the young men away from their ballroom habits and attached them to more spiritual enjoyments.[23] Years later D. S. Miller, rector of St. Mark's Church in Philadelphia, reported proudly on his strategy of employing women's talents to draw husbands, brothers, boyfriends, and especially the city's unchurched young men, old boys, and blue-collar workers into church. He promoted the seduction of men to Christ by the same means that could seduce men to sin: "Those natural endowments, which draw so many away from goodness, could not fail to exert a mighty influence in leading them back."[24]

It was not a large step, and it had been taken by 1830, from seeing women as savers of souls to seeing them as savers of society; the agents of moral transmission became the agents of cultural transformation. This is the most profound development in the doctrine of spheres in the nineteenth century. Added to their duties as guardians of morality and custodians of conversion was a millennial vocation as the cornerstones of the new society that America's Evangelicals were confident of building. A correspondent to the *Revivalist*, urging British Evangelicals to catch up with the American example of offering at least one female prayer meeting in almost every town "where religion flourishes," quoted a tract ("On Female Influence and Obligations") by the American evangelist N. S. S. Beman, who adjured women to take seriously their mission to redeem their families. "It will always depend much upon female influence whether religion shall prevail in the family or not," Beman wrote; "If females were all Christians, and such Christians as they ought to be, a hope might be cherished that the world would soon be converted."[25]

A partnership in millennial ministry was established between women and Evangelical clergy in which women and home became, in Sandra S. Sizer's words, "the primary vehicle of redemptive power." This sense of messianic motherhood, the belief that "a mother's influence . . . is second only to God himself," generalized into a sense of messianic womanhood, the belief that "next under God woman is the creator of the race,"[26] resolved the inherent paradox of the doctrine of spheres in favor of the advancement of a public vocation for women. We may criticize women for surrendering their egos to an abstraction, but it was this messianic abstraction and millennial vision of motherhood that justified their public activities and transformed them into power-brokers of religion, morality, and society.

The women's sphere doctrine—universalized, moralized, millennialized—took some women by inexorable steps into the public arena. Moral character, a cornerstone of millennial society, was formed by women. Religious progress, another cornerstone, depended upon women's engagement in the work. The popular *Lectures to Young Women* by the Presbyterian William Greenleaf Eliot (1854) informed them, "The only hope for the advancement of society is to keep woman in the advance-guard. Let her point the way and lead it, and the right progress is assured."[27] Even lectures to young men reminded them of the limits of the male sphere, touting women as the ones who "hold in their own hand the sceptre of empire of the social world, and whose influence does more to form the mind, to furnish the elements of moral character, and to control the destinies of the earth, than any other influence this side of heaven."[28] There can be no greater truism than this," ventured an article in Alexander Campbell's *Millennial Harbinger*, "that anyone who seeks the elevation of man, must devote his chief attention to that of women."[29] Although some women found their role as the world's cornerstone more akin to a millstone or even a tombstone,[30] for the moment Evangelical women capitalized on their millennial vocation to heighten their self-image and provide the rationale for their public activities.

"Les races," the French naturalist Georges Buffon was widely quoted as declaring, "se feminiscent." The virtues of women's sphere coincided with the values of the millennium. Man worked with the material; woman worked with the spiritual. Man molded matter; woman molded minds. Man lived by the *lex talionis*; woman turned the other cheek. With both Christ and woman, Julia Ward Howe lectured, "weakness and power strangely change places."[31] Man's genius was mechanical invention; woman's, moral influence. Man's strength was physical; woman's, spiritual. Man lived in the present tense; women in the future. The doctrine of the spheres, in essence, had deserted the principle of sexual complementarity and embraced an apocalyptic sexual superiority. Using millennial imagery, women defined themselves as the leaders and men as the led. From Aristotle on, the family had been seen as the microcosm of the state. Now it was seen as the microcosm of the millennium—the kingdom that women built and over which feminine virtues would reign. Messianic motherhood made domesticity more than a brightening of one's own corner. It made it a beacon to the world of millennial process, structure, and energy.

As we have said, however, messianic motherhood also brought women outside the home and into the public arena; where millennialism had been raising issues of morality and religion. Evangelical women, convinced of their social and political role in bringing in the millennium, founded and fortified a galaxy of educational, reform, and religious movements. Teaching Sunday school or joining maternal societies, for example, expressed more than a maternal interest in the educational and spiritual welfare of children; it expressed an unsparing, soul-harrying earnestness to transform the world. Men would eventually burst the expanding bubble of women's public participation in American society when moral questions began to be translated into political terms and women therefore were increasingly found meddling in political matters and demanding political power. Men then fought political power for women in the name of protecting women's angel wings from the muck of politics and preserving the nation by ensuring women's continued role as "conservators of morals and manners."[32] Yet women's engagement in public affairs and many of the arguments for giving them the franchise were based on the wide and deep hope of bringing in the millennium by vote. Some doubted that female enfranchisement would be an automatic voucher for justice, progress, and social redemption: the New Eve looked too much to them like the Old Adam. But "abolition's golden trumpet," Wendell Phillips, could say in one breath, "Give woman the ballot and I do not count on the millennium the next day," and in the next, "No, it will come very gradually." The lingering power of woman's millennial vision and messianic motherhood can be seen in Frances Willard's argument for women's ordination and, into the twentieth century, in Charlotte Perkins Gilman's assertion that women were "the main line of evolution," whose *raison d'être* was "not sex service nor house service, but world-service—the carrying on and improving of the human race."[33]

II

Before anything conclusive can be said about the sex ratio of church members and pew occupants in American religion, laborious statistical research, like that done by Richard D. Shiels for American Congregationalism from 1730 to 1835,[34] must be undertaken with a careful eye to the difference between church membership and church attendance. Literary sources unveil a well-documented penchant of American women for religion, beginning with Cotton Mather's observation that women's names predominated on membership rolls of New England churches. But these accounts, while not contradictory, vary wildly in their estimations and leave one nervously recalling the historian's dictum "Beware if you find what you're looking for." In colonial America the trend appears to have been toward, as one wag put it, females in the pews and Presbyterians in the pulpit. Even though men outnumbered women in the colonies, Cedric B. Cowing argues that the proportion of women members to men in the colonial period was five to three, going as high as two to one in some New England congregations early in the eighteenth century. Cowing's figure is probably high, but it receives support from William Lumpkin's study of eighteenth-century Virginia Baptists as well as from the histories of congregations recorded by such pastors as Samuel Hopkins and Ezra Stiles. At mid-century Hopkins counted only a handful of men in his congregation, and his Newport rival Stiles could claim little more: only 20 percent of his communicants were males. Toward 1800 the ecclesiastical hegemony of women in the North so impressed Timothy Dwight that he gauged their numerical strength at two-thirds of the church. Donald Mathews's more informed and sober calculation has put their strength in the South at this time at 65 percent, in spite of the 3 percent population advantage of the men.[35]

For the nineteenth century we again have an abundance of supposition and a scarcity of hard figures. Frances Trollope's bleak picture of male irreligiosity is certainly overdrawn, but one religious periodical in 1823 stated, "The fact that there are twice as many female as male professors in every denomination of Christianity is unquestionable." Terry David Bilhartz's painstaking study of Baltimore's membership statistics reveals that by 1830 over 70 percent of the city's religious communicants were female, with males involved in rituals mainly of the "hatched-matched-dispatched" variety. Similarly, Richard Shiels has discovered a dramatic increase in female membership in Congregational churches in New England following the American Revolution. From 1800 to 1835, 69 percent of new members were women. "The feminization of church membership, which began in the Revolution," Shiels concludes, "continued through the Second Great Awakening."[36] By mid-century it was not uncommon to find women claiming that they comprised three-fourths of all American Christians. Ann Douglas has garnered similar evidence from liberal religious sources to buttress her thesis about the feminization of America's church and culture.[37] A hurried inquiry into the mid-century sex ratio of Sunday school teachers and students at an Episcopal parish (a tradition where there were fewer complaints about male absentees than elsewhere) reveals twice as many female Sunday school teachers as males, and consistently two to three times as many female as male students in Sunday school and Bible classes.[38] As the century progressed, the claims for the overwhelming statistical supremacy of women in the church became both more extreme and more excited, with general agreement that they constituted from two-thirds to three-fourths of the membership. After the striking preponderance of female prayer requests at the Moody and Sankey crusades became publicized, the noted reformer Thomas Wentworth Higginson wrote disgustedly on "The Religious

Weakness of Women." One woman's journal in 1876 worriedly considered the equal number of males and females in American churches' infant classes and the two-to-one ratio of women to men in church and Sunday school. The fact that in some traditions, like the Methodist, it was customary to separate the sexes in worship may have made the predominance of women in church seem greater than it actually was. But by the Civil War segregation at worship seems to have been in decline, thus removing it as a factor in the impressionistic reckonings of the last third of the century.[39]

The question the historian ineluctably returns to is not whether women were in the majority in nineteenth-century American churches, but how great was their lead. In fact, an intriguing but as yet unproven dimension of American revivalism was its possible use as a vehicle for returning wandering males to the fold. When the First Great Awakening was warming in Northampton, more than half of Edwards's converts were male. When the First Great Awakening came to the First Congregational Church of Woodbury, Connecticut, for the first time in its history more men than women were admitted to the church. When the Second Great Awakening came to Troy, New York, the female majority shrank with the influx of male converts. In 1858, when the Union Prayer Meeting revival came to Richmond, Virginia, Charleston, South Carolina, Columbus, Georgia, and Montgomery, Alabama, it hit the male population especially hard;[40] some historians, in fact, refer to it as the "Businessmen's Revival." It is at least plausible that "camp meetings" in the first half of the century and "big preaching" services in the second were popular because they enabled women to get their males under the tent of religion and clergy to get recruits for the thin ranks of ministry. The test of a successful revivalist may not have been simply the conversion of souls; it may have been his ability to motivate and mobilize the women who drew men to church and then to convert the men once they got there. The apparently larger minority of males in revivalistic denominations supports this hypothesis. If this is true, the entrance and exit of males through the revolving doors of revivalism may have helped to vary the sex ratio in nineteenth-century churches. In other words, the question of why religion appealed to many women may need to be complemented with the question of why it did not appeal to more men.

There has been no dearth of explanations for women's preponderance in American religion, and in a sense this book is a commentary on the issue to be piled on the stack with the others.

Cotton Mather attributed the colonial female majority in part to religious indifference among men and more free time among women. But he believed also that woman's closeness to life's natural rhythms of birth and death and her supervisory roles at the cradle and coffin bonded her to the church. Jonathan Edwards exposed the obverse side of the coin in his thesis that men's worldly interests— "more cod than God," lamented some—diverted their time and attention from the church.[41] The essentially sociological explanation of Mather and Edwards has led some historians to a theological one. The conversion process involved a passing from "death unto life." Prefacing the new birth was a relinquishment of life to death. Women, especially women who had survived childbirth, knew that they belonged to death already, and hence they were more readily able to die to self. Margaret W. Masson furthermore argues that the Puritans' main paradigm of the soul's relationship to God—the relationship of the bride to the bridegroom—appealed to women, whereas men experienced difficulty in negotiating the spiritual transvestitism necessary to become the bride of Christ.[42]

Frances Wright was the first to provide an assessment of women's attraction to the church during the Second Great Awakening. Angered by the "odious" 1828 Cincinnati revival, with its hysterical, jerking, Spirit-slain women "victims," Wright attributed the phenomenon to the intrinsically superstitious nature of religion and women's uneducated state, which made them less able to defend themselves against clerical wizards and their bag of tricks and terrors.[43] Margaret Fuller, known as the most erudite woman in America, gave an equally negative assessment, stressing the escapist functions of religion as an emergency exit from domestic monotony and existential boredom.[44] Current historians of the Second Great Awakening are interpreting the phenomenon more positively. Some point to the intellectual hunger of women, which was partly quenched in the religious arena. Others—Donald Mathews, for example—have persuasively argued that religion offered women psychological esteem, "breathing space," and a rewarding and solidifying social life.[45] Nancy F. Cott contends that women, denied satisfying employment in the home due to the onslaught of industrialism, found it in the church.[46] A variant of this thesis will be explored in greater detail in Chapter four. What I propose to do now is to take a hard look at the most widely accepted explanation for religion's appeal to women: the consistency between conversion's demand for a "melting" into submissiveness and women's socialized state of submission.

Much has been made of the fact that religion schooled nineteenth-century women in the virtues of submissiveness, meekness and obedience.[47] It is not exactly correct to say only this. Religion and the conversion experience also served to undermine conventional assumptions about the subordination of wives to husbands. This effect was often responsible for more than the "religious autonomy" that Mary P. Ryan has discovered women exercising during seasons of revival.[48] It could be a matter of direct defiance. Rebelliousness even had its patron saint in the seventeenth-century figure of Dorothy Hazard, a Puritan maverick who on Christmas Day in 1639 opened her Bristol grocer's shop to protest against the day's superstitious sacrilege. She married an Anglican minister who shared some of her sympathies, but she soon scandalized the community by refusing even to attend his church, affiliating instead with the Baptist congregation, where she did not have to hear the Book of Common Prayer.[49] Another kind of defiance was shown by the wives of Roger Williams and Obadiah Holmes, who were spouses to Christianity before they were spouses to their husbands. After their husbands withdrew from Puritan churches in Salem and Rehoboth to form Baptist fellowships, Mary Williams and Catherine Holmes continued to affiliate with the established churches until, as John Cotton said of Mary, "at length he drew her to partake with him in the error of his ways."[50]

The popular southern Presbyterian clergyman Rufus William Bailey, an early specialist in family ministries who spent the last four years of his life (1859–1863) as president of Austin College in Huntsville, Texas, said nothing out of the ordinary when he contended that the main duty of a wife was obedience. A wife's responsibility was to be her husband's "help meet, to aid, not to embarrass his course; to advise, not to command, to obey where it becomes necessary for one to yield, or where the husband chooses to exercise his authority."[51] But Bailey, like most Evangelicals, did not stop here. Nor did he push the argument further as Orestes Brownson, a Presbyterian turned Roman Catholic, did when he said, "We do not believe women . . . are fit to have their own head. Without masculine direction or control, she is out of her element, and a social anomaly, sometimes a hideous monster."[52] Rather, Bailey went on to assure Evangelical women that their husbands' authority was not absolute, that they were not expected to obey husbands "in all things," and that no woman should submit to her husband either her conscience or her mind, a point first enforced in American history when the Providence, Rhode Island, authorities deprived Joshua Verin of the franchise in the mid-seventeenth century because he refused to allow his wife liberty of conscience.[53] Women could legitimately disagree with their husbands on any matter provided they did not become disagreeable. Further, "slavish submission" to husbands' opinions and dispositions was contrary to the "happy equality" given the sexes by the gospel, wherein the male tyranny of power most often loses out to the female tyranny of purity and truth. That there was more than the ghost of subversiveness hovering over this theory became clear when Bailey addressed himself to the realm of religion, in which, he argued, "the husband can assume no authority without a presumptuous usurpation of divine right." When a man does arrogate religious authority to himself, a wife is to ward off his "usurpation" if need be by "decided dissent" or an "uncompromising resistance."[54] Disobedience to husbands thus became, at least potentially, obedience to God.

Donald G. Mathews has perceptively argued that male opposition to Evangelical religion must be seen within the context of conversion's "new birth," which provided women with a "release from the prior restraints of culture or class, role or stereotype," allowing them "psychological and social space" that was as exhilarating for them as it was threatening to their husbands.[55] For the most part, however, the way in which religion provided women with an accepted outlet for rebellion against male dominance has not been sufficiently appreciated by historians. It did not escape the attention of many nineteenth-century husbands and fathers, especially in the South. Martha Tomhave Blauvelt has written that "many Southern men seemed to have resented, rather than encouraged, religiosity in their wives. Perhaps because their slave culture made them sensitive to any loss of authority, many Southern husbands regarded the clergy as competition for their wives' allegiance."[56] This perception was not limited to the South. In every region there were some men who did all in their power to prevent their women from attending revivals or religious services and, most calamitous of all, from marrying ministers. The 1798 Methodist *Discipline* reveals that some of their fears were not groundless. At the same time that it expelled any woman who married an "unawakened" man, it also permitted women to marry without parental consent provided "a woman be under the necessity of marrying" and "her parents absolutely refuse to let her marry any Christian."[57]

Accounts are legion and legendary of women defying parental and husbandly authority by sneaking out of the house to hear Evangelical preachers.[58] Beulah Lyon, the daughter of Vermont's first governor, Thomas Chittendon, stole out of her Kentucky home to attend class meetings with her children, paying the servants hush money to hide the horses and protect her secret. Her "deistic" husband, a wealthy businessman-politician who served in Congress for twelve years, was offended by the rudeness of such Methodist itinerants as the rough-and-tumble Peter Cartwright and by the crudeness of Methodist doctrine, especially concerning amusements and apparel, which made his wife increasingly unfit for high society. This streak of female rebelliousness was passed on from mother to daughter. One of Lyon's daughters wanted to receive adult baptism and affiliate with the Baptists. Threatened by her husband with eviction from the house and separation from her children, she flouted his authority openly. When this became dangerous, she remorselessly undermined his wishes through undercover religious activities.[59]

Evangelicals even went so far as to include in their hagiographic literature for children stories of courageous young women and wives who disobeyed male authority to attend religious services, only to be beaten and sometimes banished from their homes when discovered.[60] Female children were thus taught by parents and teachers that a higher authority existed than either parents or husbands. The Rochester Collegiate Institute's support of Mrs. Burchard's children's meetings in the early 1830s suggests that such subversive tendencies were not all talk. Teachers in the Female Department granted children time off from school to attend her afternoon meetings even though parents had not given their consent.[61] The appeal of female converts to a higher authority paved the way for later Evangelical feminists to appeal to a higher authority than the church to justify disobedience to strictures against women's organizing, preaching, voting, and ordination. In the early days of the Sunday school movement, to cite but one example, many pastors and congregations were hostile to schools for (among other reasons) desecration of the Sabbath. Yet women like Mary C. Walker of Utica, who later became a volunteer city missionary, brazenly ignored the opposition. In 1816 she began calling from door to door with four other young women aged fourteen to sixteen, soliciting funds, clothing, and students for a school that her church neither endorsed nor wanted.[62]

Barbara Leslie Epstein has made an interesting case for distinguishing women's conversion experiences during the Puritan Evangelicalism of the First Great Awakening and the Methodist Evangelicalism of the Second Great Awakening. Puritan women understood the same thing by "conversion" as did Puritan men, she argues. But by the Second Great Awakening, Evangelical women experienced conversion, not so much like the men as the attainment of exemption from divine judgment on human sins, but as the embarking on a sacred journey with Jesus. It is simply pushing the evidence too far, however, to claim that women's experiences of conversion during the Second Great Awakening expressed an underlying female outcry against males.[63] Yet the psychological harassment and physical abuse Evangelical women suffered from unrepentant spouses did have a kind of warped significance. The opposition of some husbands to their wives' conversions to Evangelical religion was both an expression of fear of losing domain over docility and property rights and an act of vengeance against the way wives could oppress husbands with their relentless, tormenting piety. Mr. Jones of Mecklenburgh, Virginia, a man with a saw-toothed personality and a violent hatred of Methodists, threatened to shoot his wife if she ever went hankering after Methodist religion. His fears had been fertilized over the years by all too many cases of Methodist women who were drawn away from the home, roused to rebellion, and incited to independence by the excitement of church work until they had been rendered virtually unfit for domestic drudgery. The dread of becoming a church's widower had some grounding in reality, for as one early manual confessed, "the public means of grace among the Methodists are so numerous, that it is absolutely impossible for our people to have sufficient leisure for family and private duties, unless they be very careful to redeem every moment of time."[64] Believing that resistance to husbands was at times as much a duty as obedience, Mrs. Jones attended a Methodist service anyway. As promised, her husband's rifle met her at the door. When she defiantly greeted the gun—"My dear, if you take my life, you must obtain leave of my heavenly Spouse"[65]—he knew immediately that his fears had not been figments of the imagination but fragments of the reality of religion's hold on women. Wives who got religion gave many husbands the shivers, for they knew that a contest had begun between them and God, and the trophy was the wife's allegiance.

Some husbands realized that this was a battle they could not win, and so they accorded their wives autonomy in religious preference and activities.[66] Others, like the reverently agnostic "Anticlericus," held preachers personally responsible for domestic disquiet and every wifely act of insubordination and independence. When Charles G. Finney visited his home:

> He stuffed my wife with tracts, and alarmed her fears, and nothing short of meetings, night and day, could atone for the many fold sins my poor, simple spouse had committed, and at the same time, she made the miraculous discovery, that she had been "unevenly yoked." From this unhappy period, peace, quiet, and happiness have fled from my dwelling, never, I fear, to return.[67]

A Warren County, Georgia, minister paid dearly for his successful evangelization of women. He was shot and killed in 1858 by an irate husband whose wife had recently been converted and joined the church.[68]

Women's high-voltage religious experiences seemed more likely to have the effect on many men of churning their stomachs rather than warming their hearts. The notorious disruptions of services by rowdy youth and furious husbands, as well as the less public forms of opposition to Evangelical preachers, attest both to the hidden sensuality of the female-preacher relationship, identified by Frances Trollope and some female novelists, and to the autonomy, self-confidence, and new values engendered by an Evangelical religion that proved inceasingly attractive to women.[69]

Chapter Three

"She Hindered Not My Work"

Peggy Dow and the Sacrificer Model

> It cannot be doubted that if we had a history of the uncomplaining meekness with which, in unnumbered instances, beauty, refinement, accomplishments, have been offered on the altar of a husband's usefulness, it would bring tears to the eyes of the most thoughtless taskmaster who ever exacted labor from the muzzled ox.
>
> The *Independent*

The first duty for the minister's wife in nineteenth-century America was never to stand in the way of her husband's vocation. She could either get out of his way or walk with him in it. The first method produced the Sacrificer model of the minister's wife, represented by Peggy Dow, the wife who through her privation, suffering, obedience, and self-abnegation became an object-lesson in spirituality: she taught Evangelicals how to die. The second method was associated with the Assistant model, represented by Lydia Finney, who through her public activities, visitation, and benevolent projects became a living epistle in consecrated service: she taught evangelicals how to live. This is not to suggest that the women who adopted the latter model did not suffer or were not servants. As we shall see, all ministers' wives drew from the same well of loneliness, sacrifice, and dedication. But the Peggy Dows, unlike the Lydia Finneys, achieved their identity through quiet suffering and passive servanthood.

Peggy Dow has lived for almost two hundred years as one of American history's footnote characters. Often such figures deserve to remain at the bottom of the page. Peggy Dow is lifted from the footnotes to the text because she lived out in her thirty-nine years many of the "vicissitudes" shared by ministers' wives. She also portrayed, through her popular autobiography and collections of poetry, hymns, and camp-meeting songs, an image of the minister's wife as a suffering servant that was adopted by a significant minority of women in the ministry, especially those married to itinerant evangelists. She represents the might-have-been of American Evangelicalism, the power of the sphere doctrine's glorification of self-sacrificing service to obstruct women's emergence from dependency and subservience.

I

Peggy Holcomb fixed herself up nervously as she prepared to enter the room and join the overnight guest. She was a simple, meek woman, "plain as a pipe stem," and the twenty-two pages of her life's short chapter (she was born in 1780) turned laboriously from one tragedy and illness to another. Even to herself she was a starkly tormented character. But for the grace of God and a sickliness that kept her on the strait and narrow, her past had been enough to set her feet on the wide path that leads to destruction. Her mother died when she was five months old, and her father wasted no time in remarrying, scattering his six children in different directions and sending Peggy (who would never see him again) to live with her older sister Hannah and her husband, Smith Miller, in a village on the Mohawk River called Western, the site of Finney's first big revival victory in 1825. Peggy was not quite able to determine whether her place in the household was one of adopted daughter or domestic servant. Her brother-in-law was to her thinking "a man not calculated to gain the world," and he alternated between states of inebriation and indolence. Three years before she and her sister had mustered enough strength to defy him and join a nearby Methodist society. Through their prayers he too had eventually "embraced religion," making them for the first time a "happy family" whose life revolved around the refreshing ways of holiness. Now they had the privilege of entertaining in their home the famed wanderer Lorenzo Dow, the man deluged in his day with such adjectives as "eccentric," "crazy," "quaint," "singular," and "mad." Smith Miller had persuaded him to rest at their place before journeying on to Canada after an exhausting camp meeting thirty miles away and a three-hour revival at Western that had converted a hundred people.

Peggy had never seen the likes of Lorenzo before. Even in a crude and rude age, Lorenzo stood out. He looked like the very devil, some people said. He was tall for the day, five feet ten inches, stoop-shouldered, with long, lanky limbs and a pock-marked baby face that was as homely as a hedge post. His hair, parted in the middle, cascaded carelessly in ringlets down to his waist. He never shaved, and his beard covered a heaving, asthmatic chest. His dress unkempt but colorful—a long cloak was draped over the rags that passed for clothes—his odor rancid, the wild-mannered Dow spoke with the voice of a canary and the personality of a hawk. "I was very much afraid of him, as I had heard such *strange* things about him!"

Just how strange things could be with Lorenzo became apparent as Peggy approached the room, where he seemed to be interrogating her sister, asking all sorts of personal questions, like "How long had I professed religion?" and "Whether I kept wicked company." Peggy walked into the room just as Hannah was quoting her to the effect that "I had rather marry a Preacher than any other man, provided I was worthy, and that I would wish them [sic] to travel and be useful to souls." Lorenzo then turned his dark, cavernous eyes on Peggy and spoke to her for the first time. Did you say what Hannah said, he demanded? "I told him I had." Lorenzo then asked her to marry him.

> I made him no reply, but went directly out of the room—as it was the first time he had spoken to me. I was very much surprised. He gave me to understand, that he should return to our house again in a few days, and would have more conversation with me on the subject; which he did, after attending a meeting ten or twelve miles from where I lived. He returned the next evening, and spoke to me on the subject again, when he told me that he would marry, provided that he could find one that would consent to be travelling and preaching the gospel; and if I thought I could be willing to marry him, and give him up to go, and do his duty, and not see him, or have his company more than one month out of thirteen, he could feel free to give his hand to me. . . . Yet I felt willing to cast my lot with his, and be a help, not a hindrance to him, if the Lord would give me grace, as I had no doubt but he would, if I stood as I ought—and I accepted of his proposal.[1]

II

Dow's proposal, even apart from the circumstances, was bizarre.[2] Everyone understood that an itinerant Methodist preacher had no business with a wife. Dow was not officially a Methodist, but he was Methodism taken to its emotional conclusion. He wanted Methodism, but on his own terms, which did not include being a team player or climbing onto denominational bandwagons. Methodists wanted Dow, but they were not about to approve anybody they could not control. Methodist elders repeatedly employed him, but sent him home four times; annual conferences reviewed his candidacy for ordination, but rejected him thrice. Still, as George Peck has written,

"Dow was a Methodist in doctrine and feeling,"[3] and Peggy Dow always remained a faithful member of the church.

If the regimen required by itinerancy was not a rediscovery of the ancient monastic vows of chastity, poverty, and obedience, it was undeniably a near miss. In the words of the southern Methodist bishop Enoch Mather Marvin, "Two of the deepest instincts of our nature must be violated—the love of money and the love of home." To be sure, John and Charles Wesley were married, but they shared a fundamental ambivalence about matrimony, enhanced by John's disastrous marriage, that is nicely captured by Robert J. Lowenberg:

> Wesley was adamant that celibacy be observed by Methodist preachers, but he was equally convinced of the need to keep Methodism a social religion, resistant alike to sectarianism and asceticism. The social aspect of Methodist worship which Wesley had in mind was not limited to the spiritual sphere, but included the full spectrum of religious life. A Methodist preacher should be, as Wesley was, an exemplary man and a family man as well as a tireless preacher. These goals, theoretically compatible, nevertheless seemed to require the use of methods that were incompatible: marriage on the one hand and celibacy on the other. What seemed perfectly sensible in theory became awkwardly and embarrassingly contradictory in practice. John Wesley, a tireless preacher, was also a married man.[5]

In the American setting Methodist ambivalence was erased in favor of an aggressively ascetic attitude toward marriage. Bishop William McKendree, explaining his own bachelorhood, once asked how any self-respecting itinerant could find the time to get hitched to a woman if he was properly hitching his horse to preaching posts and his sermons to texts. Early Methodist preachers were a proud band of bachelors. They both protected each other from interesting relationships with the sisters and disciplined the weak brothers who backslid.

Bishop Francis Asbury's opposition to married itinerants was proverbial, and his frank avowal of preference for a single preacher over a half-dozen married ones struck fear into any contemplating matrimony. Bachelorhood was one of Asbury's qualifications for promotion to a Methodist presiding elder. Once an elder's elder, one was expected to serve as a scarecrow, frightening off the flocks of women who fancied becoming the wife of a minister. Particularly to be guarded were the young preachers, for it was believed that they had not been sufficiently hammered and hardened on itinerancy's anvil to withstand the sweet whispers of wives eager to escape the mortifications of the traveling connection. Pleading at least for the fallback position of late marriage, one crabbed old bachelor in the Cumberland Presbyterian Church exclaimed, "Young preacher, stop! Turn your back upon that pair of flashing eyes; expel from your mind all thoughts of that voluptuous form; exorcise the evil demon of passion from your breast, and wait, wait, until you become a man and a preacher before you think of matrimony."[6] The New York Conference discontinued any preacher who married during his first year of probation, and marriage during the second year of trial status was punishable by a one-year extension of the probationary period.[7] The beleaguered Jesse Lee tried once to exchange his call to the ministry with a call to the married state. Praying that God would prevent him from finding a wife if he was truly called to the itinerancy, Lee approached his selection and explained to her the situation. Annoyed at being an object rather than the subject of matrimony, she turned him down. Lee joined the itinerant ranks.[8]

Although the *Discipline* meted out no penalties to traveling preachers who married, there was the Wesleyan injunction to "converse sparingly with women." Strict constructionist bishops who sensed the violation of this rule saved their brothers by appointing them to wilderness or mountainous areas where women were scarce.[9] The preacher who forsook completely the brotherhood of bachelors often enjoyed with his young wife a honeymoon among the coyotes. Marriage was a decision that caused a couple to "go far" in the ministry—often about as far in the wilderness as one could get without having wild animals and whippoorwills as the only congregation. Itinerants who married faced the whip of being "read out" to poor appointments, a harsh punishment that read many out of the itinerancy as well.[10]

It is tempting, though it would be wrong, to attribute solely to the itinerancy this state of affairs, in which wives became encumbrances at best and evils at worst. For Methodist historians, the itinerancy has functioned much as the frontier has in the past for American historians. It is the source of all that is good—the Samson's hair that was the secret of Methodism's colossal gains. It is the source of all that is bad—the whipping boy on whom all the severity insensitivity and oddity of the Methodist system can be blamed. The truth, as always, lies somewhere in between. The wives of clergy were indeed seen in the early years as Delilahs who would shear the system of its strength. When the Genesee Conference circuit rider William Colbert scowled at Samuel Budd for getting married and going off to visit his wife, warning, "The curse of God [is] to follow the men who leave the work of God for the sake of a woman,"[11] he was expressing both the church's fear and its frustration. The Methodist system was briskly parsimonious toward the families of clergy, forcing many itinerants to "locate" (that is, leave the itinerancy and become local preachers of the tent-making type in order to support a growing family). "If the great end of the itinerancy," one author explained to the wives of itinerants, "were to make provisions for ministers and their families, it surely ought to be immediately abandoned as a complete failure." But the itinerancy was designed to "spread scriptural holiness and reform this continent," an end that justified sacrifice and hardship.[12] The Methodist hierarchy was especially resentful of the embarrassing stigma placed upon it by reports of early marriages, starving widows, and unsupportable families. And it was without much sensitivity to the peculiar problems of men who married. One itinerant, whose wife had almost died giving birth in 1835, pleaded with his bishop not to appoint him presiding elder because the job would take him away from home too much. The bishop appointed him anyway.[13]

From the episcopal point of view, the very survival of the church was at stake in the epidemic of marriages that began to afflict the itinerant ranks and forced many to locate. An old study of the 650 preachers whose names appeared in the denomination's minutes prior to 1800 revealed that 500 died as local preachers and most of the remainder had left the itinerancy and located at one time or another.[14] The bishops addressed the problem in their 1844 episcopal address, lamenting the easing of strictures against early clerical marriages and the growing number of preachers with "local embarrassments" (that is, wives, children, and property).[15] Bishop James O. Andrew, whose own wife, Ann Amelia, introduced into southern Methodism two great innovations—through her novel marriage in 1816, the preacher's wife, and through her continued slave holding in 1844, the Methodist Episcopal church, South—placed the issue of Methodist marriages in clear perspective two years earlier. Marriage for Methodist preachers, he contended, transcended an emotional decision; it was most importantly a moral decision that had far-reaching implications for the church.[16]

But the opposition to marriage must not be interpreted solely within the context of the church's resentment of the overloading of its efficient machinery with the increased expenses necessary to sustain wives and families. For Francis Asbury, itinerant marriages threatened the very integrity of marriage itself:

> Amongst the duties imposed upon me by my office was that of travelling extensively, and I could hardly expect to find a woman with grace enough to enable her to live but one week out of the 52 with her husband; besides, what right has any man to take advantage of the affections of a woman, make her his wife, and by a voluntary absence subvert the whole order and economy of the marriage state, by separating those whom neither God, nature, nor the requirement of civil society permit long to be put asunder? It is neither just nor generous.[17]

The full story of the transition in America from a celibate to a conjugal Methodist ministry is in need of an author. Although almost any stick was good enough to beat Methodist ministers who stepped toward matrimony, itinerants married in increasing numbers as the nineteenth century advanced. They took the blows because even worse were the beatings of the flesh and loneliness. Further, Julie Roy Jeffrey has argued cogently that the emergence of the notion of female character as distinctively religious "helped to establish a climate of opinion where clerical marriage could be seen not as a necessary evil but, in fact, as a desirable goal."[18] But only after thousands of itinerants' wives—Sacrificers and Assistants alike—showed that they would not stand in the way of their husbands' vocation did opposition to marriage diappear, and then it did so with a venegance. For by the 1860s there had emerged the opposite pressure: pressure from the congregation and the hierarchy for ministers to marry.[19] Denominational legislation sometimes lagged behind ecclesiastical expectation. In 1860 there was still on the books of the Ohio Annual Conference a rule that forbade itinerant marriages until after two years of conference membership. But Charles Cardwell McCabe, later Bishop McCabe, wrote with insouciance, "I married first and read the rule afterwards."[20] Methodist itinerants in 1860 were expected to marry. It was only a matter of proper timing and careful selection.

In 1802, however, Lorenzo Dow was doing something very unusual: he was getting married and remaining an itinerant. By saying yes, Peggy would also be doing something quite remarkable. There were few contemporary Methodist models for a woman making a life out of being an itinerant's wife.

III

As if giving Peggy a chance to change her mind about sharing in his vagabond life, Lorenzo did not return to take his bride until two years after his proposal. Satisfied that she was aware of the implications of marriage to a scourge sent by the Lord of hosts to the lords of hell called "Atheism, Deism and Calvinism," twenty-seven-year-old Lorenzo then married the twenty-four-year-old woman one September evening in 1804. A friend to no one, though he had itinerated in all seventeen states of the union, Lorenzo's only witnesses to the wedding were Peggy's family. The next morning he left to fill four thousand miles of appointments in the Mississippi territory, "the first Protestant who expounded the gospel in Alabama and Mississippi."[21] A pamphleteer ever ready to promote his eccentricities, Dow flooded the frontier with his sermons and thoughts. Seven months later he returned, only to leave again after two weeks, to be gone another three months . . . a pattern that repeated itself over and over again in Peggy's life. She learned quickly, if she had not already felt the full weight of the realization, that the wives of circuit riders must stay in homes that were not their homes and wait for the return of husbands who were not home long enough to be husbands.

Peggy spent much of her life either traveling to meet Lorenzo at appointments, if only to be together for a short while, or waiting for him to return. In their early years together she often traveled with him, riding at breakneck speed forty or fifty miles a day, living on horseback, keeping house in saddlebags, and listening daily to five or six sermons on the mount. She shared with Lorenzo the mattress of the earth and the diamond-patterned quilt of the sky, journeyed through prairies and wilderness roamed by the wolf, the bear, the panther, and the deer, and traversed Indian paths and frontier territory that, according to an old western proverb, "is a good country for men and horses, but is death on women and oxen."[22] Lorenzo had a reputation for being death on horseflesh. When his horse could not take the pace any longer, he discarded it and found another. When sickness caused Peggy to slacken their speed, Lorenzo left her behind with friends.[23] She sat dutifully in churches, barns, and school-

197886

houses during his two-and three-hour sermons and was known on rare occasions to close one of his services with prayer.

In 1814, at an African church, she tried her hand at exhorting when the congregation's eagerness to hear from Dow's wife forced her into it. She found the experience satisfying and resolved to "take up my cross" more. Lorenzo, who supported the right of women to preach and even traveled with the Yorkshire Quaker preacher Dorothy Ripley during his 1818 visit to England, must have encouraged her in these thoughts.[24] But Peggy charted for herself a different course as a minister's wife. She became an appendage to his ministry, one that would never burst with complaints or demands, sharing his trials but stopping short of participating in the joys of service. She dutifully traveled with Lorenzo on his 1805 European raid, which ranged throughout England and Ireland, but she hated it. She found herself pregnant, trudging through the muddy streets of Dublin seeking shelter from the rain and wind with the "first American professional religious revivalist to visit England in the nineteenth century." All she wanted in life was to be Lorenzo's wife and housekeeper, but when he finally did settle her for a while in their own home, "the wilderness appeared almost like a paradise to me."[25]

Peggy knew what it was to support a man, as she had supported her bibulous brother-in-law. She did not fear that. But she did fear the loneliness of being a circuit rider's wife. She longed to find "one real *female friend*," though her reclusive temperament prevented friendliness. She secluded herself in her home, venturing out only to church and class meetings. Here, at home, many circuit rider's wives felt most secure and happy. Here their husbands deferred to them in matters domestic and economic, as William Colbert did when discussing with his wife whether to sell their house or to invite his junior preacher on the circuit to live with them: "Believe me I never mean to cross thy mind."[26] Here Peggy could indulge the two joys of her life, writing and music (indeed her fatal illness was contracted while attending a writing school). She combined these interests in her collection of poems and hymns, all of them reflective of the sober and melancholy disposition of their compiler.[27] Her autobiography is the gloomy portrait of a woman with frail health and frayed nerves, bewildered by the events of her life, troubled by fears, loneliness, depression, and bitterness, who chose to sacrifice everything dear to her on the altar of her husband's ministry.

She loved her husband deeply, and their relationship (as was true of most itinerant marriages)[28] was marked by moments of great tenderness and warmth. The vast distance between them was geographic, not emotional. Peggy found that Lorenzo, who liked to be around no one, could be "affectionate and attentive" toward her, especially when she was sick. In Ireland he remained by her bedside for twenty days during one of her "nervous fevers." When he did finally go, she repressed her bitterness and curved it upon herself:

> Although I felt willing for him to go and blow the gospel trumpet, yet my heart shrunk at the thought of being left in a strange land, in my present situation, so weak that I could not put on my clothes without help, and my sweet little babe at a considerable distance from me and amongst stangers.[29]

Although Peggy seemed constitutionally predisposed to martyrdom, Lorenzo helped prepare her for this exalted state. His bloodcurdling resolution to marry no one whose demands might interfere with the ministry is exemplified in one of the many rumors that buzzed about him. Facing a prospective itinerant recruit, he said, "'Young man, God has a work for you to do, and if you take any step which will hinder you in that work, God will curse you.' Then addressing himself to the suspected object, he said, 'Young woman, if you cause this young man to neglect that work, God will kill you.'"[30] He himself had told Peggy that if she ever said, "Do not go to your appointment," or in any way stood in his way, "I should pray to God to remove you, which I believe he would answer."[31] This monomania perhaps helps to explain Peggy's woeful response to Lorenzo's declining health after the birth of their first child, Letitia Johnson: "I often cried to the Lord to take my child or my health, but spare my dear husband." According to her dreary theology, "The Lord took me at my word and laid his afflicting hand upon me."[32] As if it were not enough to lay down one's life for the ministry, some wives of itinerants actually felt guilty when they spent time with their husbands and apologized for the pleasure. Betsy Colbert, the wife of William Colbert, then a Philadelphia Conference itinerant, wrote to her husband about his upcoming visit home in 1805:

> Be assured my love it will be pleasing to have thee with me, but I have no desire to discourage thee in missing any part of thy duty on my account. I am very sorry to be the cause of any persons

neglecting any part of their duty, especially one so near and dear, but as it seems to be convenient for thee, I am much pleased to hear [of] thy coming soon, though I do not expect the time will be very short to either of us. I do hope thou dost not harbour such a thought, as that I wished thy stay longer.[33]

For Peggy Dow, the life of a minister's wife was one of unrelieved gloom. Some of her journal entries begin with the surprised and mournful observation "I am yet alive."[34] As time went on, she sank further and further into despair, disgusted by "this world of affliction," tired of its struggle, and at home living on the edge of eternity. Her only joy was knowing that she did not hinder her husband in his work. This minister's wife, who began her marriage as one who "rejoiceth not in iniquity," ended it as one who rejoiced in infirmity. "My cry was—Lord, help me to be willing to suffer all thy goodness sees best to inflict."[35] Submission and faithfulness were the expressions of her philosophy. Suffering and resignation were the expressions of her character.

In 1819, during Lorenzo's last transatlantic journey, a mission to infuse new vigor into the Primitive Methodist Convention, which he had helped to establish in the countryside of England during his 1806 trip,[36] Peggy wrote to him of her declining health. Once again, she placed herself second to his sacred errand.

> I think yesturday, my desire to God was if it would be more for his glory, for you to return in a few weeks, if you might, if not, so let it be—GO MY LORENZO, THE WAY YOU ARE ASSURED THE LORD CALLS: and if we meet no more in this vale of tears, may God prepare us to meet in the realms of peace, to range the blest fields on the banks of the river, and sing hallelujah for ever and ever.[37]

Sensing that something was wrong, Lorenzo cut short his tour by a year and returned in 1819 to find Peggy in the throes of tuberculosis. Already without an ounce of warmth toward anyone but Peggy, he apparently expended her allotment in returning and immediately carted her away with him on a revival tour through New England. She begged him never to leave her until she either died or recovered. While they were in Providence Lorenzo returned from an appointment to find her weeping uncontrollably. After much prodding, she told him what was wrong: "The consumption is a flattering disease! —but I shall return back to Hebron and tell father Dow that I have come back to die with him."[38] They returned in September to Hebron and Lorenzo's father. Lorenzo held his wanderlust in check long enough to remain with her until she died.

It was the sixth of January, and what there was of Peggy's family gathered around her for the final ritual. Lorenzo sat by her side on the bed, holding her hand. Someone asked if she was in any pain. "She answered in the negative—and that one thing attracted her here below—pointing her finger toward me as I supported her in my arms. When I replied, 'Lord, Thou gavest her to me! I have held her only as a lent favor for fifteen years! And now I resign her back to Thee, until we meet again beyond the swelling flood!' Peggy said, 'Amen.'" She had come into the world, and lived her life, with a cry. She now left it with a gentle sigh.

Her husband's tribute to his long-suffering "rib" was etched on a white, square, upright stone on Burroughs Hill in Hebron, Connecticut, where legend says that Lorenzo, who always had an apocalyptic gleam in his eyes, buried her standing up and facing east in readiness for the Second Coming. It was a tribute that Peggy probably would have written for herself, for the greatest laurel that could be given to her was "self-sacrificing."

PEGGY DOW
SHARED THE
VICISSITUDES OF
LORENZO
15 Years &
DIED
Jan. 6, 1820
AGED 39 YEARS[39]

In what was even for his day indecent haste, Lorenzo then found a replacement for Peggy. Three months after burying her, he married, again under the strangest of circumstances, the staunch Methodist Lucy Dolbeare, a hardy, garrulous, handsome woman of contrary disposition and independent outlook, the very opposite of Lorenzo's beloved Peggy except for their common dislike of traveling.[40] Now as Dow itinerated during the first year of his marriage, he had two things to introduce to his listeners: his new thirty-four-year-old wife and his new patented remedy, "The Family Medicine," which furthered his reputation as an entrepreneur as well as an evangelist.[41] One day Lucy retired from a life of resentfully borne suffering and settled permanently on the farm her father had left her at Montville, a few miles south of Hebron. Although the farm was known to the townspeople as "Lorenzo Dow's place," Lorenzo gave it his own title, He painted in big white letters above the gate to the house: "WOMEN RULE HERE."[42] One is left to ponder why. Was it his way of surrendering in the tug of war between a wife married to a husband and a husband married to a career? Apparently that which Lorenzo had feared most had happened: he now had a wife who hindered him in his calling.

IV

The wives of Methodist itinerants were not the only ones to adopt the Sacrificer model, although Methodists were often the most outspoken and outlandish in its defense. Enoch Mather Marvin, for example, a southerner, unemotionally selected for his wife a woman who would not stand in his way and then insisted that her wedding vows include: "To be willing to go wherever he might be appointed."[13] A perusal of obituaries in nineteenth-century periodicals will reveal story after story of a deceased clerical wife, chosen for her devout character and not her leadership characteristics, who adorned the ministry with her absence, helped to support the family financially, confined her usefulness to the domestic circle, presided only in strictly private dramas like that at the family altar, and exhorted with tears.[44] The formalization of the Dow image had occurred by the early 1850s, when a marriage manual included directions on how to fulfill one's heroic mission of cheerful sacrifice if one was marrying a minister:

> The minister's bride must study to feel the grandeur of her husband's mission. She must view it in its relation to the sublime path of redemption. She must gaze on the majestic results growing out of his labours. She must view, by the eye of faith, the endless gratitude of the souls who will become the seals of her husband's ministry, and above all, she must tremble before the idea of *dragging her husband out of the pulpit into hell!* Let her never forget that no man's salvation is in greater peril than that of a minister, who through the lust of money, the love of indolence, or the persuasions of a wife, leaves his appropriate sphere, and buries himself in the obscurity of private life.[45]

If a ministry was ever found curdled into a premature conclusion because the wife had soured it with her peckish spirit, woe to that woman.

You shall see God *set his face against you and him:* domestic bitterness will poison your enjoyments; misfortunes will haunt your steps; God will curse you in soul and in body, and in all probability both you and he will fail of heaven. O then, beware, young bride, how you treat your husband's high vocation.[46]

By nineteenth-century standards of success and status, it would be hard to imagine a less inviting future than that made visible through marriage to an itinerant. Yet itinerants never seemed to want for marriage partners. One steps into the murky realm of human motivation gingerly, and there were probably as many reasons for this fact as there were itinerants' wives. One can only make educated guesses, and then still marvel. If the crux of dependency is economics, then the Peggy Dows among ministers' wives enjoyed large measures of independence. Their economic status was largely self-determined. The unspoken contract in conventional marriages called for financial support from the husband in return for domestic service from the wife. But the wives of many Baptist, Methodist, and Presbyterian itinerants were denied the securities of this arrangement. Itinerants who settled their families in one spot (moving costs were prohibitive, parsonages were few and far between, and many of those existing had no furniture) might leave it up to their wives' ingenuity to supplement meager salaries and provide for their own and their children's welfare. "A man needs grace and faith," Heman Bangs wrote, "to leave all, and be an itinerant Methodist preacher—to have a growing family, and depend on the cold hand of charity for their maintenance." The journal of his wife, Sally Burritt Bangs, reveals that it took much more grace and faith to be the wife of an itinerant Methodist preacher.[47]

The parting scene was duplicated over and over. An itinerant, after only a short spell at home, was saying goodbye to his family once again. They knelt in prayer and then arose, each one embracing the one called by God to preach the gospel. Mounting the horse and starting down the path, the itinerant turned for one last look and waved at his weeping family. Human nature said stay. But grace proved triumphant, and he rode on. The Cumberland Presbyterian itinerant Alexander Anderson left his farm, his wife, and seven children to God's mercy in the early 1800s while he preached and attended camp meetings.[48] The Methodist bishop Robert R. Robert was called the "Log-Cabin Bishop" although it was his wife, Elizabeth Oldham, and his mother-in-law who maintained the log-cabin homestead and worked the farm in his absence.[49] Even when the preacher was home, his presence might be worthless to his household. Used to perpetual motion, he was unable to stop and be content. The Cambellite itinerant John Smith left his family of seven to support themselves on their own while he was away; the farm work had to be either hired out or done by his wife with an infant in her arms. Eventually she extracted a promise from him to check in weekly and share in the responsibility of providing for their family, but he proved to be of no use to her. His mind was so obsessed with the gospel that his hands could not grasp temporal matters for even a moment.[50]

The novelist Harriet Beecher Stowe satirized the minister who was so heavenly minded that he was no earthly good in her story "The Minister's Housekeeper." While the Reverend "jest sit stock still meditatin' on Jerusalem and Jericho," the Reverand's wife had total command of the household. Even when the Reverend was home, he was absent. "But the Lord marcy he didn't know nothin' about where anything he eat or drunk or wore came from or went to: his wife jest led him round in temporal things and took care on him like a baby."[51] Eighteenth-century women married to ministers who were seldom home also took on the management of the household. The difference was that ministers in the eighteenth century expressed remorse and regret at their relinquishment of responsibility, while those of the nineteenth century rationalized it.[52] More than once a family like that of Griffin Sweet, abandoned with only a half bushel of potatoes and no meat or bread in the house, was forced to contemplate the awful privilege of being a part of the gospel ministry.[53]

There was no doubt in the minds of most ministers' wives about whom their husbands were beholden and betrothed to. The awakening could be jarring. Deborah Millett waited patiently at the altar in October 1819 for a groom who never appeared. It seems that Edward T. Taylor, who would later become famous as the organizer of the Boston Seaman's Bethel Church, had become so engrossed in his parish duties in Hingham, Massachusetts, that he forgot his wedding day.[54] The perceptive Cora Harris, whose Episcopalian background gave her a measure of objectivity rare among the wives of Evangelical clergy, based the following observation on her own experience:

There is, in fact, a highly developed capacity for heavenly infidelity to earthly ties in most preachers, and the martyrdom of forsaking father and mother and even his wife in the spirit appealed to his spiritual aspirations. Many a woman has been deserted in this subtle manner by her minister husband.[55]

The nineteenth-century clerical phenomenon of "heavenly infidelity" needs further attention. Someone must explain why itinerants drove themselves so ruthlessly, why they took an almost perverted pride in burning themselves out in the frontier and burned-over districts. At a time when religion was allegedly becoming "feminized," when "it was much the practice to ridicule ministers of the Gospel; to treat them decently as it were out of pity, as debilitated beings, half-way between women and children,"[56] itinerants and their camp-meeting religion reflected an image of the faith that was robustly muscular and aggressively masculine. It may not be unwarranted psychologizing to interpret itinerant masochism and machismo as overcompensation for membership in a world increasingly dominated by women. The noisy bravado of so many miles ridden, so many streams forded, so many sermons preached, so many months away from home, flaunted one's physical stamina and endurance as much as one's spiritual stamina and dedication. Itinerant braggadocio even had a sporting element to it. Benjamin Slight, a swaggering circuit rider stationed at Melbourne, Canada, bullied a Congregationalist minister who had claimed that in 1850 he "preached 153 sermons; attended 42 temperance, church and prayer meetings; visited, read and prayed with 298 families, and baptized 14 children; preached 5 funeral sermons; received into Church 32 new members; travelled 3400 miles; spent 114 days and nights from home." Slight paraded his own statistics in comparison: "I preached in this circuit each year about 350 sermons; special, church and other meetings, from 130–150; pastoral visitations, numerous, funeral sermons, 8 or 10; marriages, 8 or 10; received on trial, about 30 to 40; travelled about 5000 miles or more; spent about 150 nights from home, and about 300 days."[57]

At first reading Joseph Pilmoor's journal entry for 1 January 1770 sounds a typical note of resolutions that come in one year and out the next: "O that this may be the beginning of years—a Gospel Jubilee to Zion! My soul longs for the increase of the Redeemer's Kingdom in the world; I feel a willingness to spend all my strength, and even to die, for the Lord Jesus."[58] But then one pauses, for equestrian evangelists did just that. They spent themselves, they died, and the more hardships they suffered, the more they rejoiced. E. Robb Zaring found in his study of Indiana itinerants that the first thirty assigned to the territory stayed in the ministry an average of ten years and died at an average age of thirty-eight. [59] There was something heroic, but also hectoring, in the teary singing at the beginning of Methodist annual conferences of the old hymn "And Are We Yet Alive?"

Itinerants' indifference to their own well-being was matched only by their insensitivity to the welfare of their families. "She is alive now; at least I left her alive the other day," Peter Cartwright flippantly remarked of his wife of sixty-three years while thanking the Illinois Conference for the gift of an easy chair to commemorate his sixty-five years in the itinerancy and his fifty years as a presiding elder. [60] Of course, Methodists could, and frequently did, point to the admonitions of their founder after his marriage in 1751: "I cannot understand how a Methodist preacher can answer it to God to preach one sermon or travel one day less in a married than in a single state."[61] Joshua Soule wore as a badge of dedication his absence at the births of his eleven children. He was so seldom at home (between 1804 and 1806 he spent only three weeks with his wife) that his children did not recognize him when he did manage to show up. [62] When children were born, baptized, or buried, itinerants were not usually around to celebrate, to weep, or to lift the burden. [63] The New England itinerant George Pickering scheduled visits to his family just as he set appointments to preach. Even when he found himself within a half-mile of his home, he was too conscientious to stop before the appointed time. [64] Many were the wives, sick and bedridden, who were left to nurse themselves by husbands unwilling to miss or even be late for an appointment. [65] One wonders how many children of itinerants went through life with memories that stung, like those of the fifteen-year-old daughter and twelve-year-old son of Minnesota's "snow-shoe itinerant," John Dyer. While their father traveled the circuit in the 1850s, they lived alone in their cabin, a mile from the nearest neighbor, listening to the horror of the wolf's howl during long, dreary nights. "Daughter says that I left no latch on the door, and that she cried for fear at night. But our God seldom, if ever, permits evil to befall us or our families if we keep preaching the gospel."[66]

Not all itinerants left their wives and children at home. The sentimental novelist and spinster Catherine Maria Sedgwick was not the only one to live what she called a "boarding-round life."[67] Sarah Wesley, the wife of Charles Wesley, traveled with him in the early years of his itinerancy, and both of the wives of Thomas Coke shared in the "ministerial nomadism" of this "Foreign Minister of Methodism."[68] John Wesley's understanding of the role of the minister's wife clearly favored their journeying together: he wanted such spouses yoked together in ministry.[69] But there were also numerous reasons consistent with the Sacrificer model for wives to accompany their husbands on hazardous circuits. As Julia C. Bonham has shown in her study of seafaring women, whose lives closely approximated those of itinerants' wives, loneliness drove many women to forfeit earthly comforts and join their husbands on dangerous voyages.[70] Indeed, loneliness was one of the reasons the wives of clergy became so strangely and deliriously happy when it came time for synods, annual conferences, and other denominational assemblies. These were substitutes for vacations and honeymoons, times of socializing and recreation, times of freedom from parisioners—which helps to explain why lay delegation was opposed so strenuously for so long.

Economics also led some wives to traverse the circuits with their husbands. The only way to survive as an itinerant was to cut down expenses, and a prime way of doing this was to take the family and poach off the hospitality of the people. Homes usually welcomed the preacher warmly, but the wife was likely to be greeted with less enthusiasm. The southern Methodist bishop James O. Andrew noted that his wife was sometimes criticized for itinerating with him rather than staying at home and working.[71] Cyrus S. Carpenter, who was assigned in 1830 to the Black River circuit in Arkansas, made quite a picture when he set out with his family:

> Being the owner of a small wagon and horse, he would put his cat and dog on board, and then his trunk, wife and child, and tying his cow behind the vehicle with a long rope, so as to follow, and start out for a month's campaign among the saints. Some were much pleased to see the caravan, and made the brother and his family welcome; a few others, being fastidious and more penurious, were somewhat displeased, and wondered why he did not have his sow and pigs along with him.[72]

Chloe Bailey Sawyer earned for herself a priggish reputation and sneers from the pews by bringing with her supplies of a different sort.

Her distaste for dirt and bugs was so great that she carted her own bedding and tableware with her, refusing to let anyone else's hands wash her cups and saucers.[78] Especially in the South, a traveling preacher's wife could be the least popular person in a community. She increased the expenses of the station.

Even in their day, the hardships and suffering of wives who itinerated with their husbands provided the grist for folklore and legend. This is why some women traveled with itinerants: the lure of adventure within a socially acceptable context that maximized the female virtues of suffering and servanthood. A newlywed minister and his wife, Frank and Helen Edmonds were met at their first circuit by a women who, after inspecting the wife's soft skin and creaseless face, turned to the preacher and said: "Your little wife don't look as if she'd seen much hardship, but she'll get used to it before she's been a Methodist minister's wife many years."[74] Ministers and their wives could be sent to circuits where there were no churches, no parsonages, and no official members. The mountains were the only pulpits, and the heavens the only sounding boards. The wives slept with their husbands on "Jacob's pillow" by night, and by day they caught colds with their husbands fording "Jericho rivers." Many a minister's wife wept in some desolate forest, cradling in her arms a dead child. Many a minister's wife had to bury her children hundreds of miles apart; some had no two children occupying the same cemetery. More than a few wives of preachers dropped like autumn leaves.

An itinerant come calling on a daughter bedazzled by romantic, Currier-and-Ives notions of a minister's life was a dreadful sight for many parents. Preachers, generally, and Methodist itinerants, in particular, were the curse of every doting father.[75] Helen R. Cutler, whose well-to-do father ("Squire Strickland") had pampered his only daughter and hoped that life's coddling would continue through her marriage to a wealthy neighborhood bachelor, crushed her father's heart, disobeyed his will, and broke off communication with him in order to marry a dashing Methodist itinerant with "a well-developed figure and a free, open face" named Frank Edmonds, consoling her ashen father with the bromide "It is better to marry a man without money than money without a man."[76] In fact, itinerants themselves proved to be among the most protective fathers. One veteran minister recited a standard speech whenever putting up a young preacher in his home:

> Now brother, yonder are the stable and corn-crib for your horse; here is a room and a plate for yourself but if I ever catch you making sheeps' eyes at my girls, remember there's the door, and never enter it again. One woman in a family is enough for the wife of a Methodist preacher. It is hard for us, but a heap harder for them.[77]

"Is she a fool?" was all the black Methodist preacher Reverdy C. Ransom could get out of his mother when he told her of his intention to marry a West Virginia native, Emma S. Connor, during his senior year at Wilberforce.[78]

So catastrophic were the implications of the itinerancy that some women whose husbands experienced a sudden call to preach refused outright to hear of any such thing. Brother Henry Summers, licensed to preach the gospel, could not obtain the consent of his wife to join the conference, notwithstanding the united efforts of the preachers and their wives, and the class leaders and their wives.[79] Daughters of Methodist ministers were especially prone to take the vow never to marry a minister, and when they found themselves married to someone with the urge to preach, they exercised every veto power known to woman to squash it.[80]

Not all wives who married ministers felt comfortable in Peggy Dow's Sacrificer role. Fanny Newell began as a yoke-partner in ministry but slipped in later years into a Dow role because of physical handicaps or illnesses that prevented travel.[81] Others, like Mary Elizabeth Thompson, fell into the role through inertia. Thompson's wedding notice, which, she observed wryly, was printed on the funeral page, was truly her obituary. "For after that, if I was not dead to the world, I only saw it through the keyhole of the Methodist *Discipline*, or lifted and transfigured by William's sermons—a straight and narrow path that led from the church door to the grave."[82] Still others were like Paulina Bascom Williams, the wife of a Vermont minister in the 1830s, forced by financial circumstances to be a Sacrificer. Her story is tragic. It is one of soaring hopes and dreams and ambitions to be useful as a missionary of the gospel, blasted by the stinginess, callousness, and downright cruelty of churches. A slice of life taken from her history gives a graphic picture of what it was like to be a Peggy Dow against one's will.

Paulina knew when she "convenanted to be an Evangela"[83] that the lot of minister's wife would be a hard one. She expected it also to be a useful one, like so many Evangelical women who welcomed marriage proposals from ministers, itinerants, and home missionaries. Julie Roy Jeffery has perceptively described the "highly visible" and "genuinely shared ministry" of many frontier itinerants' wives,[84] and it was to this type of missionary career in Vermont that Paulina had thought she said, "I do." She expected her life to be filled with such duties as visitation, counseling, evangelism, teaching, and organizing, as well as the expected home responsibilities. It might have turned out that way had congregations seen it as God's responsibility, not theirs, to keep the pastor "poor and humble." Her dream of being a teammate in ministry turned into a nightmare of being only a partner in privation. Forced to leave a church because of delinquent salary payments, her sickly husband, who spent almost as much time in bed as out of it, accepted a call to a neighboring town, a place known as a graveyard for ministers' wives. She felt guilty at having ceased a ministry for economic reasons, for it seemed to be a tacit tenet of Evangelicalism, although observed mainly in the breech, that "a minister's family, probably ought never to leave a people simply from want of support."[85] Trembling for the future, she wrote:

> I feel a kind of pensiveness that frightens me. I look out of my windows in my chamber and everything looks like a dreary maze. There is a vacancy on all I behold. I feel a distrustfulness in everything; even in the safekeeping of God. It seems as though I should be left to dishonor my husband, my profession, and my God! Though there is nothing that peculiarly besets me now, but there will be very soon and that I am given up to the buffetings of Satan and everybody knows it, though I have told no one.[86]

Her misgivings proved well-founded, for she soon discovered that when her new parishioners were not engaged in "invectives and insinuations" about her, creating "a serious objection to my convenanting with this church," they were fighting among themselves over freemasonry. It appears, she wrote, that the Holy Spirit had "taken its upward flight."[87]

Most agonizing of all for Paulina were the contestant urgings of ministry and motherhood, which the Evangelical transformation of motherhood into a ministry did not completely resolve. Paulina suffered from split initiatives, poring over diapers, drapes, butter, and budgets when she felt that she should be spending more time pouring herself out in service to others. She simply could not do all that she felt called to do, and domestic duties were the last to suffer. She struggled all her life to find a balance, but economic necessity always seemed to tilt the scales in favor of the home over the church: "I am unhappy. I cannot endure the thought of not being useful to myself or others. Domestick cares engage all my time. I cannot think the Lord designs our stay here."[88]

Supported by a recommendation from her husband's physician to move "to the purer air" of Vermont, they left their boarding-house residence for relatives in Orwell, Vermont, hoping to find a church. There she was greeted by "saints" who blamed her family's poverty on her poor household management: "A strange thing indeed that we should not get rich on less than $200 a year."[89] Almost a year later her enfeebled husband had still not found a church, but she had fought the good fight and kept the faith. "The trials that I have forded through I shall not attempt to describe. No language is adequate. Suffice it to say that the Jordans have been deep and many."[90] The clouds lifted for a moment after her husband accepted a call from a parish in West Haven, especially when the intelligence reached her that they were building for Pastor Williams and his family a new parsonage. But she found herself so entangled in keeping the family alive on their meager salary that the original vision of her "professional" duties faded completely. "Feeling little of the Spirit of the Ancient Churches that contributed to Paul that he might administer to the weak and preach the Gospel to the poor," she became so discouraged and distraught that "it seemed to me that I had but one desire to live and that was to train up my little daughter."[91] Unable to attend church for months because she did not have the clothing or the shoes to wear "or many other articles equally important," she began hinting around to the ladies of the church that they needed more money, only to be rebuffed with barbed sarcasm. Her refuge was prayer: "Dear Saviour, help me to endure the cross, despise riches, and be contented in poverty if that be thy will concerning us."[92]

The day she had been waiting for came, and the church moved them into the new parsonage. It was in the dead of Vermont's winter, and she was in her eighth month of pregnancy.

> Such a looking place who ever saw! Workbench, tools, boards, shavens, mortar, etc. It was extremely cold. . . . No fire. Lucy froze, myself chilled. . . . House newly plastered and wet, had to open the windows and doors to prevent suffocation, however lived through this and much more. We have no cows and are out of provisions of every kind.[93]

Within six months they were once again forced to leave a church for lack of support. "So fatiguing to be moving from place to place with my little ones and feeble husband. Every move takes much out of my clay Cottage and pushes me along to the Temple above."[94]

Perhaps the most encompassing of all grievances for ministers' wives like Paulina Williams—one shared by the Assistants—was the repeated lashing their souls bore from critical members of the congregation. The Boston wife of a Baptist minister, Susan Huntington wrote in 1811:

> The wife of a clergyman is more narrowly watched than almost anyone else. Her deviations from duty are seldom overlooked; her opinions are minutely examined and often repeated. She is thought to take her notions of things, to a considerable extent, from her husband; and, of course, he suffers if she is imprudent. When I reflect on the responsibility of this situation, I tremble.[95]

Within a single week Susan Huntington found herself accused of spending too much time outside her family in benevolent pursuits and too much time with the family without regard for the public duties of the minister's wife.[96] Few women proved impervious to such criticism. One is left to wonder why Nathan S. S. Beman's free-spirited second wife, Caroline Bird Yancey, the mother of the secessionist William Lowndes Yancey, was suspended from his Georgia church, although given her history one is not surprised that their relationship was tumultuous or that she shunned his congregation at Troy's First Presbyterian Church and refused to take communion.[97] Public censure could be especially brutal to those who did not fill their rightful place in church affairs as the wife of a minister. Henry Ward Beecher's wife, Eunice White Ballard Beecher, discovered this when her husband's Second Presbyterian Church of Indianapolis struck out at her for what they believed were feigned illnesses. Her novel about the parsonage, *From Dawn to Daylight*, is flavored with her sour observations about the indignity and unfairness foredestined for the minster's wife.[98]

The problem was, of course, that everyone seemed to have a different opinion about her rightful place. The most difficult task of her career was the attempt to please everyone, even people she despised: the "cultivation of a state for disagreeable people."[99] Yet she had to avoid the spaniel syndrome—"What can I do to make everyone like me?"—and realize that "it is utterly impossible, in the nature of things, that any one course of conduct, however judicious, should be acceptable to all."[100] Helen Cutler, who felt acutely the pressure of constant surveillance by parishioners, was criticized by some for not being cheerful enough (she admitted in her journal to "similating cheerfulness") and by others for frivolity.[101] Parties were particular horrors for the minister's wife. Here subjective codes of conduct were most operative and the occasions for invidious criticism were greatest. She could be criticized for not speaking to someone even though 150 people were at the party; she could be judged adversely for seeming to favor by her speech and comportment a certain church faction that was feuding with another.[102] And she stood in constant fear of appearing unsuitably attired, an especially trying problem when economics dictated that her kitchen cupboard be filled instead of her clothes closets. The criticism was almost unbearable when her husband, abundant with compassion for parishioners, showed a scarcity of charity at home.

VI

In a sermon before the Maine Congregational Charitable Society in 1864, a Congregationalist minister from Portland, George Leon Walker, looked up and down the block of rural parishes in New England and concluded that charity ought to begin at home, among rural pastors' wives.

> The wives of New England's hill-side ministers! They are a class whose achievements have been seldom celebrated or sung. Self-denying, over-worked, placed in a station of critical difficulty; tasking every virtue of prudence, every grace of humility; struggling, with scanty means to preserve an atmosphere of refinement for the gospel's sake in a household where poverty makes narrow the ribbon and threadbare the coat; patient, zealous, benevolent; the angels of the bedside of suffering, the unfaltering helpmeets of the preacher of the word; —if ever there was a class whose virtues deserved the tribute of eloquence and reverent admiration, they are the wives of our country ministers.[103]

Just how poor were ministers' wives and their families? Did they live on "starvation salaries," as many of them claimed, and did they often find themselves having to "pray in" food and other provisions? Were clergy characteristically, as John Milton put it, under "the wardship of an overweening fist," a fist that remained tightly clenched when it came to handing out money to the pastor and his family? Were many ministers' wives married to the likes of Lorenzo Dow, who would accept nothing for preaching although he usually had someone peddling his books in the vicinity of his preaching-stand? Or were clergymen and their wives, as some contended, an especially grabby lot, seldom satisfied with their living conditions and, in the eyes of critics like those who attacked Dow for profiteering, in the business of overseeing other people's eternal affairs as a means of improving their own earthly accounts? The documents about the provisions of antebellum evangelical churches for their ministers are everywhere, in local church attics and closets. But that is part of the problem. Since the evidence is everywhere, it is toilsome to get at and to generalize about. Furthermore, clerical salary schedules are difficult to deal with, not only because of the many hidden subsidies and the inequality of urban and rural parishes, but also because of the disparity common to all religious traditions between the promised allowance and the amount received.

Salaries have stood in American religious history as major sources of friction between ministers and their congregations, and thus between ministers and their mates and between mates and congregations. The Parson's Cause and Jonathan Edwards's hasty departure from his Northampton church partly because of the resentment created by his high salary in the midst of a sagging economy are but two cases in point. John Cotton used to complain that nothing was cheap in New England but milk and ministers, and one 1706 appeal for tithing confessed that "experience does show that many People have a backward spirit to recompense their Minister."[104] In 1710, according to James W. Schmatler, Congregational clergy went on a crusade for better salaries.[105] Some clergy are even known to have "struck" for promised or higher salaries. John Wolcott (alias "Peter Pindar") delighted in sneering at the cloth's greed and arrogance, and he composed a popular poem about the Presbyterian minister David Rice, who refused to serve his congregation communion until they paid him the guaranteed salary.

> Ye fools, I told you one or twice
> You'd hear no more from canting Rice;
> He cannot settle his affairs,
> Nor pay attention unto pray'rs,
> Unless you pay up your arrears.
> O how he would in pulpit storm,
> And fill all Hell with dire alarm!

> Vengeance pronounce against each vice,
> And, more than all, curs'd avarice;
> Preach'd money was the root of all ill,
> Consign'd each rich man unto Hell;
> But since he finds you will not pay,
> Both rich and poor may go that way.
> 'Tis no more than I expected,
> The meeting-house is now neglected—
> All trades are subject to his chance,
> No longer pipe, no longer dance.[106]

Only a handful of clergy struck at their delinquent churches through job inactivity, but many struck through job relocation, which only added to their debts and to the strain on the wives who had to supervise the moving.

With the exception of a few traditions like the Disciples of Christ, Evangelical denominations believed in what Thomas and Alexander Campbell called a "hireling ministry." The Presbyterian theologian William R. Wicks insisted early in the nineteenth century that the Bible contained minute instructions for clerical salaries, which should amount to four times the average salary of parishioners.[107] Yet Evangelicals exhibited considerable ambivalence toward paying clergy for their ministry. Charles G. Finney presented to his students the motto "Work for the Lord and he'll board you" and at the same time claimed, "I have no sympathy with the spirit that denies, in theory or practices, that the laborer is worthy of his hire."[108] This ambivalence was reflected in the silent warfare between congregations, who expected their ministers' families to trust the Holy Spirit for board, and minister's families, who trusted their congregations to board them.

Salary support differed from denomination to denomination, with the Episcopalians and Congregationalists at the upper end and the Methodists and Baptists at the lower, both latter groups arguing that, as one Baptist put it:

> It is altogether best for the peace, for the purity, for the safety, and for the growth of the church, that her public teachers should possess but little of the world's goods; and that, while they do their duty, they should have no prospect of thereby accumulating a large estate. We wish to have them so circumstanced, that their choice of the ministry shall not be excited by the hope of worldly gain.[109]

In churches other than the Methodist, salary was fixed by contract and tended to vary much more wildly than today from place to place: urban salaries were higher than rural; salaries in the South higher than those in the North. In the mid-1840s Presbyterian salaries ranged as high as $4,000 and as low as $100 a year, with the average estimated at $400.[110] Charles G. Finney's 1827 salary was set at $600 by the Oneida Evangelical Association, but by 1832 he was making $1,500 a year as pastor of a Presbyterian church in New York City.[111] Average Baptist salaries in New Jersey in the mid-1840s were estimated at $350, and average Methodist salaries, if one factors in housing, were about the same.[112] By the mid-fifties average clerical salaries in the Evangelical churches had probably climbed to $600.[113] These set salaries compared favorably to some vocations, but were considerably lower than those commanded in professions like law and medicine. Clerical salaries had slipped relative to others since the eighteenth century. Clergymen earned roughly one and a half to two times as much as textile workers, a little more than factory workers in iron casting or wrought iron, and quite a bit more than the average male schoolteacher.[114] Because set salaries were not always paid in full, it is difficult to say with precision just how much clergymen received and how they ranked in the socioeconomic ladder. The evidence does not confirm the stereotype of Methodist and Baptist clergymen as pathetic, starving preachers who brought the gospel to people who did not ask for it and hence would not pay for it, but were nevertheless unstarvable—"they will live where a dog would starve to death," as someone put it.[115] Some starved, and some were unstarvable. But most appear to have lived in comfortable moderation, thanks to the ingenuity and generosity of women, especially clergymen's wives.

The more tangible Methodist sources are useful in this inquiry because Methodist preachers up until 1860 set their own "support" (they did not use the mercenary-sounding word "salary" after 1808), and all theoretically were paid the same minimum allowance (including bishops). The unstated ideal of the strictly egalitarian Methodist system was one of frugal moderation. John Wesley grew up under the tutelage of a father whose only extravagance was an "immoderate fondness for snuff and his pipe," and Wesley refused to countenance even this luxury. George Whitefield might have spoken for any number of Wesleyans when he complained on one of his seven trips to America about the stench of clergy spoiled by high salaries.[116] Francis Asbury gave the doctrine of frugal moderation its social rationale: "We must suffer with, if we labor for, the poor."[117] Bishop Beverly Waugh gave it its ecclesiastical rationale: "Methodism is a system that is intended to do the greatest good in the shortest period of time, at the least cost."[118] This "least cost" argument applied to the selection of wives as well. Freeborn Garretson's marriage into wealth and consequent ability to preach for fifty-three years without drawing any salary from the conference was lifted up as a mark at which preachers should aim. If itinerants absolutely had to marry, one humorist offered, they should make wealth a prime qualification for a wife. "I know some have blamed poor itinerants very much for marrying rich girls; but perhaps the greatest affliction with the complainer usually is, because he himself is not equally successful."[119] If clergymen did not marry women of wealth in larger percentages than members of other professions, they talked about doing so often enough to lend at least a tithe of truth to Achille Murat's observation that marriage "is indeed a profitable speculation for young preachers."[120]

The wives of Methodist clergy were allotted by the Christmas conference £24 ($64), which included all gifts but excluded traveling expenses. The 1785 *Discipline*, however, let the wives know in what spirit this allocation was given: "Question 38: What shall annually be allowed the Wives of the married Preachers? Answer: 24 pounds . . . if they need it, and no more." An allowance for children was also made, although it was discontinued in 1787, since it was "not pleasing to our societies."[121] The allowance was revived in 1800 ($16 for each child under seven, and $24 for children between seven and fourteen), when the salary for a minister and wife went up to $160. It stayed there until 1816, when it decreased to $100. In 1836 the minimum salary was raised to $200. Annual conferences did, but only rarely, send married men out with a single man's salary of $100.[122] Not included in these figures were traveling expenses and table expenses, which were supposed to be provided. Furnished parsonages were also recommended, but not required. A motion requiring rental subsidies for clerical families serving circuits without housing was defeated.[123] Another major source of hidden income was marriage fees, from which one did not grow rich but which could be quite considerable. One Kentucky Baptist minister averaged $34 per year from 1824 to 1856 just in wedding fees, while another Kentucky Presbyterian minister averaged $384 per year from 1845 to 1855 in presents people lavished on him as an expression of their love.[124]

On paper at least, most religious traditions and congregations, even the warm-hearted but tight-fisted Methodists, provided sufficient financial support to maintain their pastors at a level of, at worst, respectable and comfortable poverty. The problem was generally not a conflict between clerical families who believed that a preacher was worthy of his hire and congregations who believed that the best things in life were free. The problem was more the *manner* of payment—its spirit and form—than the *amount* of payment.

Many changes were occurring at this time in the sociology of church financing. In the seventeenth century ministers had been paid mainly in produce like whiskey, tobacco, grain, or some other crop that was readily bartered or transferable into currency. The glebe, or parish farm, provided for their tables and more. In the eighteenth century the town constable paid the preachers a lump sum out of the town taxes. But reflecting the nagging shortage of currency throughout the century (econometricians contend that the American population still enjoyed the highest standard of living in the world), the clergy received supplemental benefits in the form of land, housing allowances, wood and fuel allotments, funeral favors, silk scarves, gloves, and gold mourning rings as well as numerous other handouts. Ezra Stiles tallied up his for one year as follows: "a cow, a calf, a milking pail, a load of hay, a velvet cloak for his wife, a coat for himself, a cradle for his baby, a cheese, a turkey, a side of beef, a bridle."[125] The commercialization of the American economy which began in the last third of the eighteenth century and the first third of the nineteenth, produced a wage society; people were less and less self-sufficient and more and more cash-dependent. Congregations, however, continued to supplement clerical salaries with fringe benefits that were not cash-transferable and with clerical perquisites like special fees, love gifts, free services from physicians and lawyers, and discounts by taverns and transportation companies. Jonathan Edwards's demands for a "clear salary understanding" were still unfulfilled a hundred years later. While clergymen talked "salary" and thought "cash," congregations talked "salary" and continued to think of services and produce as acceptable supplements to whatever cash they could raise.

The slowness with which money was collected in all traditions placed a grievous burden on pastors' wives, who were charged with the management of household finances. The burden of the Methodist clergy was increased by the method of payment. Since at least the third century, some form of monthly payment to ministers of the gospel had been common practice. Beginning in the 1770s, however, and continuing until 1860, Methodist preachers received their salary in the form of what was originally called "quarterages," money collected by the stewards at class meetings and ultimately distributed to the preachers at quarterly conferences.

The misunderstanding and confusion created by this system of payment (still around today in the form of the parsonage system) were tremendous. Clerical families faced severe cash-flow problems, which caused many of them to go deeply into debt. Depending on what time of year it was, the cupboard could be bulging or bare. At the end of the year, when the discrepancy between promised salary and performance became most apparent, there was usually a concerted push to make up the difference, although sometimes the minister's wife had to rattle a tin cup. But for those expected to live simply and frugally, delinquent payments meant impoverishment for much of the year. Evidence is abundant that at the final accounting many clergymen fell short. Only three times in sixty-five years of itinerating did Peter Cartwright receive the full salary allotted him. And by 1850, 30 percent of the preachers in the Black River Conference of the Methodist church still were receiving less than full support.[126] But the main reason so many clergymen had to "let their hands hang down" in moonlighting jobs as teachers, farmers, and beekeepers,[127] why some indeed were "starved" into locating or leaving the ministry entirely, and why taking in boarders or establishing female seminaries became such a thriving cottage industry among preachers' wives,[128] was that the clergymen of America's voluntary society were caught—perhaps more than any other occupational group—in the crunch of a household society giving birth to a wage economy.

There were, of course, psychological factors involved as well. The fact that clergymen had to raise their own salary in some ways added to the clash over money. Every Methodist preacher was also a bookseller, with one side of his saddlebag filled with clothes and the other with books. He received between 15 and 25 percent of the proceeds of book sales as salary payment, to be deducted from whatever the circuit owed him. Pastoral visiting also had, in all traditions, salary-raising aspects. One minister's wife pointed this out as she described the unseemly mendicancy of the ministry: "William rarely returned from an appointment or from visiting among his flock that he did not bring with him some largesse of their kindness. This made pastoral visiting an amiable form of foraging and had its effect on character."[129]

Part of its effect on character was to create feelings of resentment and bitterness toward those who allowed such indignities to happen. When thanksgiving was offered in church for "free salvation," ministers' wives thought their experienced ears caught a reference to finances as well as faith. It was very difficult for a woman to listen with appreciation and spiritual benefit as her husband's parishioners testified and prayed when she thought of the financial hardships those same people were causing her. And it was equally hard for itinerants to go on ministering to people after returning home and finding their families living on bread and water while wealthy parishioners idly watched.[130] Roxanna Foote, wife of the Litchfield, Connecticut, Congregational minister Lyman Beecher, knew what it was to move because of inadequate salaries, and she took in boarders and taught school to supplement her husband's $300-a-year salary. In fact Lyman believed that her untimely death in 1816 was the result of "undue exertions" in erasing debts. Her only recorded words of bitterness protested against the "very low estimation which people appear to have of the blessing of the Gospel ministry"; by her calculation, the people of East Hampton, Long Island, spent more money on tobacco than on her husband's salary.[131] In over fifty years of ministry, Sue Dromgoole Mooney remembered acidly, only once was her husband's salary voluntarily raised.[132]

While congregations might feel that their ministers were generously provided with perquisites, ministers' wives felt that these perquisites were more than offset by added demands to which other families were not subjected. Ministers' wives, to give but one example, were the innkeepers of American evangelism, providing a rendezvous for preachers on the trail and a refuge for preachers in time of trial. They welcomed weary evangelists, night or day, to share whatever the cupboards contained. The wives of preachers accepted it as a given that their homes would be, as one called hers, "Itinerants' Rest," not to mention a travelers' rest as well. It was possible to travel through New England on free hospitality, Harriet Beecher Stowe observed of the olden days, and ministers' wives entertained their share of freeloaders.[133] They were also expected to do more entertaining of people in the church and community than even their wealthiest parishioners.[134]

A final method of payment especially demeaning to ministers' wives was the "donation party," also called a "surprise visit" and, later in the century, a "pound social." These parties illustrate, in bold colors, the injurious and degrading salary system of American Protestantism. The members of a parish, striving to meet the designated salary for the minister and his family, would sponsor a "party," generally held at the minister's home. Each parishioner would bring to it a donation, preferably food or clothing, sometimes furniture, as well as money for an offering plate humiliatingly passed around during the festivities.[135] The value of all the donations would then usually be deducted from what the congregation needed to meet the minister's salary. "We have had a *donation party*," Helen Edmonds wrote, "one of the episodes in a minister's life, fraught with fear, and expectations, and hope, and anxiety, and sometimes followed by regrets as well as gratified feelings."[136] Donation parties were "fraught with fear" because what was one to do with seventeen pairs of mittens, second-hand shoes in no one's size, a mish-mash of undesired produce, and grease spots on the carpet and floor? They were filled with "expectations, and hope" because someone just might bring the needed frock for the child or suit for the minister or sugar for the table (provided those attending the party did not eat up all they had brought). They were times of "anxiety" because they often became little more than excuses for members to scrutinize the parsonage and pry into how fastidious a housekeeper the minister's wife was. They were anxiety-producing, too, because how does one maintain self-respect and still lavish thanks on people for payment that is rightfully one's own? And how does one stop such festivities from degenerating into popularity contests? They were followed by "regrets" because donation parties—like the rest of the clerical payment system—transformed justice into charity, ministry into beggary, pastors' wives into hypocrites, and the honest debt of ministerial support into a charitable donation. And yet sometimes they were followed by "gratified feelings" because the socializing was important, especially for the young people who needed substitutes for dances, and the church did at least "feel benevolent,"[137] even if it was a bogus magnanimity. On the whole, however, most ministers' wives shared the sentiment of Emma Smith Brown after attending, in 1836, a "donation" in Rochester, New York: "I cannot feel that such parties are profitable."[138]

Chapter Four

"What Women These Christians Have!"

Lydia Finney and the Assistant Model

My dear, when you marry me, you must marry my parish.
>   John Fletcher to Mary Bosanquet

I must say that in Bolton, we made the acquaintance of several of
the finest and best women we saw in England—Mrs. Best, Mrs.
Smith, Mrs. Bell, Mrs. Barlow and many others. We were particularly struck with the fact that the Wesleyan ministers were as a
body so much blessed in their wives. As a class we did not meet
their equals in England. I have often thought of this, as a marked
providence of God.
>   Charles G. Finney

The legacy of the Companion was a life devoted to her husband,
children, and home. The legacy of the Sacrificer was a life that
piously endured the privations and encumbrances of ministry. Not
until Lydia Finney did the change in the minister's wife's legacy to
the world become clearly apparent. It would become not merely a life,
but a career.

The prevailing model of the minister's wife in eighteenth-
century America was the helpmeet, defined positively as a clergyman's one-person, all-inclusive support system and negatively as a
suffering servant who never made a scintilla of demand on her
husband's vocation. But when William E. Dodge, a wealthy New
York businessman and loyal patron of Charles G. Finney, lauded
Lydia Finney as "in every sense, his helpmeet,"[1] he was not just
praising the soldierly virtues expected of one who found herself
attached to a husband whose high calling meant low marriage benefits. Without openly renouncing the earlier understanding of the role
of the minister's wife, Charles and Lydia Finney transformed the
concept of helpmeet into a role that allowed ministers' wives great
opportunities for public leadership and personal growth while serving as extensions of their husbands' ministry.

The "help" in helpmeet came to refer as much to the sharing of
pastoral functions as to the shouldering of all the parenting and
domestic duties. To be a help that was meet for a minister, a woman

had to be willing to add new roles to her old ones. Finney's assistant pastor, the Oberlin New Testament professor John Morgan, identified the change that the Finneys had wrought in the job description for the minister's wife when he asserted, "She may be, and should be a helpmeet for her husband, and besides this exert an independent influence."[2] The use of the word "independent" is significant; by the mid-nineteenth century the masculine trait of "independence" was frankly, even ostentatiously, encouraged among Evangelical women. No longer was "masculine" necessarily a pejorative tag when applied by Evangelicals to female minds and spirits. At her death in 1827, Sarah K. Clarke, who had served as Sunday school superintendent at Utica's First Presbyterian Church, was heralded by her pastor as "so masculine in her understanding and so feminine in her instincts and loveliness, as to be the truest, best picture of a 'strong-minded women.'"[3] Evangelical acceptance of the Assistant model is further evidenced in the popularity of two novels written for children by the minister's wife Harmony Cary Gardner. Through their main characters, Ellinor Grey and Augusta Carrol, both novels present children with female models esteemed for their masculine independence.[4]

"Unqualified independence," which was deemed not inconsistent with meekness and humility, was so important a qualification for the minister's wife that an 1835 manual for the "wife of a clergy man" devoted an entire chapter to it.[5] In one of her lectures on the qualifications and temptations of the clerical wife, Alice Welch Cowles, the principal of the Oberlin Female Department as of 1836, echoed Morgan in adding independence to the qualities customarily expected of a minister's wife, such as common sense, discretion, impartiality, piety, love for people, and a knowledge of human nature.[6] By "independence" she meant independence of thought and action; a minister's wife was expected to visit the sick, teach the women and children of the parish, energize and direct women's groups, pray publicly, counsel the afflicted, convict the complacent, and seek the lost. Thus, when Finney, who often wept from the pulpit, wept through the pages of the *Oberline Evangelist* over the death of Lydia in mid-December 1847 and "the loss of [his] precious help-meet," he was speaking of a professional as well as personal loss.[7] Long before feminists began speaking out against the imprisonment of wives in kitchens of dependency and for women's right to manage financial affairs, assume business responsibilities, make important decisions, and converse intelligently with their partners, ministers' wives had learned to embody these values and virtues. The image of "the Model Woman" invoked by the wife of the Wesleyan Methodist Orange Scott in 1874 was one Lydia Finney had helped to create: "to be an independent woman and yet a most devoted wife."[8]

The Assistant model was deeply indebted to British Methodist antecedents and sources, although its spirit went back to the earliest days of Christian history, when a pagan observer paid tribute to the first women of Christianity with the exclamation "What women these Christians have!" As Winthrop S. Hudson has observed, Finney's theology became Methodist in all but name.[9] In fact, Finney's attitude toward the deployment of women by the church reveals him as one of Wesley's truest disciples, albeit a most reluctant one. Keith Melder has studied the early pattern of women's organizations in the nineteenth century and concluded that these mostly para-church structures owed much to the eighteenth-century Evangelical Revival in general and the "energetic example" of Hannah More in particular.[10] If Robert Wearmouth is granted his contention that "the emancipation of womanhood began with John Wesley,"[11] then it can be just as forcefully argued that Finney blazed the path for the emancipation of women in America.

To find in Finney's defense of his "new measures" no direct mention of Wesleyan precedents is odd but inconclusive. When it came to female praying and speaking in "promiscuous" assemblies, Finney and Wesley were kindred spirits and pursued revivals with the same principles, presuppositions, and passion, ultimately sharing a joint unconventional inventiveness born of necessity. Finney did, however, argue that his new measures, especially the participation of women in public worship, were not all that new, an assertion that historians have not taken seriously enough. Even Howard A. Morrison, who has emphasized as strongly as anyone the continuities of the new measures with earlier patterns of revivalism, exempts female leadership functions.[12] Yet from the time that Barbara Heck exhorted her wayward brother in the presence of his card-playing buddies, convened the first Methodist congregation and class meeting in America, and arranged for the building of America's first Methodist church, Methodist women could be found testifying at love feasts, praying during worship, conducting prayer services at quarterly conferences, exhorting congregations, and in a few cases serving as class leaders.[13] The importance of these religious

"aberrations" must not be overlooked, and the Methodist antecedents to Finney's most contentious new measure deserve a moment's
notice, especially since the lives of many of these women were
popularized and granted heroic or even—in the case of Susanna
Wesley—mythic status in nineteenth-century Evangelical circles.[14]

I

Of all the early Methodist "saints," Susanna Wesley is the most
famous and at the same time the most elusive.[15] John Wesley was
"the son of Susanna"—a minister's wife cited by some as the greatest
woman of her century. Susanna Wesley, herself the twenty-fifth
child of a minister's wife, has been widely recognized as a role model
for nineteenth-century mothers, but she was also an important reference point for ministers' wives within the Evangelical Protestant
tradition. While her home was her only parish, within it she created a
prototype of the Methodist system.[16] By so doing she greatly expanded the roles of her sex in general and of the minister's wife in
particular. The "Mother of Methodism" valued an educated laity (she
knew Greek, Latin, and French), insisted that girls be taught to read
fluently before they were allowed to work, led worship services,
counseled her husband's unruly parishioners, composed a catechism for her children, and wrote unpublished theological treatises,
including commentaries on the Apostle's Creed, the Lord's Supper,
and the Ten Commandments.[17] These were certainly not the standard attitudes and activities of an eighteenth-century Anglican
minister's wife, but then Susanna Wesley was not formed by the
standard molds. By thirteen she had already demonstrated her independence by withdrawing from her father's congregation and renouncing the dissenting theology that had driven him from his
parish in 1662. Susanna did not shrink from suffering with her father
a life of persecution and hardship, but she would not suffer for the
sake of what was to her a contrary theology.

The story of how Susanna Wesley overcame cultural barriers is
revealing. The transformation of the role of the minister's wife into a
vocation originated in the frustration of her desire to become a
minister or missionary. As Susanna tells it, her voracious appetite for
books led her to an account of the lives of two Danish-Halle missionaries named Bartholomeus Ziegenbalg and Plütschau, who were
sent out early in the eighteenth century by King Frederick IV of
Denmark to convert the heathen at Tranquebar in southern India.

The life of a missionary as reported in their *Propagation of the Gospel to the East* (1709) shone for her with all the brilliance of the Holy Grail. "I was never, I think, more affected with anything than with the relation of their travels," she exulted, confessing that "for several days I could think or speak of little else."

> At last it came into my mind, though I am not a man nor a minister of the Gospel, and so cannot be employed in such a worthy employment as they were; yet, if my heart were sincerely devoted to God, and if I were inspired with a true zeal for His glory, and did really desire the salvation of souls, I might do somewhat more than I do. [18]

Susanna Wesley experienced what in a man would have been termed a "call" to the ministry. Her call, however, had to be channeled in directions that would not threaten social mores. "I thought I might live in a more exemplary manner in some things; I might pray more for the people, and speak with more warmth to those with whom I have the opportunity of conversing. However, I resolved to begin with my own children" [19] Thus began Susanna's famous individual theological conferences with her children—John's night was Thursday—and her kitchen revival.

Quickened by her religious experience, Susanna conducted with greater freedom and intensity her Sunday evening family devotions in the Epworth rectory kitchen while her husband was away in London. Soon the altar of family prayer became an altar of revival. The services for her children and servants began attracting the attention of neighbors and soon were attended by as many as two hundred of her husband's parishioners. Many had to be turned away. Finally, Susanna's revival elicited the anger of a rejected, incompetent curate named Inman (who could only preach tedious sermons about paying debts) and her absentee husband, Samuel, whose sermons she may or may not have been reading in her services. Susanna responded to the reproof of her husband, whom she always dutifully addressed as either "Sir" or "Master," with an imposing letter. She would consent to abstain from conducting services if he would emphatically command her to cease and stand in her place at Judgment Day. [20] Susanna, ever a cunning controversialist, won the argument.

John Wesley grew up in a home where the dominant presence

was female, and where the female was assertive, outspoken, independent (politically and theologically), and the intellectual peer of
the male. All of these qualities became associated with the leadership
function of the minister's wife. Susanna Wesley should not be regarded as the first Methodist woman preacher, for when she led
public services she was more like a passive mirror reflecting the
readings, collects, and the "most awakening" sermons she could find
in her husband's library. Whether she prayed from the heart or the
prayer book is still uncertain. What is certain is that those early
Methodist women who followed her example in opening up their
kitchens, parlors, and dining rooms for devotions commended their
congregations to God with unscripted words and prayers. As a model
of womanhood and of the minister's wife, Susanna Wesley blazed a
wide trail for the women of early Methodism.

Her influence was most immediately felt, however, not as a role
model, but as a teacher. She changed people's ideas about where
preaching could take place and who could do the preaching; field
preaching and lay preaching were the results. Susanna had shocked
her son by lecturing him on the meaning of "call" and "ministry." Lay
preaching could be validated as much by the uplifted hands of
converted souls, she argued, as by the laying on of hands by the
ordained ministry. Wesley's support for women's preaching, and for
lay preaching in general, derived from his mother's instructions.
Both were functions of necessity, which knows no laws, and of
results, which legislate only success.

Wesley appointed women as class leaders in Bristol as early as
1739. When a class of twenty-six on one Sunday became a congregation of two hundred the next, as happened to Sarah Crosby in 1761,
the style of counseling-leadership required by a small, sharing group
was clearly no longer appropriate. Although Wesley initially refused
to allow women to preach, expediency won the day, and he began to
encourage women like Sarah Crosby, Sarah Mallet, Alice Cambridge, Mary Sewell, Hannah Harrison, Penelope Newman, Mary
Barritt, Elizabeth Ritchie, and Mary Fletcher to preach, at first on
condition that they call it not preaching" but "witnessing,"[21] and then
on condition that they could claim, like male lay preachers, an
"extraordinary call."[22] Thomas Mitchell, one of Wesley's most persecuted preachers (he was once thrown into a pond by a mob of
anti-Methodist women), pragmatically defended women preachers
against those who would suppress them with the dry observation: "I

know not what you would do without the good women, for all the fish they catch they put into our net."[23]

Even those women who could not boast any felt dispensation from what Wesley called "the ordinary rules of discipline"[24] were given services to perform during the Evangelical Revival. The Methodist historian Earl Kent Brown has classified the wide variety of roles available to eighteenth-century Wesleyan women as follows: "women became public speakers, class and band leaders; intimate advisors to the Wesley brothers and other male leaders; school founders and teachers; visitors to the sick, the prisoner, and the backslider; ministers' wives; leaders in female support-groups; itinerants; patrons; and models of the Christian life for male and female alike."[25] One such Methodist woman was Sarah Bentley. Known around York as "the pious housemaid," Bentley labored at the crossroads of decadence and destitution as a counselor to the rich and the poor while serving as class leader to three class meetings.[26] Another woman disciple of Wesley's was Hannah Ball of High Wycombe, who started the greatest lay educational movement in the history of Christianity, the Sunday school. Concerned for the education of neglected youth, she established the school in 1769 and corresponded with Wesley about her work. This was the first of many weekend schools founded mostly by lay women years before Sophia Cooke (later the wife of the Methodist preacher Samuel Bradburn) inspired Robert Raikes's widely publicized Gloucester endeavor in 1781.[27] In fact, Wesley worked so closely with women and traveled, labored, and corresponded with so many of them (he spent three times as much time writing to women as men) that his yellow-eyed wife, Molly Vazeille, became crazed with jealousy, subjecting him to domestic and public indignities until the two separated in 1758 after seven years of marital horror.[28]

The Evangelical Revival in England gave women positions of leadership and responsibility unprecedented in the history of the Christian church.[29] The administrative functions performed by London's Lady Selina Shirley, countess of Huntingdon, were so far-reaching that Earl Kent Brown has called her "the first woman Methodist bishop."[30] Wesley had the clearest vision of anyone up to his day of the benefits an active and committed minister's wife could bring to the ministry. "The light wherein my wife is to be chiefly considered," wrote the frustrated bachelor, is "as a fellow-laborer in the Gospel of Christ."[31] In the late 1740s Wesley believed that God had sent him such a person in the form of Grace Murray, a widow whom he first appointed to manage his preachers' house in Newcastle and then sent out into the northern counties and Ireland, where, as he says:

> She examined all the women in the smaller societies and the believers in every place. She settled all the women-bands, visited the sick, prayed with the mourners, more and more of whom received remission of sins during her conversations or prayers. Meantime she was to me both a servant and friend, as well as a fellow-laborer in the Gospel. She provided everything I wanted. She told me with all faithfulness and freedom if she thought anything amiss in my behavior.[32]

After listing the attributes that would make Murray an ideal wife ("chaste, modest, temperate," "gentle and longsuffering," "compassionate," "zealous of good works"), Wesley assessed her professional dowry:

> She has a clear apprehension and a deep knowledge of the things of God; she is well acquainted with and exercised in our method of leading souls, having gone through all our little offices, and discharged them all entirely well. She has a ready utterance, a spirit of convincing as well as of persuasive speech, a winning address, an agreeable carriage in whatever company she is engaged. By means of all which she is exceedingly beloved almost wherever she goes, and is dear, in an uncommon manner, to great numbers of the people. I never yet heard or read of any woman so owned of God; so many have been convinced of sin in her bands and classes, and under prayers. I particularly insist upon this: if ever I have a wife, she ought to be the most careful woman in the kingdom, not barely one who probably may be so, (I could not be content to run such a hazard,) but one that undeniably is so.[33]

For John Wesley, the status of the minister's wife began to promise an enlarged usefulness, an inducement to marriage that one of Lady Selina's preachers did not hesitate to use on a reluctant Frances Mortimer in 1782.[34] But minister's wives were often chosen not for their potential but for their achievements. The wealthy Mary Bosanquet Fletcher was, at forty-two, a celebrated leader of Methodism even before her marriage in 1781, with its consequent grand merger of ministries, to fifty-two-year-old appointed successor, John

William Fletcher. A leader of prayer groups, bands, and class meetings, banished from home by her father because of a stubborn defiance of his religious wishes, Fletcher was perhaps best known for her Christian Community and Orphanage, which she established with her alter ego Sarah Ryan at Laytonstone and then moved to a large farm at Yorkshire's Cross Hall in 1768. Perhaps modeled after Francke's orphanage operations at Halle in Germany, the Laytonstone project employed sufficient numbers of Christian women to prompt some detractors to dub it a Protestant nunnery. Fletcher herself drew up the rules for a Methodist Society at her new home and supported the preaching efforts of her friend Sarah Crosby. From the dilapidated barn she called her "preaching-room," she exercised weekly during her four-year marriage her own preaching skills and style, which an admiring Wesley described as "fire" (a metaphor he employed to characterize his own preaching), After Fletcher's untimely death she took charge, with Wesley's encouragement, of many of her husband's parish duties at Madeley, preaching at times to crowds as large as three thousand. Clergymen were regularly seen in her congregation, thus making her a "minister to ministers."[35] Other early Methodist minister's wives, like Mary Holder, who itinerated with her husband, George, and often exhorted after he preached, were equally active in the entire spectrum of ministerial labors.[36]

The lives of these women, popularized through tracts and biographies, provided inspiration and models for nineteenth-century American women, especially women preachers.[37] Of all the Wesleyan women who pioneered in religious leadership, however, it was Hester Ann Rogers, the wife of an itinerant, who most caught the imagination of American Christians. Selections from her journals, published along with the funeral sermon Thomas Coke delivered upon her death on 26 October 1794, were widely read and discussed, especially among Evangelical women. Nathan Bangs, a prominent Methodist leader, wrote, "Of all the females in modern times, I consider her as standing first on the list of Christian women."[38] Born on 31 January 1756, Rogers was the daughter of an Anglican minister. Her father was bent on making the stubbornly pious girl into a theological and biblical prodigy. After his death when she was nine, her "seriousness" about religion waned, and she reached out for all the things that Evangelical parents strove to keep away from their children: dances, novels, cards, plays, and frivolous attire. The more frolicsome her life, however, the more "melancholy and mopish" her disposition, until she feared a mental breakdown. Finally, at age fifteen, she found God's forgiveness among the group of Christians her father had warned her about and her mother abhorred—the Methodists. One of her Methodist friends, the wife of the itinerant James Rogers, died shortly after giving birth. After some scheming by John Wesley, Hester married the widower on 19 August 1784. Later, the aged and lonesome Wesley made her husband assistant rector at City Road Chapel in London, mainly in order to surround himself in his dotage with the comfort and care of pious young women like Elizabeth Ritchie and Hester herself, both of whom were eyewitnesses at his death. The Rogerses lived for two years in Wesley's parsonage. She proved to be more popular with her husband's parishioners than he was. Her days were filled with visiting the sick, the dying, and the poor, as well as some occasional preaching, but it was as a leader of bands and classes that her ability as a workhorse for her less talented husband became particularly prominent. When Rogers entered a circuit, he would present his wife with a few names and direct her to gather up enough other people on her own to form a class. Then, as soon as her classes reached thirty or forty people, "her almost cruel husband," as Thomas Coke called him, "would transplant all the believers to other classes, and keep her thus continually working at the mine."[39] In spite of this difficulty, at one time she had nearly a hundred souls under her care.[40]

Wesley had justified female preaching only as an exceptional expedient, and no theological or biblical rationale had been fashioned to sustain a public leadership role for women. Thus, when necessity no longer ruled, women preachers were no longer countenanced. Mary Barritt, the closest thing to an itinerant woman preacher in early Wesleyan Methodism, was married in 1802 to the Methodist itinerant Zechariah Taft, whom one colleague caustically chided for "taking a female to assist him in the ministry." Her success in the counties of northern England, where hundreds were converted, forced the conference that met shortly after Wesley's death to take note. The 1803 conference publicly frowned on women preachers, noting ungratefully that there was now an adequate supply of Methodist preachers. Grudging allowance was made for those with an "extraordinary call" (Jabez Bunting deprecated this exception as "every fanatic's plea"), but they could preach only to their own sex. A similar shrinkage in public usefulness occurred in other areas of women's involvement in the church. A few women—including Harriet Elizabeth Webster, Sophia Steigen Berger, and Mary Taft— gamely ignored the injunction and continued their "irregular" activities, but not without ridicule. William Atherton, eulogizing the ministry of one of Mary Taft's converts, wrote: "God often works by strange instruments. Balaam was converted by the braying of an ass, and Peter by the crowing of a cock; and our lamented brother by the preaching of a woman on Good Friday morning."[41]

The factors that led to a sharp decline in leadership roles for women spared the minister's wife, as the crowded life of Dinah Morris Evans, the wife of a local preacher, reveals.[42] But the seed of women's religious leadership had been sown, and in the fertile soil of necessity it would continue to sprout. The precedents and standards set by Wesleyan women in the eighteenth century were thus of great historical consequence. American Evangelical women, planted in similar soil in the early 1800s, drew from this tradition, modeling themselves on its strong, enterprising, effective women. Annis Callon Peck, mother of a dynasty of Methodist itinerants, was proudly described as follows: "She had the administrative power of Queen Victoria . . . the popular power of Joan of Arc and Charlotte Corday . . . the deep piety of Mary Fletcher and Hester Ann Rogers," and the influence over her children of a Susanna Wesley.[43] With this distinguished lineage, it is little wonder that many Evangelicals grew to like their women active, intelligent, independent, forceful, deeply spiritual, and humble.

II

American ministers' wives were able to exercise public leadership because of certain changes in the theology and sociology of American religion. As Winthrop Hudson and others have observed, the nineteenth century was the "Methodist Age" in American religion.[44] The triumph of Arminianism, itinerancy, and an emphasis on "organizing to beat the devil"[45] created shock waves that shook the retiring domesticity of the minister's wife. Itinerant evangelists who married, for example, quickly confronted the question of what to do with their spouses. Charles G. Finney wanted his wife, Lydia, with him during his revival labors, although this was not immediately apparent to her. A few days after their marriage in October 1824, Finney abandoned his bride at her father's house, promising to return in about a week from a preaching tour. Six months passed before he returned.[46] But that incident was not indicative of their relationship, for until a few years before her death on 8 December 1847, Lydia accompanied Finney on many of his evangelistic tours. "She participated in my labors, and trials, my rejoicings and sorrows," Finney wrote of her, "through many of the most searching and powerful revivals of religion that I have ever seen, or of which I have read or heard."[47] People who invited Finney to labor in their towns quickly became aware that they were soliciting a package deal and promised accommodations in private homes that would cater to their needs and provide care for the children if Lydia brought along the family, as she did when Anson G. Phelps invited the Finneys to stay in his home during the New York City crusade.[48] Indeed, one of Lydia's friends complained that she traveled so much with her husband that one was at a loss to know where to send letters.[49]

The rationale that permitted Lydia to travel and toil alongside her husband was the energetic doctrine of Christian usefulness, or, to use a later term reclaimed from the Wesley brothers, "practical Christianity," the nineteenth-century expression of the Protestant work ethic. "We should never be idle; no, not for a moment" is how Amey Scott put it.[50] But it was not a "secularized" expression that "had all but nudged out God," as Daniel T. Rogers contends.[51] Rather, the ideal of usefulness was the nineteenth-century counterpart to the Puritan concept of "calling," which had thrived in the theocentric, theocratic soil of Calvinism but was inappropriate to the increasingly democratic, anthropocentric outlook of the nineteenth century. The utilitarian cast of New Haven theology, in which even the happiness of heaven was defined (by Timothy Dwight) as "voluntary usefulness," blended smoothly with the Arminian Evangelicalism of the Methodist Age.[52] Finney's ministry, which was most decisively shaped by these two theological forces, appropriated the Wesleyan notion that the seal of conversion was action, and action was the center of the life of the church. In an occasional lecture entitled "Employment of the Church," Finney outlined nineteen recommendations for a vital church, each one based on the doctrine of "usefulness."

1. All should contribute to support the Gospel according to relative ability.
2. All should have something to do.
3. The church should be so organized as to employ each one in active labor.

4. He is the best general who makes the best work of the army.
5. Christians can not live without labor.
6. You cannot prevent dissension if you feed them and require no labor.
7. Don't spare them in giving to benevolent objects because they are poor and can't hardly pay your salary.
8. Sectional or class meeting indispensable.
9. Encourage female meetings.
10. D[itt]o. Benevolent effort.
11. D[itt]o. Visitation and personal labor.
12. Trust them to great prayerfulness.
13. D[itt]o. To great and continual activity.
14. Put young men forward, and let them not be kept back by old conservatives.
15. Each church should be a missionary society.
16. D[itt]o. A temperance society.
17. Sometimes more can be done by having such societies for the younger members in addition to the general society of the church.
18. Sometimes the unconverted members are too numerous to allow the church, as a body, to act as such societies.
19. In such cases societies should be formed of the living members.[53]

The engines of human initiative and industry propelled the church forward with boundless confidence and millennial briskness. Indeed, action was seen as the great Archimedean lever that would move the world toward the millennium. Usefulness thus became, as Ian Bradley has shown in his study of eighteenth-century Evangelicals in England,[54] the most highly prized trait of the Christian, who was increasingly seen more as an agent than as a being. "A life of Christian usefulness," the Presbyterian pastor William B. Sprague declared on the death of one of his parishioners, "is the highest glory of a women."[55]

One of the reasons women dominated churches in both America and England was that Evangelical religion gave women something of universal significance to do with their lives at a time when economic and social forces were sabotaging their traditional roles. Encouraged by millennial-minded clergy, women transformed the acquiescent eighteenth-century ideal of "duty" into the nineteenth-century vision of "usefulness." Some historians have seen the feminine ideal of idleness ("expressed positively as gentility") as a substitute for the alleged social integration and economic usefulness of eighteenth-century women.[56] No doubt this ideal was around, as Alabama's *Sumter Democrat* made clear in 1852 editorial summarizing the role of women in society: "To dress, to sing, to play the piano, to speak French and German, and to preside gracefully at the tea table."[57] But to the extent that this neurasthenic secular alternative to Evangelical womanhood existed, it was spurned and scrapped as women passed through the conversion process. As Joseph Kett has aptly put it, the notion that female conversion "hammered down the nails on the coffin of domesticity" is inadequate.[58] Conversion meant obedience to God, but for women it also meant rebellion against social patterns of idleness, decoration, and subordination. A Massachusetts schoolteacher, Eleanor Emerson, who married Rev. Joseph Emerson of Beverly, Massachusetts, in 1805, testified in her writings that conversion smashed her image of woman as a "parlor ornament" and spelled the defeat of "the transient charms of personal beauty" at the hands of the substantial treasures of richly cultivated minds, capable of everlasting enlargement and increasing glory."[59] What has often been missing in discussions of the conversion phenomenon in nineteenth-century America is the recognition that conversion—which Finney stressed was the beginning, not the end, of the Christian life—was a vocational decision. Conversion put people to work for the kingdom. Both male and female converts stood under divine injunction to get busy in some voluntary society, teaching in Sunday school, visiting the sick, praying in social meetings, exhorting the lost. "The discharge of duty," wrote the southern Methodist bishop and editor Linus Parker, "is generally the first and often the severest test of the new convert."[60] And "duty" entailed the rejection of earthly enjoyments for heavenly employments.

Usefulness took on a different cast for women than for men. Usefulness for men was defined primarily in economic terms; usefulness for women, in spiritual and moral ones. Thus, the self-denial required of useful, productive men involved the stoical acceptance of tiresome drudgery and a life of disciplined toil.[61] For useful women, on the other hand, self-denial meant "bearing one's cross" submissively, usually defined as enduring periodic forays into public roles, away from the retiring anonymity of domestic duties. Although the value of women's work in the family had been disrupted by the development of a market economy, commodity fetishism, and industrial capitalism, the ideal of usefulness promised to replace stylish idleness or aimless busywork with purposeful activities. Domestic chores as well as social activities were now invested with millennial meaning. In short, Evangelicalism appealed to women because it made them feel useful. Amelia Ann Norton, whose husband, Herman G. Norton, would become an Oneida Association evangelist, wrote Lydia Finney an ecstatic letter describing the change Finney's Troy revival had made in her life. She was attending female prayer meetings, visiting the sick and poor, distributing tracts, and engaging in numerous outlets of service: "I never was happier in my life."[62] Every woman was made into a missionary, teacher, and minister (although not a preacher). It was not God's will that home and husband should delimit the extent of woman's concerns. And just as the father was increasingly circumscribed by the economic role of breadwinner, so the mother was increasingly seen in the spiritual role of soul-winner.

A life of usefulness defined in terms of soul-winning and kingdom building is what Evangelical mothers desired for themselves and their children. "Usefulness is the most desirable term in our language," wrote one manual for ministers' wives.[63] Evangelicals sent their daughters to Oberlin, Mount Holyoke, and female seminaries that deemed "ornamental" education abusive of women and aimed instead to instruct them in the "useful branches" of knowledge and prepare them for such useful vocations as minister's wife, missionary, or schoolteacher. "The ultimate object of all education should be usefulness," intoned Rufus Anderson in 1839, at the second anniversary celebration for Mount Holyoke Seminary. The theme of Anderson's address was the importance of the missionary wife, a fitting subject for a school Lucy Stone believed was founded with the express intention of educating the prospective wives of missionaries.[64] Female education must prepare for usefulness in two spheres especially: the sphere of human character formation, which was no small assignment given the reigning social philosophy of the nineteenth century, and the sphere of benevolence, which, Anderson argued, was for the Christian woman "coextensive with that of the Christian man—it is THE WORLD."[65] Many Evangelical parents nourished in their daughters the dream of becoming a missionary wife and Narcissa Prentiss Whitman (who with another missionary wife Eliza Spalding became the first white women to make the overland journey) was not the only young woman who read at her mother's knee the standard textbooks for ministerial candidates.[66] The greatest wish that Samuel W. May could offer for Lydia Finney's daughter Helen was "O may she become a Harriet Newell here," and when at seventeen, she abruptly married an Oberlin professor, William Cochran, a crushed and somewhat spiteful Lydia and Charles decided that if she was not to serve on a mission field, they would dispose of her piano in such a way that it would perform some missionary service.[67]

The most common vocational fantasies of Evangelical women in nineteenth-century America involved becoming a minister's or a missionary's wife. Both roles represented lives devoted to soul-winning, and both permitted women a public, assertive form of usefulness: the wives of missionaries functioned as missionaries (the American Board of Commissioners of Foreign Missions officially designated them "assistant missionaries"), and the wives of ministers functioned as ministers. The aspiration to become a missionary was frequently a by-product of a Finney revival. Paulina Kellog Wright Davis yearned for the life of a missionary after Finney's Leroy revival, and the Clinton revival produced two prominent recruits to the mission field, Emilie Royce Bradley and Laura Fish Judd.[68] Finney's Oberlin College also nourished among women the dream of a career in the ministry. The wife of the poet and mathematician James Abraham Martling persuaded him to enroll in Oberlin's theological course of study, which she hoped would change his career plans in the direction of the ministry.[69]

If one was not lucky enough to have a minister-father (three of Peter Cartwright's six daughters married ministers) or parents who ran a "Methodist Tavern" (a home that served as a clerical hotel), other steps could be taken, whether intentionally or unconsciously, to maximize one's chances of becoming a minister's wife. A signal of interest to ministers and missionaries was attendance at a female seminary or academy. Gideon Draper, the first presiding elder of the Genesee District in New York, saw to it that at least four of his daughters married ministers by providing all of them (at great expense to both his pocketbook and his career) with educational advantages.[70] Another tactic for catching the eye of a minister was to immerse oneself in religious activities, starting sewing circles, visiting the sick, promoting conversions, and exhorting in public. These were the notorious "prayer-meeting virgins," as one minister's wife called them, who so naturally keep their lamps trimmed and burning before the pulpits of unmarried preachers. These are really the best women to be found in any church. They never go astray, they are gentle maiden sisters of all souls, the faded feminine love-psalms of a benighted ministry who wither and grow old without ever suspecting that their hope was marriage no less than it is the hope of the giddiest girl.[71]

Women who married ministers or missionaries often chose not a husband, but a career, and the men who married them were much like John Fletcher, who interpreted his marriage to Mary Bosanquet as choosing a wife for the church. Mary Tucker's reputation as a fitting and willing candidate drew a quick proposal from Thomas Wait Tucker, who popped the question at their first meeting. She entered into the agreement in a mechanical, businesslike fashion and "commenced preparations at once for the career before me," determined, as she put it, that "if I could not labor like my husband in a public manner, I would devote all my energies to smooth his rough path, and strengthen his hands for the great work of saving immortal souls."[72] The Arkansas schoolteacher Ann J. Marshall was another wife who unabashedly chose her husband's vocation and then resolved to love the husband. Admitting an absence of feeling for her fiance, she nevertheless believed that one day her emotions would bow to her decision. "Next to a Missionary's life," she explained, "that of a pastor's wife was the most to be desired."[73] There was more than facetiousness in the occasional introduction at the annual conference of an itinerant's wife as "the new member." For as the southern schoolteacher Sue Dromgoole Mooney put it, her marriage day was also her ordination day: on that day "I joined the Methodist itinerancy."[74]

Both Lydia and Charles Finney were instrumental in matching ministers and missionaries seeking partners in ministry. Asked on numerous occasions to keep an eye out for suitable candidates, the Finneys also presided over negotiations in the parlor of their Oberlin home between missionaries ready to go into the field provided they found a wife to go with them, and women willing to go provided they found a missionary with the desired qualifications.[75] Such courtships were often short, but the ensuing marriages sweet. Somehow deep affection grew out of marriages built not on feelings, but on commitment. Anne Tuttle Bullard's novel *The Wife for a Missionary* (1834) describes a missionary's search for an "active and efficient" wife who would dedicate herself to "a life of real usefulness." His quest ended in the selection of a woman engaged in home visitation and tract distribution.[76] Evangelical ministers and missionaries went the biblical admonition "Be not unequally yoked together with unbelievers" one better. Their primary criterion for selecting a spouse was not love or faith, but a joint vision of usefulness.

Many letters to Lydia from friends, recent female converts, and young women seeking admission to Oberlin reveal secret ambitions of becoming a missionary and a sublimation of those desires in teaching, whether in district or private schools or Sunday schools.[77] Sarah T. Seward, whose desire to become a missionary burned unabated even after she had organized Seward's Female Seminary in Rochester, confessed to her friend Lydia that her motivation for attending Emma Willard's Troy Academy and becoming a teacher "centered in one great object—the salvation of souls."[78] Seward's passion for soul-winning had initially been awakened by Finney's 1827 revival in New Lebanon, New York. During their two months of labor at Silas Churchill's Lebanon Society, Lydia, Charles, and his prayerleader "Father" Daniel Nash took special interest in the spiritual formation of this intelligent, energetic, and promising new convert.[79] The pioneer women's organizer and educator Isabella Graham taught an earlier generation of Evangelical women that "the missionary is the nearest to the apostolic," and Sarah Farquhar, one of her assistants, became America's first missionary through her 1806 marriage to a British missionary to India.[80] Evangelical women like Graham saw the schoolteacher as a missionary, the school district as a mission field, and pupils as members of their congregation.[81] This was the idea behind Catharine Beecher's appeal to the wife of President James K. Polk for support in training urban women workers abused by ruthless "capitalists" and deploying them in the West as "missionary teachers."[82] The merging of educational and evangelical motives among female teachers is illustrated by the frequent scenes of religious revivals in educational institutions for women during the first half of the nineteenth century, and ministers encouraged pious young women to open up schools in which an hour a day would often be spent in Bible teaching.[83] Lydia herself was an enthusiastic supporter of missions, corresponding with Laura Fish Judd about her labors in the Sandwich Isles and harboring a special love for mission endeavors in Africa.[84]

Usefulness was such a desired quality among Evangelical women that Lydia's unique opportunities for soul-winning as a minister's wife inspired envy among some correspondents. One lady who witnessed the 1826 revival in Rome, New York, wrote: "O my dear Mrs. Finney, if there are any beings on earth, whom I could envy, it is those who are actively engaged in winning souls to Christ. No I will not envy. I will pray for them."[85] Other women wrote to Lydia asking for prayers rather than offering them, beset by dreary feelings of worthlessness caused by domestic responsibilities that prevented them from doing any more praying and pining for the conversion of sinners.[86] We are now beginning to appreciate how women took words like "duty" and "usefulness," long seen as serving to keep them in their place, and turned them on their heads to expand and extend female roles.

Lydia's position enabled her to promote the Assistant image of the minister's wife. First, as wife of the premier revivalist of the day, Lydia naturally shared the limelight. Second, Lydia was a prominent participant in the Female Department at Oberlin, where women who hoped for lives of enlarged usefulness came to study. There she was able to impose her conception of "independent" assistance on a generation of students. The class of 1841 included the first three women to receive the degree of Bachelor of Arts. Each of "the dauntless three"—native daughter Mary Hosford, Elizabeth Smith Prall from New York City, and Caroline Mary Rudd from Huntington, Connecticut—married a minister.[87] Just as Finney sired at Oberlin "a new race of ministers," Lydia bred a new race of ministers' wives. A recognized mother-confessor and spiritual advisor to students, Lydia instructed young women in educational, spiritual, and vocational matters. She was a member of Oberlin's Female Board of Managers, a small, self-perpetuating coordinate body mainly composed of the wives of faculty members, who, as Frances J. Hosford revealed of her student days there, "managed the girls; incidentally they managed the boys; occasionally they managed the faculty, and now and then they managed the president."[88] Lydia was not bashful about throwing her weight around to get what she wanted. She spearheaded the drive to remove as principal of the Female Department Mary Ann Adams, a pretty but punctilious woman who was not afraid to defy the Female Board and who tried to alter, perhaps by her resolute support for Antoinette Brown's bid to study theology, what Lydia felt was the best pattern of female education.[89]

III

The increasing tendency of ministers' wives in the antebellum period to define themselves as Assistants and for congregations to think of them the same way is evident in the clothes ministers' wives wore, the journals they kept, the manuals written for them, and the emerging Evangelical consensus on the qualities required of them.

If the sociologist Erving Goffman is correct in stating that dress functions as an "identity kit," and if antebellum clothes revealed a definition of women as frivolous, delicate, submissive, and inactive,[90] then the minister's wife's reigning fashion of modest simplicity stood as the shibboleth of dignified resistance. The first half of the nineteenth century witnessed a desultory debate between those who would bring fashion within the pale of taste and those who would drag it into the purview of morality. Among the former were those who argued that since the scriptures legislated no dress code and "the kingdom of God does not consist in meat, or in drink, or in dress," everyone might dress as he or she chose, provided the habiliments were modest and tasteful.[91] Among the latter were those who denounced with garment-rending intensity the immorality of spending time and money on fashions at the expense of more meretorious attractions.[92] It is impossible to establish this with certainty, but it appears that most ministers' wives, although often fastidious to a fault in their modest simplicity, lined up squarely behind the latter position. The apparel of a minister's wife ought to "appear as a sort of compromise between a saint and a Quakeress," one wrote. Methodist women probably came closest to their goal, for their *Discipline* ruled: "Give no tickets to any that wear high heads, enormous bonnets, ruffles, or rings."[93] But only the Quakers managed to establish an identity of dress and address. Evangelical ministers' wives were left to follow their own moral judgment in dress, realizing that "while some attention to the usages of society is essential to our usefulness, economy may be practiced, either by prohibiting variety, or by limiting our expenses to a certain sum."[94]

A modest simplicity became the norm. Costly jewelry and gaudy frills were forbidden. The wife of a minister ought to so dress that the poor would feel welcome in church, the reasoning went.[95] The money that went to purchase that piece of jewelry might have better gone to send tracts to China: "In this age of missionary enterprise, the wives of ministers should be the last to indulge in ornaments."[95] Furthermore, it was believed that fashion squandered a woman's time and diverted her energies from morality to manners, from substance to style, from reform to recreation, from values to vanity, and from intellectual and spiritual improvement to social dissipation. A few clerical wives were known for wearing their husbands' raises on their backs and transforming their churches into temples of finery,[97] but most, making their own clothes and practicing "habits of strict economy," shunned both spartan and extravagant extremes.[98] Their modest simplicity announced their active, serious, sturdy, and independent vocation.

The brief journal of Amey Scott chronicles her pilgrimage from a Dow to a Finney conception of the role of the minister's wife. When she married Orange Scott in 1826, she brooded over her duty not to obstruct her husband until she was in tears: "O, forbid that I should prove a dead weight to thy servant—a stumbling block in the way of sinners—or a hindrance to the prosperity of thy cause." Within eight years, however, she had discovered that the best way to avoid being a "dead weight" was to be a live wire in the ministry, praying publicly, exhorting, visiting the sick, organizing benevolences, and attending and assisting at prayer meetings on Tuesday and Friday evenings, class meetings on Wednesday and Thursday evenings, and three services on Sunday.[99]

Both churches and clergy came to appreciate the value of women in the ministry, and any woman who showed the promise of being "a sympathizing companion, a prudent counsellor, and a general female evangelist" was in special demand.[100] John Burgess, who set down ahead of time the characteristics he was looking for in a wife ("devoted to God," "modest and retiring," "fond of her husband," "a true helpmate," "strong support in the ministry") found the perfect candidate in 1846 and married her. While her independent spirit meant that "often we have slightly diverged—sometimes in thought, in plans, in actions," her ministry proved to enhance his immeasurably.[101] One manual for ministers encapsulated the Assistant model clearly when it stated that the requirements for the wives of clergy "should correspond in all important respects with those demanded in pastors themselves."[102]

Inherent in the Finney model, however, was the victimization of the minister's wife as an unpaid servant of the church. This issue was confronted gingerly by the first American manual for the wives of the clergy, published in 1835. "Some . . . have supposed that parishes have no claims on the exertions of a minister's wife," wrote Catherine L. Adams, a Presbyterian minister's wife from Maine, "that parishes stipulate for the services of the pastor, and with these services, they ought to content themselves."[103] When the cross fire of arguments ceased, she contended, the issue was "holiness of heart and life."

> You are the first to become acquainted with the great plans of benevolence, which are ushering in the latter days of millennial glory; the first to hear of the wants of the heathen, and of the openings for useful exertions in your own vicinity; and from the comparatively holy atmosphere that they breathe, society has a right to expect that the wives of ministers will be holy and devoted first in every good word and work. [104]

The manual was written to install Procrustean bedsteads in American parsonages—to encourage all ministers' wives to fit the same mold. The nature of the mold is what makes the book interesting. Adams instructed the wife of a clergyman on how to fulfill those daily duties that were "requisites for usefulness" if she was to become an "assistant to [her] husband." [105] Meekness and humility were enjoined, not as code words for gender subordination, but as general Christian virtues especially required of persons in ministry, who must continually "calculate upon meeting with meddlesome, officious people" and not lose their credibility with outbursts of "resentment" and "vulgarity." [106] "To be a good housekeeper is the way in which a minister's wife can best serve God," she averred, not because her calling was to keep house, but because unless she managed the household efficiently and economically, she would dishonor God by spending all her time there ("God undoubtedly, placed us all here for far higher purposes"), dishonor her husband by diverting his attention to finances, and dishonor religion with "the reproach of unpaid debts." [107] She was called to be "independent," "intelligent," and involved, diffusing "a spirit of active benevolence," especially among the young. Her curiosity was to be directed to the gospel rather than the neighborhood gossip, and she must be ever vigilant before her family and flock. [108] She must visit, assume leadership in the Sunday school, preside at female meetings, organize women's societies, and generally strive to exert "a powerful influence upon her husband's ministry." [109] If she ever found herself weary in well-doing and sinking into inertia, she was to remember her calling: "When you married a minister, you did not calculate upon a life of ease, or upon leisure for the gratification of selfish pursuits." Besides, "rest ought only to be looked for in heaven. God has placed us here to labor." [110]

The servant was seen as almost less important to God than the service, a harsh perception that was carried to its logical conclusion by Phoebe Palmer. The reason so many ministers' wives have "pined out a short existence," she contended, was that God disapproved of their performance in their sacred profession. "For this cause many are sickly, and many die."[111]

H. M. Eaton, a Methodist itinerant who also lived in Maine, published in 1851 a handbook for clerical wives that gave their professional requirements a distinctly Wesleyan slant. One stated purpose of the book was to discourage the faint-hearted and weak-minded from undertaking this career in the first place. Another was to encourage the wives of clergymen already in the work by enlisting the sympathy of their husbands. "While, therefore, we would sympathize with the itinerant, and from personal experience acknowledge that his labors are truly burdensome, we are still constrained to confess that his companion deserves a yet deeper sympathy."[112] What the Methodists thought about the minister's wife is especially important for the historian because they, most among all the traditions, had procedures for enforcing their conception. The Methodist *Discipline* made it mandatory for clergymen contemplating marriage to consult with "the most serious of their brethren" about their plans. There was also some attempt at regulating the function of clerical wives through the stationing committees of the annual conferences, which required presiding elders to deliver a report about the wives in their districts.[113]

Eaton's list of qualifications began with "common sense" and then proceeded to "literary culture." She must be educated, informed about the Wesleyan tradition, able to "form an opinion for herself," and well-read ("there is no danger that she will know too much"). It was, of course, a given that she would be pious, but since she would be leading the women of the church, she needed a piety that was "ardent," "cheerful," "uniform," and "benevolent"—for which she had models in the lives of Mary Fletcher and other wives of early Wesleyan preachers.[114] Her duties were threefold. Her duty to her husband included praying for his success and offering him "pious counsel" ("though 'in subjection' to their husbands, it is still their right and their duty to give advice"). Her duty as a mother included complete responsibility for managing the household economy and raising and educating the children, since the father was at best an "occasional visitor." Finally, her duty to the church was summed up in the phrase "foremost in every good work."[115]

Church visitation received considerable attention in Eaton's book and wherever anyone talked about the duties of a pastor's wife, and for good reason. Visitation quickly became an addiction for women in the ministry. The nineteenth century knew four types of "housecalls,"[116] although it is admittedly difficult at times to know which one is being talked about. Family visitation was restored by John Calvin to replace the confessional. Once the pastor had rounded up the family and servants, he conducted a religious inspection, educational interrogation, and theological inquisition. The Baptist president of Brown University, Francis Wayland, recommended that the interviewing take place individually;[117] others saw value in having the entire family undergo the process together. Evangelistic visitation involved a community dragnet of door-to-door calls that at times had less to do with mission "outreach" than with pew-filling "indrag." Pastoral visitation focused on the sick, shut-in, and dying. Finally, social visitation emphasized the pastor's role as a friend; he was to get to know his congregation in their own homes and on their own terms. The clergy were most heavily involved in the first two types of calls, and their wives in types two, three, and four.

Women came to dominate evangelistic, pastoral, and social visitation because of clerical default. While some Puritan clergymen would spend several afternoons a week visiting families, reserving one day a week for counsel in the home, others, like the Mathers, tended to shunt aside pastoral duties and concentrate on studying and preaching.[118] Above the door to Cotton Mather's study were placed the solemn words "Be Short"—a protective imperative that allowed him to produce at least 444 published items and become perhaps America's most prolific author. Jonathan Edwards, who reportedly spent thirteen hours a day reading and preparing sermons, refused to make any parish visits unless personally invited.[119] The emphasis on the scholarly pastorate persisted, and the Protestant sacrament of preaching continued to be the centerpiece of the Methodist Age as it had been that of the Puritan Age, although the quantity of sermons delivered was accented over quality (nineteenth-century lay exhorters and local preachers did more preaching than the ordained pastor of today). One Methodist itinerant, repulsed by the unwillingness of his colleagues to do anything but preach, decided to emphasize pastoral visitation. He soon found himself mired in poor appointments, penalized by the hierarchy, and able to extricate himself only by renewed attention to preaching.[120] It is not necessary, as a recent biographer of Henry Ward Beecher has done, to relate a lack of involvement in visiting the sick and dying of the parish to a personality dysfunction.[121] The reason was given in a prominent textbook in pastoral theology, a discipline that tended to stress "private" labors of a pastoral nature over more "public" labors like preaching: "If people can not have many visits and good sermons also, let them lack the visits."[122] Protestant laity in New York lacked visits, the European observer George Lewis noted in 1848, because "every minister gives his chief strength to the pulpit."[123]

"A home-going pastor makes a church-going people" was an eighteenth-century Evangelical saying that became an aphorism of Victorian America. The nature of the "home going," however, was dramatically altered from one century to the next. Whereas it was increasingly defined toward the end of the nineteenth century in pastoral and social terms, "home going" originally meant evangelistic and family visitation.[124] John Wesley, who revitalized these latter forms of home visitation, learned from his father's solemn, systematic household searching ("Who can read?" "Who can say their prayers and catechism?" "Are family prayers conducted?") that visitation should involve more than friendly conversation.[125] Isaac Watts called it "parlor preaching," and its adaptation to the American setting was revealed by George Whitefield in 1738 when he described his method of visitation during his four-month sojourn in Georgia and South Carolina:

> I visit from house to house, catechize, read prayers twice and expound the two second lessons every day; read to a house-full of people three times a week; expound the two second lessons at five in the morning; read prayers and preach twice, and expound the catechism to servants, etc., at seven in the evening every Sunday.[126]

When antebellum clergy said that it was "as necessary that a pastor should visit his people, as that a physician should visit his patient,"[127] it is often this family visitation that they are referring to. For it was a probing examination of the spiritual state of the entire family, accompanied by prayer, religious instruction, and prescriptions of Bible passages, tracts, and books that might promote spiritual growth.[128] Some lay people were uneasy about these stern, formidable inquisitions. Indeed, the very sight of the preacher standing at the door was enough to strike terror into a sinner's heart, especially if that preacher had the manners of James Gilmore, a Methodist itinerant who roamed western New York in the early nineteenth century. "He came in, and without being seated, asked, 'Have you any religion here?' If the answer was not satisfactory, he added: 'You must repent or you will go to hell. Good-by.'"[129] Faithfulness in pastoral visitations was for some a redeeming quality, but most Evangelicals judged a minister by his preaching, not his calling.[130]

Charles G. Finney encouraged women to take a lead in every form of visitation except social and family. He rejected social visitation for them because it was a waste of their and his precious time[131] and family visitation because it smacked too much of exercising authority over males, although he managed to take the edge off the interrogations and involve women in them by transferring them to the church, segregating parishioners into "classes" (male heads of families, female heads of families, young men, young women, children, merchants, lawyers), and calling them "inquiry meetings."[132] It is often forgotten that ever since John Wesley encouraged women to assist their pastors in visiting the sick and shut-in,[133] women dominated the performance of many "pastoral functions." It was pious females who were summoned when someone new moved into the community, when someone was sick, impoverished, in trouble, in need of food, or crying out for help to make it through the night. And it was these same females who, when their health failed, passed on to their daughters the duties of neighborhood visitation.[134]

In some cases women brought their minister with them; this seems to have been especially characteristic of Episcopal women. Mary G. Harley of South Carolina, for example, died while riding in a buggy with her pastor as they made the rounds visiting the sick.[135] But much of the time, when the Evangelical clergy were not preaching, they were tracking settlers in the forests of the New World, fording rivers, fighting blizzards, and tenderly caring for their horses. While they made special efforts to attend to the souls of the dying, "pastoral" shepherding was mainly left to the cradling touch of women, who increasingly saw this as their preserve: "How little man can do at the bedside of the afflicted! His hand is hard and his arm is heavy. His voice is gruff, and his movements awkward." In the

Methodist tradition, class leaders functioned as pastors to the twelve members of their class and thus were charged with visiting the sick. But even here there was a tendency for class leaders to appoint "lady assistants" who would perform much of the pastoral labor for them. Even without the title, Eunice Cobb made it a practice to visit every family in her home town of Cazenovia once each year.[136] During the 1830–1831 revival in New York City, one woman gathered together the people she visited and conducted weekly prayer meetings.[137] The official recognition given to the Ladies' and Pastors' Christian Union by the Methodist Episcopal church in 1872, as well as the late nineteenth-century trend toward designated "parish visitors," "Sunday school missionaries," and "deaconesses" in other denominations, was only institutional acknowledgment of what everyone knew all along: "Ministers almost invariably find WOMEN their principal helpers."[138] As one church official stated in the early twentieth century about women who gave two afternoons a week in home visitation: "May the tribe of such pastors' assistants increase."[139]

Shortly after Henry Ward Beecher arrived in Lawrenceburg, Indiana, to begin his first pastorate, he outlined in his journal the hopes and goals he cherished for the church. If he expected to reach the goal of a "large congregation" he must first "Preach well uniformly" and second "visit widely and produce a personal attachment; also wife do same."[140] Manuals for ministers' wives were insistent that they visit the sick, the poor, the rich, the young, the old—if possible with their husbands, but if need be alone. Often serving as visiting nurses, dispensing health aid and advice to those they visited, the wives of clergy risked their lives alongside their husbands in nursing parishioners visited by epidemics.[141] When death itself became the final healing act, it was often the minister's wife who superintended the shrouding of the corpse and provided for the physical needs of the mourning family.[142] The visits of a pastor's wife were not "fashionable calls" for idle conversation or backyard gossip.[143] A minister's wife, no less than her husband, was required to direct all her energies and efforts to building the kingdom.

There is ample evidence that daily visits consumed a hefty portion of the time of a minister's wife.[144] This was as true for Evangelical wives like Lydia Finney as it was for Unitarian wives like Hannah Huntingdon.[145] Especially during revivals, Evangelical women spent their mornings canvassing homes, counseling with Christian wives who had not yet brought their husbands to their knees, and praying for disturbed souls.[146] Indeed, Lydia Finney seems to have worked with her husband in mobilizing women for campaigns of evangelistic visitation, a mode of evangelism quickly adopted by other Finneyites.[147] Finney was not the first to employ women in this fashion. In 1810 Eleanor Dorsey, the wife of a prominent judge in western New York and a patron of Methodist itinerants, accompanied a circuit rider in house-to-house visitation. Their day's labor yielded forty new members for the fledgling Methodist society in Lyons, New York.[148] Nor was Finney the last. The Buffalo, New York, YMCA undertook in 1853 a citywide Bible and tract distribution project and used women as colporteurs.[149] But Finney, through his wife, Lydia, was the first to integrate female visitation into the machinery of revivalism.

The lives of service scripted for ministers' wives in the manuals by Adams and Eaton presumed that many would have domestic servants,[150] a submerged subject in the history of the parsonage but an important one if we are to understand the economics behind the triumph of the Finney model. The availability of cheap black or immigrant labor (mostly Irish, Swiss, and German) coincided in the 1830s with the rise of the commercial middle class and the cities.[151] The massive exploitation of household help that ensued, the northern version of slave labor, brought outcries from Evangelical women, ranging from Catharine E. Beecher's proposal to educate and relocate unemployed domestics as teachers in the West to the American Female Guardian Society's sponsorship of what may have been America's first effort at a "Christian Yellow Pages," an employment agency where over 2,000 female domestics registered to find work with Christian employers.[152] The employment of domestics by those living in homesteads or parsonages, coupled with declining birth rates all through the century and the tendency for ministers' wives without parsonages to live in boarding houses, freed many women from much of the actual labor, if not the administration, of housewifery and afforded them sufficient time to pursue their calling's "broad and extended field of labor."

In a sense, the inclusion of domestics within the parsonage was a throwback to an older tradition. Katherine Luther supervised a retinue of servants who performed most of her housework, and John Wesley learned as a child to direct requests for food at the table not to his mother, but to the servants in attendance, servants he used as an adult to test the intelligibility of his sermons.[153] But domestics released the energy of earlier wives so that they might be directed to entertaining her husband's guests and pupils or rearing her children, not serving the church. There is evidence to suggest that nineteenth-century ministers' wives sometimes paid for the boarding of domestics out of their own pin money, that the clergy themselves more often hired servants to help their wives, and that churches in rare cases included the services of a domestic for the minister's wife in the fringe benefits of their salary package.[154]

Considerable ambivalence and revealing anomalies sometimes attended this departure from household labor. Like Harriet Beecher Stowe, who defended the dignity of housekeeping while dreading its drudgery even when aided by servants, Lydia Finney leaned on servants to do her housework while sustaining the ideal of doing it herself. Her niece, a Congregational minister's wife from Michigan, wrote to Lydia that "I often think how trying, with your views of housekeeping, to have so many different ones do for you. I have been able but a very little to do my own work since we commenced housekeeping, but much prefer it were it possible."[155] But Lydia appears to have panicked when she was without servants, and her successors, Elizabeth and Rebecca, were never without at least one.[156] So commonplace had it become for the wives of clergymen to be assisted by domestics that William Andrus Alcott, who campaigned for "the young wife" to do her own housekeeping, aimed a special attack at the wives of ministers for influencing young women in the opposite direction:

> How rare it is for a minister to marry a lady who understands, and above all, who loves the domestic concerns of a household? ... I have known many a minister's wife, whose hands performed all the labor of her family, while in good health. Nor was this labor incompatible with a good degree of mental improvement. ...
> But it is not so now.[157]

A final bit of telling evidence for the triumph of Lydia Finney's model of women's ministry was the phenomenon, beginning in the 1830s, of ministers' wives organizing themselves into state and local societies. An early association of ministers' wives in New England took the form of a maternal association; another assumed the guise of a prayer meeting; still another fashioned itself into a benevolent society. But all of them were designed to bring the wives of clergy-

men together for vocational communication, edification, and reinforcement. Catherine Adams dedicated her manual "to the wives of
clergymen in Maine, comprising the 'Society for Mutual
Improvement,'" and her book purposed to stimulate the founding of
similar state and local organizations. Whether Lydia Finney was ever
a part of one we cannot be sure, but a friend of hers, also a minister's
wife, corresponded with her about the efforts of Congregational
ministers' wives in Ohio to establish separate meetings while their
husbands attended the general association.[158] A common ministry
began drawing the wives of ministers together.

IV

The establishment of the career of the minister's wife was not without opposition. Emerging most strongly within the Presbyterian
tradition, disapproval developed toward churches for expecting su-
perhuman performances from the wives and toward the wives for
assuming too much official authority. The Union Theological Seminary professor John H. Rice wrote to his daughter, who had recently
married one of his Presbyterian students, some advise on how they
both could be "very *happy*, and very *useful*." Since "the life of a
minister is the life of a student," the minister's wife should cultivate a
"cheerful spirit," display a "conciliating," even temperament in all
situations, refrain from burdening her husband with small talk, and
discreetly correct his "striking and offensive *mannerisms* or impro-
prieties." When Rice came to talk of her public role, he issued a stern
warning: "Many ministers' wives destroy their influence entirely by
seeming to think that they have also a sort of official character, which
gives them authority to dictate, prescribe, recommend, or oppose
measures to be adopted in the congregation." The course to be
followed in her leadership capacity, he counseled, was that of "meek,
gentle, and affectionate insinuation."[159]

Others reacted to the welter of conflicting and unattainable job
expectations of the local churches. Unable to find in the scriptures
any requirements for the wives of ministers, the *Presbyterian* turned
with tongue in cheek to "that other rule of faith and practice, public
opinion." It mandated that the wife of a minister be a composite of the
best attributes of various biblical heroes, plus "be apt to please
everybody." The only way out of such unstated but entrenched
understandings, the article concluded, was to "set apart women, and
educate them for minister's wives"; screen the wife as well as the

pastoral candidate for vacant parishes "to ascertain whether she be able or willing to perform the labor of five ordinary women without any compensation"; and publicly admit that "a minister's wife should be always at home and always abroad; always serving God and always serving tables," as well as "a little more prudent than our Savior, for he had favorites among his disciples, which in her is unpardonable."[160] The editor of a Presbyterian publication out of Philadelphia did not use satire when detailing the role of pastors' wives in the church. Instead, he bluntly urged all churches to consider the following three recommendations:

> First. The relation of a pastor's wife to a congregation is the same as that of every other woman; her marriage with a minister invests her with no office, and gives her no pre-eminence.
>
> Secondly. Her duties are the same as those commanded by Paul to be performed by every other Christian woman in the married state;—no more, no less.
>
> Thirdly. When she performs these to the best of her ability, nobody ought to complain.[161]

Chapter Five

"Take Up Thy Cross and Follow Me"

Praying Women and Antebellum Revivalism

Of late I've been requested in silence for to keep,
Because I've grieved the Pastor and likewise his dear sheep;
But if my Savior calls me to speak in his dear name,
I can't obey the Pastor, although a man of fame.

I do respect his person, his faults I can forgive,
But to refrain from speaking, I cannot do and live;
If I am called to speak for Jesus and his cause,
I can't obey the people which make such human laws.

. . . .

I must join with Mary and tell to all around
That Jesus Christ is risen, for I his grace have found,
And if I am reproached because these things I say,
My work is to forgive them and humbly watch and pray.

Polly M. Stevens

As almost every historian of American religion has observed, Charles G. Finney was a pragmatist's pragmatist. Success was the prime sanctioner of his strategy, and even of his theology. In one of his sermons he declared, "But some of you will say, this is not consistent with Finney's theology. What do I care for Finney's theology? I can change my mind ninety-nine times in a minute, if I see reason for doing."[1] Finney was a prospector for truth, particularly truth that worked. He would abandon old shafts that did not yield sufficient returns on his revivalistic investment as quickly as he would discard nuggets of truth after overturning larger chunks of ore. His remarkable insouciance about theological consistency was matched by his disregard for social conventions that stood in the way of converting all who were guilty of unbelief and statutory piety.

There was one thing about which Finney never changed his mind, however, although it cut against the grain of social convention: the power of prayer, especially female prayer, and most especially Lydia's prayers. Finney knew that the prayers of pious women worked in the conversion of sinners because it had been Lydia's prayers that brought him to his knees. Lydia Root Andrews had been converted at age eleven under the ministry of John Frost of Whitesborough, a pastor who would later become one of Finney's strongest defenders and closest confidants. When she was eighteen, Lydia first met a tall, handsome lawyer with sharp flashing blue eyes, a nasal voice, and a sallow complexion. She became infatuated with him and began praying in secret for his unredeemed soul. Within a few months Finney had passed through the stages from conviction to coversion to calling. He abandoned his law practice, reportedly telling one client whose case was to be tried the next morning, "I have a retainer from the Lord Jesus Christ to plead his cause, and I cannot plead yours."[2] While traveling from door to door pleading for the salvation of souls, Finney discovered (he never tells us how) that he had been ushered to the mercy seat, like multitudes of males before him, on the wings of a woman's prayers. This pious young woman with whom he had been "slightly acquainted" for a few months had spent the time since their meeting laboring before the throne of grace for the salvation of his soul. As Finney put it, "The knowledge of this fact led to a still further acquaintance which resulted in our marriage."[3] It was Lydia's prayers that led Finney to the altars of conversion and matrimony.

Finney never forgot this lesson on the efficacy of prayer. When he published in 1835 his classic *Lectures on Revivalism*, he devoted nearly a quarter of the volume to prayer, the "prayer of faith," and prayer meetings. Nine prayer meetings a day, or more, were not unheard of; new measures revivalism offered a veritable dawn-to-dust smorgasbord of prayer meetings for starving souls and hungry soul-winners: inquiry meetings, union meetings, home meetings, sunrise, afternoon, and evening meetings, children's meetings, and meetings for "young men," "young ladies," "male professors," and others.[4] Celia R. Ladd remembered how Finney "attributed his success in soul saving largely to the fact that he had always been favored with helpers who knew how to pray."[5] The helpers he leaned on earliest and most often were women. On 17 March 1824 the Female Missionary Society of the Western District of the state of New York gave him a three-month commission to labor in nort'iern Jefferson County, the scene of sweeping revivals nine years earlier. Finney's first stop was the small rustic village of Evans Mills. He arrived at the home of his hosts, the Hopkinses, who asked if they might take his overcoat. Squirming out of it, Finney inquired, "Any praying women around here, Brother Hopkins?" Hopkins replied, "Yes, I believe there is one, at the other end of the village." Without even sitting down, Finney thrust his arm back into his coat and set out to meet this praying woman.[6]

It would be difficult to overestimate the evangelical importance Finney attached to prayer. When Finney was asked by one of his 1827 female converts to inscribe her autograph album, he wrote, "Sarah, My Dear Sister, 'Pray Always.'" When Finney preached at Rochester in 1830–1831, perhaps his most successful mission, each day for six months, between eight hundred and a thousand people would gather for prayer at 10:00 a.m., and those who could not crowd into the sanctuary of an evening would kneel outside in the snow and pray during the service. When Finney preached at his own church in Oberlin, devoted parishioners would stay at home and prayfully "hold on" for him while he preached.[7] Prayer was the rock upon which Finney built his revivals, and ministers' wives were some of his most faithful praying women.

I

Prayer meetings have been represented as the most elementary form of associative activity available to Evangelical women.[8] That may be. But Finney viewed their importance and impact as elemental, and thus they became. For a proper understanding of why the words "praying women" were Finney's basic recipe for revivalism, we must first divest ourselves of the unfortunate association of "prayer" with words like "private," "personal," and "passive." Finney believed that prayer, like love, was in its truest form not an attitude but an activity, and, as Sandra Sizer has shown, a predominantly social activity at that.[9] Revivals were the stimuli, and prayer meetings the means, of faith in action; Evangelicalism's large standing army of women was mobilized to sally forth from female prayer meetings, fortified by sororal encouragement and solidarity, and do battle against the evil forces that held their husbands and children hostage to sin. Weekly female prayer meetings were more than social parantheses or pious pep-rallies. When animated by the hope of revival, they became directed gatherings, pulsating centers of creative energy and zeal. Earlier Evangelicals had learned to value and encourage female zones of prayer. Francis Asbury, who learned to shout from the vigorous sisters in his mother's fortnightly women's meetings, gave the following prescription "to the sisters" for whatever ailed them and their churches: "I recommend more frequent prayer-meetings."[10] But it remained for Finney to make female prayer meetings intentional, investing them with major responsibility for conversions. Finney expected praying women to go after their prey, stalking sinners wherever they lurked, whether at home, on the streets, or in the shops.

Female prayer meetings, the solar plexus of new measures evangelism, were meetings in both the psychological and organizational senses of the word: people encountering one another on a level of intimacy and adventure, and groups organizing to do business. Prayer meetings allowed women to share with other women the condition of their own souls and those of their significant others; at the same time, they expressed organizational impulses that could most comfortably be fulfilled within the framework of religion and aided in the development of the strategies, skills, reciprocities, and disciplines requisite to organizing revivals.[11] The rumor that a prayer meeting had drafted a constitution—odd as that might appear to us—evoked Lydia Finney's serious interest, and she penned a note to the church women of Troy in 1827, asking to learn more about their efforts. The Troy women responded that they had formally structured their prayer group and convenanted with one another around four points: "that we will attend unless necessarily detained; . . . that we will commence at the hour though but two should be present; that all shall lead in prayer each in turn; that we will live together as dear sisters in the Lord."[12] In Little Falls that same year, the women agreed that if for some reason they could not leave their houses to attend the weekly Tuesday prayer group, they would keep the covenant with their sisters by praying at home in their closets during the time the rest of the group was meeting.[13]

As a social activity, prayer brought Evangelical women into collusion with other women who shared similar concerns about their unredeemed families and communities. Although one slightly paranoid but prescient clergyman was reported to have insisted on leading the prayer at his church's female prayer meetings (because "there's no telling what these misguided females would ask for in their prayers"),[14] most Evangelical women fenced themselves off from intruding eyes and ears. Their prayers became vehicles for self-discovery and investigation into ploys for promoting conversions and getting around their menfolk. It was in the accepting ambiance of these ladies' prayer meetings that women like Margaret Prior, one of the first managers of the New York Orphan Asylum, developed skills and gained confidence in public speaking.[15] When unable to pray in gender closets, women locked themselves in their home closets for seasons of "secret prayer" (Susanna Wesley did so for two hours a day). In either case they were physically separating themselves from their unconverted children, husbands, and neighbors and theologically setting themselves apart as the major intercessory agencies of human regeneration. Female meetings were occasionally thrown open to men, as the holiness theologian Phoebe Palmer's famed New York Tuesday Meeting for the Promotion of Holiness was in 1839. But this happened only after the women had met long enough (in Palmer's case, for four years) to satisfy their own needs and attain sufficient levels of poise and independence.

A composite picture of these prayer meetings reveals revivalism's debt to women. Women were the experts in methods of evangelism, and they displayed great revivalistic polish. In preparation for a revival, and often directed by a revivalist or in anticipation of his coming, one praying woman would seek out another, who would find still another, until enough had been gathered to form or revitalize a meeting. Emilie Royce Bradley was sixteen and never-been-converted when she joined one of the circles designed to pave with prayer Finney's road to Clinton, New York.[16] Often a minister's wife would be the sparkplug who got the engines of evangelism running.[17] Soon a young people's meeting might follow, as maternal pressure began to bear fruit. In some cases the young men and young women were organized into separate prayer groups, though young men's prayer meetings, like those of their fathers, were much rarer than those for girls or their mothers. There was even what might be called a female provincialism. "I do not know anything about the male members," Mrs. H. C. Green of New York City wrote to her friend Lydia Finney, after recounting in graphic detail the activities of the women of her church.[18] Young ladies' prayer meetings flourished and multiplied like their mothers', until Lydia's sisters, Mary Ann Andrews and C. S. Andrews, found themselves in 1826 attending five young ladies' prayer meetings in the little village of Whitestown.[19] Once prayer meetings were securely organized, women would begin in earnest to work on their husbands and neighbors. Sometimes they would do it through fasting or private urgings in the home, and at other times through more public means of persuasion, such as praying by name for family members in mixed prayer meetings or marching through the congregation and laying siege to unsuspecting sinners, falling on their knees with tears streaming down their faces, and relentlessly begging them to repent.[20] After a few reported cases of influential citizens coming under "conviction," social pressure would take hold and a whole community would find itself swept up in a revival.

Thus, for Finney and other new measures revivalists, female activities were a major sign of revival readiness. Finney's disciple Edward Norris Kirk was about ready to leave Albany, New York, after being ousted from his church because of his new measures evangelism, when he was informed that a band of praying women had spent the night in prayer beseeching God that Kirk not depart from them. "I would go to the gates of hell with such a band!" Kirk replied, and went on to form Albany's Fourth Presbyterian Church. Another pastor who declined the call of the church was persuaded to change his mind and become its pastor when informed of the existence of a praying trio of women in the church.[21] Many of those who solicited Finney's services pointed to the presence of praying women as evidence of the revival ripeness of their community.[22] Lydia herself monitored through correspondence the vital signs of communities that were being considered for a Finney revival, and she kept a tight finger on the pulse of female activities both before and after one.[23]

Lydia was of immense help to Finney, both in starting female prayer meetings in communities where Finney decided to conduct revivals and in reviving comatose groups. In fact, when Lydia was unable to accompany Finney, as happened during his Troy revival in 1826, the women of the community felt cheated: they had been denied her services. When she did labor with him, the familiar postrevival lament that the fires had cooled with Finney's departure also referred to Lydia's efforts. Henrietta Platt of Stephentown reported to her that the female prayer meetings she had started a few months earlier still continued: "We only want your presence to make them as interesting as ever." A year later her complaint was pitched much higher, and she contrasted the vitality and popularity of the meetings when Lydia conducted them with the present "nonanimated" and thinly attended gatherings.[24] Such news, as spiritually disheartening as it was, must also have been psychologically gratifying. Her work made a difference. She was needed. And the same mystique that mantled the revivalist began to wrap around her as well.

The invitation from Ellen and Elisabeth Knight to conduct

female prayer meetings at their church in Reading, Pennsylvania, is only one sign of Lydia's emerging importance among the Evangelical sisterhood.[25] It was a tribute to her influence that she did not have to remain in or even visit a community to provide female prayer circles with encouragement, support, and advice. Her surviving correspondence reveals a minister's wife with a deep female consciousness, an intense hunger for news of female religious activities, and a prized store of advice on how to infuse new life and spirit into barren women's meetings.[26] Her epistolary conversations were never circumscribed by domestic concerns. She engaged in theological disputations over issues like original sin and perfectionism, interpreting the latter doctrine to people who often seemed, as Finney later phrased it, more afraid of sanctification than sin.[27] The wealthy merchant and abolitionist Lewis Tappan discussed with her as an intellectual peer his nascent conviction that abolitionism was beginning to replace revivals in the church.[28] Catherine Huntington of Troy especially enjoyed discussing recently published theological tracts and books with Lydia.[29]

Lydia was, of course, sometimes used as a conduit to her husband, especially by those women and ministers' wives who sought Finney's service in their church. As Lydia Gilbert of Wilmington, Delaware, put it, "According to an old saying that the wife is the neck of the head of her husband, we depend much on your influence."[30] But most of Lydia's correspondents wrote because she was a worthy, intelligent, admired model of Evangelical usefulness with whom one could counsel and communicate ideas. Lydia saved her most preferential treatment for the women with whom she labored during her husband's revivals, and she expected these friends to keep her informed on their activities and prayer meetings.[31] Other ministers' wives—C. C. Copeland, Rhoda Churchill, Lydia Gilbert, Amelia Norton, Ann F. Cole, Emily S. Bartlett, and others— corresponded with her about their frustrations, failures, and successes and the questions produced by their attempts to establish an effective ministry in their husbands' churches.[32] Through her correspondence as well as her leadership at Oberlin, Lydia served as the spiritual preceptor and vocational counselor of ministers' wives.

II

The new measure that made new measures revivalism controversial was the praying of females in the presence of males. Although this practice had stirred tongue and pen long before Finney, his endorsement heightened Evangelical sensitivity to the issue. In fact, his extraordinary success at converting and mobilizing the women of New Lebanon, New York, may have evoked the unanimous vote of the trustees and deacons of the New Lebanon Society in 1827 "to supply Dr. Lyman Beecher and the honorable Asahel Nettleton all monies necessary to stop up the satanic Charles Finney." The church's pastor, Silas Churchill, who had sponsored Finney's revival in the community was now forced by his church's lay leaders to sponsor the convention designed to silence him.[33]

Once the dust had settled from this shootout on revivalism, compromise agreements were standing on every issue except female public prayer. Finney's opponents reached for their guns whenever they heard the words "women speaking." The issue was not the spiritual and intellectual equality of women, however, or their involvement in promoting conversions. Gardner Spring, pastor of New York City's Brick Presbyterian Church for over fifty years, had in common with Charles G. Finney only a denomination and an early career as a lawyer. Yet Spring celebrated his wife's "fine intellect" and verified that she was "no incompetent counsellor to the awakened and convinced."[34] Many ministers, like Spring, respected their wives' minds but opposed their praying in public. The bone of contention was whether women should exercise spiritual authority over men in public as they were already doing in private.

The opposition to this new measure was significant, for Finneyite revivalism relied on social prayer, testimony, and exhortation, and the women who led them, to create a "community of feeling" conducive to conversions.[35] For Asahel Nettleton, the opposing bloc's premier revivalist, a little feeling went a long way. He wrote to the Oneida Presbytery in care of Lydia's former pastor, John Frost, of his conviction that Finney's "great secret" in arousing the passions that produced a revival "is to get females to pray in school houses and circles where men, and ministers especially, are present to see and hear them pray for them and others by name."[36] Finney and his cohorts, men like Nathaniel Beman and Samuel C. Aikin, perceived the value in appropriating the increasingly sentimentalized "female influence" for revivals, and they persisted in this belief and practice in spite of the early social warnings of Yale's president, Timothy Dwight, and his student Lyman Beecher, the theological arguments of New Lebanon, and the ecclesiastical admonitions of the Oneida Association (1827) and the General Assembly (1832).[37]

Finney was only heeding the ancestral voices of women. Three Baptist sisters in Sturbridge, Massachusetts, shored up the First Great Awakening with their public utterances. Quaker women like the wife of John Cranston, the seventeenth-century governor of Rhode Island (she was the woman who scandalized Providence's founder, Roger Williams, by breaking into the middle of one of his speeches with prayer)[38] have a well-known history of liturgical leadership. Less appreciated is the fact that Baptist and Methodist women, and especially ministers' wives, not uncommonly prayed and exhorted in public. Two brothers-in-law, Shubal Stearns and Daniel Marshall, are widely recognized for their extension of the Baptist faith into the South in the mid-eighteenth century. It is less well known that Daniel Marshall's second wife, Martha, Stearns's sister, was jailed in Windsor, Connecticut, for preaching and exhorting. She launched the southern tradition of female exhorters among separate Baptists.[39] The colonial Baptist leader Isaac Backus sought to douse what he called the "wildfire" of women exhorters. Thus, further studies may reveal the custom to be far more pervasive than historians have realized.[40]

American Methodist women could also be found giving public expression to their Christian faith in the late eighteenth and early nineteenth centuries. Earl Kent Brown's important study of John Wesley's female associates and followers helpfully categorizes the forms assumed by early Methodist women's public address: "Casual conversation, talks or prayers in band and class meetings, prayer in society or other public meetings, testimony, exhortation, expounding, biblical exegesis and application."[41] Early American Methodist history abounds with examples of women engaged in all but the last two of these activities. Methodist women were called on by their pastors to pray publicly. They led prayer meetings at quarterly conferences. They narrated their conversion experiences during worship. They testified in love feasts as frequently and fearlessly as men.[42] As any visitor to a revival or camp meeting could see, the Pauline injunction "Let women keep silent in church" had no meaning for Evangelical women. They were, the outspoken Unitarian Theodore Parker observed from his outpost in Boston, "always the most noisy" in prayer, testimony, shouting, singing, and congregational feedback.[43] A Presbyterian who refused to attend a camp-meeting love feast because "*You allow women to speak in these public meetings*" was sharply rebuked by the Methodist who extended the invitation.

The truth is, my brother, you and your creed belong to a by-gone age, when woman hardly dare speak in the presence of her husband,—when silence and inaction were enjoined on account of her (supposed) inferiority. That day has passed. Woman has been redeemed by the blood of Christ, and exalted to equality with man in the privileges and blessings of the Gospel dispensation.[44]

Perhaps the freedom allowed in these Methodist services explains why "women in those days often rode on horseback forty, and even fifty, miles to a quarterly meeting, received a powerful blessing, and returned rejoicing."[45]

In fact, both before and during Finney's new measures revivalism, the Methodist class meeting (which became so popular in the American setting that other traditions adopted its small-group format)[46] served as a school in the art of public address. Every member of the class was urged to speak. Since most classes were mixed, women found themselves in effect being pushed by the church to address men. Mary Boardman, who would later develop with her husband, William, a Partner ministry, was first convinced by a Presbyterian minister in 1840 that she had an obligation to pray before others. She struggled with this conviction until, after reading the holiness testimonies of Finney and Asa Mahan, she sensed that her own experience of sanctification hinged on her giving her voice to God.

"Surely it cannot be that thou dost want me to speak in any public way, when the Word says women are to keep silence in the churches! I talk to individuals; I do pray in small circles; and what else can I do?"

It sounded in my heart, "You must tell what I am to you wherever I wish; Your lips are Mine, and must be fully surrendered."

"But there is no opportunity," I argued. This objection was very quickly overruled, as the answer came to me that the Methodist class meeting was open to me.[47]

Her attendance at the class meeting quickly confirmed her inner urgings, for she was told that if she did not publicly proclaim the blessings of holiness, she would lose it.

Many Evangelical women were encouraged in the class meeting to develop expertise in public speaking. E. S. Jones, whose 1868

Address to Class Leaders was intended to lift the flagging spirits of a vanishing breed of "assistant pastors," recollected having met a woman in the 1840s who expressed an interest in Methodism. Jones invited her to his class. She hesitated, saying, "I cannot go to class because I cannot speak in class." Assuring the tongue-tied woman that he would not embarrass her, Jones nursed her along in his class until she could rise and speak as forcefully as anyone else.[48] Jones need not have reached back into the past for such a story. A similar tale was told by Maggie Newton Van Cott, who became in 1869 the first Methodist woman to get a preacher's license. She at first shunned class meetings because they required women to speak, but the experience she received there enabled her to develop the dynamic, commanding preaching style that prompted one contemporary to describe her as "today the most popular, most laborious, and most successful preacher in the Methodist Episcopal Church."[49]

Converted women had a story to tell, and nineteenth-century Evangelicals encouraged them to tell it. Ministers' wives most often were the first to step forward and to break down the barrier between exhorting sinners, which was not technically defined as preaching, and expounding the gospel, which was. To call Frances Wright the first woman public speaker in America is to ignore countless Evangelical women. One of the pioneers was the beloved Fanny Newell. At the close of the afternoon sermon at an 1810 quarterly conference, Ebenezer Francis Newell shed his determination to remain single and married Fanny Butterfield. When her friends clustered around to congratulate her on her name change, she began exhorting them to undergo a name change also—from heathen to Christian. As Newell itinerated through Vermont and Maine, his wife and two children traveled with him. But her responsibilities to the children did not deter her from what her husband called "united efforts in public and from house to house," and the churches and schoolhouses were often filled with people who had come to hear the famed preacher's wife exhort and invite sinners forward to "come to Jesus."[50] Similarly, the second wife of the New Jersey itinerant William Baker closed his services during the 1830s with "powerful exhortations" that brought many to Christ.[51] The marriage of the scrappy Elizabeth Cantrell to an Arkansas Baptist preacher did not stop her from being a "shouting Methodist." She would travel from church to church on her husband's circuit during revivals and "pray, exhort, and shout till the victory would result."[52] Hannah Pearce

Reeves, wife of a Methodist circuit rider, achieved considerable fame as "The Lady Preacher."[53]

Amey Scott, the twenty-one-year-old Vermont native who married the Methodist itinerant Orange Scott in 1826, did not ease into public speaking as effortlessly or as quickly as Newell, Baker, and Cantrell. It was not until she underwent the experience of sanctification that she "gained some important victories—particularly in speaking and praying in meetings and especially in the presence of my husband." The years of her enlarged efforts of exhorting, speaking, praying, visiting, and aiding the poor by dressing simply became for her "the most highly favored of my life."[54] The incredible Bangs family, which sired five Methodist itinerants (the most prominent of whom was Nathan Bangs), also produced a minister's wife, Mrs. Joseph Gatchel, who eyewitnesses said equaled her husband in eloquence and exhorted "like a streak of red-hot lightning." Rachel Evans, the wife of an African Methodist Episcopal preacher in New Jersey, had a reputation that reached up into the episcopal hierarchy and down into local congregations for being a better preacher than her husband.[55]

There were also more eccentric clerical couples, like the coarse-grained, mercurial Presbyterian revivalist Jedediah Burchard and his maverick wife. After losing their only child, a seven-year-old daughter, Mrs. Burchard embarked on a crusade for the early conversion of children. She accompanied her husband and originated meetings for mothers and children throughout western and central New York in the 1820s and 1830s. Her efforts were quite successful in stirring Evangelicals to labor for the conversion of children under seven, the presumed age of accountability, after which one could not ride the parental coattails into heaven. Finney and such prominent lay patrons of revivalism as Judge Emerson of Windsor, New York, at first applauded their labors. By 1833, however, many had backed away from the Burchards' "theatrics," which included brandishing a Book of Numbers containing the names of all their converts and bragging about the count from village to village.[56]

It was not only in exuberant and unrestrained revivalistic settings that women exercised their lungs. Everywhere, especially where male religious leadership was lacking or lagging behind, Baptist and Methodist women eagerly took up the slack, no matter how unconventional the task.[57] Some practices became standing traditions of local church life. Before Finney's new measures were even heard of, it was the custom of a popular Rochester Bible class teacher, Lorena Kelley, to speak in prayer meetings and revival services. When reprimanded by a deacon for violating Paul's strictures against women speaking in church, she "remained standing and casting a withering look at the interrupting deacon, replied: 'I differ with St. Paul on that subject,' and resumed her exhortation."[58] In another city congregation, the Ebenezer Methodist Episcopal Church in Washington, D.C., a woman named Elizabeth Speiden was an unofficial prayer leader.[59] For charismatic women like Kelley and Speiden, prayer and exhortation were ways of becoming a public figure and celebrity.

Both white and black city pastors leaned on women to provide their services with excitement, serendipity, and energy. When the black domestic Jarena Lee found Jesus in the "English Church" during the preaching of Philadelphia's esteemed Richard Allen, "That moment, though hundreds were present, I did leap to my feet and declare that God, for Christ's sake, had pardoned the sins of my soul. . . . For a few moments I had power to exhort sinners, and to tell of his wonders and of the goodness of Him who had clothed me with His salvation."[60] Lee quickly joined the Methodist class meeting, where she began to develop her stirring oratorical skills.

By far the most celebrated of the Methodist dual ministries was that of Edward Taylor and his wife, Deborah Millett, both of whom labored to build the famous "Seamen Bethel Church" in Boston. She was known as "the Reverend Mrs. Edward T. Taylor" because of her eloquence and proficiency in exhortation. Ever since her conversion at fourteen, Deborah had hoped to marry a minister. Her chance came in 1819 when she met Taylor, a "saddle-bagger" (a southern itinerant bent on the redemption of the North), shortly after he had left Newmarket Seminary, the only Methodist school in America at the time. Deborah Taylor, who numbered among her closest friends the wives of Horace Mann and Nathaniel Hawthorne, joined her husband in establishing close ties with Boston's Brahmins, and laborers, sailors, and common people. "The Reverend Mrs. Taylor" did not preach her first Sunday sermon until 1859, and the setting was Boston's Bethel Chapel, where men sat together in the middle section and women occupied the side pews. But she had begun forty years earlier to found women's societies (most importantly the Seamen's Aid Society), pray publicly, and exhort in her husband's church and elsewhere.[61] Thus, the assertion by some historians that women got used to the sound of their own voices and learned to address audiences primarily in female antislavery societies mistakenly slights the religious provenance of women's public speaking.[62]

The most intense debate over whether women should pray and exhort in public took place in Calvinist circles. In all her labors up and down the eastern seaboard, only in Maine did the itinerant evangelist Nancy Towle meet a female preacher who was a "rigid Calvinist."[63] The itinerant temperance lecturer Catherine S. Lawrence worshipped with the Methodists, although retaining her doctrinal Calvinism and membership in the Reformed church, because they supported the right of women to pray and speak in public.[64] Presbyterian and Congregational women, reared to revere dignity and order, were somewhat restrained in asserting themselves publicly. But as Stephen Peet, a Wisconsin Presbyterian missionary and later one of the founders of Beloit College, admitted to a colleague in 1837, the dearth of "praying men" and the frequency of union services with Baptists and Methodists reduced the typical Reformed reserve and encouraged female presumption.[65] Alexander Campbell, while serving as a Seventh-Day Baptist missionary to West Virginia in 1833–1834, conducted "conference meetings" where women exercised their "Christian liberty" in speaking. Congregational churches called these occasions—when women were neither spare in testimony nor sparing of unsaved souls—"experience meetings."[66]

The prompting of new measures revivalism was all many women needed to open up, and Antoinette Brown was not alone in the 1830s when she began praying and speaking in her Congregational church in western New York.[67] Theodore Weld testified from personal observation that "all over the region nothing is more common in revivals of religion," although Whitney Cross is probably correct in his impression that female public prayer was more likely to occur during Sunday worship in Methodist and Baptist circles, and during weekday meetings in Presbyterian and Congregational ones.[68] Narcissa Whitman had grown accustomed to women taking part in public prayer while growing up in the burned-over district, and found it cruelly frustrating when missionary reinforcements arrived in 1838 who squashed the practice.[69]

To be sure, some areas were much slower than others in adopting these practices. Lucy Drake, whose first twenty-one years of life (1844–1865) were uneventfully spent as a Massachusetts Congregationalist, began attending Methodist services with her friends. Experiencing the baptism of the Spirit, she felt constrained to testify and pray publicly, which immediately made her feel "the weight of all the Congregational churches in Massachusetts," not to mention her family and friends, "pressing upon [her] shoulders." Women who had tried it before had been driven from the church. "On the other hand, I knew I would lose standing with my dear Methodist brothers and sisters if I decided that the Bible was against the public testimony of women." Finally, she steeled herself to begin public prayer and testimony in her Congregational church. "That first night after speaking I could not sleep for sheer joy until two o'clock." She soon discovered that she also could not sleep for sheer exhaustion. She began attending as many as seven services on Sunday, speaking at four of them, often having to walk three miles to church because her family would not transport her unless she promised to keep her mouth shut.[70] By the 1860s, however, the Presbyterian and Congregational prejudice against women praying and speaking had so faded, especially in rural areas, that some congregations "seem quite astonished when told that it is anti-scriptural, anti-Presbyterian, and unprofitable; and some are ready to wage war upon any ministry or ruling elder that dares to oppose it." Women from the Reformed tradition may have tended to be more decorous and ordered than other Evangelical sisters. They exhorted, from the altar, with their bonnets on. But they were now speaking in public just like the Methodists and Baptists. Alarmed clergymen began to panic; in one Old School presbytery, there was "scarcely a church in which there has not been more or less of it."[71] By the Civil War there had emerged a backlash movement designed to bring the full weight of Presbyterian authority against the trend. Unless they moved quickly, some believed, there would be no turning back.

Lyman Beecher, next to Finney perhaps the most renowned preacher of his time, deemed female public prayer capricious in nature and pernicious in effect. He called it what it was, a discreet form of public address: "There *is* generally, and *should* be always, in the female character, a softness and delicacy of feeling which shrinks from the notoriety of a public performance."[72] At a time when a typical prayer lasted from ten to twenty minutes (Finney usually prayed from twenty to thirty minutes),[73] the line between praying and preaching was precariously blurred. This also was the position of Parsons Cook, pastor of the Presbyterian church in Lynn, Massachusetts. Cook found his church in the mid-1830s embroiled in debate over the "practice of female speaking in mixed religious assemblies." For him, as for Beecher, the issue of women's involvement in public worship boiled down to the question whether they should be allowed to preach. Cook's answer to the women of his parish took the form of a remarkable sermon that is notable both for the faithfulness of its reproduction of contemporary positions and for the ferocity of its indictment of women's public speaking.[74]

Some argued that women spoke as they were moved by the Holy Spirit; Cook denied that God's Spirit was doing any such moving. The "standing defense" of the practice was based on 2 Corinthians 3:17 ("Where the Spirit of the Lord is, there is liberty"); Cook condemned such exegesis as a perversion of the text. To the argument that other traditions allowed female preaching, Cook retorted, "Am I justified in transgressing the plain law of the Bible, because others have done it?" He had to agree with the pragmatic argument that female public prayer and exhortation promoted revival and did much good, but with two qualifications: first, "I believe the good is far less than many people suppose," and second, "God often brings good out of evil but never suffers us to do evil that good may come." The contention that the ground is level at the foot of the cross and the "common complaint that we degrade woman from her proper rank and influence, by excluding her from the pulpit" Cook found sufficiently answered by St. Paul.[75]

Fears related to the subversion of male authority and female purity were at the heart of Cook's opposition to female preaching. The notion that God-given talents ought to be nurtured and employed by the church was offset, when those talents were oratorical and the recipients female, by the usurpation of male authority inherent in public address. Women stood and spoke; men sat and listened. Female authorship was permissible, while female preaching was not, because reading a book did not require male deference: a female author did not usurp men's authority because "hearing is more of their own procuring than hers." Yet what Cook most feared was female preaching's subtle arousal of male sexuality. The closest parallel to a female preacher, he believed, was an actress, and he demanded that Evangelicals combat the surging interest in theatrical women as they fought other forms of female public address. Cook likened the attraction of women preachers to that of the "public stage

dancer" who "entertains men with the . . . exposure of her person."
"To the unsophisticated ear, the term female orator, in whatever
cause the oratory be displayed, . . . has a sound too nearly aligned to
another that may not be named. And all approaches to the character
of a female public speaker, proportionately detract from the honor
appropriate for females."[76]

Mary C. Wilber, whose title at Cincinnati's Wesleyan Female
College was "governess," but whose unofficial status was copresi-
dent (with her husband, the Methodist minister Perlee B. Wilber),
turned Cook's argument to the advantage of women public speakers.
How could men censure Evangelical women for giving public
addresses when they "encourage and applaud the gifted songstress
and the eloquent actress" as well as countenance "the lady salesman
at the fair table in the public hall?"[77] Similarly, two antebellum
female evangelists, Deborah Peirce and Nancy Towle, used to their
own advantage the argument that whenever one was moved by the
Spirit to speak, whether in prayer, testimony, exhortation, or singing,
one was in effect preaching. Jarena Lee rejected the notion that
because Mary did not cite a text on Easter morn, her jubilant message of Christ's resurrection was not a sermon.[78] Those who believed
that silence in church was an absolute Pauline injunction squirmed
when they were asked why women were allowed to speak to inquirers and sing—and if singing, why not praying?[79] New measures
revivalists like Finney had to do their own fidgeting, however, when
it was pointed out to them that women were exhorting and delivering
theological monologues while praying—and if exhorting, why not
teaching and preaching?

The issue of women's role in public worship, which would
become even more contentious after the Civil War, was never really
judged by either side in antebellum Evangelicalism: it was merely
fudged. The official Presbyterian line on female public prayers was
presented by the 1832 General Assembly in a pastoral letter distributed to all the churches. On the one hand strongly condoning
women's societies, on the other it condemned any woman who
through teaching, exhorting, or leading in prayer failed to maintain
careful custody of her tongue in church.[80] It must have been mildly
exasperating for men like Dr. Ashbel Green, in 1824 moderator of the
General Assembly and later president of Princeton, to stand before a
female society and tell them to keep their mouths shut for Christ

while asking them to keep the rest of their bodies busy for him.[81] Of course, it was even more exasperating for the women, but many of them simply shut their ears instead.

Finney's patronage of women's public speaking has sometimes been overdrawn. In 1877 the clergymen who blocked the Methodist local preacher Anna M. Oliver from speaking brandished the Finney banner, quoting him to the effect that any man who favored women's preaching was prompted by "an aberration of amativeness."[82] Antoinette Brown lamented in her autobiographical essay that the Oberlin College faculty frowned on public speaking by women.[83] While women and men recited in the same classes, women were not allowed to read their own essays on public occasions because they would be sharing a platform with men. In class after class, female petitioners sought experience at public speaking, but professors of rhetoric continued to read the women students' essays both at monthly rhetoricals and at commencement exercises. It was not until 1859 that five women who graduated from the classical course were allowed to read their own essays, and not until 1874 that women were permitted to speak rather than read from manuscripts.[84]

Prevented from public speaking, Oberlin's sandpaper duo, Lucy Stone and Antoinette Brown, organized in 1846 what was probably the first debating and speaking society ever formed among college women.[85] In staggered singles and pairs so as not to arouse suspicion, the half-dozen members of the debating club walked to the home of one of Stone's black pupils on the outskirts of town, where they would hold informal debates. Sometimes they adjourned to the woods, with sentries posted, for increased protection and voice projection.[86]

The conservative wing of the Oberlin faculty, led by John Morgan, remained adamant against public speaking by women, causing Lucy Stone to say, somewhat excessively, "I was never in a place where women are so rigidly taught that they must not speak in public."[87] There is evidence that the faculty was not of one mind on this matter. Indeed, thanks to Stone and Brown, the situation improved markedly. Of the clergymen associated with Oberlin, John Keep and John Jay Shiperd were perhaps the most liberal on this issue. Both of them even agreed to participate in a stillborn ordination service set up for Brown by James Tefft, a prospective missionary to Liberia.[88]

The former Lane rebel, antislavery propagandist, and Oberlin professor of rhetoric James Thome supported the right of women to speak before mixed assemblies. So also did Oberlin's president, Asa Mahan. Both were blocked, however, first by the faculty (who refused even to allow Mahan's daughter Anna to read her own essay before her male peers), and then by the young women themselves. During Brown's last year as an undergraduate, Thome allowed her to take the rostrum in his rhetoric class for a debate with Lucy Stone. But the event drew such a crowd that the faculty vetoed any encore performances.[89]

The issue even divided families. Henry Cowles's first wife, Alice Welch Cowles, principal of the school's Female Department, opposed public speaking or instruction by women; his second wife, Minerva D. P. Cowles, supported it in principle and in deed, presiding personally over the 1853 Ohio State Women's Temperance Convention, where a thousand men and women sat in attendance. Henry himself was opposed, arguing that women who spoke before large public assemblies violated the "natural sense of propriety which God has given us, or the real sense of scripture."[90]

Of all the members of the Oberlin faculty, Brown felt the greatest support from Finney. Her admission into the theology department in 1847, along with the retiring Lettice Smith, provided a test for Finney's softening views on female public speaking. He admitted her to his theology class ("the most helpful class that any of us ever attended"), drew her name out of a hat for recitation with odds-defying frequency, invited her to relate her religious experiences, and called upon her to speak in public meetings. In conversation with her, she recalled, "he certainly seemed to forget that he was talking to a woman." Finney believed that women were not "usually called upon to preach or speak in public because the circumstances did not demand it, still that there was nothing right or wrong in the thing itself, and that sometimes she was especially called to speak."[91] Whether or not she possessed this "extraordinary" or "special" call to preach could only be confirmed by results in the field, however, and this is where Brown balked:

> Oberlin educated me; but it will neither license, ordain, or encourage me as a public speaker. As an exception to the general rules against woman's preaching many of them have been will-

ing to regard me; but then to prove myself such an exception, I must be successful as an evangelist or rather a revivalist. My temperament would not adapt me to this class of labors.[92]

III

Pragmatism had always justified exceptionalism in Finney's mind. In his early years he encouraged women to pray and testify in the presence of men, not because of biblical and theological convictions concerning the equality of women in the church, but because women were effective in stirring up sinners to repentance.[93] The absence of revivals usually chilled Finney's support for public displays of female leadership. Nevertheless, evidence points to an environment that was generally permissive toward female involvement in public worship during the Second Great Awakening. Some of this permissiveness was due to Finney's own pragmatism and some to his followers'. One of Finney's most famous converts, the abolitionist Theodore Dwight Weld, began openly challenging females to pray and speak in public gatherings a week after he was converted during the 1825–1826 winter revival in Troy.[94] In many cases, however, women took the initiative themselves. E. P. Barrows, principal of the Hartford Grammar School, wrote to Finney about his bewilderment at the increasing female domination of city mission worship services.[95]

Where Lydia fits into the debate over public prayer by women is difficult to determine. No record exists of her thoughts on this subject. There is no direct evidence that she spoke publicly, although, as we have seen, there was ample precedent in Evangelical circles for the wives of clergymen to engage in public speaking. Finney's reference to her "taciturn and reserved" disposition and "mild, unobtrusive and calm type" of religion may in fact mean that Lydia shunned the new measure of female public prayer.[96] Her friend Lydia M. Gilbert was the wife of Eliphalet Gilbert, pastor of the Second Presbyterian Church in Wilmington, Delaware, whose theology did an about-face during Finney's 1827 revival there. In her opinion Lydia's besetting sins were too little "zeal" and too much shrinking from public forms of ministry. In a stirring letter she chided her for her reticent, retiring manner and faulted her for not "rousing" herself to "warn, exhort, and instruct poor lost sinners."[97] It is likely, however, that the opprobrium that greeted Eliphalet Gilbert's encouragement of women like Anna Maria Jones to exhort publicly in his Wilmington church would threaten any woman with Lydia's sensitivity to criticism.[98]

One walks along a precipice when generalizing on the basis of a few letters, but the difference in Lydia's outlook and mood before and after the controversy at New Lebanon appears to be more than a chronological coincidence or a reaction to the news that her brother Philip was facing a possible death sentence after his arrest in Canada for counterfeiting.[99] Before New Lebanon, friends from western and central New York wrote to her gleefully about the anxious prayer meetings in which, as the wife of M. S. Wright of Rome would later put it, "the sisters are often called upon to pray, the D.D.'s notwithstanding."[100] After it, Lydia's spirits went into a tailspin. She admits to chafing under an unnamed burden. Succumbing to depression and self-pity, she retreated from many of her public activities.[101] Whether she was suffering with her beseiged husband, or whether she took personally the denunciations of female prayer in mixed assemblies is uncertain. What is clear is that Lydia's style of helpmeet ministry involved her less in assisting her husband through public prayer and exhortation and more in distributing tracts and visiting homes, as she did during Finney's 1830–1831 Rochester revival, and in organizing the women of a community into various societies.[102]

V

What is amazing about this period is that female preachers were not hard to find, and not just among the Quakers. One did not meet them every day, but there were not so scarce that only a few people heard or knew about them. Once we look away from institutional history and toward popular religious life, we see that the folk phenomenon of female preaching boasted a surprisingly large cast of characters: from the Methodists, Zilpha Elaw, Susan Hermes, Mrs. Thompson, Judith Mathers, Jane Perry; from the Congregationalists, Harriet Livermore; from the Christian church, Ann Rexford; from the Primitive Methodists, Ruth Watkins and Anne Wearing; from the Reformed Methodists, Salome Lincoln; from the independent black Methodist churches, Rebecca Cox Jackson, Mrs. Cook and Jarena Lee; from the Universalists, Maria Cook and Sally Barnes Dunn; from the United Brethren, Charity Opheral and Lydia Sexton; from the Free-Will Baptists, Almira Bullock, Hannah Fogg, Judith Prescott, and Mrs. Quimby. Often accompanied by female traveling companions,[103] women preachers made regular visits to towns and villages throughout the North and South. Their visits to frontier areas were especially frequent and especially relished, but they also appeared in urban settings, especially during revival seasons. The holiness preacher Harriet Olney, for example, was active in New York City during the first phase of the Union Prayer Meeting Revival in 1857–1858.[104] We know few of their names and still less of their experiences. For the most part their lives are preserved only in the form of stray references in scattered sources. Their personal histories have fallen through the cracks of religious history, but we know enough to say something. And something must be said about female preaching in popular American religious history if we are to begin to understand, first, the social context, which was more receptive to the preaching of ministers' wives and other women than has heretofore been imagined; second, the reaction ministers' wives who preached could expect from the community and church; and third, the grounds on which women in the ministry justified their preaching.

"Preaching" here does not mean merely public praying, exhorting, or testifying, all of which, as we have seen, became common practices in antebellum Evangelicalism, although historians' concentration on reactions against such measures has tended for a long time to make us think otherwise. By "preaching" is meant the deliberate, undisguised proclamation of the gospel, derived from an announced text and delivered from a pulpit or its equivalent. The difference between the two is revealed in Charles D. Burritt's account of an incident in Ithaca, New York. Burritt, who personally had no opposition to allowing women like Phoebe Palmer and her sister, Sara Lankford, to speak and conduct meetings, was wary about the support for female preaching that he admits had become "current in some quarters." He tells of the popular Nancy Towle, an unaffiliated itinerant "prophetess," who drifted through the open gates of permissive itinerancy into Ithaca and asked to speak before the local Methodist society. She was supported in her aims by a majority of Ithaca's Methodist, and openly opposed only by a prominent physician. The pastor, who disliked seeing women exercise ministerial functions but disliked even more offending his congregation, negotiated a compromise. At first all went according to plan. The Methodist pastor delivered a short sermon, while Towle sat "with impatience." Then he shut the pulpit desk, walked down to the altar area, and convened a social meeting, inviting all the sisters to stand up and testify. At this point things began to go awry. Towle rose from her seat, walked past the altar to the vacated pulpit, announced her text, and began preaching. "We never fully recovered from it."[105]

The justifications women offered for their preaching reflect a religious climate whipped by the winds of pragmatism, millennialism, and perfectionism. The first defense was the ancient one of necessity and expediency. Peter Martyr had been one of its earliest architects: "In the planting of churches anew, when men are wanting, which should preach the gospel, a woman may perform that at the first; but so as when she hath taught any company, that some one man of the faithful be ordained, which may afterwards minister the sacraments, teach, and do the pastor's duty faithfully."[106] When a minister could not preach because of a last-minute illness, he could, rather than break an appointment or dismiss an unfed congregation, ask his wife to substitute for him.[107] When a minister was away, many wives seized the opportunity for leadership and conducted worship. Sarah Roszel of Loudon County, Virginia, prayed, sang solos, led the singing, read sermons, exhorted, and gave the benediction.[108] Lois Murray, a Kansas church school superintendent, spoke at meetings, read sermons in the Sabbath school, and officiated at funerals; the last function was frequently performed by women evangelists, although they were not allowed to officiate at marriages until 1875, when Maine passed the necessary legislation.[109] In fact, the expediency argument was so pervasive that it could lead historians to assume that the shorthandedness of the ministry constituted a sufficient explanation for the frequency of female preaching, though this is clearly not the case. Invitations to preach at the regular worship services conducted by the chaplains of the Senate and House of Representatives were coveted, and yet it appears that some women received these. Sir Augustus Foster, Secretary of Legation to the British minister in Washington in 1804–1806 wrote from personal observation that "though the regular Chaplain was a Presbyterian, sometimes a Methodist, a minister of the Church of England, or a Quaker, or sometimes even a woman took the speaker's chair."[110] The impassioned preacher Harriet Livermore, whose father and uncle were United States senators, preached in the Hall of Representatives in 1827, with President John Quincy Adams in attendance. During the presidencies of Andrew Jackson (1832), Martin Van Buren (1838), and John Tyler (1843), she preached to Congress, and one senator from Massachusetts, who heard her in 1832, wrote,

"I have heard but few better models of correct speaking." She also spoke before several state legislatures, including those of Massachusetts and Pennsylvania.[111]

That success sanctifies innovations was the second argument women used to vindicate their preaching. The concession "God's ways are often not our ways" was granted to two pioneer women preachers who reaped a successful harvest of souls in the West. Either they were chosen by God, or else one was obliged "to admit what is abhorrent to every Christian; namely, that the Holy Spirit will sanction and set its seal to work brought about by improper agencies."[112] The argument of success also provided the foundation for the justification of female preaching by the Seventh-Day Baptist Alexander Campbell, who dismissed the popular doctrine of the divine call to the ministry but cautioned that only women whose preaching had evidenced unusual results could legitimately proclaim the good news.[113] Ordination by success seems also to have dominated the Free-Will Baptist criteria for evaluating calls. In 1821 Nancy Towle made her debut as a preacher in Stratham, New York. She was overcome by the experience of preaching from a text, and her speech foundered. The sermon fell flat. She was criticized by those assembled, not for being a female preacher, but for evidently lacking a call "to the Work."[114] The belief that initially worked against her worked for the great black preacher Jarena Lee. Forbidden to preach from a text herself, she found herself one day listening to a bland sermon on a particularly vital passage. She stood up and began to "exhort" on the preacher's bungled text. Her ability to hold the hearts of a congregation in her hand so impressed Bishop Richard Allen, who happened to be in church that day, that in Lee's words, he "rose up in the assembly, and related that I had called upon him eight years before, asking to be permitted to preach and that he had put me off; but that he now as much believed that I am called to that work, as any of the preachers present."[115]

Third was the apocalyptic argument. At a time of great millennial conviction, female preachers reminded Evangelicals that Joel prophesied, and Peter later reiterated the prophecy, that "it shall come to pass in the last days, saith God, I will pour out my Spirit upon all flesh; and your sons and your daughters shall prophesy" (Joel 2:28; Acts 2:16–17). Throughout Christian history millennialism has expanded boundaries for women. As heaven moves to earth, the ideal criticizes the real and the future exorcises the present. Such tendencies have long been acknowledged in such eccentric manifestations of the apocalyptic mentality as the Montanists and Collyridians, the Shakers and the Oneida Community. Increasingly, however, historians are appreciating the extent to which mainstream culture has been formed by millennial impulses.[116] It was last-day convictions that helped convince Deborah Peirce, who initially had opposed public speaking by women that she was "without excuse" for ignoring the call to preach the gospel. Ellen Gould White and other female followers of William Miller, moreover, held that their adventist convictions justified their public ministries.[117]

The preaching tours of Harriet Livermore were also inspired by millennial impulses, which grew stronger as she grew older. Of all the women preachers, Livermore was the most traveled, prolific, and interesting; her fame was due in part to John Greenleaf Whittier's unflattering portrait of her as the "half-welcome guest" in "Snow-Bound."[118] She was a pioneer premillennialist, and there is strong evidence that she conceived of herself as one of the two witnesses prophesied in the eleventh chapter of the Book of Revelation. Convinced that the Second Coming was to occur in 1847 (when she was fifty-nine), she set about in the 1830s to bring the news of Jesus' return to the American Indians, although her efforts to settle among them were stymied by the commissioners on Indian Affairs when she reached Fort Leavenworth. Livermore produced four issues of *Millennial Tidings*, a periodical intended for Native Americans and full of apocalyptic forecasts and messages. She also visited Jerusalem four times, hoping to convert the Jews and welcome Christ back to earth there. Because William Miller, the other noted premillennialist of the day, did not believe in a literal restoration of the Jews, she resolutely dismissed his movement.[119]

The apocalyptic argument often gave female preaching an eschatological significance because it was female and so tended to work against the notion that gender was irrelevant in the proclamation of the gospel. But not always. Contesting positions, for example, are evident in the writings of the lay Methodist evangelist Phoebe Palmer and the founder of the Salvation Army, Catherine Booth. Phoebe Palmer defended her preaching as important to Christ's Second Coming precisely because it was female. Catherine Booth, who cited the same texts in defending Phoebe's preaching in England, emphasized that sexual equality was provided for in Christ's first coming. She even gently quoted Phoebe Palmer to Phoebe Palmer to this effect.[120]

The fourth argument was the one of the "extraordinary call." More than anything else, the conviction of an extraordinary calling was the rod and staff of women who preached. The ordinary rules of ecclesiastical governance as established by the apostle Paul restricted female activities in the church, Zilpha Elaw admitted. But the winds of the Holy Spirit blew where they would and could even overturn the ordinary obstacles preventing "female Evangelists or Oracular sisters."[121] Women like Elaw claimed to have been to the back side of the Mount of God, to Moses' smoking mountain, and there received an extraordinary commission. To the question of how women knew whether a call to preach was "extraordinary" enough, Deborah Peirce provided her sisters with an interior checklist to try the Spirit:

> [If] poor sinners appear before you in their sins, exposed to the wrath of an angry God, and their disobedience and destruction cause your flesh to tremble, your soul to mourn and your sleep to depart from you, and the scripture seems to sound in your ears, and open to your mind, then go forward and obey the impression. If it brings peace to your mind, and you feel comforted, and relieved, then it is your duty; while on the other hand, if when you neglect you feel gloominess upon your mind, all nature seems to mourn, Jesus hides his smiling face, your soul is in distress, the worth of souls lies with weight upon your mind, the devil tempts you, your flesh shrinks at the cross, and lukewarm professors oppose you, . . . then speak.[122]

The doctrine of an extraordinary call allowed Evangelicals to keep faith with both the letter and the spirit of scripture. It also permitted especially courageous women to subscribe to a somewhat different version of the American Evangelical vision of a righteous empire. God works in mysterious ways, women preachers reminded their congregations. So does the devil, retorted their opponents.

VI

The popular climate was somewhat hospitable to women's preaching before the Civil War and antagonistic to it afterward. The difference is revealed in the changing course of Lucinda Barbour Helm's conviction that she was called to win souls. Before the Civil War she could be found conducting Sunday afternoon services in back-country Kentucky farmhouses, preaching to both men and women. After it her soul-winning activities were exclusively routed through her pen and her work with parsonage societies and home and foreign missionary societies.[123] It was religious forces—not secular, social ones—that tended to legitimate female public speaking. This is one of the reasons why female preaching and exhorting were more accepted than the reform lectures of Frances Wright, Abbey Kelly, and Sarah and Angelina Grimké, the last two hired in 1836 by the American Anti-Slavery Society as the first professional women lecturers in American history. "I know that in some denominations, she is permitted to preach the gospel," observed Angelina Grimké of her religious comrades who had pioneered in blasting the barriers to women's public speaking. "But permissiveness is granted not from a conviction of her rights, nor upon the grounds of her equality as a *human being*, but of her equality in spiritual gifts—for we find that woman, even in those societies, is allowed no voice in framing the *Discipline* by which she is to be governed."[124]

What led to the antebellum increase of female preaching in circles outside the Quaker and Free-Will Baptist traditions, where women had been preaching all along? First, the air was charged with millennial hopes. As John Humphrey Noyes recalled, "In 1831, the whole orthodox church was in a state of ebullition in regard to the Millennium."[125] Strange sights and wonders were expected prior to the arrival of the kingdom, and, as was noted above, when millennialism is at its height, social barriers are at their lowest.

Second, this was a period of great evangelistic thrust, an emphasis that seems to stimulate unorthodox female behavior. Caught up in the millennial optimism of converting the world in a generation, and maybe even in three months,[126] the call some women felt to spread the gospel did not bring with it the cumbersome cargo of fine distinctions between what is and what is not acceptable in public speaking that weighted down the male mind. Not wishing that any should perish, some women and men simply felt that the end justified the means so long as the means were successful. Lorenzo Dow, with whom many female preachers felt a special kinship because he, like them, was something of a religious side-show oddity, wrote the preface for Nancy Towle's moving autobiography and asked how anyone could judge her labors when the fruitfulness of her ministry had obviously proved the divine smile.[127]

Third, the Second Great Awakening prescribed an expanded role for the laity. Whenever this happens, as Olive Anderson has argued, it creates "spiritual and material conditions" favorable to female preaching "by diffusing the belief that public preaching need not be confined to the clergy, and greatly increasing the number of missions and undenominational assemblies which required the services of a succession of visiting special preachers."[128] Ministers' wives were in the right place to benefit from this revolution in the involvement of laity in ministry. Women preachers went out of their way to encourage clerical wives and assert themselves in preaching, and they applauded those who held forth in spite of their husbands' opposition. They also grumbled loudly about the tragedy of neglected opportunity, especially when they saw ministers' wives failing to seize open pulpits or writing sermons for their husbands to read on Sunday while on Monday silently watching them resist female preaching. This was the backdrop for Nancy Towle's lament: "It is for the most part, I see with much painfulness, that those females who are the companions of ministers, possess but a very small degree of vital piety."[129]

Fourth, this was a period that popularized the doctrine of holiness, which was, as Timothy Smith, Nancy Hardesty, Lucille Sider and Donald Dayton have demonstrated, often a call to arms for radical causes like women's equality.[130] The grammar and imagery of perfectionistic theology projected on the divinity the sexual stereotypes of humanity, thus making it easier for men to accept edification from women. It was not the sanctified believer, but the Spirit of God working in the believer, that did the witnessing. As one sanctified female preacher pointed out, surely the Spirit of God could not be accused of usurping male authority.[131] In a comparative look at the black female preachers Rebecca Cox Jackson, Jarena Lee, Elizabeth and Amanda Smith, Jean McMahon Humez has discovered that holiness ideology occupied a prominent place in all four of their theologies.[132]

The holiness movement itself bears compelling witness to women's desire, encouraged by perfectionist theology, to shuck the shackles that bound them to retiring spheres of service. The last page of the first issue of *The Guide to Christian Perfection*, founded by the Boston itinerant Timothy Merritt, contained a special appeal:

> A WORD to the Female Members of the CHURCH. —Many of you
> have experienced the grace of sanctification. Should you not

then, as a thank-offering to God, give an account of this gracious dealing with your souls, that others may be partakers of this grace also? *Sisters in Christ*, may we not expect that you will assist us both with your prayers and pens?[133]

Evangelical sisters also assisted the holiness movement with public testimony and exhortation. Many men and women were moved to seek perfect love by the public appeals of women during protracted meetings and camp meetings.[134]

The holiness connection to female preaching manifested itself in other ways. Melinda Hamline, the wife of a Methodist bishop, believed that immediately after the experience of sanctification a woman ought to be challenged to become a "witness to holiness."[135] Popular holiness authors liked to tell the story of a woman, perhaps originally Mary Boardman, wife of Rev. William E. Boardman, who "tried to run around the corner, and refused to pray and speak in public. When she came to seek the blessing of holiness, this duty was the thing, above every other thing, over which she had the greatest struggle."[136] The 1853 ordination sermon for the first woman ordained in America, Antoinette Brown Blackwell, was taken from the text of Galations 3:28 by Luther Lee, one of the patriarchs of the holiness Wesleyan Methodist church. The Nazarite revolt against the smell of spiritual death in New York's Genesee Valley, emanating from the formal, respectable worship services of Methodist churches in the late 1850s, was led by ministers and their wives who, in true apostolic fashion, labored two-by-two with almost unlimited freedom to revive the living dead.[137] After the holiness Free Methodist church was organized in 1860, its founder, B. T. Roberts, who believed in team ministry and developed one with his wife, Ellen Lois Roberts, wrote two of the nineteenth century's most cogent defenses of women's religious rights, "The Right of Women to Preach the Gospel" (ca. 1860) and *Ordaining Women* (1891).[138] The new denomination Roberts founded had almost as much trouble with his views as the church that had expelled him, but his witness was not lost on the likes of Melissa Booth Carter, a holiness preacher whose popularity was such that during a nine-week 1877 revival crusade in Oswego, New York, four policemen had to be stationed at the church to keep the crowds from trampling one another.[139]

Finally, women in general and ministers' wives in particular were allowed many liberties that would later be denied them because the ministry had not yet been professionalized. Biblical institutes, seminaries, preachers' aid societies, book rooms—all were in their infancy. The clergy tolerated deviations from the norm because professionalization had not yet put them on the defensive. A cognate explanation points to the autocratic tendencies of institutions as opposed to the anarchic tendencies of movements. This was a time of numerous religious movements: movements across denominations, movements within denominations, and movements in the process of becoming denominations. As soon as the movement became institutionalized, whether independently or within existing structures, the relaxed, indulgent atmosphere was replaced by an uncompromising demand for conformity. This is what happened to the Free Methodist church in 1860 and 1861, in spite of the wishes of its guiding spirit, B. T. Roberts. The Nazarite movement allowed women an equality of ministry with men unparalleled in antebellum history, but when the Free Methodist church was formed in 1860, as Mariet Hardy Freeland, a minister's wife, put it, "Woman was not counted in, and at the second conference [1861] she was officially counted out."[140]

Significant social and historical questions beg to be raised at this point. In what climate did women preachers function? Were there any differences between the clerical and the public response? How did female itinerants manage to set up speaking appointments? When were denominational doors opened to them, and whose? We have to settle for some very preliminary probings. Few women, it appears, received the ecclesiastical patronage accorded two black Pennsylvanians, Jarena Lee and Zilpha Elaw—Jarena Lee by her spiritual father, Bishop Richard Allen; Zilpha Elaw by a host of clergymen, white and black, Methodist and Baptist.

A woman with only three months of formal education, Jarena Lee cornered Richard Allen to discuss her call to preach, most likely shortly before her 1811 marriage to the pastor of the Snow Hill Methodist Society near Philadelphia. Allen's response seemed to her to be a warming of the water before drowning the cat:

> He replied, by asking, in what sphere I wished to move in? I said, among the Methodists. He then replied, that a Mrs. Cook, a Methodist lady, had also some time before requested the same privilege; who, it was believed, had done much good in the way of exhortation, and holding prayer meetings; and who had been permitted to do so by the verbal license of the preacher in charge at the time. But as to women preaching, he said that our *Discipline* knew nothing at all about it—that it did not call for women preachers.[141]

Lee's ambitions could not be drowned, however, and for the next eight years she held her breath and waited patiently for Allen to change his mind, exhorting when occasions arose and conducting prayer meetings in her "hired house." The strategy of patience prevailed. For by the 1820s the first female preacher of the African Methodist Episcopal church could be found delivering sermons periodically at "Mother Bethel" church at Bishop Allen's invitation, accompanying Allen to annual conferences, where she often spoke at his request, raising up new AME societies in most of the principal cities of the Northeast, and preaching at his behest to both black and white churches and camp meetings, most notably a camp meeting that Allen had arranged in Lewistown, Delaware, at "Governor Paynter's Woods," which the governor himself attended. While Lee itinerated for two and a half years, Allen welcomed into his home and educated as his own son her only surviving child. Until his death on 26 March 1831, Bishop Allen gave Jarena Lee substantial encouragement and aid; he did everything but ordain her. And these four facts—that his elders often took her along on their circuits; that some of his ministers agreed to come second and give exhortations after she had preached; that his successor continued to set up preaching appointments for her; and that she was able to preach over a hundred sermons a year—attest to the fervor and faithfulness of Allen's patronage.[142]

Zilpha Elaw, a contemporary and neighbor of Jarena Lee's, was also a black female Methodist preacher. A sweetly modest woman who had been orphaned at thirteen, coverted at fourteen, and married to a fuller at sixteen, Elaw felt a divine summons to visit Elias Boudinot, one of the wealthiest citizens in Burlington, New Jersey, and witness to him about her expanding faith. It was not unheard of for black women, even southern slaves, to testify publicly before whites in Evangelical circles, especially before the chill that gripped the South at Nat Turner's insurrection. The example of a women slave recounting her faith in God before a Methodist love feast, reported a Sunday school volume intended for advanced youth, "opened the way for the white females" to preach and pray publicly.[143] Elaw consulted her Methodist minister, and he advised assent to the summons. A few years later another call seized her: this time she was to be a traveling preacher. Once again she sought light from the Methodist clergy, though she kept her husband in the dark: "I laid my case in reference to my call to the work of the ministry before the ministers; and they greatly encouraged me to proceed, and to preach wherever and whenever opportunities offered."[144] Elaw was able to itinerate throughout New Jersey, Maryland, Washington, D.C., Virginia, Cape Cod, and England, preaching to people of all ranks and races, because she did not press Methodism for official recognition and maintained a ministers-know-best relationship with the clergy, never trespassing on their turf without permission, ever seeking their mind and guidance. The degree of her success can be seen first in Commodore Rogers's offer to subsidize her living expenses if she settled in Washington, D.C., and second in the discreet, distant smile from Bishop Elijah Hedding that blessed her ministry.[145] Given our current understanding of antebellum society, the support Lee and Elaw received from the clergy and the overall lack of opposition to their ministry are a revelation.

More predictable were the experiences of "Elizabeth," a gritty, outspoken black Methodist preacher whose reminiscences are mostly resentments. Born in 1766 to Methodist slaves, she was freed thirty years later by a Presbyterian owner who believed in indentured servitude but not slavery. At forty-two she began preaching, first in Maryland and then in Virginia, Michigan, and Pennsylvania, and she continued these "exercises," as she called them, for another half-century. Her autobiography curdles into bitterness toward virtually everyone but the Quakers, as it recounts the frigid reception and scurvy treatment the clergy meted out to her as a "speckled bird." Elizabeth's boisterous crankiness, "nervous susceptibility," abrasive rigidity, and cry-baby disposition did little to win friends and influence people, even her own. "It is not from the worldly, so called, that I have endured the most, but from high professors, mostly amongst my own people."[146] She collected abuses as many itinerants collected conversions. For all her courage in withstanding the buffets of social prejudice and the bullets of personal abuse, at 100 years of age Elizabeth had reached the stage of sainthood for some, and schizophrenia for others.

Relations with the clergy usually fell somewhere between those of "Elizabeth" and those of Jarena Lee. Harriet Livermore, a champion of women's rights in the church, was born again as a New England Congregationalist, again as a Quaker, and again as a Free-Will Baptist, with an unstated Methodist conversion in regard to sanctification and simplicity of dress. She carried with her enough letters of commendation from individual clergymen and general annual conferences of Free-Will Baptist elders to keep her busy preaching almost seven days a week. In the early 1820s she delivered sermons to rural Baptist folk in crowds of up to 1,500 throughout Canada, Massachusetts, Rhode Island, and Connecticut.[147] But by her own pained admission, she was often at worst a laughing-stock, at best a "gazing-stock," a kind of traveling side-show that drew few serious listeners and many curiosity-seekers eager to gaze at the "eccentric," "crazy" female "enthusiast" with short-cropped hair.[148] She became so discouraged that she once resolved to abandon the ministry and return to teaching school, a new career that lasted a total of three days. Livermore was also plagued by financial woes, although whether this was due more to special ecclesiastical shunning than to general itinerant indigence is doubtful. The sales of 600 copies at twenty-five cents each of her 1824 publication, *Scriptural Evidences in Favor of Female Testimony*, an early American defense of sanctuary service for women, subsidized her travel expenses for a year. Her father, a U.S. senator, "spent what I might call a decent fortune" in underwriting her labors. Yet these sources were quickly drained, and with them receded her dream of traveling to western New York, where female preachers were reportedly already involved in the work. Impecunity now forced her to travel on foot to keep appointments.[149]

The clergy forged vital links in the chains that bound one community to another through the custom of writing letters of recommendation for itinerant clergy. These letters were instrumental in setting up appointments for preaching and served as passports to foreign parishes and unknown pastors. Many Evangelical clergy—either by their own wishes or in response to public demand—were inextricably involved in the appointment-making process. Women preachers had little difficulty in obtaining letters of recommendation, and it was not unheard of for female evangelists to be selective about the letters of recommendation they accepted. One such letter was written by John Winebrenner a few years after he founded the General Eldership of the Church of God. A peace, abolition and temperance crusader, Winebrenner also joined his friend Lorenzo Dow in supporting women preachers. The letter he wrote for Nancy Towle and her traveling companion, Thomasine O'Bryan (daughter of William O'Bryan, general superintendent of the English Methodist Reformers), throws a beam of light on the degree to which one's reputation was staked on these letters.

Shippensburg, 30 January 1832

My Dear Brother—This is to introduce to your acquaintance Miss Nancy Towle and T. O'Bryan, and request an appointment for N. Towle to preach in your place. She has preached with us for about two weeks, and much to the edification and profit of the people. Yesterday she preached in this place, and the people were much pleased. She comes well recommended; and is doubtless, an able, useful Preacher. By giving her an appointment and a lodging—and by receiving her (as Paul said of Phebe) "as becometh saints," you will much oblige,

Your Brother in the Lord,
John Winebrenner[150]

Nothing can be said conclusively about the overall public response to women itinerants until more sources are unearthed and more studies undertaken. Unsystematic searches suggest tentative observations that conflict with expectations. One is not amazed to see Horace Bushnell refer to female preaching along with female suffrage as "the reform against nature."[151] One is not surprised to learn of opposition to paying women for doing what they had allegedly always done for free; as a man said after hearing his first woman preacher: "Oh, the sermon was all right, but you see I hear a woman preach six days a week, and on Sunday I like to get a rest."[152] One is not taken aback by learning that the clergyman James A. Garfield, later president of the United States, responded negatively in the 1850s both to female ranters who "screamed loud, frothed at the mouth, pounded, etc.," and to the more respectable pulpit utterances of Antoinette L. Brown: "There is something about a woman's speaking in public that unsexes her in my mind, and how much soever I might admire the talent, yet I could never think of the female speaker as the gentle sister, the tender wife or the loving mother."[153] Totally unforeseen, however, are the discoveries that in Camptown, New Jersey, a chapel was built expressly for Ann Rexford; that women preachers were asked by families to conduct funeral services; that before the Civil War many Baptist and Methodist churches welcomed women evangelists into their midst, even for the prime-time slot of Sunday morning, with various Methodist presiding elders sponsoring them and quarterly conferences inviting them to preach; that it was more than curiosity that brought vast crowds to hear a woman preach; that "many were much tried" with James B. Finley for silencing at a Methodist quarterly meeting a sister who suddenly, in the middle of his pulpit declamation, stood up, removed her black calico bonnet, stepped into the aisle, "took up her cross," and spoke her mind, taking the service out of the preacher's hands as confidently as if she had been sent from God; and finally that Nancy Towle was able in Harrisburg, Pennsylvania, to preach to congregations of Lutherans, Dutch-Reformed, Baptists, Methodists, and members of the state legislature, and after ten years of itinerating could claim that only in Frederick, Maryland, did the preachers prohibit her from speaking in their churches, and only in Charleston, South Carolina, did she find a large city where the people refused to allow her a preaching place, if not in a church, then at least in a schoolhouse, boardinghouse, courthouse, or Masonic hall.[154]

Ever since the Boston midwife Anne Hutchinson outraged seventeenth-century authorities by conducting "gospelings," or women's meetings, in her home and delivering expositions of the week's sermons, sometimes disagreeing with the minister's theology and countering with her own, the issue of how American parishioners and pastor interact with and transform each other has searched for an analysis. It is one of the great unasked questions in American religious history: How did the pew affect and alter the pulpit? How did the perceptions and attitudes of the congregation shade and shift the nature and functions of ministry? It appears that women preachers often received a warm response from the people along with the cold opposition of the clergy. Women parishioners especially appear to have spearheaded drives to get their pastors to sponsor women preachers and arrange appointments for them. Soon after Nancy Towle arrived in Painesville, Ohio, she learned that some of the Methodist preachers had decided to postpone the scheduled four-day protracted meeting because of "colds." "Their colds I found were toward female speaking," she later wrote. Towle quickly packed her bags, not wanting to be an "eyesore" or to further aggravate their allergies. When the people of Painesville awoke to what was happening, they put such pressure on their spiritual leaders that they relented and offered Towle odd-hour preaching appointments.[155]

Some women preachers reasoned that denominations were abominations and the less they had to do with them the better. Noisy popularity was a peculiar danger, for it could bring them close enough to church hierarchies to cause them trouble. Such was the case with a "Miss Miller," a woman of "fine literary attainments" (that is, she did not shout and stomp and preach as if she were swatting a swarm of bees), "ardent piety" (she judged all her actions by the yardstick of usefulness), "tasty eloquence" (she used bookish words that sounded nice although not everyone knew what they meant), and "highly accomplished manners" (she stood at the altar, not the pulpit, to preach).[156] Miller itinerated in Methodist circles without official sanction but with widespread popularity among both laity and clergy, eventually marrying a minister named William A. Smith from the Virginia Conference of the Methodist Episcopal church. Armed with impressive recommendations from distinguished preachers, Miller used as her home base for an evangelistic tour in 1826 or 1827 the Steubenville, Pennsylvania, home of Dr. David Stanton, father of E. M. Stanton (later secretary of war). With Stanton's sister-in-law Nancy Norman as her traveling companion, and with the Steubenville Methodist pastor George Brown as her guiding and guardian escort, Miller preached in the surrounding towns to large and responsive crowds.

Swept up in the public acclaim for this woman preacher, citizens of Wheeling, Pennsylvania, invited her to speak at their next quarterly conference Sunday morning service. After Miller arrived on the island prepared to preach, she learned that Bishop Joshua Soule and his family were also planning to be in town for the conference. Not desiring a head-on collision, particularly since the bishop had opposed her ministry and uncharitably referred to her as "that strolling country girl," Miller begged to be released from her preaching obligations. A delegation consisting of Wheeling's presiding elder, stationed preacher, and most prominent church member refused to excuse her, insisting that "they represented the wishes of the church and of the entire community of Wheeling," and besides, they had not invited the bishop to preach. Miller finally agreed, "with tears in her eyes," to preach at the morning service; the bishop would preach in the afternoon.

As soon as Bishop Soule arrived and learned of his upstaging by this uncertified and upstart female, he put the fear of the Lord into his preachers, demanding that they retract their invitation. Terrified, they acquiesced. As one participant put it disgustedly, "A great bull has come to town and given a roar, and scared all the preachers." Many of Wheeling's residents, however, denounced the bishop for his high hand and the preachers for their weak knees, insisting that the bishop should be publicly embarrassed by having Miller compete with his morning service: "None doubted but the lady preacher would carry off the multitude and leave the bishop with a very slender congregation." Cooler heads prevailed, and a compromise was worked out whereby the bishop preached at the Methodist church in the morning, and Miller's afternoon appearance at the local Protestant Episcopal church was announced at the conclusion of the service. Her three o'clock service, much to the bishop's dismay, drew so many people that as many worshippers were forced to stand outside the church as were packed inside.

Antebellum woman preachers like Miss Miller were often caught in a dilemma: without mass popularity their ministry was threatened by the absence of credentials and finances; with mass popularity their ministry was threatened by clashes with antagonistic clergymen and denominations. Either way they lost. By the time of Reconstruction, itinerant women preachers had become virtually extinct, and praying women were an endangered species.[157] In 1873 women were prohibited from speaking to mixed assemblies by the organizers of the new tenting on the old camp ground that took place at Chautauqua, New York, where Sunday school teachers (delicately referred to as "rare pearls in rough shells") from across the nation gathered for a summer session of continuing education.[158] Public speaking by women surged in the postbellum years, but women were speaking less in religious circles and more in lecture tours, conversation societies, and women's clubs, like the New England Women's Club in Boston and the Sorosis in New York City. The prim and sober women's club movement had replaced the more worrisome, because more venturesome, revival movement as the nursery of women public speakers.

Women preachers in the first half of the nineteenth century paid an incredible price in tattered nerves, shattered reputations, and psychosomatic ailments.[159] Their autobiographies are tortured testaments to the psychological abuse heaped on women who dared to preach. It is no wonder that these brave pioneers uniformly referred to their call to preach as "taking up a cross." Women preachers who felt called by the Lord but not by the church were often beset by suicidal impulses and nervous breakdowns.[160] Some became connoisseurs of suffering. The price was too high for most women in ministry, as well as for most women in the ministry. Tragically, preaching could only be a burden to bear, not a gift to receive. But each of them who accepted it stretched her cross, like a bridge, across the troubled waters of antebellum society.

Chapter Six

"She Hath Done What She Could"

Lydia Finney and the Institutional History of Women in Ministry

From no one class of females are the expectations of the public so large and so unreasonable, and yet with an occasional exception which but establishes the rule, no one class of women so nobly and even heroically come up to the high demands of Christian duty.

The *Independent*

It is no mere historical happenstance that the nineteenth century was called both the "Practical Age" and the "Woman's Century."[1] When people of the 1800s expressed a desire for a "practical religion," they did not mean that they wanted religion to help them attain the desires of their hearts. A "practical" faith, rather, was one that stretched beyond itself in active and benevolence service toward the millennial future that was America's decision before it was America's destiny. Faith was sanctified sweat, and preachers left their congregations not so much with thoughts as with tasks. The century belonged to women because they were for the first time being both seen and heard, creating what Emily Faithfull, the English businesswoman who visited America and sensitively recorded the changing position of women in American life, called "the most difficult problem presented by modern civilization." Just how difficult it was, according to the Unitarian reformer Thomas Wentworth Higginson, could be seen in the fact that "during the last half of the century more books have been written by women and about women than during all the previous uncounted ages."[2]

The Woman's Century was the Practical Age because generations of women who were supposed to be tied to the home were spending lots of time outside it. Not content like their earlier sisters to sit at the Master's feet and listen to the truth, they also bustled about furiously to spread it. The conversion process during the Second Great Awakening truly caused many women to perform an about-face, turning them away from the pursuit of happiness, the eighteenth-century ideal of the "lady," and toward the happiness of pursuit, the nineteenth-century ideal of "evangelical womanhood." Evangelical women thus became an army in search of battles. This then is the tale of some of the battles that Evangelical women and their generals, ministers' wives like Lydia Finney, chose to fight. We shall also be looking at the supply trains that reached them at their mission outposts, their armory, and the formations in which they organized themselves. For a long time historians examined the involvement of women in political organizations at the expense of their participation in social, religious, and labor associations.[3] The pendulum is now going the other way. Scholars are awakening to the realization, first, that the historical sequence was from benevolent to reform to political activities, and second, that the women's movement as a whole and American feminism in particular are inexplicable without an understanding of the sisterly *esprit*, self-esteem, political experience, and expertise in wielding power gained through the women's benevolent organizations that abounded in the nineteenth century. As we have seen in previous chapters, female activity and creativity were not quarantined either in households or in gender groups. But our knowledge of women's institutional history is so embarrassingly limited that, for example, the precise significance of the phenomenon that Carroll Smith-Rosenberg and Janet Todd have respectively called the "homosocial network" and "female bonding" is difficult to fix.[4] We have spent great amounts of time examining attitudes toward women within religious traditions. We have given insufficient attention to the activities, experiences, and beliefs of women within those traditions.

The English history of organized Protestant female alliances had its beginning in 1670, when the idea of a Protestant convent for women dropped in and out of the mind of Edward Chamberlayne. Five years later Clement Barksdale tried unsuccessfully to promote a similar project in female education and piety, though he covered the convent idea with a curtain of words, calling it a "college of Maids" or a "Virgin Society." The opposition to women's forming their own organizations was still vigorous enough twenty years later to knock down Mary Astell's efforts to revive Barksdale's plan. Not until 1711, in Wolverhampton, England, did there arise a lasting female religious association.[5] Less than a century later such societies would be commonplace in American life. In fact, female voluntary societies, whether they were antislavery, colportage, temperance, or antidueling, outnumbered virtually all equivalent male societies. By 1876 women's societies had so cornered the philanthropic market that New York was forced to recognize their importance by appointing Josephine Shaw Lowell as "state commissioner of charities." She was New York State's first woman officeholder.[6] Philanthropy had become big business, and women played a prominent part in managing it.

Nineteenth-century American, according to Alexis de Tocqueville, had taken on the character of a voluntary society for the promotion of voluntary societies. It has been less obvious, however, that America's major volunteers were women. Women were the genius and goad behind the voluntaristic system and hence were responsible in large measure for one of the century's more creative forms of ministry. Through a general survey of female associational activities and the role of ministers' wives in organizing them, and a more detailed probing of Lydia Finney's achievements in forming women's networks, I hope to cast further light on this phenomenon of voluntarism: How important to the churches were ministers' wives and the voluntary societies they headed, and by what financial, moral, spiritual, or educational standards can one measure their importance? To what extent did revivalism nourish affiliative urges? Were women's organizations ecumenical or denominational in orientation and structure? To whom were they accountable, if to anyone, and under whose patronage, if anyone's, did they operate? Were they directed to women's concerns as defined by women? On what basis was sorority solidified—common feelings, common experience, common gripes, common ideals? How were they organized—loosely or tightly, with a clear hierarchy or an acephalous, broadly based leadership? What duties did they perform, what tactics did they employ, and how powerful were they? Did they serve as pressure groups on men and especially the clergy, and were they effective in circumventing and confounding America's patriarchal system? Did men look on women's networks with fear, fascination, indifference, admiration? Finally, as women made their own place in church, did they make their own church as well, an *ecclesiola in ecclesia*? These questions will be addressed within the context of the sociological research on voluntary associations by Gregory H. Singleton, Don H. Doyle, and Walter S. Glazer, all of whom have emphasized the integrative role of these mediating structures in giving order and stability to a nation constantly on the move.[7]

I

Donald G. Mathews has argued in a seminal article that the Second Great Awakening was a social movement that "organized thousands of people into small groups" and indeed "may have been the greatest organization and mobilization of women in American history."[8] The question of why an unprecedented explosion of women's societies began around the year 1800 has exerted an enduring fascination. First to raise the issue were the British travelers Harriet Martineau and Frances Trollope. Both were unpleasantly struck by the involvement of American women in religion and by the sight of "women bracing hurricane, frost, and snow, to flit from preaching to preaching; and laying out the whole day among visits for prayer and religious excitement among the poor and sick." The wages of sin is boredom, they believed, contending that women used religion as a stimulant to relieve the ennui and emptiness of American existence.[9]

It is true that the rise in industrialism and the decline in economic opportunities for women after the American Revolution (a phenomenon not reversed until the mid-twentieth century)[10] put some women on the lookout for meaningful activities outside the home. But if one is to seek a psychological cause for women's prominence in religion, it is better to look at how the relentless round of religious activities provided them with an antidote to depression. Depression was as much the common cold of mental illness in the past as it is in the present, although it often went by other names. The Puritan theologian Cotton Mather diagnosed all of New England as within the throes of "melancholy," and David Hume declared that he had never met a pious person who was not depressed. Yet women seem to have been especially prone to depression and plagued by its debilitations, especially those caught between society's expectations that they find meaning and purpose in domestic chores and their own religiously reinforced needs to carve out blocks of time for writing, reading, and thinking. Prominent Evangelical models like Eliza Hessel, Hester Ann Rogers, Barbara Heck, and the Baptist missionary to Syria, Sarah Lanman Smith, boldly testified in their autobiographies to their dark nights of the mind. "Life has appeared to me short, uncertain, and insignificant; and heaven worth any sacrifice," Smith wrote to her sister in the 1820s. The only antidepressant that seemed to work for her was a heavy dose of benevolent activity. "Confinement and solitude are extremely injurious to mind and body. Activity and social enjoyment are imperative duties."[11] Ultimately, however, the notion that women used religion to paper over their boredom and depression leaves the historian unsatisfied, for it fails to take seriously the religious integrity and deep spiritual commitment exhibited by Evangelical women.

A second explanation has been offered by Keith Melder, who stresses the transatlantic influence of elite British reformers and their role in inspiring many of the early efforts at organizing women's societies, such as the Quakers' Female Society for the Employment of the Poor (1793), Female Association (1801), and the later Female Hospitable Society.[12] There is little doubt that American women saw as heroic models such British reformers as Elizabeth Fry, who was noted for her work at Newgate with female institutions (hospitals, lunatic asylums, schools, and prisons), and the philanthropist Hannah More, whose stories and tracts were so widely reprinted that as late as 1835 Harriet Martineau was amazed at their circulation.[13] There is also little doubt that the momentum of women's activities on behalf of soldiers, widows, and orphans during and after the American Revolution was carried into the nineteenth century. Women discovered their economic power through antitea boycotts and rudimentary consumer organizations and their general resourcefulness through running business affairs while the men were away.

But it must not be forgotten that major encouragement for founding women's societies now came from men. The New England clergy, who in the eighteenth century would have deemed public activities as a violation of female delicacy, were in desperate need of help to restore their denominations in the aftermath of the Revolution. Moreover, the population boom of the early nineteenth century (between 1800 and 1860 the population increased sixfold), combined with the omnivorous frontier, created a serious shortage of clergy; this is why so many of the early female societies beat the bushes and sewed miles of seams to raise money for funding western missionaries. After responding to the Savior's command "Follow me," women no longer struggled to find how it could be obeyed. The clergy showed them.

The vigorous, near-volcanic growth of women's societies after 1800 must, however, be primarily interpreted within the context of revivalism. Why did the revivals of the nineteenth century stimulate women's organizations and not the revivalism of the eighteenth? First, the revivalism of the nineteenth century was Arminian, not

Calvinist, and the do-good theology of Arminianism gave women a vocation by putting them to work building the kingdom. Second, women were seen by the emerging spherist ideology as especially suited to benevolent endeavors. Before, women were willing to support charitable activities through organizing their husbands; now they organized themselves. Third, the revivalism of the Second Great Awakening was strenuously optimistic. It expected the moral machinery of entrepreneurial evangelism to bring in the millennium. Because women dominated religion—as Frances Trollope observed, "There is no country in the world where religion makes so large a part of the amusement and occupation of the ladies"—they became the dominant labor pool for the millennial task. Again and again the clergy praised their voluntary societies as spokes in the wheel that was rushing toward the millennium.[14] Yet the clergy sent women mixed signals. The assertion of women's bent toward benevolence, the proclamation of their right to take public action and organize societies, and the hosannas of praise heaped upon the heads of female pastoral assistants, while they "represented a break with the past,"[15] nevertheless were laced with admonitions to preserve their modesty, submission, and humility. Confronted with such conflicting messages, women picked up the signal most congenial and advantageous to them, thereby resisting the tendency of voluntarism to reinforce traditional female role expectations.

II

If we are to understand the history of women's institutions and the role of ministers' wives in them, we must begin with a split-level analysis that recognizes both the manifest and the latent functions of women's societies. Unlike male voluntary associations, women's were exclusively religious[16] and devoted to the performance of visible acts of benevolence. The female association movement originated in Boston in 1800 with a flurry of societies: first the famous Boston Female Society for Missionary Purposes, started by the handicapped laywoman Mary Webb, who in her green baize wheel chair organized fourteen Baptist and Congregational women in this pioneering endeavor; then the Female Cent Society; then the Boston Female Asylum, organized by a minister's wife, Hannah Stillman; then the Boston Female Society for Promoting the Diffusion of Christian Knowledge, started by praying women to enhance the efforts of the newly formed Massachusetts Missionary Society.[17] Within a few years the wind of religious gender groups had turned into a gale. We refer to such groups collectively as "Dorcas societies," named after a woman of Joppa who was "full of good works and almsdeeds" (Acts 9:36). The societies had various names: Female Sewing Society, Female Mite Society, Female Missionary Society, Female Charitable Society, Female Harmony Society, and Colored Female Dorcas Society. "Ladies" gradually replaced "Female," as in Ladies' Benevolent Society and Ladies' Aid Society, but in all of them the sewing needle was the tool, the home the workshop, and women the workhorses for benevolent activities.

Clerical wives who subscribed to the Assistant model of ministry were often the instigators of these societies, priming women to repay Christianity for their exalted rank in society with their activities and associations. Ministers' wives also pioneered in devising new kinds of women's societies: the wife of an Ohio Presbyterian minister, James Hoge, responded to Columbus's cholera epidemic in the 1830s by forming the city's longest-lived charitable organization; Women's Bible Bands were started in the 1880s by a Baptist minister's wife from Scranton, Pennsylvania. Finally, they were the most likely to revitalize ailing or defunct groups, like the AME church's "Mite Missionary Society," into which Fanny Jackson Coppin breathed new life in the 1880s.[18] Even when other women managed to upstage the pastor's wife in founding a society, she often ended up with the most votes when it came time for the election of officers. Sarah Royce, who gathered together seventeen women in May 1837 to organize the first women's society in Batavia, New York, took a back seat to Amanda Gillett, who headed the list of charter members and was the wife of the Presbyterian minister Erastus J. Gillett.[19] Just as ministers could expect a vacated pulpit when they moved to a new church, the minister's wife could usually expect that once she had chosen the circle in which she would become active, there would shortly be a vacancy in the office of president.[20]

Ministers' wives worked with church women for a variety of missions. Sometimes they dispensed charity—fuel, clothing, food, seldom money—to the poor. Sometimes they packed food, furniture, quilts, and clerical shirts for "indigent but pious" seminary students. Sometimes they supported "wornout preachers." Sometimes they served as auxiliaries for bible, tract, and prayerbook societies. Sometimes they subsidized missions, both foreign and domestic (in the early years, because of the period's apocalyptic bent, they showed a penchant for American Indians and Jews). Sometimes they supplemented a missionary's meager salary with love-gifts: boxes and barrels tenderly packed with clothing, quilts, medicines, seeds, needles, buttons, and utensils. Sometimes they raised money for church repairs and new buildings. Frequently they combined these projects, as did the Female Benevolent Society in Orange, New Jersey, organized in 1817 for the "Relief of the Poor and Distressed, the Education of Pious Youth for the Gospel Ministry, the Distribution of Bibles and Religious Tracts, and to Supply Funds to the Extension of the Gospel Truth."[21]

Although the manifest function of female organizations was religious, latent functions were also at work. These organizations nurtured a sense of sororal community and encouraged solidarity with other women. Ellen DuBois argues that this sense of community reached the point of "caste consciousness," and she ascribes to it "prepolitical," "proto-feminist" underpinnings.[22] William L. O'Neill refers to the outlook that developed in women's associations as "social feminism." Keith Melder finds in them the "beginnings of sisterhood." And Nancy Cott calls them the "bonds of womanhood," a mischievous pun that calls attention to the paradox that voluntarism and the doctrine of women's sphere tied women together as it tied them to subordination. Cott and Melder are somewhat closer to the truth than DuBois and O'Neill, for one must be careful not to claim too much for these groups. Participation in or support for benevolent societies were not in themselves a sign of liberal views on women's place in the world or sensitivity to the abuses and debilities suffered by the sex. Ronald W. Hogeland has written of the restrictive, "ornamental" view of womanhood subscribed to by the early Princeton professor Samuel Miller and Ashbel Green, later president of the College of New Jersey. Yet their wives were instrumental in establishing and endorsing female benevolent societies that were applauded by their husbands.[23] Lucy Stone uttered a cry of frustration at the amateurishness of church women's politics, marveling that they could marshall resources and organize sophisticated structures to collect $2,000 a year for the poor, but could not use their solidarity and skills to advance their own political interests.[24] The sisterhood of women's societies was founded not on self-interest, political consciousness, common grievances, or common history, but on common ambitions and prayer: "Thy Kingdom come on earth."

Yet a female consciousness and orientation toward women's needs did develop. How this happened can be summarized for our purposes. Because the wives of ministers were often the "heart and soul" of a town's benevolent impulses, the parsonage developed into the hub of women's organizations and activities.[25] As the Dorcas Society (or its equivalent) became the center of a church's home life and thus a church woman's social life, conviviality and friendships developed within a context of gender differentiation. As women sat around a table covered with broadcloth, ribbon, gilt paper, and minikin pins, they might listen to the minister's wife read and pray, but most often they talked. In that circle of conversation they discovered a homosocial support system that was a tightly woven fabric of ego strength, identity, community, and common goals. At a time when the men of industrial capitalism were learning how to choke each other in competitive combat, the sense of community among women was growing as never before.

When forced to do without female communities, women felt less alive. Letters written home in 1840 by Almira Raymond, recently married to a Methodist missionary stationed in Oregon, reveal the psychic pain inflicted by her uprooting from female intimacy. The ladies of Rochester, New York, had in 1834 established a society to train infant school teachers and send them as missionaries to the West. Rochester's Evangelical women looked at prospective candidates from female seminaries and selected Raymond as one of the first young ladies to be sponsored by them. But she found the withdrawal from her female world traumatic. After her dangerous northwestern journey over the mountains in a wagon, it was not her family, safety, or the culture of Rochester that she missed most; it was "female society."[26]

It is thus not surprising to see the objectives and orientation of women's societies becoming more gender-specific as the decades rolled on. Some were this way from the beginning—the Boston Female Asylum, organized in September 1800, had as its first rule: "This Charity shall be confined to FEMALE ORPHAN CHILDREN"[27]—but most proceeded gradually to sharpen their focus on women's concerns. It took two years for the women of the First Presbyterian Church of Newark, New Jersey, to shift their attention from the "Relief of Poor and Distressed Persons" (1803) to the "Relief of Poor and Distressed Widows and the Instruction of Poor Children" (1805).[28] It took about eighteen years for the parent women's voluntary society, the Boston Female Society for Missionary Purposes, to direct its home missionaries James Davis and Dudley Rosseter to labor among Boston's poor, especially "that unhappy class of females who have 'wandered into the paths of vice and folly, and forfeited their good name and reputation.'"[29] The Illinois Baptist Female Society, organized in 1841, opted to support the *daughters* of poor Baptist preachers and the cause of female education.[30] The growing gender consciousness can also be seen in the attempts of some female societies to forge links between "sister" societies.[31]

The same gender agenda led to the establishment of a column in the Methodist *Ladies' Repository* to highlight female worthies and track down milestones in women's history and to the formation of a Women's Cooperative Printing Association in San Francisco to support the employment of female printers. It was first evident in the rallying of Evangelical women in the early nineteenth century behind Catharine Beecher's plea for help in founding female seminaries in the West.[32] It was also increasingly evident in the involvement of ministers' wives in supporting women missionaries and foreign women, which did more than anything else to widen women's horizons. As one new member of a female missionary society exclaimed, "Just think of it! Now I no longer belong merely to my own community, but I am part of the whole world!"[33] Being a global citizen sometimes necessitated women's societies taking political positions. Women's sewing circles had been sending money and clothes to "aid suffering Greece" for years when Emma Willard organized in 1833 the Troy Society for the Advancement of Education in Greece, which raised $3,000 for a teacher-training school in Athens and made support for the Greek revolt against Turkish rule fashionable.[34]

It is possible to argue that the increasing tendency of women to support women was a sign that male prescriptions for female nurturance and dedicated motherhood had triumphed. Such historians as Kathryn Kish Sklar, Nancy F. Cott, and Anne M. Boylan, however, have demonstrated that "women-directed" most often meant "women-defined," a point that has ample corroboration.[35] The Female Cent Society in Thompson Ridge, New York, voted to divide its funds between Princeton scholarships and its own Female Library, in spite of heavy juridical pressure from the Presbyterian hierarchy to contribute to needy seminarians at the newly formed Princeton.[36] Women's societies appear to have realized that total self-interest would have been self-destructive. Thus, they accommodated the wishes of the men, up to a point. The New Hampshire Missionary Society complained in its 1817 Trustees' Report that scores of Cent Societies, formed presumably to aid it, were channeling some of their funds elsewhere: "We are sensible that people have a perfect right to direct their own charities, yet we cannot refrain from reminding the pious females of New Hampshire that the Cent Societies were at first instituted to aid the funds of the Missionary Society."[37] Evangelical women's societies did not always go according to plan—the plan of male benefactors, that is.

Another latent function of women's societies was the development of organizational, executive, political, public relations, financial, and leadership skills. As the women's movement became politicized, these early benevolent associations would provide training and models of institutional inventiveness. The organizational complexity of these societies varied, though not as much as one might expect. The Female Orphan Asylum of Portland, Maine, like other homes for orphans, was incorporated, employed a staff, and was funded through its Ladies' Board of Managers.[38] Virtually all women's societies, no matter how simple, required some sort of constitution and by-laws, minutes and records, business meetings, elections for officers and managers, the collection and disbursement of funds, fundraising and promotional campaigns, and annual meetings and reports. Most were deferentially, though not rigidly, hierarchical within a democratic framework. Women knew that their talents must be either disciplined or dissipated, and so they instituted codes of conduct and methods of group discipline (such as fines on tardy or absent members or punishments for moral indiscretions) to ensure cohesiveness, stability, and sustained commitment. After paying initiation fees, the earliest source of revenue, women often made weekly, quarterly, or annual pledges (Florence Hayes estimates the average gift as a cent a week, though some in the South gave as much as 6.25 cents a week).[39] At a time when women's prescribed sphere prevented their having much to do with money or business, religion provided them with a wealth of first-hand experience in both financial and administrative management. Those "Just like a woman" slurs could never sound the same after such training. It is not surprising to find a churchworkers' manual published in 1917 beginning with the sentence: "For devotion, persistence, intelligence and general efficiency the women's organizations of the average local church are in advance of every other department."[40]

Although women's societies ostensibly challenged class boundaries by urging women to identify with the oppressed and needy, they also worked to confirm social status and define the local structure of female leadership. When Frances Trollope was describing the routine of a typical upper-class Philadelphia family, she had the lady of the household direct her footman to "drive to the Dorcas Society," where she spent the bulk of the day in sewing, gossiping, and rating ministers.[41] This final latent function is confirmed by a look at the career of a wealthy New York City widow and schoolteacher, Isabella Marshall Graham, who deserves if anyone does the title of patron saint of woman's work for women in America. She and her companion Sarah Hoffman presided at the formation of numerous societies for women, all of which proudly drew into their ranks ladies of wealth and social status. In 1796 Graham instigated the establishment of the New York Missionary Society, one of the first of its kind in America and the creator of a new method of evangelism called the "mission family," which integrated the services of the missionary's wife into the mission. In 1797 the Female Society for the Relief of Poor Widows with Small Children was organized in her home, and for the next ten years she served as its first directress. Within a year of its formation, 190 ladies were donating a minimum of three dollars annually, and many were giving much more, enabling them eventually to purchase a home in which the helpless children of widows could be preserved from dreary futures. In 1804 she drew together twenty-five young women who were, she was pleased to announce, "in rank the first in the city" and organized them into a school for the education of orphans and the children of widows. Graham's daughter, Joanna Bethune, and her wealthy women friends like Elizabeth Hamilton (widow of Alexander Hamilton) established the first orphanage in New York State in 1806, the Orphan Asylum Society. In 1811 Graham was elected president of the newly created Magdalene Society. Her last gift to women's societies came in 1814, when she and other women of high social standing formed the Society for the Promotion of Industry among the Poor, complete with an employment bureau for widows and a tandem effort directed at factory workers called the Sabbath Morning Adult School.[42]

In urban areas like New York City, sewing circles were not joined by the kind of woman Henry Ward Beecher described as so poor that only the needle stood between her and hell. Rather, the wives of clergy and property owners, increasingly women of similar age with shared concerns and common class interests, dominated associations that sought to do something for the poor rather than with them. The pattern differed little in smaller communities. Mary F. Kihlstrom discovered that the Presbyterian women who joined their pastor's wife, Mrs. Samuel Fisher, in founding the Morristown (New Jersey) Female Charitable Society in 1813 "represented some of the wealthiest and most prominent families in the community."[43]

Antebellum strategies of benevolence, the economics of pity and piety, willy-nilly drew pious attention to the softened hearts and generous hands of the patron while pitifully softening the pride, hardening the hearts, and crippling the hands of the poor. This is why the Social Gospel movement revolted against *noblesse oblige* charity.[44] The wealthy women who formed charitable societies reinforced their social standing while relieving their consciences when they separated the sheep from the goats, the deserving from the undeserving poor, through door-to-door visitation in lower-class neighborhoods.[45] In some cases, as in Boston's Mount Vernon Congregational Church in the 1840s, benevolent sewing circles became blatantly elitist, allowing membership "by invitation only."[46] Some historians argue that there was a "leveling" tendency, so that by the time of the moral reform movement, women's associations were markedly more socially heterogeneous than in the earlier years.[47] In fact, these societies identified for the community, church, and clergy not so much a social elite as a power elite of influential women, women whose opinions had to be consulted because they controlled interlocking directorates on various benevolent committees and magnified their power by multilayered involvements.[48]

Just as women's societies promoted dependence on women, they promoted independence from men. David Schuyler has pointed out that in the homes of middle-class families in the Northeast, women often did have a "room of their own."[49] They enjoyed rooms of their own in religious life too. It is difficult to generalize about the thousands of women's societies that speckled the landscape in antebellum America, but it seems clear that most excluded males, and some were so desirous of pride in their own proceeds that they even debated whether to accept male money. In most cases the concern for the money's destination won out over regret about its genesis. But even when men could become dues-paying members of a society, they were generally not admitted to meetings: the ladies' society at the Mother Church of Methodism in Washington, D.C., was unusual in permitting male officeholding. Even when men were allowed to attend the meetings, many women's societies apparently forbade them to speak. Pastors who opened the meeting with prayer were expected to leave afterward. Only at the annual "public meeting" was it common for men to be present and preside, often providing booster sermons: "Women are generally the first, the most efficient, and most successful in the causes of benevolence." The tradition of male exclusion at Cincinnati's Pleasant Ridge Female Auxiliary Society was so firmly established that as late as 1870, "if a man so much as set foot in the room" while the women were meeting, "business was suspended, a hymn was sung, and the man was kindly but firmly invited to leave." In the early years the husbands excluded from meetings were nevertheless honorary guests at the suppers that followed, a reward for their generosity in driving their wives the long distances to the meetings.[50]

Women's institutional exclusivity had the potential for creating major frays within the religious tapestry of antebellum America. The danger was exemplified by the experience of the downtown Methodist Episcopal church in St. Louis. Some of its "wealthy and influential ladies," inspired by Phoebe Palmer and her "Guide to Holiness," began holding in their parlors, meetings for the promotion of holiness. Soon the group began to function as a church within a church, soliciting its own speakers, passing judgments on other programs, and generally exerting a divisive force within the congregation.[51] That few women's societies went this far, although, as we shall see, they exercised considerable power, was due to the prominence of ministers' wives in their leadership and the genuine desire of women to serve as a loyal tribe of pastors' assistants. Of considerable importance also was the fact that most women's societies were irenically ecumenical in constituency and purpose (before the Civil War there was only one nationally organized denominational women's society, the Free Baptist Missionary Society, founded in 1847), uninterested in theological debates, and united in a millennial world view. The Presbyterian Isabella Graham and the Episcopalian Sarah Hoffman were proudly nonsectarian as they walked together down the squalid streets of New York City's poorest section, distributing Bibles and tracts long before any Bible or tract society existed.[53] Where widows and orphans lived, where the sick and dying cried, there hastened the footsteps of ministers' wives and dedicated benevolent women of whatever denominational persuasion.

Men could be found endorsing women's societies from beginning to end, though more often at the end. In the beginning there were reservations about the propriety of "ostentatious" women and deep fears about what this development portended for domestic tranquility. When the elders of the Old Presbyterian Church in Gilbertsville heard in 1817 that the ladies of the church were organizing one of the first missionary societies in New York, they shook with fright and convened a secret meeting to plot how to stop it. "If it is allowed to go on," they said, "women will be completely unsexed and will get the notion of having money of their own."[53] Other men greeted the growth of ladies' aid societies with "God-bless-them" condescension, derisive epithets ("Ladies' Raid Societies"), or a willingness to accept their money but not their meetings. But it was self-interest linked with social fears that created much of the hesitancy and opposition. Sunday schools are nice, and maternal associations are helpful, but the primary place for a woman's influence is in the home, said John Abbott, who believed that women were spending far too much time outside it. This was also the contention of William Andrus Alcott, a veteran of counseling's covered-wagon days, who advised young women, if they had an irresistible urge to do good, to do good at home, their greatest mission field:

> For the friends of the Maternal Association will expect you to join them. Of the Sewing Circle, you must, of course, be a member. The Moral Reform Society will expect you to be one of their members. The Female Society for Promoting Education in the West will put in its claims. Then you are also expected to be a member of the Peace Society, the Temperance Society, the Tract Society, the Bible Society, the Foreign Mission Society, the Anti-Slavery Society, and perchance the Sabbath School Society and the Society for Ameliorating the Condition of the Jews.[54]

It is unclear how prevalent such opposition was among husbands, families, and ministers, but overall there was clearly far more encouragement.

One of the reasons for the encouragement was, of course, that women's societies had made themselves economically indispensable to local churches and to the entire network of voluntary societies. "The Cent contributions is one of the happiest expedients which has been devised," said the New Hampshire Missionary Society in 1817 of the more than fifty female societies that were emptying their purses into its pockets.[55] "Hints for Female Education Societies" were given to Episcopal women in 1825 by the Society for the

Education of Pious Young Men for the Ministry of the Protestant Episcopal Church, in hopes that more would be established. Its twenty-five female auxiliary societies in Washington, D.C., Maryland, and Virginia were already raising by 1825 half of the society's annual receipts of $2,455.[56] The Presbyterian General Assembly was the first denominational voice to go on record as approving ("with lively pleasure") the organization of benevolent females.[57] The contributions of female societies to the support of needy students at theological seminaries were crucial. Four societies with this purpose had been formed by 1815, and twelve by 1824.[58] Of the six sources of revenue for the American Education Society, organized in 1815 to boost America's supply of ministers, at least four were dominated by women within five years.[59]

Even in the South, which has been seen as bereft of voluntary societies and women's associations,[60] formal associations for women can be found flourishing. In only three years (1816–1819), the 130 members of the Charleston, South Carolina, Congregational and Presbyterian Female Association for Assisting in the Education of Pious Youth for the Gospel Ministry raised over $3,000, of which $2,500 went to endow a "Charleston Female Scholarship" at Princeton. The rest was distributed as aid to prospective ministers from five denominations in eleven states, who were studying at eleven different academies, colleges, and theological schools. "Animated by the laudable example of our fellow Christians of our own sex, in various parts of our land," they declared, Charleston's women spent another $2,060 in similar support over the next four years.[61] Following in the wake of such fundraising successes came warm recommendations from denominational agencies, like the 1840 General Association of Baptists meeting in Elizabethtown, Kentucky.[62]

In short, ministers' wives and their women's societies funded the nineteenth-century benevolent empire. Congregations may have left the maintenance of church buildings in the hands of men, but fundraising for new buildings, as well as mission and outreach, was largely left to the women. For small, struggling churches, the presence of a women's society often made the difference between life and death, between surviving and thriving.

III

Like most Evangelical women, Lydia Finney loved female companionship. In fact, wherever she went, a women's society was sure to follow. Five Oberlin women's organizations were founded in 1835, not incidentally the year of her arrival there.[63] Lydia's interpretation of the Assistant role included the belief that ministers' wives should assert themselves to establish benevolent endeavors without deference to or dependence on their husbands or other males.[64] At first she limited her independent activities to infant schools and maternal societies, both of which reflected interests at the center of woman's proper sphere. But she also began to move toward the periphery and became a force behind the more radical crusades for moral reform and abolition.

Part of the attraction of infant schools and maternal associations for Lydia and other ministers' wives was that they enabled women struggling to be assistants in their husbands' ministry to balance what Julie Roy Jeffrey has called the "pressures of conflicting domestic and religious demands."[65] That is, they allowed ministers' wives to remain active leaders of the church while raising children and fulfilling their domestic responsibilities. But the infant schools, maternal societies, and moral reform movement must be seen pre-eminently as the women's phalanx in the nineteenth-century Evangelical campaign to establish the millennial kingdom on American soil. "A ray of millennial light has shone on us," exulted the Boston Infant School Society in 1843, "and reveals a way in which poverty, with all its attendant evils—moral, physical, and intellectual, may be banished from the world."[66] By schooling children in the rudiments of piety, nationalism, and learning at an early age (as early as eighteen months), Evangelical women felt that they were both giving their children a greater chance for a life of usefulness and winning themselves opportunities to leave the home for acts of service and benevolence. Joanna Graham Bethune, who pioneered in the education of children under six in the 1820s, organized the 1827 Infant School Society of New York City as a religious day care center for the children of laborers, but middle-class Evangelical women heavily involved in volunteer work dropped their children off as well. Lydia not only sent her children to infant schools, but founded them in towns where her husband conducted revivals, and inquired about costs and the improvements that other areas had implemented.[67] Lydia Finney did not exhibit the organizational genius of an Emma Willard or a Catharine Beecher. Without a formal structure to control her creations, however, she was nevertheless able to exert her influence informally on infant schools and other female societies through the faithful maintenance of private correspondence with key members of these groups.

Perhaps closer to her heart than any movement other than revivalism itself were the maternal associations, and particularly the Oberlin Maternal Association, formed in 1835 by mothers who were "deeply impressed with the great importance of bringing up our children in the nurture and admonition of the Lord."[68] Even before Lydia joined her husband's church on 9 July 1837, her name had been entered into the membership list of the Oberlin Maternal Association (on 7 July 1836). Within a year she became recording and corresponding secretary, a position that she held for two years. In 1842 she was elected first directress of the organization, and she piloted it through its banner membership year—150 mothers and 472 children, a long way from the 5 or 10 members who had founded it eight years previously.[69] Finney himself considered the association either worthy enough or powerful enough to announce its meetings from the pulpit of First Church.[70]

The maternal association movement provides graphic evidence of the degree to which motherhood had become a distinct profession. Founded in 1815 by Ann Louisa Payson, the wife of a Portland, Maine, Congregationalist minister and the mother of the novelist Elizabeth Payson Prentiss, maternal associations aided mothers through the development of professional standards, certification, specialization, and continuing education.[71] Unlike other women's societies early in the nineteenth century, the maternal societies that flourished from the 1820s through the 1840s did not confine their activities to the raising of money, perhaps for their minister's pet project. Rather, through maternal associations women accepted and celebrated their common roles as custodians of conversion, especially the task of educating their children for eternity as well as earth, and covenanted together to lead exemplary, pious lives befitting their exalted vocation. The maternal associations lend institutional credence to Donald B. Matthews's argument that given the catechetics of conversion as taught in Evangelical homes, historians of Evangelicalism have made too much of the distinction between crisis and gradual conversion.[72] Responsibility for conversion rested not on the shoulders of roving revivalists or settled pastors, but squarely in mothers' laps. Years before Horace Bushnell's *Christian Nurture* appeared in 1848, Evangelical women had already written much of the book. Revivalists were expected to perform the task of "bringing in the sheaves," but only after women had nurtured, cut, and bundled the harvest.

Perhaps because there was no national governing body, local maternal associations were more tightly organized than many of their sister societies. In Oberlin a directress was elected yearly to conduct annual and quarterly meetings and generally to superintend the society's operations, although by 1840 the increasing demands on the society's leadership led to the inauguration of a trinity of directors. In spite of the hierarchical structure, the women practiced leadership rotation; each month different members were given the responsibility of conducting the meeting around a designated theme. Monthly meetings took place in members' homes, although Lydia appears to have hosted far more than her share. Each meeting began with a prescribed liturgy of prayer, singing, reading, and reports form the recording secretary, the corresponding secretary, and the librarian-treasurer, who were also elected yearly. Detailed annual reports, sometimes excerpted in the *Oberlin Evangelist*, reveal a sisterhood of pious, self-disciplined women who, within an organizational context that was almost as sophisticated and efficient as any of their husbands' associations, expressed genuine care and concern for one another, kept track of one another between meetings, tallied the positive and negative features of each other's children, shared child-rearing success stories, and kept precise tabulations of the increases in the population of New Jerusalem due to their initiative and industry. With Argus-eyed vigilance they collectively monitored their sons' and daughters' spiritual and social development while promoting by every means available the voluntary acceptance of Christ at the earliest age possible.[73] The popular biography of Elizabeth Janeway and a spate of spiritual biographies written by the pastors of pious young females were as filled with early conversions as with early deaths, excommunicating the belief that there was anything miraculous in the conversion of children.

Preparing children for "immediate conversion" and a life of "eminent usefulness," Lydia argued, ought to be the first, though not the exclusive, goal of Evangelical women. She reinforced the spiritual responsibilities of motherhood in a rather stern lecture delivered in 1842 to the Oberlin Maternal Association, which she was then serving as first directress. Many of the "Mothers in Israel" among them were becoming "weary in well-doing," she scolded. Busy with college, church, and community activities, not to mention their unending labors for benevolent societies like the Oberlin Female Anti-Slavery Society, the Female Society of Oberlin for the Promotion of Health, and the Oberlin Female Moral Reform Society, women were neglecting their physical health as well as jeopardizing the spiritual well-being of their children. Their pressing millennial vocation might take them outside the home, but there was no millennial exemption from mothering. She did not, however, charge mothers with full responsibility for children's spiritual tuition. A frustratingly obscure but suggestive feature of Lydia's term as first directress was the establishment of the short-lived Oberlin Paternal Association, to stimulate fathers' interest in the spiritual education of their children. One searches the records in vain for insight into why the fathers met weekly and the mothers monthly, how the women responded when the fathers addressed the mothers at their joint meetings, and why the paternal association appears to have burned out in 1843 after only two years.[74] Yet it is clear that however much Lydia might have wished for more masculine involvement in child rearing, she esteemed a mother's spiritual training her most important endowment for her children. Even the conversion of a child should not mark the cessation of worry over his or her spiritual condition, Lydia warned, for temptations cling firmer and longer to converted children than to unconverted ones.[75]

One can see Lydia practicing what she preached in her solicitous regard for the unsanctified state of her eldest child, Helen, even after her marriage at seventeen to a thirty-two-year-old Oberlin professor of logic. One might have expected Lydia to express greater concern over her new son-in-law, William Cochran, an academic success and a social embarrassment who had a difficult career at Oberlin both as student and as faculty member. Instead, shortly after their marriage in 1846, Lydia asked William, who had helped promulgate the doctrine of Oberlin perfectionism in the pages of the *Oberlin Quarterly Review*, now to promote the experience of sanctification in the life of his bride, and "see to it *dear William* that Helen meets me in Heaven." Lydia felt deeply that Helen's defiant resistance to sanctification meant that she as Helen's mother had failed in her "faithfulness to my covenant vows," confessing to Helen that her overbearing, disputatious reaction to her daughter's "feigned indifference" to Christian perfection was unhelpful and "all but contemptible."[76] The danger in Evangelical mothers' overwhelming concern for the conversion of their offspring was, of course, that the children would cease to be subjects and become objects. The extent to which Lydia's concern for ther children's spiritual health eclipsed all other concerns was made ruefully manifest three weeks before her death on 17 December 1847, when she called her children to her bedside and there conducted her last prayer meeting. From then on she was no longer interested in conversing with them, explaining to a bewildered Finney that "her work was done with and for them. . . . [She] had said all she had to say. She had given them her last advice."[77]

The tactics used by maternal associations to produce early conversions ranged from loving, gentle inducement to gross intimidation. Motherly sacrifice was a favorite technique. Mothers would set aside their children's birthdays and annual meetings as seasons of fasting and prayer for the children's conversion. Psychological pressure was also used, as evidenced in a letter Lydia wrote during the 1842 Rochester revival to her children, Helen, Charles, Julia, and Norton, who were being cared for by Adaline Chapin, a would-be missionary:

> Dear little Julia, last sabbath when I was at meeting I saw a little girl, just about as large as you are. I was struck by her calm, sweet heavenly little countenance, and felt that she had been taught of God. I soon perceived that she had but one hand. . . . I then thought, surely the Lord had suffered her hand to be taken away that he might save her soul, and perhaps to eternity she will bless his name for the loss of that *little hand*. Dear Julia, will you love the Lord with both your hands? or will he have to take one or both of them away to make you think about Jesus Christ? We had a very pleasant ride from Buffalo to Rochester.[78]

The enormous pressures exerted by Evangelical mothers reflect the pressure they themselves were under. A mother's work was not complete until her children, saved and sanctified, rose up and called her blessed. For in the words of a minister speaking to the Amity Street Baptist Church Maternal Association in New York City, "The son unguided [is] his mother's shame."[79]

Maternal associations like the one at Oberlin also served to pressure the clergy to take children more seriously in their ministry through visitation and sermons written for a child's level. Nancy F. Cott has correctly observed that the 1830s phenomenon of "evangelically oriented child-rearing books" spurred the institutionalization of the "developing consciousness" of mothers.[80] But it is equally true that maternal societies prompted such publications. "The Mother's Hymn Book," for example, was expressly written for maternal associations and family prayer sessions by the composer of "Rock of Ages," Thomas Hastings, Finney's Utica friend whom he brought to New York City to serve as his music director and song leader. Hastings's wife, significantly, presided at maternal association meetings at Chatham Street Chapel in Lydia's abscence.[81] Particularly irritating to Evangelical women was the seeming indifference of clergy toward the need for children to hear sermons they could understand. One women correspondent to the *Oberlin Evangelist* complained that in over thirty years of listening to over two thousand sermons, she had heard only a handful designed and delivered with children in mind.[82] Sunday morning children's sermons as we know them today do not appear to have surfaced until the last quarter of the century.

Oberlin women made sure that the clergy would heed their wishes by arranging for quarterly exercises at which the children (who were now constitutionally members of the association) would be addressed by a minister especially invited for the occasion. Contrary to Joseph Kett's contention that maternal associations limited their concern to the child's pliable years, transferring to the father's spiritual care and control children over ten, the Oberlin Maternal Association patterned itself after the widely imitated maternal association of Portland, Maine, in defining its constituency, and brought to these quarterly meetings female children between three and sixteen and male children between three and fourteen.[83] Furthermore, at a time when it was deemed indelicate and unladylike to speak of conception even in hushed tones, Lydia and other mothers agreed that the sexual education of children was their responsibility, and that it should begin as early as the child's understanding permitted. In fact, an 1841 compact entered into by the mothers of the maternal association, no doubt inspired by the moral reform movement, bound them to read daily with their sons from the Book of Proverbs to break the ice for frank discussions of the social implications of the seventh commandment.[84]

A gradual enlargement of scope characterized the Oberlin Maternal Association during Lydia's twelve-year involvement in it. By 1840 it had spread its wings to cover the spiritual growth of domestics employed by members of the association and had resolved to embrace and provide relief for "all orphans," not just the motherless members of the society.[85] As a concrete embodiment of its desire to be a "mother to motherless children," the association arranged to receive and rear the children of Dr. Dan Beach and Emily Royce Bradley, missionaries to Siam, after her death in 1847.[86] Yet the need for a sharing, discussion, and literary group and the yearning for child-rearing support systems were never forgotten by the sisters. Lydia's friend, Amelia Ann Norton, wife of the first pastor of the Union Presbyterian Church in New York City, a church founded by wealthy businessmen to preach the gospel to the poor and promote revivals, expressed her exultation after attending a meeting of the maternal association that she had just helped to organize: "I always feel a *confidence*, and *firmness*, in going forward and endeavoring to watch over my children, and discharging my duty to them, after returning from a meeting of our society which I didn't feel before."[87] They shared experiences, reviewed books, debated theological issues like conversion, perfection, perseverance, and the Abrahamic covenant, invited missionaries to speak to them, discussed and distributed the *Mother's Magazine* and *Mothers' Assistant*, and assigned one or two women each week to compose essays on the topic to be discussed at the next meeting (subjects chosen included female education, corporal punishment, property rights for children, proper dress, the use of tea and coffee, means of promoting purity, usefulness and unselfishness, and the difficulty of getting children excited about the Sabbath).

Lydia's contributions to the Oberlin Maternal Association and, more importantly, the maternal association movement were most distinguished and did not go unrecognized by her peers. In the words of a tribute to Lydia written years later on behalf of the sisters, they had been "aided by her judgment, and encouraged by her counsel, profited by the frequent contributions of her pen and blessed by her example and her prayers."[88] Besides holding executive offices and presenting papers and lectures, Lydia, along with Alice Welch Cowles, had the coveted task of selecting books for the association's library. Her sisters' esteem was further manifested in the debate over whether force or moral suasion was more effective in raising children. Lydia's aversion to physical punishment, except in cases of "determined obstinacy," held sway within the society.[89]

In terms of nineteenth-century Evangelicalism, Lydia was a woman's woman. Outside the society Lydia was seen as an authority on both maternal associations and child development. Evangelical mothers looked up to her for wisdom, and Lydia responded with letters of advice. She even composed letters to their children, filled with spiritual admonition and counsel.[90] As a one-woman clearing-house of information and ideas on maternal associations, Lydia arranged for model constitutions to be sent to interested churches, communicated directly with other societies, especially those in difficulty, tackled the problem of churches that did not dance to the tune piped by the minister's wife, and kept herself on top of developments in this diffusive grass-roots movement as best she could, even tracking the progress of missionary wives in establishing maternal societies in the mission field.[91] Lydia firmly believed that essential to a vital maternal association was the benefaction of a supportive minister's wife who faithfully scrutinized the pages of the *Mother's Magazine*. That Finney seconded her opinion is evident from his expenditure accounts, which reveal that he had paid subscriptions to three magazines—*New York Evangelist, Biblical Repository,* and *Mother's Magazine*.[92]

The more radical movements against slavery and for moral reform also owed large debts to Lydia's organizing abilities. In supporting these two causes she reinforced the already existing identification of the names of Finney and Oberlin with the crusades for abolition and women's rights. Lucy Stone believed that the founding of Oberlin in 1832 marked the birth of "the idea of Equal Rights to education," and in her short memorial tribute to Charles G. Finney, she featured perfectionism, abolition, and coeducation as the distinguishing marks of the career of this "eccentric, original, and acute" man.[93] Similarly, William Lloyd Garrison assured Oberlin's founder, John Keep, that in his projected volume, *A History of the Anti-Slavery Struggle*, "I shall not forget Oberlin—its origin, its struggles, its anti-slavery testimonies and examples, its deliverance from the spirit of complexional caste, and its wonderful growth and extended influence in shaping the destiny of the West, and with that the destiny of the country."[94] The scant records of Lydia Finney's anti-slavery activities show her as a guiding light in the Ohio Ladies' Anti-Slavery Society, and in 1839 she and Alice Welch Cowles joined their husbands as representatives to the Ohio Anti-Slavery Society Convention. It was Alice Welch Cowles who was chosen as the first president of the Oberlin Moral Reform Society in 1835, but it was Lydia, fresh from founding the New York Female Moral Reform Society in May 1834, who exerted the greatest influence over the controversial movement that would proliferate during the 1830s and 1840s into over four hundred chapters.

Historians of women have so superbly analyzed the moral reform movement that one wonders if any further insight is possible. Carroll Smith-Rosenberg, Keith Melder, Nancy F. Cott, Mary P. Ryan, Barbara Berg, and Paul Boyer have written perceptively of the movement's objectives: eradicating prostitution, equalizing public contempt for courtesan and customer, and generally diffusing moral purity throughout the nation in pursuit of millennial perfection.[95] Everybody agrees that more than any other movement except, perhaps, abolitionism, moral reform served as the nursery of feminism. Everybody is right. The invocation of women's power, the attempt to redefine sexual relationships, the encouragement of a distinctive sense of female outrage and grievance vis à vis male values, the abolition of the double standard, the celebration of female moral superiority—all these are properly cited as evidence that moral reformers "contributed substantially to the feminist spirit" and "moved toward asserting women's rights."[96] Yet is must be remembered that the vast majority of moral reformers, like Lydia herself, did not become feminists in the militant or political sense of the term. Indeed, Melder's contention that conversion was equalled in importance and eventually eclipsed by reform is simply not accurate. Moral reformers could envision no lasting reform without conversion.[97] For example, Margaret Prior was a wealthy Methodist, a pioneer social worker in the Bowery, and the most famous city missionary employed by the American Female Moral Reform Society. She dispensed band-aids of charity (often from her own purse or from the pockets of her wealthy friends) in visits to an average of 350 destitute families per month in 1838. Yet what she was honored for and proudest of was having more conversions to her credit than most ministers in New York City.[98]

The radical innovation of the moral reform societies was to free Evangelical women from laboring for the millennium on their knees, through their purses, or with their aprons on. After years of exhortation to escort the world into the millennial kingdom as a guardian angel leads a child—prayerfully omnipresent but unseen—women were challenged to act in public as Gabriels of the good news. (Some moral reformers went even further and acted as avenging angels against male salaciousness.) Women's energies were no longer directed into maternal or ecclesiastical channels. For the first time, they undertook direct, physical, even political, involvement in building the millennial kingdom through conversion and reform. Women, whether they knew it or not, were outward-bound.

The Finney connection behind the moral reform movement has been ably documented by Carroll Smith-Rosenberg.[99] Sponsors, supporters, officers, and managers of the New York Female Moral Reform Society were Finney's disciples, and the society was founded and held its meetings at Finney's church, the Second Free Presbyterian Church. Finney personally threw his weight behind the women in a rousing speech delivered shortly after the society's formation. He emboldened and empowered the women present to act as posses of purity, always ready to bring male seducers to justice, always ready to extend a helping hand to wayward women. The limited, indirect influence women exerted in the home and church, Finney contended, must now be traded in temporarily for more direct assertions of power in society. Moral reformers must not shy away from personal contact with prostitutes and their sinkholes of sin or think that removing prostitutes from the streets and containing them in asylums would convert them. "Visit these houses and fill them with Bibles and tracts, and make them places of religious conversation and prayer, and convert these wretched inmates *on the spot.*" With a typical flourish of optimism, he concluded: "Let Christians only go to work and they may accomplish the whole in three months."[100] Oberlin's President, Asa Mahan, echoed Finney's summons in an address before the Oberlin Moral Reform Society in July 1842. Only a "false delicacy" would judge the public condemnation of moral impurity inappropriate for women. Virtue and chastity were moral issues, he reminded those whom society upheld as arbiters of morality, and the greatest moral sermon ever uttered, the Sermon on the Mount, was "spoken in a promiscuous assembly."[101]

The history of the Young Men's Moral Reform Society of the Oberlin Collegiate Institute demonstrates another feature of the movement. Organized months before the November 1835 formation of the Oberlin Female Moral Reform Society, the men's group was never able to arouse much enthusiasm, especially in comparison with the excitement stirred up among the 166 charter members of the female society. Though traces of its existence can still be found in 1845, the impact of the young men's auxiliary was minimal.[102] Its history was typical. The failure of men's societies to become viable moral reform groups is significant. In analyzing the vital support of

Finney and his disciples and the diminished gender insularity of this movement in comparison with some of its sister societies, one must be careful to underline the dominant, female cast of the crusade, which gave moral reform a direction and identity somewhat different from those envisioned by its male patrons. Lydia and her good friend Mrs. H. C. Green were more than plenipotentiaries for their husbands. Lydia was the national society's first directress (the highest executive officer), one of its earliest managers, and in later years a vice president. Mrs. Green served under Lydia as second directress and succeeded her as first directress when the Finneys moved to Oberlin in 1835.[103] Both imposed their own agendas and personalities on the societies of which they were a part and promoted the movement's transformation first from male- to female-orientation (that is, from protecting men as victims to pointing the finger at them as villains) and then into a social service agency for the helpless, hapless, and hopeless. Moral purity, as Elise Boulding has pointed out, "was not a cramping, inhibiting concept, it was a releasing one."[104] As an ethic of both abstinence and continence, it proclaimed woman's right to control over her body and protected her from unwanted pregnancy and the epidemic dangers of venereal disease.

Lydia and Alice Welch Cowles (who died in 1843) dominated the meetings of the Oberlin Moral Reform Society with their speeches and insights. Sometimes they invited male speakers, a concession that a few other societies were unwilling to make. Mary Tucker, for example, the active wife of a Methodist itinerant stationed in Holliston, Massachusetts, recommended during her 1839 term as president of the local moral reform auxiliary that male lecturers not be invited. She was chosen as lecturer.[105] Lydia's influence was not so monopolistic, but she did assume major responsibility for conducting the liturgy at the opening of each meeting. Composed mainly of religious women from both the Oberlin community and the campus, an ecumenical feature that characterized the entire movement, the Oberlin auxiliary had by 1837 the fourth largest membership of any of the 268 local chapters of the New York Female Moral Reform Society. Absorption in local activities did not lessen Lydia's interest in the national body that she had helped to establish. In the year of her death, Lydia wrote an admonishing letter to Margaret Prior's amanuensis, Sarah R. Ingraham, rebuking the ugly, fractious spirit that had reared itself among a band of women members of the American Female Moral Reform Society.[106]

Residents of the "Houses of Refuge" established by moral reform societies for destitute women and prostitutes were seen precisely as refugees from urban license and male licentiousness, which the Oberlin constitution deemed "more guilty" than female licentiousness.[107] Lydia and other moral reformers were unsparing assailants of the double standard, which since its eighteenth-century acceptance in literature had permitted men to inhabit a different moral universe than women.[108] "As he is first in fault, he shall have our first frown," said the Oberlin moral reformers, as they turned the tables on past inequities in every way possible.[109] The Female Moral Reform Society went along with the idea, first through its proposal, since adapted by New York City police, to publish the names of men (especially socially prominent ones) seen frequenting brothels, and second through its determination to inspect all potentially licentious liaisons, even between clergymen and slaves.[110]

The vehemence of this reaction to male moral turpitude was both a measure of women's long-suppressed hostility toward men and a means of legislating women's standards of morality on the male community.[111] In Lydia's hands moral reform became an instrument for redefining the boundaries of social conventions and regulating the relations between the sexes—on the basis not of sexual equality, but of a distinct sense of female superiority. In her speeches Lydia fastened her attention on all aspects of cross-gender relationships, including fornication, adultery, dancing, theater, long engagements, shotgun marriages, proper conversation and calling hours (no male visitors after the "hour of retirement"), the dangers of moral laxity while traveling (especially associated with steamboats and hotels), the necessity to guard children against improper reading material (including trashy, frothy novels that stimulated day-dreaming and fantasy), and the obligation of mothers to join maternal associations for support in offering their children frank, detailed sex education, starting at an early age ("Ignorance is not purity").[112] The blending of moral with physiological reform manifested itself in the society's opposition to short sleeves, low necklines and tight lacing, though Lydia's motto, "Dress in such a manner as not to attract particular attention one way or the other," stood somewhat at variance with her husband's agreement with Lewis Tappan that the Christian's dress should be a visible sermon on the simplicity and plainness of his or her religion. Lydia's dress code actually provoked attack from those who sought comfort and convenience without regard for fashion.[113]

Ironically, the most radical of the Oberlin women's activities was their defiance of accepted norms of female behavior by joining other members of the society in circulating a resolution calling on the state legislature to impose legal sanctions against seduction. In the first half of the nineteenth century, women symbolized morality and the withdrawal from politics. Oberlin women's participation was ironical because here, when they were acting most vigorously on behalf of morality, they were also, most decidedly, acting politically. Their action was radical not just because it brought women into the political process (though perhaps it was this feature of moral reform that attracted to the Oberlin Society the militant women's rights advocates Antoinette Brown and Lucy Stone),[114] but because the distribution and signing of petitions (whether antiseduction or anti-slavery) was, according to Sarah J. Hale's *Ladies' Magazine*, a violation of feminine modesty.[115]

V

"The language of moral reform," Nancy F. Cott has written, "evoked women's power; power to avenge, power to control and reform."[116] The issue of women's societies and the role of the minister's wife in them inevitably leads to a discussion of power. The most beguiling question of today in women's history is related to power: symbolically, the first number of the influential quarterly *Signs: Journal of Women in Culture and Society* was a theme issue on "Power and Powerlessness,"[117] How much power did the wives of clergymen and the women's societies they so often headed have in the church? Power is an extremely complex subject, a difficult phenomenon to analyze because it is so imprecise. Any discussion easily falls into the swamp of presentism and hence is precarious.

The lexical definition of power is twofold: first, "the ability to do something or anything"; second, "a position of ascendancy; ability to compel obedience."[118] If real power is defined constitutionally and politically as the "ability to do something," like vote for the officials of church boards and voluntary associations, then clearly women possessed little power, though even here they had more than historians have supposed. The congregational franchise was generally limited to white male contributors (or pew holders) over twenty-one years of age. Aside from such fringe millenarian groups as the seventeenth-century Fifth Monarchists and the nineteenth-century Shakers, the Quaker and Baptist traditions can boast the best history of giving

women equal suffrage in church affairs, though by no means all
Baptist churches extended women the franchise and allowed them
to sign church covenants.[119] In the church pastored by Isaac Backus,
the leader of the colonial Massachusetts Baptists, women could not
vote in church affairs, at least if the 1770 evidence is decisive.[120] A
variety of complex psychological and sociological contingencies—
prominent among them the expanding number of black members—
converged by 1800 to create a tide of southern Baptist antagonism to
female suffrage, a trend that does not appear to have been paralleled
in the North. Often, however, northern women had to fight to keep
what was already theirs. This was the predicament of the women of
Philadelphia's First Baptist Church in March 1764, when they
learned that the men of the church had decided to continue to allow
women a voice in the church's business meetings, but no vote. On
behalf of the women of the church, a little over a month later,
Johanna Anthony gave a speech that bristled with indignation. "We
know our former rights and we beg to know who had a Right to
deprive us of them," she demanded.

> According to the former rules of our Baptist church sisters had a
> right of giving their suffrage or disapprobation in all which they
> have been totally omitted. We do assure the brethern we will not
> attempt to teach or usurp any authority in the church of God;
> neither would we be so ignorant as to shut our eyes at all times,
> when our rights, which we never did anything to forfeit, are
> denied us.[121]

As for the complaint of the brethern that the women did not speak up
sooner, it was because they had already spoken to the convener who
had omitted them from the notices of the meeting, and he assured
them that he would look into the matter of their attendance and
voting. Anthony sat down with a stab of sarcasm: "Since when
promise we have waited with all due subordination."[122]

In the congregational tradition, women usually attended the
church's business meetings but were without the rights of speech or
suffrage. Lutherans politely excused the women and children
whenever important business was about to arise. There are scattered
examples of churches enfranchising their women, usually prompted
by the monumental unfairness of requiring women to support a
minister without participating in his selection.[123] But in most cases
the closest that churches came to recognizing their women members

constitutionally was in allowing them to affix their names to church covenants and articles of faith, and not all did this.[124] In short, although theoretically the church franchise was no more or less democratic than the civil franchise, in actuality, given the overwhelming preponderance of women members, congregational elections were far more restrictive than political ones.

A few railed against these restrictions. In 1805 Eliza Dunlap appealed to the General Assembly the ruling of the Synod of New York and New Jersey that prohibited her from the "distinguishing privileges of our church."[125] Most women were content to build their own pockets of power through a vast network of societies and activities. Clearly, men held the decision-making positions, but they realized that they left women out of the decision-making process at their peril. This is why the notion of elevation through enfranchisement, which played such a prominent part in the debate over the civil franchise, was missing in the mid-nineteenth-century debates over giving women the church franchise. Their presence and power were already felt in the functions of church government. Quantifying such power defies ordinary standards of measurement, but everyone believed that it was there. For better or worse, wrote one aggrieved outsider in 1855:

> it is the women who are the tribunal of any question aside from politics or business. It is the women who give or uphold a literary reputation. It is the women who regulate the style of living, dispense hostilities, exclusively manage society, control clergymen and churches, regulate schemes of benevolence, patronize and influence the Arts, and pronounce upon Operas and foreign novelties.[126]

By the mid-nineteenth century, men had begun to feel twitches of guilt over a state of affairs where they held all the offices, but women did all the work. Elizabeth Wilson, writing at mid-century, estimated that women were enfranchised in half of the Presbyterian churches in the United States.[127] The prevailing, albeit "covertly expressed," sentiment in favor of women's ecclesiastical suffrage, if Wilson can be believed, ought not to obscure the fact that suffrage was granted not as a given right, but as an expression of the magnanimity and condescension of pastors and church officers. By the mid-1870s many of the major denominations had enfranchised their women,[128] although a few denominations, like the Disciples of Christ, sustained the opposition of their founders.[129] In sum, the majority of American church women did not have the power to vote or hold office in their local churches until the last third of the nineteenth century. If this is what we are to define as power, then clearly women did not have it.

But what if power is defined unofficially, in terms of judgment and accountability? That is an entirely different story, one that is illuminated by James D. Thompson's theory of "inner circles," and its adaptation to local churches by the sociologists James G. Houghland, Jr., and James R. Wood. Church policies as they develop do not necessarily follow the channels of church constitutions, and Houghland and Wood have demonstrated that churches have "unofficial centers of power." This was equally true in nineteenth-century America.[130] Women were without vote, but they were not without voice in religious matter. Sometimes voice dictated vote. The Methodist Church in Hingham, Massachusetts, had little trouble adjusting to having a woman run things when Anna Howard Shaw served as a student pastor there in 1877 because women had been unofficially running the church all along. It was standard practice during board meetings, before an important vote was taken, for someone to volunteer to poll the disenfranchised: "Hold on till I can go over and see Miss Cozneau."[131] When women spoke, the Methodist officers in Hingham believed, let all the earth keep silence before them.

Churches that operated under a call system, though they usually gave women no vote in selecting the pastor, were often careful to consult them. In the eighteenth century Virginia's Albermarle Baptist Church gave the sisters equal voting rights with the brothers. When the men were hopelessly divided over whether to call Andrew Tribble as pastor in 1777 and began looking elsewhere, the sisters raised such a river of rage and tears that the church was swept into calling him.[132] Pastors themselves were reluctant to accept or continue a call without a female vote of confidence. Abraham Camp, fresh out of Yale, showed his esteem for women's power. A unanimous call followed his probation sermon in 1773 at the First (Standing) Baptist Church in Middleborough, Massachusetts, but he refused to commit himself until the females in the congregation had been polled.[133] Henry Melchior Muhlenberg, who in 1746 organized the first permanent Lutheran synod in America, denied the women of his church the franchise. But when a dispute arose in 1762 over the extension of his call at Philadelphia's St. Michael's Church, he asked the women to participate in the ballot.[134]

Two examples from the nineteenth century reveal the accountability of pastors to women. At a party in Mobile, Alabama, the Scottish Presbyterian visitor George Lewis overheard some Presbyterian ladies talking about their pastor. When he discovered that they had helped to elect the pastor and exercised equal privileges in the church, he expressed his amazement. Huffily they informed him that if anyone was indispensable to the church, they were. Besides, who was better equipped to deal with the theological complexities inherent in a ministerial election? "We might have a Socinian one day, and a Universalist the next, for anything some of the gentlemen know or care."[135] Many a church lived to rue its failure to search the mind of its women. Many a pastor lived to regret having lost their patronage. His job depended on it. When Isaac Pardee, pastor of Wilmington's Trinity Episcopal Church, married Boadicea Bennett, daughter of Governor Caleb P. Bennett, in May 1834, he countermanded the advice of a prominent church woman. Phoebe George Bradford, wife of the *Delaware Gazette*'s editor, Moses Bradford, denounced the marriage as an "unholy alliance" and resolved to replace Pardee as her pastor. Within six months he was gone, and soon her candidate was hired.[136]

Even more powerful than the imposition of their will in ecclesiastical affairs was the psychological and institutional hold that women had over the clergy. These patterns of patronage deserve some exploration. Isabella Graham's 1797 donation to John Mitchell Mason's seminary may have been the first gift in the history of American theological education.[137] But the ties of accountability and deference that bound the clergy to women were characteristically more subtle. In countless communities across America, women provided the main religious stability in the midst of hit-and-run evangelism. They also proved to be in many cases the factotum of American Evangelical. Upon graduation from Lane Seminary in 1837, Henry Ward Beecher went to Lawrenceberg, Indiana, to pastor a twenty-member church, nineteen of whom were women. The call was extended by Martha Sawyer. "She collected the money, she was the treasurer, she was the manager, she was the trustee, she was the everything of that church."[138] Women were often the first converted, the first baptized, the first organized, the first to sponsor preachers, the first to start revivals, and the first to establish churches.

The first stirrings of Baptist and Methodist sentiment in America owed their existence to women. Lady Deborah Moody, an intractable woman of wealth, education, and independence, deserves equivalent standing with Roger Williams for pioneering Baptist views in the colonies. Williams's own short-lived Baptist views were inspired by the theological arguments of Anne Hutchinson's sister. In 1642, two years after Lady Moody purchased a plantation from an England-bound magistrate in Lynn, Massachusetts, she took a stand against infant baptism and succeeded in persuading some women in her Salem church to refrain from baptizing their children. Undaunted by ecclesiastical censure and public reproof, she moved to Long Island in 1643 and settled among the broadminded Dutch, taking many sympathizers with her but also, to the consternation of Massachusetts authorities, leaving many behind.[139] One of the women Lady Moody was accused of converting to Anabaptist views was Mrs. Eaton, wife of Connecticut's first governor, who stood at the head of the long succession of New Haven women that included Abigail Dorchester in the 1760s and Mrs. Wooster, who founded the Baptist cause in the city, in the early 1800s.[140] A search of Westmoreland County, Virginia, in 1783 would have unearthed only two Baptists, as would a similar census of Louisa County in 1788, and both stray pairs were women—women who acted as true "Mothers in Israel" in their bold hospitality amid hostility and opposition.[141] Partly as a result of their patronage, Baptists had become a major presence in Virginia by 1800.

Methodism began in America under Barbara Heck's patronage, and numerous other Barbara Hecks ushered it to a front seat in American religious life in the nineteenth century. The first Methodist class, formed in 1789 on the first circuit in New England, was composed of three women, Mary Wells, Ruth Hall, and Mrs. Risley. The reluctant doors of Vermont were openned to Methodism through the strong patronage and tireless evangelism of Mrs. Peckett, a former housekeeper to John Wesley and a "band-mate" of Mary Fletcher. In Long Island, Mrs. Azuba Wicks, Mrs. More, and a praying band of females planted the seeds of Methodism in the late eighteenth century, long before Methodist itinerants arrived to reap the harvest. Lucy Walker Wentworth, the Barbara Heck of the West, sponsored Methodism in Chicago. The wife of a tavernkeeper, Wentworth singlehandedly rounded up congregations to hear the itinerant preacher William See, scheduled appointments for him at her home, and formed with three of her children the first class meeting in Chicago. The wife of a Methodist blacksmith in Chatham, Ohio, began a revival in her home that swept through the entire town.[142]

The debt clergy owed to women is graphically illustrated in the vast network of female patronage accorded Francis Asbury. Methodists in England were accustomed to the patronage of "Mothers in Israel,"[143] but the experiences of Asbury and his Methodist preachers support the assertion of a European traveler that American women of wealth collected itinerants as fashionable Frenchwomen collected literary artists.[144] When in upstate New York, for example, Asbury had the pleasant option of staying with either the Livingstons or the Van Cortlandts. Joanna Livingston Van Cortlandt, wife of the New York's long-standing lieutenant governor, kept a "prophet's chamber" in Van Cortlandt Manor, her estate, and built Asbury a Methodist chapel.[145] Margaret Beehman and her husband, Judge Robert R. Livingston also extended to Asbury a standing invitation to stay at their estate. The Methodist itinerant Freeborn Garrettson's wife, Catharine Livingston, a daughter of the New York Livingston dynasty, turned Rhinebeck (or Wildercliffe), her magnificent estate overlooking the Hudson, into a resting place for restless itinerants like her husband. In sheeted poster beds in rooms filled with art treasures slept the smelly, rain-washed, coarse-grained men who traveled the circuits from Canada to the Carolinas in their round-breasted coats and wide-brimmed fur hats, some as big as a parasol.[146] In western New York Eleanor Dorsey, wife of Judge Dorsey of Lyons, entertained the organizing session of the Genesee Conference in 1810 as well as two other conference sessions, catering for up to thirty preachers at once. Asbury had a home in New York City at the residence of Ann Grise, where his most famous portrait was taken.[147]

Mary White, the wife of a wealthy judge in Delaware, made their mansion a preaching place on the southern Methodist circuit and an asylum for itinerants. She hid in her house Asbury and other Methodist preachers hunted by authorities suspicious of their Tory sympathies; the Whites' association with the presumably disloyal Methodist eventually led to the judge's seizure and imprisonment.[148] It was at the Whites' home that Asbury first met Ann and Richard Bassett, a couple who did much to promote the impression that sponsoring Methodism was a cult of the cultivated. Their three homes, especially the 18,000-acre estate called Bohemia Manor, served double duty as Methodist hotels. Here Methodist preachers came to eat, to rest, and to die.[149] The Maryland equivalent of Bohemia Manor was a vast estate on Maryland's western shore called Perry Hall, a second home to Asbury and the living quarters of Asbury, Coke, Whatcoat, Vesey, and others while they prepared for the Christmas Conference in 1784. At first the fabulously wealthy Henry Dorsey Gough, who married Governor Ridgely's daughter, Prudence, forbade his wife to even listen to Methodist preachers. But eventually he joined his wife as a devout convert, and they built at Perry Hall a chapel with the first bell heard in an American Methodist church. Every morning and evening it rang, summoning to worship the Gough family and servants, a congregation of over a hundred people. It summoned annual conferences as well.[150]

Farther south Asbury enjoyed the hospitality of Patrick Henry's sister, the wife of General William Russell of the Continental army. If any itinerant passed through the Holston River Valley and did not stay in the home of Elizabeth Henry Campbell Russell, it was through no fault of hers.[151] Out west in Ohio, Asbury's home was in the house of Mrs. Edward Tiffin, wife of Ohio's first governor, or in the more humble dwelling of Jane Trimble, whose son would later become the state's governor.

The financial dimension of female patronage can be seen in Asbury's friendship with Rebecca Dorsey Ridgely, wife of the sea captain, planter, builder, and politician Charles Ridgely. Rebecca supplemented Asbury's annual salary of $150 with periodic outpourings of affection. Since she could not have children, Asbury told her, he would become her "almsgiver" son, and the poor she helped would be her "adopted children." At least in the extant letters, Asbury never asked for money directly, but his pleas for support were only thinly veiled. After describing the crying needs of Methodism, he wrote," Oh, mamma, Let not your company, nor Cattle, keep you from Christ: Your Houses and Lands. God has blessed you, only acknowledge God in your house. In Domestick life you have commanded thousands of your own, and other Families. Be regular, and fervent, in your returns of duty."[152] The accountability Asbury felt toward her is suggested by the fact that he sent her annual minutes and personal progress reports on the growth of Methodism.[153]

All these "Shunammites" of Methodism had their counterparts in other traditions. The Presbyterians, for example, had Paulina Read, later Paulina LeGrand, whose massive estate in Charlotte

County, Virginia, known as "Retirement," constantly sheltered preachers and, indeed, whole presbyteries.[154]

Through Dorcas societies even women who were not wealthy had become financial sponsors of the clergy, at first indirectly, as auxiliaries to state or regional voluntary associations, and then directly, as their employers. In fact, many of the first missionaries to labor in the western states were sent there or supported by women's missionary societies.[155] The women of the Boston Baptist Female Education Society outlined in their 1818 annual report the qualities they were looking for in candidates for scholarship money.[156] Both coming and going, many revivalists were held accountable to women. Their first salaries were paid by missionary societies; invitations to conduct services contained such key phrases as "the Elders of the church and the leading females here are very anxious for your coming"; their services were infiltrated by female spies like Catherine Huntington Williams, who accompanied her pastor in reconnoitering a Finney revival to determine its worthiness of patronage; and if perchance the passions aroused during a revival were those not of worship but of wrath, it was often the women who formed an angry hornet's nest bent on revenge.[157]

Women began to direct and criticize the clergy with social impunity in the eighteenth century. John Adams did not think it indecorous of his wife to instruct her minister to preach up the colonial cause.[158] Evangelical women of the nineteenth century judged their pastors as they never had before.[159] When women's societies liked an address given at their annual meeting or commissioned by them, they often requested its publication.[160] When they were unimpressed by the message delivered and the method of delivery, they let the minister know it. Page Putnam Miller has shown that women's sponsorship of speeches and sermons was really a two-way street: clergymen got their sermons published, and women got clerical recognition for their societies and activities.[161] The "Apostle of New England," Jesse Lee, found out how censorious women could be when he preached in Fairfield, Connecticut. The women of the town complained that he preached so loudly that he made their heads ache. Since it was no longer possible to banish critical females, Lee's response was a prayer asking God to help him hereafter to speak so as to make their hearts ache."[162]

Evangelical clergy in settled churches had to get used to pious women who evaluated their calling, criticized their ministry, and sometimes stood up against them.[163] There were those who had difficulty adjusting. Calvin Colton gave as one reason for abandoning the Presbyterian fold for the Episcopal church in the 1830s the periodic "visitations from women to instruct [the pastor] in his duty" that characterized the congregational system.[164] But most clergymen learned to accommodate themselves to pressure from their wives and other women; some even agreed to serve on a Board of Counsel after submitting to an election by the women's Board of Managers. In Cincinnati advertisements for female meetings were dutifully read in all the churches of the city. And in most cities Evangelical clergymen complied with the request of the women's charitable organization to preach an annual charity sermon in aid of its funds.[165] Such accommodation reached comic proportions later in the century, in 1875, when the clergy of Buffalo, after having had their arms twisted by the Women's Branch of the Society for the Prevention of Cruelty to Animals, agreed to preach one sermon a year in support of the organization.[166] It was before this backdrop that a nineteenth-century writer claimed:

> Expel women as you will, she is in fact the parish. Within, in her lowest spiritual form, as the ruling spirit she inspires, and sometimes writes the sermons. Without, as the bulk of his congregation, she watches over his orthodoxy, verifies his texts, visits his schools, and harasses his sick. . . . The preacher who thunders so defiantly against spiritual foes, is trembling all the time beneath the critical eye that is watching him with so merciless an accuracy of his texts. Impelled, guided, censured by women, we can hardly wonder if, in nine cases out of ten, the parson turns woman himself, and the usurpation of woman's rights in the services of religion has been deftly avenged by the subjugation of the usurpers. Expelled from the temple, woman has simply put her priesthood into commission, and discharges her ministerial duties by proxy.[167]

Relations with women were matters of professional life and death for both revivalists and settled clergy. Revivalists quickly realized that they would survive and succeed only through a partnership in ministry with women. Success as a revivalist in antebellum America was defined in terms of the number of revival notices and noses one could count. Evangelical clergy came to respect, and the Universalist clergy to imitate the ability of "Limitarians" or "Particularists" to draw youth to revivals and new members away from other religious traditions, and their secret was the "well-directed energies of some half-dozen active and zealous females who form societies."[168]

There is another form of power, the power of economics. When this is taken into consideration, women again appear far from weak. Widows, with whom Francis Asbury spent inordinate amounts of time, were the primary source of endowments for the early Methodist churches. The story of the loaves and fishes is the only suitable analogy for the incredible ingenuity of women in multiplying their pin money until it filled the benevolence baskets of the churches. State missionary societies were often little more than clearinghouses for the funds received from female auxiliaries. The New York Female Missionary Society of the Western District, which sent out six of its own missionaries, raised the incredible sum of $2,000 in 1818 from forty-six towns and villages in ten counties.[169] The fairs, bees, suppers, and bazaars sponsored by women not uncommonly raised substantial amounts of money, which was used to supplement pew rents, furnish the church and parsonage, fund benevolent projects, or build new churches, with women carrying stones in their aprons and even pitching in at the construction itself.[170] Women were the expert fund raisers of the nineteenth century, and their societies were the backbones of religious philanthropy. The money-making power could translate into wonder-working power was not lost on them.

Nor were women afraid to throw their weight around to get what they wanted. Emboldened with the self-confidence and experience gained from gender groups, women can be found approaching public and political figures with requests and recommendations and appealing to women's societies for support. Catharine Beecher lobbied for assistance in sending female teachers to the West, and later in the century the women missionaries and teachers themselves would make personal appearances before women's societies. Emma Willard petitioned the New York state legislature, and in the early 1830s Sarah L. Huntington overcame various political roadblocks to squeeze $900 out of the Connecticut legislature for an educational project: "I am the more encouraged in the pursuance of my determination, from the fact, that my own sex are sometimes successful in the cause of humanity, while others are 'turned empty away.'"[171] The notion that women were content to use their power indirectly, either through their children or through their husbands is simply not substantiated by a study of Evangelical women in the nineteenth century. These were women who used their influence indirectly and directly—but always collectively. That women's societies, with all this power, did not clamor harder, more impatiently, for administrative, legislative, and juridical power as well may perhaps be partly due to the fact that they became entangled in their own networks of power, trapped by their own success, afraid to jeopardize what they perceived to be de facto hegemony for de jure equality. Wendell Phillips couched his support for women's suffrage in precisely these terms.

> I do not ignore the power of woman; it is too great. I want it lessened. I am not going to give the sex anymore influence; I am going to diminish it. Her influence is hidden and all but omnipotent. Uneducated and irresponsible, it is terrible. I want it dragged to the light of day; I want it measured and labelled; I want it counted and criticized; I want it educated and put on record; I want to be able to find it and indict it, which I cannot do today.[172]

• Chapter Seven •

"Satisfied with Favor"

Elizabeth Finney and the Partner Model

> The revival of this age, as well as of every other age, has
> been marked by this endowment, and the labours of such pious
> and talented ladies as Mrs. Palmer, Mrs. Finney, Mrs. Wight-
> man, Miss Marsh, with numberless other Marys and Phoebes,
> have contributed in no small degree to its extension and power.
>
> Catherine Mumford Booth

"Many say, 'Mrs. Finney, *your mission* to England is almost if not *quite* as important as that of your husband's,' and I really feel that God has opened to me a wide and I trust an effectual door of influence." Elizabeth Atkinson Finney, Charles's second wife, thus described to a Rochester friend her perception of her labors during Finney's first English revivals.[1] Charles G. Finney knew, as Lorenzo Dow before him and Dwight L. Moody after him, that successful transatlantic labors were necessary before American Evangelicalism's highest honors would be bestowed upon his ministry.[2] What Finney did not know when he and Elizabeth set sail for England was that she also had embarked on a compelling odyssey of confirmation. In England she would find validation for her expanding sense of being an integral part of a team ministry with her husband. Elizabeth believed just as strongly as her husband that converts baptized one's ministry, and the balmy reception awarded her "Ladies' Meetings" sanctioned her labors existentially just as Finney's acceptance in England as an established theologian as well as a glamorized revivalist sanctioned his ministry ecclesiastically. The English revival of 1849–1851 meant that henceforth the eyes of the American ecclesiastical community gazed on Finney as the brightest star in the Evangelical firmament. For Elizabeth, the English revival meant that what she called "my work" in "woman's mission" was henceforth acceptable and anointed, both in her own view and that of her husband.[3] But whereas Finney returned to find that American pastors who had growled at sharing their pulpits with him were now scrambling for his services, Elizabeth returned to neglect from the American press.

Lydia Andrews Finney and Elizabeth Atkinson Finney were as different as a Schubert symphony and a Beethoven concerto. Whereas Lydia, as John Randolph once said of Martin Van Buren, rowed to an object with muffled oars, Elizabeth was more likely to splash furiously. While Elizabeth fastened her eyes on the shere appropriate to a woman, every stroke of her oar took her in the opposite direction. Lydia was reserved, humble, and unobtrusive, plagued by a negative self-image, depression, and "weak nerves." Elizabeth had a highly developed sense of self; she was supremely confident and poised, plucky in demeanor, and witty in speech, and her wise, cheerful face masked an iron resolve. Lydia's religious pilgrimage was marked by mountain highs and valley lows, seasons of sedate assurance and tormented questioning. Security of salvation did not come to her until after the move to Oberlin, and sanctification some time later. Elizabeth's faith was just the opposite of Lydia's "mild, unobtrusive and calm type," as Finney called it. Elizabeth was always secure in her faith, and her "consistent," "sober," "rational" walk with God prompted Finney to exclaim, "I never saw a more uniform Christian."[4] Visitors to the Oberlin home of Charles and Elizabeth came away appreciative of the "spiritual intercourse" they shared there, not just with Charles, but also with Elizabeth.[5]

Less constrained by cultural presumptions and pressures, less fearful of transgressing social boundaries, Elizabeth crafted a public woman's mission without allowing men to realize just how public it had become. In public speaking, Lydia was faltering, Elizabeth fearless. Lydia shrank from public duties, preferring to work behind the scenes with small groups of women in causes within woman's traditional province. While she enlarged the duties of a minister's wife and presented an image of energetic usefulness to a generation of Evangelical women, Lydia did so within a conventional sexrole.

Like Lydia, Elizabeth began her work with mothers, children, and other womanly concerns. She did not embrace female societies, however, though she dutifully became Lydia's successor as a leader in the Oberlin Maternal Association and the Oberlin Moral Reform Society. Elizabeth's mind was elsewhere for three reasons, historical, sociological, and psychological. First, maternal associations and moral reform societies, as a national phenomenon, were burning themselves out by the 1840s. Second, the vacillating membership patterns of both societies seem to reflect their status as a function of revivals. When revivals seized the Oberlin community, membership swelled in women's groups; but by the time Elizabeth arrived in Oberlin, revivals were becoming less and less frequent. It is true that moral reform elicited more of Elizabeth's interest and involvement than any other cause, but by the time of her election as president in 1849 and again in 1851, the vitality of the society had clearly drooped, and she found herself addressing a dwindling circle of females.[6] Third, the female friendships so important to Lydia were not cultivated with the same lavish care by Elizabeth. Her ego gratification derived not from small, intimate circles of which she was the first among equals, but from large, formal groups of which she was the center.

Lydia built small, cozy fires that invited other women to sit up close and keep each other warm. Elizabeth built huge bonfires that drew and dazzled vast crowds but forced people to keep their distance. Promoting a more openly public role for the minister's wife, Elizabeth supplemented her lectures to small groups of women with the performances she clearly relished most: addresses to mass audiences, mostly female, but sometimes including males as well. Elizabeth was most alive when she was preaching. Lydia felt most secure as convener of an ensemble, and she was a reluctant conductor; Elizabeth thrived on solo work. Lydia worked closely with the churches that were sponsoring her husband's revivals. Elizabeth both struck out more on her own and integrated her efforts more fully with her husband's. Lydia's sentiments regarding religious careers for women were identical to those of an Oberlin professor who wrote to Lucy Stone's brother, Rev. William Stone: "If Antoinette [Brown] will be a Mrs. Sigourney, a Mrs. Ellis, or a Mrs. Ingraham, I will say Amen, most heartily, but if she tried to be a Finney or a Webster, I must say Alas! I hope she has too much sense to choose the latter course."[7] Elizabeth, on the other hand, encouraged the ambitions of both Stone and Brown, and further, she espoused a self-conscious, religious feminism based on the scriptural support for women's equality and believed it her mission to challenge women to open their lips and pray, even preach in public. The contrast between Lydia and Elizabeth reveals the transition from the Assistant to the Partner, virtually an equal participant in ministry.

I

Elizabeth Ford Atkinson was the schoolteacher widow of William Atkinson, one of Rochester's pioneer settlers, a prosperous merchant miller on the east side of the Genesee River and a Masonic-Episcopalian partner in Josiah Bissell's predominantly anti-Masonic Presbyterian venture in Sabbath-keeping transportation, the ill-fated stage and boat "Pioneer Line." The Atkinsons were among the most active Episcopalian couples in the city. Elizabeth's husband served on the incorporating vestry of St. Luke's Episcopal Church in 1817, was elected warden yearly from 1820 to 1827, and spearheaded with her the 1827 project to build a sister congregation, St. Paul's Episcopal Church, for those living on the east side of the river. Along with twelve other communicants from St. Luke's, William and Elizabeth transferred to the mission church in May 1827, at which time William was elected to serve with Giles Boulton as the church's first wardens. On a lot which she and William originally owned, and with a $2,000 mortgage to the Atkinsons, St. Paul's Gothic structure was consecrated on 20 August 1830.[8]

From its very inception the Atkinsons sought to open the doors of St. Paul's to the new breezes of the spirit that were wafting their way throughout the burned-over district but seemed unwelcome in the parish district of St. Luke's. This was one of the reasons why St. Paul's founding vestry approached the Princeton-educated Charles Pettit McIlvaine to be its first pastor, an invitation that so alarmed St. Luke's vestry that it sent a distress signal to Brooklyn's prominent priest (and later bishop) Henry U. Onderdonk. Angered by the inroads made by low churchmen, Onderdonk took it upon himself to warn St. Paul's that McIlvaine was a "half-churchman, a zealous promoter of schemes that would blend us with Presbyterians." Admitting that McIlvaine possessed superb preaching skills, Onderdonk nevertheless contended that preaching "certainly is but the lesser half of a *pastor's* qualifications."[9] The Atkinsons could not have agreed less, which is why they zealously promoted Finney's first Rochester revival. Affirming the importance of the laity by dressing not in the clerical garb of the day but in a gray business suit, Finney was never known for preaching good sermons in the conventional sense of the term—sermons that went over a person's head and hit a neighbor. Finney let fly with unpardonable accuracy sermons that stung the soul, seared the mind, bit at the heart, and, in Rochester at least, literally brought down the rafters. In October 1830 the weight of the multitudes crowded into the First Presbyterian Church to hear Finney preach caused the ceiling to collapse and the people to panic as they jumped from the galleries to safety. Given St. Paul's identification with Finney's new measures, it surprised no one that the vestry invited the Presbyterians to worship in their sanctuary during repairs to the structure. The Atkinson's affection and respect for Finney were unshakable, enduring even Finney's embarrassment of Elizabeth's foppish brother Hobart Ford, whom Finney hailed from the pulpit as the evening congregation stood to leave: "Mr. Ford, have you given your heart to God? You are too proud! too proud!"[10]

For reasons that are not clear, it came to pass that Elizabeth expanded her course offerings in June 1841, moved to the northern part of the city near the Lower falls, and opened the Atkinson Female Seminary. Perhaps the financial panic of 1837 led to financial reverses in William's milling business and caused him to embark on a new career as a land agent and Elizabeth to throw more of her energies into teaching, or perhaps competition from the public schools threatened the enrollment in her select school. Rochester was noteworthy in that a higher proportion of its females attended school than males, and the Atkinsons were connected to two of the four seminaries in the city: Elizabeth ran one, and, according to the Rochester directory, William served as secretary of another, the Rochester Seminary, a public school that specialized in training teachers and clergy and included a female department. Elizabeth's venture was aided considerably by two endorsements: the local newspaper testified to her competence ("The high character of Mrs. Atkinson is a sufficient guarantee that the Institution will be all that could be desired for the education of young ladies"), and Lydia Finney's close friend Sarah Seward, forced by ill-health to close her seminary just as Elizabeth's opened, paid public tribute to the new enterprise.[11] By April 1842 it appears that Elizabeth had moved once again to larger quarters, for she advertised for more female boarders and day scholars at a new address.[12] The prestige of her seminary, her activities as a member of the State Street Congregational Church, and her unremitting solicitations of subscriptions for the *Oberlin Evangelist*, wherein she encouraged her friends and pupils to study Finney's views of Christian perfection, made her a prominent disciple in a city that boasted more of Finney's spiritual children than perhaps any other. An 1843 typhoid epidemic, which forced Elizabeth to bury two daughters next to four sons she had lost earlier, took her fifty-three-year-old husband's life as well.

On 13 November 1848 the "precious promises" of singular influence that God made to Elizabeth after the death of her husband began to be fulfilled.[13] For on that day, President Asa Mahan of Oberlin presided at the marriage ceremony in Akron, Ohio, of forty-nine-year-old Elizabeth and fifty-six-year-old Charles. Little is known of the circumstances that ushered these two people into what Finney once labeled a "dangerously happy" relationship except that Finney admitted after her death that he had not sought her, but that God had "sent her to me in a remarkable manner."[14] During their brief courtship, in order to stave off any semblance of impropriety, Finney's daughter Helen addressed his letters to Elizabeth while Elizabeth in turn adressed her letters to Helen.[15] The Oberlin community gasped in shock when Finney arrived with his new wife, but their hearts were soon melted at the afternoon service on Thanksgiving Day, when Finney burst into tears while introducing his unblushing bride, pointing out the depth of his loneliness and the agonizing difficulty he faced in raising a family alone.[16] Oberlin was happy for Finney, most happy for the children, and reservedly curious about the new wife.

Finney once offered his own personal evaluation of Elizabeth's importance to his ministry: "She accompanies me," he explained in response to a plaintive request for his services, "and holds meetings with the females and gets them into the work. Her meetings often become large, and one of the most important instrumentalities in the promotion of a revival."[17] Elizabeth's labors became Finney's guarantee that there would always be an adequate pool of those praying women on whom he depended to undergird his revivals. "We have no trouble now to find the praying women," she wrote.[18] Within a year of their marriage, the Finneys arrived in England for what would be, according to the historian of transatlantic revivalism Richard Carwardine, "the first occasion when a revivalist with an established reputation in both countries had arrived to do more than adorn conventions or repair damaged health."[19] At first Elizabeth hesitated to assert herself through public speaking during these revivals, which Finney likened to the ones he conducted at the beginning of his career.[20] It may be that pulmonary problems, serious enough to prompt a concerned son-in-law to warn that unless Finney sent Elizabeth home he would be signing her death certificate, prevented the employment of her services.[21] Entrenched British prejudice against public speaking by women may also have played a part. It is more likely, though, that Finney's winter campaign was a stacatto affair, jumping from one backwater British town to another as the

Finneys moved from the home of one wealthy patron to another, and therefore not permitting the continuity Elizabeth needed to establish her novel meetings.[22]

Elizabeth's sustained, public involvement in Finney's revival labors dates from his nine-month campaign at London's Moorfields Tabernacle, a metropolitan church where a century earlier George Whitefield, "the Great Awakener," had conducted his services. Elizabeth did some "awakening" herself, for shortly after Finney began preaching in the pulpit of the prominent Congregationalist pastor and editor John Campbell, she initiated daily female prayer meetings. At first only two turned out, reflecting the low state of piety in England's metropolitan, manufacturing centers uncovered by the great religious census of 1851, which found fewer than one person in ten occupying a pew on Sunday morning—and this even after the Finneys successful revival labors.[23] But the longer Elizabeth labored, the more people "prized her worth and were stimulated by her zeal," until eventually she found herself presiding each morning over a meeting of forty or more women. "Many that never opened their mouth in public prayer," Elizabeth was thrilled to report, "can do it then, for their own comfort and the edification of those present."[24] The remaining hours of the day Elizabeth filled with speaking engagements to temperance societies, ragged and private schools, and tea meetings, as well as numerous addresses to mothers, poor women, and other congregations, where men were often in attendance. The measure of London Tabernacle's estimation of Elizabeth was fully evident in the valedictory tea given in the Finneys' honor at the Royal British Institution. Elizabeth was celebrated by the 600 people present, in the words of the *British Banner*, as "a woman of wholly kindered spirit with her husband; she sees everything in the same light, estimates all matters by the same standards, and by the same means seeks the same ends." The love and respect that enveloped Elizabeth this evening was due not to her position as consort to the great Charles G. Finney, but to her "own personal worth." John Campbell focused on this equality of esteem when, after paying tribute to Finney's services, he turned to Elizabeth and said, "My dear friend, will you permit me to beg that you will apply to yourself what has just been uttered respecting your husband." Presenting her with a copy of Ingram Cobbin's enormously popular *Commentary on the Bible*, Dr. Campbell explained why the inscription her gift bore was an exact counterpart of that placed on her husband's gift of an English hexapla:

> As every way one, you cannot be separated, and assuredly it is not the wish or intention of those whom I now represent to attempt it. But although one, you have your distinct personal identities, attributes, characters, and claims. I have, then, to assure you, on their behalf, you are highly esteemed not simply for your husband's role, but for your own.[25]

Elizabeth's London legacy was a lasting one. The prayer meetings she founded were sustained even after her departure in the spring of 1851. Elizabeth maintained a link with the congregation at Tabernacle House by sending them a copy of an as yet undiscovered journal she had written during the return sea voyage, a manuscript that was widely circulated and deemed profitable and "interesting."[26] Indeed, Elizabeth had placed the stamp of her personality so forcefully on Campbell's congregation that two years after the revival he marveled at how people still "think of her, often talk to her and always with respect and pleasure." In a judgment that some considered too modest, he concluded, "She raised for herself amongst us 'a good degree and great boldness in the faith.'"[27]

After the London revivals it is perhaps inappropriate to speak of "Finney's labors"—it was now "the Finneys' labors." At least Henry Ward Beecher thought so when he sent greetings to Elizabeth from Liverpool.[28] In fact, Charles and Elizabeth Finney were, if not a clerical couple, at least one of the closest things to one in the nineteenth century. Upon her return to America, Elizabeth's personal battle against the battering of women by social definitions of inferiority and unworthiness began to absorb all her time and energies. During their Syracuse tour Finney took to writing to the children on her behalf. "Your mother has an important meeting with the Ladies and cannot write now," he explained to his daughters concerning her efforts at the First Presbyterian Church to awaken slumbering women from a variety of religious traditions to their full leadership potential. A month and a half later he apologized once again: "Your mother is well, . . . but can not yet [find?] time to write to you." It appears though, that she took the time to ask the girls, through Finney, to tell Mrs. Rosebrough that "the Ladies' Meetings are daily increasing in numbers. I miss her very much in making them interesting."[29] The story was the same in Hartford, Rochester, and a year later in their first Boston crusade.[30]

By January 1857, the beginning of Finney's *annus mirabilis* holiness crusade in Boston, Elizabeth had perfected a style of ministry that both allowed her an independent arena for her talents and permitted her to work in tandem with her husband until he became dependent on her services as a primer for his revivals. The day after Elizabeth arrived in Boston (Charles had already been there for a couple of days), their joint ministry got under way. She began her visiting, rounding up women for daily prayer meetings that would eventually overflow the halls in which they met. "These meetings became so crowded," Finney wrote in his autobiography, "that the ladies would fill the room, and then stand about the door on the outside, as far as they could hear on every side."[31] Some things had not changed. Finney was still writing the letters to the children: "Your mother is just come in from one of her prayer meetings. She will write when she has time." Some things had gotten worse, as Finney revealed with some exasperation in a letter to his daughter Julia: "Your mother is gone almost constantly. This morning before 11 o'clock she had gone to the third meeting."[32] Elizabeth's work, though ignored by the religious press, won for her scores of friends and loyal followers in the Boston area. Her female prayer meetings, her lectures to mothers, her sessions with children, made her labors, as one obituary startlingly admitted, "scarcely less memorable than Mr. Finney's preaching in Park Street Church."[33] On their departure from Boston in late April 1857, a thanksgiving gift of $1,500 was presented to both Charles and Elizabeth Finney.[34]

II

The team approach to mass evangelism developed by the Finneys manifested itself most clearly in the British phase of what some historians have called the "Third Great Awakening." Indeed, in view of the visibility of Phoebe and Walter Palmer, Catherine and William Booth, and Elizabeth and Charles Finney, it is amazing that historians have overlooked this dimension to the history of the transatlantic revivals of 1857–1860.[35] Horace Bushnell did not overlook it when he composed a letter of recommendation introducing Finney to the ministers in England, for he included paragraph endorsing Elizabeth's activities.[36] Catherine Booth did not overlook it when she attacked the crumbling cliches about women's place in Arthur

Augustus Rees's violent pamphlet denouncing Phoebe Palmer for preaching the gospel.[37] Many British contemporaries of the Finneys did not overlook it; they issued invitations to both Charles and Elizabeth to come and labor in their communities. Sometimes the invitation to Elizabeth was presented in the form of a tempting challenge: "The females are trying to begin a female prayer meeting. They act slowly. I think Mrs. Finney would soon bring them together."[38] Sometimes the pastor soliciting their services would blandish Elizabeth with tributes to her talents or present her, as George Redford of Worchester did, with the names of a couple eager to serve as her assistants in the work of women's outreach. Sometimes the overture came directly from the ladies themselves, in letters or by word of mouth.[39] All these people knew that one of the surest ways to get the Finneys to conduct a revival in their town was to mention Elizabeth's work approvingly.

The importance of Elizabeth's labors was also not overlooked by those expressing gratitude in the aftermath of a Finney revival. Although few of these thank-you notes have survived, it is unlikely that the deacons of Angel Street Church in Worcester, England, were atypical in thanking the Finneys for their "united services" and singling out Elizabeth's "valuable" and "precious" leadership.[40] Finney himself was not unaware of the importance of this shift in his style of evangelism. His estimation of Elizabeth was evident in more than just the displacement of the vertical pronoun by the federal "we" in his references to revival activities. Between them there existed a deep feeling of equal partnership and joint ministry, developed through times of success, frustration, suffering, and exhaustion. "The females will hang for any length of time upon every word that my wife can say to them, and while I have power to speak a mixed congregation will sit to hear me."[41]

Not surprisingly, Elizabeth came to exhibit the same monomania about revivals and the same martyr complex that characterized her husband's ministry. "Your mother's hands as well as my own are full of labors," Charles wrote to his children during the first English revival. Both riveted all their resources on the revival until they were utterly oblivious to the beauty of their surroundings, the sights of London, or the enjoyment of new friendships and readings.[42] Relentlessly driving themselves and each other beyond the limits of physical endurance, they sympathized with each other in their joint exhaustion, although clearly each relished the seraphic state of being weary in well-doing. If anything, Elizabeth outdid her husband in courting martyrdom. "My dear wife has already overdone her strength," Charles confided to his colleague Henry Cowles from London. "She has been laid up for several days. She cannot be restrained when the people are anxious to hear. I really fear that she will kill herself outright."[43] Others shared his fear and begged him strongly to intervene, but headstrong Elizabeth persisted in her belief that she had discovered the ultimate prescription for any illness, especially in women: work, and more work, which would "exercise the body and occupy the mind."[44]

For her part, Elizabeth's passion for evangelistic employment was sometimes cramped and frustrated by her husband's physical and emotional prostrations, in particular by a prolonged period during 1861 of severe depression and spiritual doubting ("nervous despondency" Finney called it). It caused her to be as inattentive at times to her husband's ailments as to her own. "She longs so much to be in the work that she would risk a good deal," Finney wrote to an Ohio pastor, speaking of his fear that his own impaired health would be seriously jeopardized if he yielded to Elizabeth's yearnings and agreed to labor in Middletown.[45] During the Bolton revival in March 1860, Finney informed his wife as she walked into the study after a morning meeting that the doctor had just warned him that if he refused to backout of conducting services at the Manchester Exchange, he just might die in the pulpit. Gazing into the pale and drawn face of his jaded wife, he asked, "If I do, what will you say dear?" "Mrs. Finney placed both hands on his shoulders, looked him right in the face, and in a solemn, impressive tone replied, 'I shall say, Rest, warrior, rest, thy warfare's ended!'"[46]

If Finney thought of himself as "the Brigadier General of Jesus Christ,"[47] some thought of Elizabeth as the Brigadier General's commanding officer. This perception was passionately denied by Elizabeth herself.[48] Her reputation as the one who ran the show, however, was enhanced by her role in the controversy that developed over whether Finney should schedule a return engagement in England. It is a story worth telling in some detail, for it contradicts the standard portrait of Finney as a steely-eyed, indomitable personality who, if his autobiography is to believed, fought singlehandedly in the mighty work of revival.[49] The episode speaks volumes about his insecurity, his indecisiveness, his dependence on his wife's judgment, and his profound respect for her calling. It also reveals clearly the granite determination and confidence of this formadable woman. Finney thus appears naked in his humanity, which perhaps explains why the story was not in his told *Memoirs.* Here he was weak and vacillating, buffeted about by popular opinion and frightful anxieties. Only his wife's ballast steadied their course.

Ever since their return in 1851, Elizabeth harbored the conviction that "our work in England was an unfinished work." A couple of times they tottered on the brink of deciding to return, and in the fall of 1857 Elizabeth tried to lure Finney across the ocean, ostensibly for his health.[50] At first her efforts were to no avail, but pressure from English friends like Potto Brown and from Elizabeth herself mounted until, during the Boston revival in the spring of 1858, Finney weakened. A rejuvenated Finney, flushed with victory at the peak of his Boston efforts, gave Elizabeth an opening by asking her to make the prospect of a second visit to England a subject of prayer. Elizabeth had already received "indications of his [God's] will that I thought I could not mistake," but she did as Finney requested. She "came to God for direction, but . . . made preparations for going." At the last moment, however, Finney balked. The Oberlin community presented a united front against their plans, and, as Finney explained to Elizabeth, had marshalled compelling objections to any travel away from Oberlin at this time. Perturbed by her husband's about-face, she was even more incensed when she learned of a remark made to Finney by a Mr. Clark: "Everybody thinks you are so under influence of your wife that if she says go to England you go, if she says go to Boston you go."[51] An enraged Elizabeth, after informing her husband that "God had shown me it was of little consequence if God was the director of our steps, whether the direction came through him or myself," angrily resolved to say nothing further about the trip. "I left him the 1st of November," Elizabeth jotted down in her journal, and she went to visit relatives, soothing her spirits with the knowledge that Finney would be the responsible party before God for their negligence of England and privately relieved at her escape from a dangerous winter voyage. After a two-week absence, "I returned quietly," Elizabeth continued, but "the next day after my return God called me to my account for my want of faithfulness, and my own conviction of duty." Called of God to minister in England, Elizabeth determined to drag her husband there if need be. Thus she dug in her heels, and braced herself for a tug of war with the entire Oberlin community. Finney expressed the essence of the situation more poetically: "We had come to the place where two seas meet."[52]

Unfortunately, Elizabeth's popularity was a casualty of the collision.[53] Blamed for being "ambitious," "self-willed," and "dominating," she nevertheless stood defiant in pleading for "England's woes." Finney fueled the flames that lashed out at his wife by admitting publicly that he did not feel the call as his wife did and that he often found himself listening to her more than to God, although Elizabeth contended that "when he was alone uninfluenced by others he saw things differently." Swaying in the breezes, Finney was blown in Elizabeth's direction by his love for her and his respect for her call and in the other direction by the imputation that "this is Mrs. Finney's doing." Prayer meetings were used to get Finney to stay, as were raillery and abuse from the faculty, students, and townspeople who reproached him for his pitiful dependence on his wife and fitful neglect of his health and pressing duties at home. In Elizabeth's own prayer circle, only one woman supported her position. Fortified by the words that came to her, "In thy light shall we see light," Elizabeth's vision of God's will enabled her to withstand enormous pressures and personal abuse from the people who told Finney that "if we went, it would be because of my influence," or that "if we went I should be punished" and Finney would fail.

For weeks Finney lived on a see-saw, one moment tilting toward his wife, and siding with everyone else the next moment after, as she put it, "his heart failed him." On 14 December he asked Elizabeth once more:

> Is your mind clear as to the duty of going to England? I replied, Yes. . . . Well, we will go then. He went out to make the necessary preparations. As soon as he had gone my heart sank within me to count the great responsibility resting on me for such a decision. I cried to the Lord, O Lord, I cannot bear this responsibility alone. He must take some of it. When he returned his decision to go had again been overruled by the remonstrance of the people.[54]

Elizabeth still did not give up, informing Finney that she was prepared "to stand alone in the decision." Hounded by his undaunted wife, plagued by fears of nonacceptance in England, and troubled that he could not "hear the voice of the Lord in this" but only his wife's voice, Finney ultimately decided to allow God's call to be transmitted solely through Elizabeth. With her, he finally concluded, all things were possible. The morning of 16 November he informed her that "if we go, we must go without saying one word to anyone. Can you be ready by ten? I replied, yes, for I thought I could not lay a straw in the way of his going." A nervous and reluctant Finney, accompanied by a wife with a fatigued body and wounded heart, sailed on the *Persia* on 2 December 1858. They were bound for a mission field to which the wife felt called, but not the husband.[55]

III

As her motto for this second English tour Elizabeth Finney appropriated the promise "satisfied with favor," partly to quench the diffidence of her sulking husband, who felt neither satisfied nor favored. But the promise proved true, for the Finneys' second transatlantic tour, if not the zenith of Finney's career,[56] was the fullest realization yet of the team concept of ministry, a concept adopted by such Evangelical prototypes of "clerical couples" as Mary and William Boardman, Jennie Fowler and W. C. Willing, Ada C. and B. F. Bowles, Ruth Augusta Damon and James B. Tabor, Mariana Thompson and Allen P. Folsom, Mary Still Adams and her husband, Hannah Pearce and William Reeves, and Minnie Baldwin and Elmer E. Selhamer.

A few days after their arrival, Finney began to conduct services in Huntingdonshire, his headquarters for two months of preaching in Houghton and Saint Ives. Elizabeth did not immediately start her ladies' meetings but began home visitations in the area, soliciting support from female "revival friends" and generally sowing seeds of friendliness and concern that would bear fruit when she summoned the women together. Sometimes, as in Aberdeen, Elizabeth asked her husband to preside at the first few ladies' meetings; her role was solely that of a participant until the third or fourth meeting.[57] In most cases, however, she officiated from the start. It is important to note that these meetings were almost daily events, quite different from the leisurely weekly or monthly gatherings that Lydia had sponsored. Further, there was a subtle shift in designation: Lydia had always called them "ladies' prayer meetings," but Elizabeth tended increasingly to call them simply "ladies' meetings," signifying an enlargement in strategy and substance. Although Elizabeth encouraged women to open up and pray publicly just as Lydia had, she also imposed a liturgical framework on these meetings that made them virtual carbon copies of her husband's evening services.

The Edinburgh revival was a case in point. It may not have been a typical example, for Elizabeth was extraordinarily successful there, but sufficient records exist to permit generalization. In late August the Finneys arrived in Scotland for a three-month tour of Evangelical Union pulpits. They began ministering in John Kirk's large Brighton Street Chapel, and on 20 August a newspaper advertisement announced the start of Elizabeth's three o'clock ladies' meetings, the first one to be held two days later at Bristo Place Hall. These were the first daily prayer meetings in Edinburgh's history. There were no set services on Saturday, a day devoted to young people's meetings in order to accommodate the work schedule of shopgirls. The first meeting drew 30; the second 70; the third almost 140; and succeeding meetings continued to increase in popularity until between two and three hundred were regularly present. Within a month the *Christian News* and *Revival Record* were carrying weekly reports on the astonishing meetings taking place in Edinburgh, the result of a deliberate decision on the part of the women to publicize their proclamation of the gospel and to lift up Elizabeth Finney as a model for Christian women.[58]

Whenever possible, Elizabeth enforced her conception of "woman's mission" by nosing out talented women and training these apprentices to overcome traditional British reserve and to assist her publicly. Especially wooed were ministers' wives, like Margaret M. Ferguson of Aberdeen and her close friend Helen Kirk of Edinburgh. Throughout the 1859–1860 revival tour of England and Scotland both Charles and Elizabeth urged wives of ministers to exert a leadership role in religion while they gently rebuked those social stereotypes which impeded "woman's mission." When Margaret Ferguson's husband asked Finney to excuse his wife from her extensive involvement in prayer meetings, Finney stiffened: "Nonsense, by no means. If the minister's wife draws back everyone will do the same."[59] Helen Kirk was a thirty-year-old woman with five children whose "energy, industry, and readiness to enter upon any work and labor of love," Elizabeth wrote, "make her a beautiful example as a minister's wife." Protégés like Ferguson and Kirk were tutored in how to work with inquirers, and Elizabeth rejoiced at how well her student Kirk conversed with inquirers as "they seek counsel of her as one taught of God and one that can teach them."[60] Finney's increasing usage during the 1850s of the inquiry meeting over the anxious seat may have implied an unspoken recognition of his wife's artful persuasiveness in these settings[61] as well as his growing sophistication in style.

Elizabeth's Ladies' Union Prayer Meetings were part of the transatlantic Union Prayer Meeting Revival that began in America in 1857 and quickly spread to England, Scotland, Ireland, and Wales through the efforts of team ministries like the Finneys themselves, the Palmers, and Booths, and the Boardmans. Elizabeth's meetings, at least in Edinburgh, were even more interdenominationally successful than her husband's revival meetings at Brighton Street Chapel, since Charles had problems getting all the denominations to cooperate with him because of the somewhat dubious theological standing of the Evangelical Union. But Elizabeth's meetings were more than just attempts to enroll women in the ranks of her husband's revivals, although clearly "one special object of the ladies' meetings was to beseech the Lord to pour out his Spirit upon the inhabitants of Edinburgh," as Helen Kirk noted in her *History of the Ladies' Union Prayer Meeting.*[62] Equally important was Elizabeth's appeal that Christ wanted his female disciples to do more for him than work in Sunday schools, raise Christian children, and teach home Bible classes. Elizabeth fumed at the prevalence of muffled ministries. Women must ask not clergy or husbands or society, but Jesus directly, "Lord, what wilt thou have me to do?" Elizabeth was convinced that Jesus' answer would be, as Helen Kirk put it, "Come forward in a public capacity and confess Christ before a multitude."[63]

Although many women were converted under Elizabeth's ministry, her primary stress was on the need for sanctification, an "*active surrender* of all that they have and are to his work."[64] Practically, a surrendered life meant the development of self-control, a systematic, not desultory, searching of the scriptures, and more efficient, disciplined methods of household management that would make women better wives and mothers. But most significantly, sanctification meant putting God first: in Helen Kirk's words, making God's work "*superior* to every earthly claim. Husbands must not be too exacting. Christian women are no longer their own, nor yet the property of their husbands in this sense. Christ claims *all* the heart. He must not have a rival."[65] The boldness that this message urged upon women became manifest in numerous ways during Elizabeth's tenure at Edinburgh; women even evaluated the sermons of the town's clergy and visited the ministers who delivered inadequate ones with the purpose of calling them forth toward higher levels of Christian life.[66]

The techniques Elizabeth used to break down women's "timidity" and "restraint" were personal variations of liturgical features characteristic of the Union Prayer Meeting Revival. Helen Kirk usually opened the service by lining out a few hymns for the congregation to sing. These were followed by spoken and written prayer requests, testimonies, participatory prayer, and perhaps "a few words" from Helen Kirk. One or two scriptural passages were read, after which Elizabeth Finney stood to deliver an address. Elizabeth filled these speeches with personal illustrations drawn from her labors in America and her personal journey of faith. She told, for example, of her own first attempt to pray in public, the fear that engulfed her, and her mother's admonition not to let fear of failure prevent her from doing her duty, since even if she did break down during her prayer, the experience would "humble her and do her good."[67] At the conclusion of her speech, Elizabeth would sometimes invite women to come forward, kneel, and present themselves for prayer—clearly her own seatless version of her husband's "anxious seat" techniques. At the conclusion of the meeting, Elizabeth and Helen challenged the women present to return to their homes in the countryside or city and start their own meetings, as some did. In fact, one of Elizabeth's converts professed to have conversed with more than six hundred inquirers and initiated a meeting where over a hundred lower-class women gathered. Elizabeth continued in Edinburgh a pattern she had established elsewhere of conducting Thursday afternoon meetings for mothers and scheduling special meetings for "poor mothers" and young converts as well as "tea meetings," "experience meetings," and Saturday or evening meetings for "factory women," who were unable to attend afternoon sessions. Those who would not come to her, she went to herself, visiting Queen Street Hall, the poor at Cannonsgate, and the "Poor's-home."[68]

On 5 November 1859 Elizabeth held her last union prayer meeting in Edinburgh. At the end of the service Helen Kirk arose to present her mentor with a thank-offering of fifteen sovereigns. "My dear Mrs. Finney," she began, "I believe I express the feelings of every heart in this meeting, when I say that we all love you." For three months they had listened to her "heart-stirring appeals" and experienced the truths of Christ that come alive not through mere appeals to the intellect, but through testimonies that "searched the heart." Yet as important as anything she said was the influence of her example as a woman in ministry. "We all behold in you a model Christian, whom God has highly honored in his glorious cause." Indeed, Helen Kirk expressed her belief that "your name will become a household word in our families, and that often the mother will be found telling her children what Mrs. Finney said, and how Mrs. Finney acted, in this or the other difficulty."

> From a distant land you have come to instruct us in the peculiar power and duty of woman's mission. You have shown us that we have not only home ties and domestic duties to attend to, but also that the Church of God has its claims upon us, as well as the world lying in wickedness.[69]

Elizabeth stood up to thank them for their tender expressions of affection and appreciation, visibly surprised by the intensity of their love and praise. She confessed, however, that the best reward she could receive from them would be continued evidence that they had "been stirred to duty." "O do not let Satan shut your mouth any longer" were some of the last words she left ringing in their ears.[70]

As sad as the ladies of Edinburgh were to see Elizabeth go, many of their husbands were glad to get rid of her. She had summoned women to revise their priorities and they responded enthusiastically, often letting "many little household duties alone" so that God's work would not go untended. Some husbands tolerated this state of affairs as a temporary aberration that would subside with the Finneys' departure. But when Helen Kirk picked up where Elizabeth left off, or, as she put it, resolved that the "effort would not be slackened even for an hour," opposition to the ladies' meetings broke out.[71] Yet the women hurdled over both the obstacles their husbands set in their way and the inevitable "falling off" of interest, about which Elizabeth had warned them. Thanks largely to the faithful efforts of Helen Kirk, who published a small volume describing the Ladies' Union Prayer Meeting movement, new meetings sprang up in the towns and countries about Edinburgh, and as late as 1861 she could be found busily shepherding fifteen new meetings through biweekly visits until they were strong enough to be weened from her leadership.[72] The 1861 chancery records from the annual convention of all ladies' meetings in the Edinburgh area reveal that "in some of the towns great and important revivals have followed the institution of the female prayer meeting.[73] Elizabeth exulted on hearing of such encouraging results.

In Aberdeen where Margaret Ferguson was charged with continuing the work, the frequency of meetings was reduced from daily to three evenings a week with Elizabeth's departure in late December. Perhaps as an admonition to recapture their past zeal, Elizabeth transmitted through Helen Kirk a letter to the Aberdeen "sisters," which was read at their meeting.[74] She followed the fortunes of her spiritual children and organizational creations with great interest and was always a prejudiced observer of their progress.

The highlight of their British expedition, and Elizabeth's finest hour, occurred northeast of Liverpool in the cotton manufacturing town of Bolton, Lancashire. They would labor after Bolton in Manchester (25 April to 27 July) and Salford, where Finney preached twice on Sunday and four times during the week and Elizabeth held meetings five times a week as well as conducting services in outlying chapels,[75] but the Bolton revival marked their crowning achievement together. According to her rendition, it was Elizabeth who once again determined that Finney should accept the invitation from the Congregationalists at Duke Street Chapel, though the crowds of twelve or thirteen hundred people quickly necessitated a move to Temperance Hall for union revival services with the Methodists and Independents. To pave the way for her visit, Elizabeth sent to the Congregational minister, Rev. Davison of Bolton, the tract "Mrs. Finney, the Ladies' Prayer Meeting," a reprint of an article about her Edinburgh labors published originally in the *Christian News*. Demand so far exceeded the initial printing of 500, and Mr. Davison was "so much interested in seeing what women can do," that with the help of James Barlow, the Finneys' Bolton host, 1,000 more copies were circulated in the Bolton area. John Kirk even advised Finney that "it might be well to form it as a standing tract."[76]

In spite of Elizabeth's advance billing, her first meeting drew only between 25 and 30 women. Before the series ended, however, upwards of 700 women from "all denominations, ages, classes and conditions of life" attended. At first the meetings were held in the schoolrooms of various chapels, but the congregations became so large that by the fifth week they had to be switched to the Temperance Hall, where Finney's evening meetings were held. Within a week after their arrival in Bolton, Elizabeth inaugurated afternoon meetings from three to four, and shortly thereafter established a six o'clock tea in the vestry, followed by another meeting in a room in the New Connection School from half-past six to half-past seven, designed for those who could not make the afternoon session. Thursday afternoon she addressed mothers; Friday afternoon she addressed young women. Saturday evening meetings were held in the Duke's Alley School. The evening tea and meeting allowed her time to converse with inquirers about their souls. These meetings also functioned in the revival as a conduit for converts, a place where Finney could send women (who made up the majority of his congregation at Bolton) for instruction in the faith and where, as Elizabeth put it, a woman would "be roused to use talents for God."[77]

Elizabeth was quick to draw other female leadership into her meetings and was especially proud of her role in leading to Christ the two women she trained to succeed her in Bolton, Alice Barlow and Mrs. Bell. Alice Barlow was the wife of James Barlow, a wealthy manufacturer of men's and women's apparel and twice mayor of Bolton. Barlow converted to Methodism while on a business trip to Ireland in 1858 and returned home to inform an astonished wife that neither of them had been truly Christian as they had supposed. Barlow entertained Charles and Elizabeth in hopes that they would be instrumental in his wife's conversion. His hopes were realized the second night of their stay, and the friendship that ensued was perhaps the most intimate that Elizabeth and Charles shared. "Finney says I do not think we were so much attached to any family," Elizabeth wrote to her "Dear Son and Daughter," seeing herself as the Barlows' spiritual mother as Finney saw himself as their father. Elizabeth found herself continually prodding the weak Alice to "call out your talents which I consider of great consequence" and propping her up with positive reinforcement: "You find you have gifts if you only use them. You know I have great respect for the gifts God has bestowed upon you my dear Daughter." It was not that Alice Barlow lacked ambition; it was just that Elizabeth feared that her ambitions leaned more toward resting in greened glades of material success and social status than roaming the streets of spiritual usefulness. Like her husband, Elizabeth believed that a Christian moved either forward or backward spiritually and never idled. While under Elizabeth's wing, Alice Barlow matured spiritually until she was assisting Elizabeth in prayer, testifying at class meetings, and teaching a class in Edgeworth. Symbolizing the bonds of affection between them, the Barlows named a daughter after Elizabeth.[78]

Elizabeth's other spiritual child, Mrs. Bell, became, as Elizabeth said of another of her friends, "a missionary spirit around the village." Mrs. Bell, a Quaker, and her Wesleyan husband had been invited to a tea given for the Finneys by the Barlows. During a prayer by Finney, Elizabeth noticed that Mrs. Bell "was much overcome and convulsed with grief." Whispering to Mrs. Bell, Elizabeth inquired whether she had found peace with God. "Oh no, she replied with a sob. I took her by the hand and led her into the dining room, motioning Mr. Finney to follow." Once again, Finney followed his wife's beckoning, and Elizabeth won for herself and her Bolton meetings another influential woman leader who was later called upon to stand in during Elizabeth's illnesses.[79]

Just as Finney experienced new burst of energy during his three months at Bolton, so the sixty-one-year-old Elizabeth worked with the vigor of renewed purpose. When not attending meetings, she filled her days with visits: from inquirers, some of whom were male; from ministers' wives who sought advice on how to organize the women of their husbands' parishes; from people who brought friends to see her in hopes that they would leave her presence converted. Her visitors were a variety of classes. Among them were thirty-two young lads, aged ten to sixteen, who were employed at Barlow's mill. In a single week upwards of a hundred inquirers were reported to have requested advise and aid in seeking Christ from the Finneys. It is probable that Elizabeth saw many of these.[80]

Elizabeth was able to labor in England and Scotland without any imputation of unseemly behavior or manly agressiveness because of her status as a minister's wife, her connection with her husband's ministry, her "winning address," and her refusal to raise political feminist issues. Newspaper coverage of her Edinburgh and Bolton meetings applauded her for remaining within "the sphere of a true lady, according to the most stringent notions of 'women's place'" and observed that, despite the English prejudice against female public speaking caused by "eccentric exhibitions" of "women's rights from across the Atlantic," Elizabeth had captured the respect of everyone who attended her meetings. It is true that she prided herself on the absence of emotional outbursts in her meetings and displayed a refined sense of belonging to a community of real ladies. But what these public accounts fail to convey is the degree to which Elizabeth stretched women's conception of ministry until it could hardly return to its original dimensions. Her major achievement must be seen in the elevation of the public's threshold of tolerance for women's ministry within the context of the decidedly feminist orientation of her message. As she observed of her transatlantic labors, "I am surprised at myself—surprised to see how much I am permitted to do and how I am helped of God in the doing of it."[81]

When a woman waxed enthusiastic about her stimulation under "Mr. Finney's sermons and Mrs. Finney's personal conversations," she inadvertently suggested how Elizabeth went as far as she did in public ministry without threatening male sensibilities.[82] Minister's wives in the nineteenth century were not stupid. Guile as well as tact decreed whether a minister's wife would be successful in eluding criticism for her public labors. Elizabeth simply called her public speaking everything but "preaching." Granted it was hard to tell the difference, but although readings from biblical texts preceded her address, she never appears to have taken a text. Rather, her thirty-minute speeches were topical, not exegetical in nature, an important distinction to nineteenth-century minds and one that she honored, thereby making her talks palatable to even the more sensitive observers. Whether she put as much work into them as her student Helen Kirk, who laboriously studied for her addresses, is doubtful.[83] What is certain is that she, like Catherine Booth, was fastidious about presenting herself, as she put it, "in such a way that *no man* can reasonably object to woman's mission." That did not mean that Elizabeth did not yearn to break free from the social standards that confined her labors. She was interested in strategies for getting men to listen to a woman speak, as Finney revealed when he wrote to his youngest daughter about Elizabeth's great interest in the story of a London Tabernacle female convert who visited 200 people regularly, sponsored teas to entice men to church, fed them when they arrived, and then spoke to the grateful audience of stomach-filled but soul-starved men. Indeed, this may have been the inspiration for a "tea" sponsored by James Barlow for 300 aged, infirm, and poor neighborhood residents selected by home missionaries. After the assembly "sat down to a bountifully supplied table," Mr. Barlow addressed them, and then Elizabeth took over and spoke for thirty-three minutes. She numbered three converts from this tea.[84] Unlike Phoebe Palmer, who was, with her husband, itinerating in Britian simultaneously with the Finneys, Elizabeth had complete control over her services and did not have to defer to her husband, the price Phobe paid to speak to united assemblies. Whether Elizabeth deemed the cost too high or simply preferred not to make herself vulnerable to social stigma is a question of interest but one on which no evidence is yet available.

Elizabeth's addresses themselves also cleverly combined molasses and medicine. According to the *Bolton Chronicle*, she "speaks with them of their common duties to husband, and children and home; of their common joys, their common sorrow; their common interest in the sympathy of the Divine Redeemer, the influence of the Gospel upon their positions and prospects, and the claims of the Saviour upon their reverential love and service."[85] Such familiar topics as the early conversion of children were standard fare at the popular Thursday afternoon "Mothers' Meetings," as warnings about worldly amusements were at the young converts' meeting on Friday afternoon. But as we have seen, Elizabeth also included in these speeches hefty doses of personal experience and belief, which drew attention to her authority as a spiritual guide and at the same time made her something of a celebrity. She had the talent that separated the great revivalists from the mediocer, just as (according to Arthur Miller) it differentiates ordinary plays from great drama: the evocation from an audience of the response, "Good Lord, that's me! that's me!" Elizabeth shared revelations about her feelings and intimate stories about others' experiences until people so identified with her illustrations that, as one woman confessed, it seemed as if "someone had been telling her about me." Just as people had fallen under "conviction" through Finney's searching reconstructions of human experience, so now his wife pursued the unredeemed, unsanctified, and unsteady by unveiling her own spiritual state as a "wounded healer": "I sometimes have compared myself in the divine life to a ship in a gale—just lying her head to the wind but making no progress—only just power to keep the direction right."[86]

A personal appeal for women to realize their talents in religious service insinuated itself into almost all of Elizabeth's coruscating lectures.[87] She was never bolder, than in her valedictory speech at the Bolton testimonial tea given in her honor on 29 March 1860. Eight hundred tickets were made available for purchase (the poor were presented with complimentary tickets), and it is estimated that 1,000 were present to pay homage to their beloved soul-winner, who was responsible for many of the 1,200 converts Finney claimed. Elizabeth Best, wife of a Congregational minister at Bolton, spoke on behalf of the "one grateful band" of women who had assembled for the final Thursday "Ladies' Tea Meeting," thanking Elizabeth "for the teachings we have from time to time received from your lips." She had taught them, Elizabeth Best testified, about the power of prayer; she had instructed mothers in how to win their children and husbands to God; she had warned young people about life's trinity of temptations—the world, the flesh, and the devil; she had challenged women to brook no distinctions in the urgent task of soul winning; she had coaxed them up the ladder of spiritual holiness, and had shown them the reigning power in weakness and the resident weakness of power. At the conclusion of this speech, the women on the platform presented to Elizabeth a "thank-offering," the ultimate recognition of her worth as a professional soul-winner. Monetary appreciation of her labors was not new to Elizabeth, for the women of Edinburgh had also thanked her, as they thanked male professional revivalists, by awarding her a love-gift of fifteen sovereigns, an act of gratitude duplicated by the women of Aberdeen (who presented Charles with a purse of twenty-two and a half sovereigns and his wife seven and a half), and later by the people of Salford at their farewell tea for the Finneys in August 1860 (where Elizabeth received thirty guineas and Charles a hundred for their services).[88] The legitimacy of the Partner approach to evangelism had finally been recognized by that most reluctant of witnesses: the purse and pocketbook.[89]

A profoundly moved Elizabeth, after regaining control over her emotions and tears, then delivered to the women of Bolton her final speech. It was much the same speech she had given to them three weeks earlier, when, in her words, she tried "to prove how dear this cause of woman's emancipation and the use of woman's power to help herself, was to my heart."[90] After uttering the expected words of gratitude about the "free-will offering," Elizabeth began to share with the ladies the undergirding philosophy of her ministry: "I trust a new era has dawned upon woman's history, and that she is now beginning to understand her power, position, and mission in this world." Created by God "to be the equal of man, and with him forming a united head for the family," woman lost her position through Eve's introduction of sin. But Elizabeth did not linger unnecessarily on woman's liability for the origin of sin. Instead, she blamed female subjugation on the masculine rule of "might makes right," which led to the introduction of polygamy, the most brutalizing and degrading force that ever beat upon woman's psyche. Through these millennia of darkness, God had nevertheless preserved the divine intention for woman and had raised up periodically "a Miriam, a Deborah, a Huldah" and others as reminders of the original design for the complete equality of male and female. The full light of God did not break upon woman until the advent of Christ, who seemed to have in Elizabeth's theology a peculiarly feminist message and mission: "Christ came to redeem her from the *curse* of the law, being made and suffering the curse for her. He began to *help* just *where* the ruin began. He seemed to say, it is enough, 'Live, for I have found a ransom.' "[91] Finding significance in the fact that Christ was born of a woman and hence had received his full humanity from the female sex, Elizabeth recalled for her audience the historic progress woman had made since the birth of Christ. "Last at the cross, the first at the sepulchre," women were the ones first chosen by Christ to preach the resurrection news. They assisted the apostles, "began to have influence even in some heathen nations," were given "places of great influence and usefulness" by Roman Catholics, and gradually were rising in stature and self-esteem until "we have now come to the place where we can help ourselves." According to Elizabeth's journal account of her earlier speech, she had said, "The day is fast approaching, when our Sons and Daughters will prophesy, and woman be restored to the original place for which God created her." Identifying with the woman who bathed Christ's feet with her tears, Elizabeth revealed that during one of her "night watches" she experienced an overwhelming desire to

> lead all the sisters—the women of the world—and bathe with my own tears those blessed feet, and say, "My blessed Saviour, we are all here to weep and to confess our sin before thee. We are all *fallen women*—some have sinned against *society*—but we are *all* fallen—we gave up our birthright for the gratification of an appetite. We bless thee thou has come to restore us to our first estate, and now we give ourselves to thee, and will do all we can to bring back this fallen world to thee, the rightful sovereign.[92]

The weight of the world's redemption rested on woman's shoulders, Elizabeth concluded. The only question was "Will you accept *this responsibility*? Will you be *true* to *yourselves*? Will you prove true to the *trust committed to you*? Will you prove true to your God?"[93]

Just as the success of their first English tour secured for Finney an aura of respectability, even among American skeptics, so their second English tour stamped Elizabeth's ministry with a seal of approval that reversed somewhat Oberlin's repugnance at her influence over her husband. As soon as the Finneys arrived in Oberlin, they began attending morning prayer services at which both men and women prayed for a revival at Oberlin and testified to its preliminary signs. Elizabeth seems to have become a local celebrity, for she was in constant demand. "On Sunday evenings I go to Ladies' Hall. There I meet a large number of ladies on Monday. I meet about 200 more Tuesdays and Wednesdays. On Thursdays I hold a general meeting for all females, and besides this have two other meetings a day every day to attend."[94] In November the prayers were answered, and a revival commenced. "I have never seen in Oberlin such scenes as we are now witnessing," Elizabeth wrote breathlessly, as she told of her three meetings a day, constant company, and the steady stream of inquirers from dawn till dusk.[95] The passing of the Oberlin revival of 1860–1861 did not ease their efforts for further revivals, for when health permitted they both attended prayer meetings daily right up until Elizabeth's death. But Finney's mental collapse in 1861 and his deteriorating physical condition thereafter deflected her energies from evangelism to nursing, and as a result her own physical condition worsened. In September she visited Clifton, New York, for the water cure, and died of a cerebral hemmorrage on 27 November 1863 while en route to Rochester to visit her son Hobert Ford Atkinson. She died in a Syracuse hotel, surrounded by her brother, two sons, and a female cousin. "I think I have never known her superior as a wife, mother, a neighbor, a Christian female, a laborer for Christ," Finney mourned. "I am left to make the rest of my journey home without my sweet companion and helpmate."[96]

Once again Finney paid tribute to a "helpmate" who had played a "prominent part" in his revivals.[97] We have already examined the numerous ways in which Elizabeth moved the sense of that word toward fuller, more equal partnership in the ministerial vocation. But Elizabeth altered the role in another important way. Lydia's style of "assistance" gave her ample room to promote the gospel and without manipulation or supervision by her husband. These areas of self-management, wherein the influence of a minister's wife could be felt directly and not merely through the husband's ministry, were possible only because her loyalty to his authority was assumed. A ministers' wife was still expected to conform to her husband's image so that where she was, there he might be also. Not only did Elizabeth work independently of her husband, however, but she was also not afraid to think and develop her theology independently and, what is even more important, to exert her influence in ways that actually contradicted his views. Her independence was especially evident in her feminist tendencies, which violated her husband's idea of woman's proper sphere. Susan B. Anthony wrote to Elizabeth Cady Stanton about a trip she had made from Seneca Falls to Schenectady in company with the Finneys. Charles rambled on about the political rights for which women were clamoring and denounced women's rights advocates as "infidels," and then "Mrs. Finney took me to another seat and with much earnestness enquired about what we were doing and the growth of our movement. Said she you have the sympathy of a large proportion of the educated women with you. In my circle I hear the movement much talked of and earnest hopes for its spread expressed—but these women dare not speak out their sympathy."[98] Antoinette Brown retrieved from her memory a similar story about a visit she paid to the Finneys in Brooklyn. During a "nice, fatherly," peripatetic talk, Finney nervously lectured Antoinette about her unorthodox tendencies in politics and religion, admonishing her "to be very prudent and maidenly." Finally, after Elizabeth had sufficiently honored his speech with her silence, she delivered her own short homily: "Antoinette, follow your own conviction." At which point Finney is reported to have "grinned and said nothing."[99]

That grin is but one indication that his views on women's public role may have mellowed under Elizabeth's tutelage. At least Antoinette Brown, whom Finney admitted to his classes and called on frequently to participate in class discussions (too frequently for her tastes), believed that Finney had "liberalized under her influence." Finney also tacitly admitted that his views on women's public speaking softened with time. When his wife began speaking in London to vast crowds that contained a few men, he expressed his worry about the social repercussions, and yet, he wrote, "I believe I did not advise her to keep still, and not attend any more such meetings; but after more consideration I encouraged it."[100] Less than two years before his death, Finney was visited by two young women seeking to borrow a book from his library. Finney's aging eyes mistook them for Miss Rice and Miss Wilcox, two students who were campaigning for the right to deliver orations. "Stick to it, girls, stick to it!" Finney is supposed to have said. "When I was President I always had to *just pull them along!*"[101] If Finney had indeed "pulled them along," it was mainly because he himself had been pulled along by his forward wife.

Tantalizing shreds of evidence suggest that such prodding was not unusual. Mary A. Thorp Bushnell, a descendant of the Puritan minister John Davenport and wife of America's most prominent nineteenth-century theologian, Horace Bushnell, was told by her husband that her "influence" over him was not to be "an ambitious noisy power; it is silent, clam, persuasive, and often so deep as to have its hold deeper than consciousness itself." The true style of her influence was made evident in 1871, shortly after Bushnell had called women's suffrage a "reform against nature" and vilified women preachers. She attended a revival service conducted by Lucy Drake and was so entranced that she insisted that Drake come home with her for dinner and meet her husband.[102]

IV

Finney's penchant for strong women was as visible in his female friendships as it was in his selection of wives. He carried on an intense and voluminous correspondences with Mary A. Parker, Elizabeth's niece, the wife of a prominent New York physician and a fiery feminist. The correspondence began shortly after Elizabeth's death, and soon Finney was speaking to Parker through the mail much as he would have spoken across the table to Elizabeth. Her letters to him were intimate, lengthy revelations of her views on a wide range of topics, and Finney, who obviously needed such exchanges with a women and was stimulated by them, responded with letters that must have seemed interminable, for even in his more hurried moments Finney was known for his unrelenting pen. "Thanks for the hasty lines you sent me," Henry Ward Beecher once greeted Finney. "I hope you may never have leisure to write long letters."[103]

Parker and Finney discussed as equals such topics as temperance, phrenology, abolition, medicine, and her pseudonymous writings (Finney assured her that she was not unread). She debated politics with him, supporting the enfranchisement of women and bemoaning the massive influx of Roman Catholic immigrants. She told Finney what he should be teaching and asked him to sing the praises of late marriage to his students. She judged preaching and was especially hard on preachers who delivered but had not derived their sermons from a text, a practice she attributed in part to the Princeton style of ministerial education, which "tied them up in a straitjacket and deadened all their powers."[104] She also discoursed about theological issues. "I cannot dismiss the Beechers as summarily as you do," she wrote. (He had perhaps repeated Lewis Tappan's observation that Finney "address[ed] the *thinking* portion of the people, and he [Henry Ward Beecher] the unthinking." Henry's "gold is not in ingots," as his father, Lyman's, was, Tappan stated, "but in goldleaf.")[105] She also took FInney to task for his unflagging postmillennial optimism; she sided instead with David Lord, an elder in her church who had just written a book on premillennialism. "It is a great comfort to me not to have to believe we must wait for the conversion of the whole world, when we make so little progress toward it and seem to go back in one place while we go forward in another."[106] Even Finney's detailed refutation of Lord's position failed to persuade her.

What is most revealing about their correspondence is that Parker, who claimed to have preached privately whenever an opportunity arose, felt free to complain to Finney about her church's "Pauline views" on women and her pastor's low estimation of women's work in the church. "I agree with you that they are important in a church," she nodded to Finney; but her church had dubbed such views "Mrs. Parker's heresy." The reason women "don't amount to much" in her church, she observed, was that a lot of the men have "weak wives," and especially the minister, whose wife "never had an independent thought in her life."[107]

In the fall of 1865 Finney married his third wife, forty-one-year-old Rebecca Allen Rayl, and the letters from Parker suddenly ceased their fortnightly flow. Their now limited correspondence revolved around the missionary labors of Parker's daughter, Katie C. Lloyd, who served with her husband in Umwoki, South Africa, and remained there after his death. Because of her father's presumed affluence, Katie Lloyd encountered great difficulty in securing needed funds and workers for her mission. Rebecca, who had long harbored an ambition to become a missionary, was moved by this need. Finney and Rebecca agreed in their fourth year of marriage that if her age was not deemed a deterrent and the way was made clear, she would join the Lloyd mission in Africa. Both Katie and her mother, somewhat horrified to think that Rebecca would consider leaving Finney in his dotage, reminded them that the marriage vow "till death do us part" was still in force, and Mary Parker declared, "It is not the duty of all to go."[108]

Once again, it appears that Finney had chosen for his wife a strong, motivated, independent woman, though the evidence about her life and character is fragmentary at best, making any conclusions tentative. In the words of Adelia A. F. Johnston, principal of the Female Department and a staunch supporter of sexual parity in education and privileges at Oberlin, Rebecca Rayl was "a woman of marked individuality."[109] She had begun her career as a teacher when she settled down as the wife of a country blacksmith. In 1856, shortly after his death, she came to Oberlin as a teacher. Her intellectual acumen, perception, demeanor, sensitivity, and felicity of expression immediately commanded the attention of the faculty and won her that same year the position of assistant principal of the Female Department, which she held until her marriage to Finney.

For the next sixteen years she served on the Women's Board of Managers. Finney's son Fredrick Norton adoringly described the wife Finney came to cherish and the mother the stepchildren and grandchildren came to love: "She was a well-rounded figure, about medium size, plain but neat and graceful, with a face full of intelligence and vivacity, very lovely eyes, and a voice of rare sweetness and charm."[110] Rebecca was both articulate in speech and conversation and skilled as a writer. Her stepson called her "a positive genius in the choice of words."[111]

Finney came to lean heavily on her writing ability during his ongoing revision of his narratives on systematic theology. Too old and infirm to fight sinners from the pulpit, as his dear friend Lewis Tappan painfully informed him, the old crusader took to penning sulphurous attacks on Masonry. For these compositions and for much of his correspondence, Rebecca served as his secretary and amanuensis. Finney's anti-masonic rantings have been seen as an odd, light-headed, unseemly ending to a distinguished and coherent life. One hardly knows what to make of them, and one hates to mention them. Yet Finney's blitz against Masonry appears quite sensible when interpreted within the context of his growing feminist consciousness.

During this period Finney patronized the itinerant evangelist and preacher Lucy Drake, who said, "Outside of my Bible, I learned more from him about practical soul-saving than from all other sources." Drake spent weeks during the 1870s at the Finneys' home, and Finney arranged for her to speak in a variety of forums during her stay in Oberlin.[112]

The same sensitization toward women's rights that led him to aid a female preacher enlisted his identification with the fears of Evangelical women over the growth of Freemasonry as a surrogate church that attracted their husbands, sons, and even ministers in great numbers to occult, masculine rituals conducted in temples that female eyes had never seen and where female power could exercise no sway. Women's role as custodians of conversion and guardians of morality was under seige by the massive revival of secret societies after the Civil War. Dorothy Ann Lipson has already shown that women were some of the most obsessed opponents of antebellum Freemasonry,[113] and this appears to have been equally true of postbellum antimasonry. The Finney Papers at Oberlin College are filled with frenzied letters to Finney from women relating horrifying personal experiences with local Masonic societies and telling him how Freemasonry had driven a wedge into their families, causing their spouses and sons to desert the pleasures of the home and the blessings of true religion.[114] The public might not be agitated on the Masonic issue, one woman wrote to him, but "*women's* minds are fully occupied by it." Indeed, wrote another, Freemasonry was the "beast" of Revelation 11.[115]

Finney came to see anti-masonry, in his words, as "the next great question of reform to which the church and nation will be forced to attend." With Rebecca's help he wrote articles and a book savaging the institution as an enemy of religion, morality, social justice, and good government ("the most dangerous enemy with which either church or state has ever had to contend") and advertising his leadership in purging Christian society from its evils as he had already helped to purge American society of slavery and intemperance.[116] 'From letters which I am daily receiving," Finney wrote to the editor of the *Independent*, "I learn more and more of the deep and widespread interest in these acticles."[117] Much of this interest came from Evangelical women who saw Freemasonry as jarring loose their power and control over the men in their lives. Finney's last great crusade once again witnessed him leading the forces of pious women into battle against sin and Satan. This time, however, his only weapon was the pen, a pen that was guided and guarded by his third wife, Rebecca.

Much of Finney's reading in these later years was a joint enterprise: Rebecca read aloud portions and then discussed them with her husband.[118] Everyone who knew Rebecca commented on how she worshipped Finney. "It was a daily custom for my grandmother," Jennie F. Woodruff reminisced, "to comb and cut my grandfather's beautiful white hair for about a half hour after the noon meal. She adored him and to my childish mind she looked as if she were administering to an angel!"[119] Even fourteen years after Finney's death, Rebecca was still the faithful disciple, apologizing for the prosaic quality of his last words: "I am dying." Last words in the nineteenth century were supposed to be words that lasted, words carefully constructed to redound in hushed quotation as an inspiration to believers and an illustration for preachers. The disappointing flatness of his expiring remarks was really her fault, Rebecca confessed, for she kept insisting to Finney on his death bed that she did not believe he was dying. If he had faced the immediacy of his death, she suggested, "his mind would have dwelt more, I presume, upon the great spiritual themes so familiar to it, and his utterances have been more indicative of that perfect rest in God, which was his habitual state."[120]

For all this adulation, however, Rebecca ever remained her own woman. Finney was highly critical of ministers' wives who failed to serve as an icon of the Christian ideal, adorning themselves in jewelry and stylish fashions rather than the more comely garments of good works.[121] Yet it is told of Rebecca that she would sit in church, "peaceful and handsome," serenely listening to one of her husband's furious sermons against frivolous flowers and feathers while her own black bonnet was festooned with red blossoms.[122] Rebecca's independence was also manifested in her lobbying efforts on behalf of the political appointment of female clerks in the nation's capital. Shortly after Finney's son-in-law James Monroe was elected a Republican representative to Congress, Rebecca entreated with him to appoint female clerks and specifically to select a "Mrs. Cadwell" for a position.[123]

V

Since members of a team are rarely equal, some ministers' wives virtually eclipsed in ministry their less endowed husbands. Ordinary preachers with extraordinary wives excel, the saying went; the obverse side of the coin warned ministers in search of mates that extraordinary preachers with ordinary wives fail. Many examples of the phenomenon could be marshalled. Robert Corson's wife, Emma, "equalled our father in eloquence," her son admitted, and at her death "the ministerial success of my father suffered diminution."[124] The Methodist bishop Leonidas L. Hamline referred to the episcopacy as "our ministry" because "I deem Mrs. Hamline's labors are, if anything, more fully blest than my own." While encouraging his wife to spend summers in New York for her health, he silently hoped that she would refuse. "I need her. I find her conversations with the preachers often do more good than all my exhortations in the conference. A remarkable power attends her prayers. Under them souls have been directly and powerfully sanctified."[125]

The most obvious case of the wife's supremacy in ministry was that of the Seventh-Day Adventist leaders Ellen Gould White and James White. "Was my part of the work important," James White wrote of his marriage, "hers was no less important." Actually, most historians judge hers to have been more important. Ellen began her public ministry at sixteen when she became a disciple of William Miller and began heralding the news of Christ's imminent arrival on earth. After Jesus failed to materialize, Ellen took some traveling companions and intinerated along the eastern coast of Maine and New Hampshire. Here she underwent numerous visions, prayed for special healings, and generally sought to fulfill her mission of interpreting to adventists Christ's nonappearance in 1843 and 1844 and weeding out errors and enthusiasts among the flock. Elder James White observed Ellen's ministry and was so impressed that he started traveling with her entourage. But the rumor mills began grinding out unflattering gossip about this arrangement until "duty seemed very clear that the one who had so important a message to the world should have a legal protector and that we should unite our labors." The arrival of children was not allowed to interfere with this union of ministries. When their eldest son was one year old, he was left with a Maine couple, who for the next five years provided for his total care ("except a present I would bring him once a year, as Hannah did Samuel," Ellen wrote). A second son's sickliness was interpreted as a "satanic" attempt to impede Ellen's ministry, and when nine months old he was entrusted to the care of a New York disciple. After a few months the Whites ventured to take him (sick or well) along with them. Both Ellen and James took part in the services they conducted, and both wrote extensively. But it was Ellen's spiritual leadership, theological formulations, and political moxie that proved most authoritative in shaping the fledgling Seventh-Day Adventist church.[126]

Perhaps the best Evangelical illustration of a Partner ministry in which the wife's impact was as great if not greater, as the husbands, was the career of Julia Jones Beecher, the second wife of the younger half-brother of Henry Ward Beecher and Harriet Beecher Stowe, Thomas Kennicut Beecher. Described by her husband as "my strong, courageous energetic Julia—to whom belongs the credit of nine-tenths of the achievement of our long life in Elmira,"[127] Julia Jones Beecher had excellence in her blood. Cotton Mather was part of her family tree, and her mother, who began her married life as the wife of a minister, was the youngest child of Noah Webster.[128] Her cousin and childhood friend was Olivia Day (or "Livy," as Julia called her), daughter of the president of Yale College and first wife of Thomas K. Beecher. Shortly after their marriage in 1853, Livy and Beecher moved to Elmira, where he had accepted the call of an aggressively abolitionist church named the First Independent Congregational Church (it became in 1871 the Park Church). Little is known of Olivia's short life in Elmira except that she joined her husband in refusing to make the visits expected of a minister and a minister's wife and did not relish the thought of having to conduct prayer meetings.[129] The very year they settled in Elmira, Livy died, and a distraught Beecher moved to Gleason's Health Resort, a water-cure sanitarium founded by Silas Gleason and his wife, Rachel Books Gleason, who received her medical degree only two years after Elizabeth Blackwell. During a study retreat at Bridgeport, Connecticut, Beecher married the thirty-year-old Julia on 21 January 1857.

Julia arrived in Elmira with her husband amid a mid-winter snow storm. As they plodded up East Hill toward the Gleason resort, where they would live for the next three years, Julia walked in the tracks left in the snow by her husband's footsteps.[130] She never followed in his tracks again, for she did not conform to any image but her own. She bobbed her hair long before Irene Castle; she trekked around town on eleemosynary errands in Congress boots. Feminine footwear and long hair were for Julia thieves of time. The bas relief portrait of her on the drinking fountain at the corner of the Women's Federation Building, the only public memorial to an Elmira woman, reveals a strong, firm face, snub nose, kind gentle eyes, and a feisty mouth betraying a rollicking disposition. She was a dynamo; her mother described her childhood as like having a rabbit in the house. Her adolescent friends called her the "belle of Bridgeport" because of her vivacity and boundless energy, and her husband compared being married to her to being "hitched to a steam engine." Whatever she did, whether it was illustrating letters with pencil drawings, sculpting "jabberwocks," sewing dolls, playing games with "Ooey" (it rhymes with "phooey": it was her name for Thomas), lifting her husband out of his frequent lugubrious moods, or doubting the efficacy of prayer, she did it with spirit. Even when she poured coffee, as one of her friends remarked, she did so with "indiscriminate fury."[131]

Fearlessly independent of mind, Julia cared not a whit whom she contradicted. She dissented from her husband's opinions at prayer meetings and social events. An ever-present white ribbon on her dress proclaimed her support for the Woman's Christian Temperance Union, even though her pool-playing husband enjoyed his glass of beer and table wine.[132] She argued with the family friend Samuel Clemens about life after death, concluding with a challenge: "Now, Mr. Clemens, if you meet me in heaven a million years from now, will you confess that you were wrong?" In spite of his repeated assents, Julia insisted on a contract, and on the three stone she produced for a durable record, Clemens inscribed the following lines:

> If you prove right and I prove wrong
> A million years from now,
> In language plain and frank and strong
> My error I'll avow
> (To your then mocking face).

> If I prove right, by God his grace
> Full sorry I shall be
> For in that solitude no trace
> There'll be of you and me
> (Nor of our vanquished race).

> A million years, O patient stone!
> You've waited for this message;
> Deliver it in a million years—
> Survivor pays expressage.[133]

Julia's influence on the Elmira community was as great as her husband's. Indeed, when she died on 11 November 1905 Elmira witnessed an outpouring of love and unity equalled only by the town's reaction to Beecher's death in 1900.[134] Julia reorganized the church's Sunday school program and superintended its 600–900 pupils while her husband wrote curriculum materials for it.[135] She presided at women's meetings, prayed publicly, visited the sick, and populated her childless home with people in need—orphans, old people with no one to care for them, a prostitute—earning the title "Elmira's Sweet Sister of Mercy."[136] Finding Park Church "icy cold" toward foreign missions, she formed the church's first missionary society, designing and crafting the chubby baby rag dolls (collectors now call them "Beecher dolls") that were sold to raise money for the Women's Board of Foreign Missions.[137] It was partly her vision of the church's mission that prompted Park Church to constitute itself as probably the first institutional church in America. "It is not too much to say," wrote one of Elmira's residents, "that although always in an unobtrusive manner, very much of what may be called the great success of the church in temporal and spiritual ways, in doing the vast amount of good that it has accomplished in almost every direction, if not in inception are due to her incessant push and energy."[138] Beecher himself put it the matter more succinctly: "She is pastor, I am log."[139] When Annis Ford Eastman was made co-pastor with her semi-invalid husband upon Beecher's death in 1900, it was a fitting climax to nearly a half-century of the Partner model of ministry.[149]

• Chapter Eight •

"One in the Work"

Women in the Ministry under Attack

Dear Posterity:

Pardon us for thus familiarly addressing you, but we must confess to a deep interest in you, strangers though we are. . . . It almost makes us tremble with awe to think how many things you know of which we are ignorant; of the questions puzzling us that have been made plain to you. For instance, you must have learned what has become of the "New Woman"—whether she had developed into the "Old Woman" or the "Old Man."

Another item of knowledge you must possess which makes us green with envy. There have been so many General Conferences since our time that it must have been decided what St. Paul meant when he said, "Let your women keep silence in the churches." We are having such a time about it! We do not know whether he meant that women are not to respond in prayer meeting when things are getting dull and pastors call upon them as a last resort, or whether they are still to do the drudgery but never have a voice in deciding upon matters pertaining to the results of their labors. . . .

With great respect,
Ellen Larrabee Lattimore
(letter found in the cornerstone of the
First Methodist Episcopal Church,
Rochester, New York)

Most women and men today no longer marry a minister: they marry a person. The Peggy Dows are all but gone, and the Lydia Finneys and Elizabeth Atkinson Finneys are around only in diminishing numbers, although search committees can still be found hiring them as part of a package deal. A tradition dies slowly, especially one that has been of such economic and institutional advantage to the church. But when the exceptionalism that permitted the minister's wife to labor in ways denied the rest of her sex was gone, so too was the woman who came into the ministry through the side door of her husband's career. Succeeding women have inherited most of the occupational hazards of being a minister's wife, but without the relative benefits that accrued to the first women in the ministry.

My present thesis, not dogmatically asserted but suggested for discussion and future exploration, is that beginning in the last two decades of the nineteenth century, there occurred somewhat of a retreat from the image of the minister's wife as a vocational partner or institutional asset and a return to the Companion image of a help-meet or psychological support system. This interpretation accords well with a recent study by William R. Leach, which argues that the most powerful, assertive, and dynamic stage in the American feminist movement was the antebellum period, and that the movement experienced a withering of vigor and vision toward the end of the century.[1] In fact, the retreat appears to have been so dramatic that by 1900 pastors' wives were commonly used in literature and sermons as models of subordination. The admonition to act like a minister's wife became a mechanism for arresting rather than activating the autonomous efforts of women in the church. Ministers' wives contributed little leadership to the revivalism of Moody and Sankey in the seventies and Sunday in the early 1900s or to the Third Great Awakening.[2] The level of leadership reached by the wives of the Evangelical clergy in the antebellum period seems to have been maintained only in the Woman's Christian Temperance Union, the American Volunteers, the Christian Americanization Program, some adventist groups, and some branches of the holiness movement, specifically among itinerant evangelists, the Salvation Army, the Free Methodists, and camp-meeting associations.

There has, of course, always been opposition to any new model of ministry, and women in the ministry in antebellum America had more than their share of antagonists. But the attacks of the late nineteenth and early twentieth centuries were especially concentrated. This did not mean that church women ceased to look for and find new and creative ways of pursuing vocations or that they stopped affirming and exercising equality. This period in American history posed fresh challenges for women as well as men, some constructive, others debilitating. Women of towering abilities, like Grace Beaven, Ida Strawbridge Nuveen, Sophia Packard, Silvia Nickerson, and Helen Barrett Montgomery, to cite only some Baptist examples,[3] wielded great influence in their religious, social, cultural, and economic arenas. Many nineteenth-century women, as Karen J. Blair and Ruth Bordin have shown, found in women's clubs and the temperance movement, especially the WCTU, effective vehicles for advancing the feminist cause.[4] But ministers' wives tended to settle tended to settle into a more traditional background role. "In the better class of churches," the *Philadelphia Times* reported in 1879, "not as much is required of the pastor's wife as formerly."[5]

The *tradition* of ministers' wives as women in the ministry continued, as assertive women like the Presbyterian Annie C. F. Cunningham kept alive the Assistant model in her husband's parishes in Philadelphia and Wheeling, West Virgina, until her death in 1897.[6] But the *movement* was subsiding. In the late nineteenth century, some ministers' wives assisted in organizing the WCTU at the local level, while others became involved in what David J. Pivar calls the "mass movement" for sexual purity.[7] But unlike their antebellum counterparts, they were neither the organizing nor the operating force behind these associations. One cannot write a history of the antebellum response to prostitution, the moral reform movement, without featuring the role of ministers' wives. One can write a history of the purity crusade of the 1880s and 1890s without highlighting their involvement. Whereas the wives of ministers were often the most influential local leaders in the antebellum missions movement, Lois A. Boyd has discovered an "interesting" trend for the "wives of merchants, politicians, and other pofessionals"—but not ministers—to be the most "active organizers of the PCUSA [Presbyterian Church, USA] women's board for foreign and home mission in the latter part of the nineteenth century."[8]

The minister's wife was increasingly seen as more of a helpmeet to her husband than to the church, someone who helped him prepare for ministry rather than someone who helped him in ministry. Sometimes she was defined in terms of what she did not do: gossip, drink, argue, play favorites, or dress fashionably.[9] At other times she was defined in terms of she did for her husband: cater to his whims, counsel and pray for him, or (as in the case of Laura Jones, the wife of a southern evangelist) hurry off to his revival sites when he got lonesome and needed comfort.[10] There were, to be sure, many ministers' wives, as an 1898 editorial in the *United Presbyterian* observed, who continued to lead the Sunday school, women's prayer meetings, missionary societies, and song services, making their "services more indispensable to the congregation than even the pastor's." But her real role as "one of the most important factors in almost every efficient pastorate," according to this same editorial, was as a counselor to her husband, reporting on conditions in the parish, ministering to his moods, and helping to control his tongue.[11]

The full extent of this change wherein the minister's wife found herself acting as a minister's wife more in the home and less in the church is apparent in Margaret E. Blackburn's 1898 manual for ministers' wives, entitled *Things a Pastor's Wife Can Do.* The wife of a Baptist minister, Blackburn denied that a prospective minister's wife need feel called in any way to the ministerial vocation, or that she needed special attributes. Saying yes to a minister was saying yes to his love, not his call. A large proportion of her book was spent on home economics and discouraging the wives of clergy from working outside the home or holding offices in the church. Rather than be a leader, she should "shrink from prominence" and be an enabler to others, serving officially only in the Sunday school.[12]

"One in the work" was losing its double meaning. The role of the minister's wife was defined less in terms of her relationship to the ministry and more in terms of her relationship to her husband. "One in the work" for Blackburn meant domestication. She tied the wife more tightly to her husband at the same time that she literally separated her from his work. Parsonages should be built away from the church, she argued, and the minister's wife ought never to develop friendships among parishioners. The wife of a minister should find her greatest pleasure in lavishing praise on him, checking any criticism that might arise, furnishing, ventilating, and dusting the parsonage, protecting the sanctity of his study, and learning generally that "no" is a Christian word when said to his parishioners. The wife of a minister was someone to come home to. "Let us, as pastors' wives, make our home cages so large, so delightful, that the one we love will not *feel* the bars, but will always be more than glad to return."[13]

It was but a short step to the stand taken by the prominent minister who, when asked about the qualifications of his wife for parish duties, inquired what salary the parish intended to pay her.[14] "She is my wife and not yours," declared another at his installation service.[15] The minister's wife "is not at the beck of anyone" submitted another. "No one has the least occasion to comment or criticize if she take an obscure place and devote herself wholly to her family and not at all to the parish." Any leadership she bestows on the church "is a gratuity on her part, it cannot be demanded, and she is within her rights in declining to give it."[16] One Reformed minister supported the idea that wedding fees belonged to ministers' wives, but his decision was based on christian charity rather than the fact that she deserved some compensation for services rendered. Indeed, if the General Assembly was to deliver an official ruling on the relationship of the minister's wife to the church, conjectured a Presbyterian journal, "It would most probably be declared that she does not sustain any official relation to the congregation different from that of the elders' wives, or of any other woman in good standing in the church."[18]

Ministers' wives themselves began to speak out about their status in the church. Church authorities sometimes chafed under the tendency for ministers' wives to become assertive in their own defense and on their own behalf. "They haven't had a call, they say; they have been promised no salary; it is their duty to take care of their husbands while they look after the congregation; a minister's wife isn't bound to be the leader in everything, and so on."[19] Perhaps the popular author Mary Virginia Terhune, herself the wife of a Congregational minister, best summed up the feelings of such wives when she wrote, "The unwritten contract is unfair, cruel and iniquitous." It is not true, argued Marion Harland (her pen name) in a bitter article in the *North American Review*, that the success of a minister is largely due to his wife. "In no other profession, vocation, or craft, do a man's domestic relations so seriously affect his success," she admitted, but the affect could only be negative. Since both ministers and their wives were now judged not on the basis of leadership qualities, but on the basis of personality and popularity, a minister's wife could through her style "mar his usefulness, even to the utter destruction thereof; but it is not given to her ever to rivet his hold upon the affection of his charge; to place or to maintain him in a desirable position."[20] The wife of a minister, she believed, was now in a position to assist her husband's career only by not destroying it.

The declining status of the minister's wife in the late nineteenth century no doubt reflected in some degree the general decline of the ministry in these years. Strong and talented women found attractive outlets for their energies in secular pursuits like the woman's club movement, the suffrage cause, the charity organization movement, and various professions, like nursing, that were now opened to women. But the reduction of the minister's wife to an illustration in one of her husband's sermons must be related primarily to overall changes in the status of women in American life.

We need look no further to begin with than the forces of immigration and industrialism. The new immigration reinforced patriarchal structures and women's tradition status; industrialism tightened sexual role definitions, lessened social experimentation, and, as Alice Kessler-Harris has argued, fragmented female bonds and pried women apart from each other by "acquistive materialism."[21] Amid the chaos of social change, the image of a pure woman as a purveyor of inherited civilization and of the sanitized home as an incubator for all that was good in life became powerful forces for stability.

Since women had proven their equality in numerous ways throughout the century, the question was no longer what a woman was qualified to do, for as the Baptist clergman W. H. Felix observed, the answer would have to be virtually anything a man could do. Thanks to Julia Evelina Smith and her 1876 "Aldersey" edition of the Bible, woman had even proved to the world her ability to translate the scriptures from the original languages. The question now was "What is her divinely appointed sphere and work?"[22] Even though there was a visible feminist component to the progressive movement, and a stripping of the cult of motherhood during the progressive era, it was Progressivism that gave home economics scientific status as a home discipline, thus reinforcing traditional social functions for women.[23] When the apostle of the science of domesticity, Harriet Beecher Stowe, lectured to women about the "cross [that] each one must carry," the cross was not a summons to speak or minister in public, but to wash the dishes without domestic help and be the home's "chief minister."[24] Toward the end of the nineteenth century, only the wives of urban America's largest and wealthiest churches could afford domestics, who had freed earlier women for service and even here servants were a vanishing breed. Pastors no longer hired domestic helpers; they married them. In the shift toward an industrialized world, where people were expected to function as part of machines, passivity tightened its grip on social behavior.

A second factor in the decline of the role of the minister's wife was, ironically, progress in women's emancipation. Higher education and slightly greater economic opportunities for women, offered ministers' wives the prospect of varied careers outside the home. A small number of hardy souls took outside jobs and renounced the notion that the wives of clergymen need be women in the ministry.[25]

Third, Beverly Wildung Harrison has shown that the feminist movement, which began in Evangelical circles during the Second Great Awakening and in which ministers' wives played a prominent part, had become secularized by the 1870s, stripped of the biblical roots and religious vision so evident in Sarah Grimké's 1838 *Letters on the Equality of the Sexes*. No longer would women's rights conventions bother to pass resolutions declaring that "inasmuch as man, while claiming for himself intellectual superiority, does accord women moral superiority, it is pre-eminently his duty to encourage her to speak and teach, as she has the opportunity, in all religious assemblies.[26] As Elizabeth Cady Stanton's *The Woman's Bible* (1898) revealed, a few feminists had come to see the church and clergy as enemies at worst, obstructions at best.[27] Although *The Woman's Bible* was not representative of the religious views of most late nineteenth-century feminists, its publication proved to many that the woman's movement proceeded from an unevangelical standpoint. When Evangelical theology ceased to undergird radical women's activity, it lost many of its women.

Fourth, this was a period of constitutionalism in women's religious history, as they fought for institutional recognition of the gains they had made in the past. Arguments embalmed in past debates were resurrected: the Lutherans skirmished over women's right to vote and speak in church, the Presbyterians over women preachers, and the Methodists over the election of lay delegates. Retrenchments sometimes occurred when churches were forced to examine the portentious implications of *faits accomplis*, as illustrated in the case of the Methodist Episcopal church. Women who had been licensed to preach—among them Maggie Newton Van Cott, Anna Oliver, Jennie Fowler Willing, and the black revivalist Amanda Smith—had their licenses revoked by the General Conference of 1880, and the General Conference of 1884 judged it "inexpedient to take any action on the subject of licensing women to exhort or to preach."[28] Early in the century women had dragged from their ministers permission to form Sunday schools. Women also managed them and, more than historians have realized, served as the commanders of the young armies of soldiers being trained to march toward the millennium.[29] The schools, which had never really been in the hands of the clergy, were formally turned over to women when the 1880 General Conference ruled that women could serve as Sunday school superintendents (this happened in 1898 in the southern church). The conspicuous hope was that women's leadership would be cloistered in Sunday school rooms. That same conference generously permitted women to serve as class leaders, an office by now defunct or meaningless in most churches, and stewards, a position being replaced by church treasurers. How far women had actually come in achieving recognition for their leadership in the field of religious education was made painfully evident with the 1906 formation of the Religious Education Association. Nine-tenths of the Sunday school teachers in America were women, but the association elected no women officers, and at its first convention no women speakers were chosen.[30]

The red-hot issue of lay delegation tells a similar story. Women were left to ponder their identity after the 1892 General Conference Committee on Judiciary determined that "laymen" and "lay delegates" referred only to males. Four women were admitted to the general conference for the first time in 1896, but they were never seated because the debate over their presence was so degrading that they left. Not until 1904 would the General Conference seat women delegates without debate. Southern Methodists did not elect women as delegates to annual or general conferences until 1920, ten years after a General Conference expressly refused to acknowledge women as laity. Moreover, church women's institutional gains in this period are eclipsed by the unofficial activities and privileges of antebellum women. In terms of institutional recognition of women's place in the church, not much was changing, and the changes that did occur were often for the worse. Partly for this reason many women chose not to knock at the doors of religious establishments and wandered instead through the corridors of the occult, listening to lectures on Swedenborg, baring their bumps for phrenologists, gathering for spiritualist seances, or joining new spiritual movements headed by women.

The women's phase of the Social Gospel movement, known as the "deaconess movement," has been accorded by historians such accolades as "a radical departure for women," "a step forward in the women's liberation process," and a sign of the church's acceptance of "the new womanhood."[31] Upon serious scrutiny, however, the deaconess was not the "new woman" who so fascinated Henry Adams and Henry James. The deaconess movement's main accomplishment appears to have been winning insitutional recognition for what American Evangelical women had already been doing as ministers' wives, church visitors, moral reform society workers, and city missionaries.[32] A compassionate German pastor and his intrepid wife, Theodore and Frederike Fliedner, initiated the deaconess movement through their work in the small Rhine village of Kaiserswerth, where

Frederike was the "moving spirit" behind the "Kaiserswerth Deaconess Institute."[33] From Germany it came to America, in 1850 through the English Lutherans in Pittsburgh, in 1855 through St. Andrew's Episcopal Church in Baltimore, in 1868 through the Episcopal Bishop Potter Memorial House in Philadelphia, and in 1873 through the Episcopal diocese of Long Island. By the mid-1870s, there were at least fifteen sisterhoods in the Episcopal church, which led the way in establishing the deaconess order in America.[35] It was in Chicago in the 1880s, however, that Lucy Ryder Meyer, a Methodist, transformed disparate, sporadic efforts into an organized, coherent movement through her founding of the Chicago Training School for City, Home, and Foreign Missions and the first deaconess order in the Methodist Episcopal church. Though never one of Methodism's official schools, over the next thirty-four years the Chicago Training School graduated over five thousand unmarried women from various religious traditions, who in turn helped to found more than forty church institutions, including deaconess houses in America's largest cities. Costumed in white ties, serge bonnets, and "conventional— not conventual—dress," unsalaried except for pinmoney, and boarded as a community in homes, deaconesses went out, as the 1888 General Conference put it when it recognized them, "To minister to the poor, care for the sick, provide for the orphan, comfort the sorrowing, seek the wandering, save the sinning."[36]

The ease with which the deaconess order was adopted as an official arm of the church, and the unrestrained glee with which bishops and other leaders greeted the prospect of corraling hyperactive, troublesome women in useful but narrow enclosures, should have cautioned historians against treating deaconesses as the flower of the "new womanhood." The deaconess movement did nothing to change the status of women in the church. It did nothing to criticize a system that, in the Free Methodist B. T. Roberts's scolding words, gave "to the deacons the dignity and to the deaconesses the drudgery." It said nothing about a church polity where deacons were ordained and deaconesses were "consecrated."[37] What it did was reinforce prejudices about where women should serve, reasserting the prominence of children's education, nursing and visitation. It gave the impression that women were making progress in the church and provided replacements to take on some of the duties that ministers' wives were abnegating, but it kept women in a setting strictly subordinate to and under the control of pastors. Deaconesses were given official status within the church. They came to an open door, and closed it.

A fifth factor in the decline of women in the ministry involved the women's organizations that ministers' wives had such a large role in founding a half-century earlier. These groups now focused their concerns ever more sharply in one of two directions. Either they were reduced to appendages of the current expense or benevolence budget of the local church, becoming permanent fund raising committees, or they became social in orientation. Women's societies, once concerned over a plethora of reforms ranging from missions to the poor to missions to the pastor, had opted for the pastor. Whereas Evangelical women in the first half of the century had transformed their homes into churches, in the second half they transformed their churches into homes. Virtually singlehandedly they presented American churches with parsonages[38] and furnished them, built Sunday school wings, pastors' offices, and parlors, installed kitchens, subsidized pastors' salaries, kept American churches supporting foreign and domestic missions, and generally served as a rescue squad that saved the churches and their benevolence budgets from insolvency. There were attempts to instill women's work with some of its original vigor through, for example, the "women's bible bands" movement, which was designed to be more than a collection or distribution agency for Bibles. In visiting homes women were to be evangelists and "open the Bible; expound its meaning; administer its consolation."[39] But this movement never really took hold. The drive for unified budgets and the consolidation of women's activities in the local church was born of a similar reformist impulse; it was a response to the cumbering concern with finances at the expense of genuine ministry outlined in the following poem, found in an undated clipping:

> The old church bell had long been cracked;
>   Its call was but a groan;
> It seemed to sound a funeral knell
>   With every broken tone.
> "We need a bell," the brethren said,
>   "But taxes must be paid;
> We have no money we can spare,
>   Just ask the Ladies' Aid."

The shingles on the roof were old;
    The rain came down in rills;
The brethren slowly shook their heads
    And spoke of monthly bills.
The chairman of the board arose
    And said, "I am afraid
That we shall have to lay the case
    Before the Ladies' Aid."

The preacher's stipend was behind;
    The poor man blushed to meet
The grocer and the butcher as
    They passed him on the street;
But nobly spoke the brethren then:
    "Pastor, you shall be paid!
We'll call upon the Treasurer
    Of our good Ladies' Aid."

"Ah!" said the men, "the way to heaven
    Is long and hard and steep;
With slopes of care on either side,
    The path is hard to keep.
We cannot climb the heights alone;
    Our hearts are sore dismayed;
We ne'er shall get to heaven at all
    Without the Ladies' Aid.[40]

The cutting edge of American religion, so sharp in the first half of the century, was blunted in the latter half by overpowering concerns about respectability and mainstream acceptance. It actually became fashionable in urban centers to be a Methodist or a Baptist. Pastors' wives were no longer under congregational pressure to identify with the poor; like other women who bought into the ethos of upward mobility, they now dressed to identify with the dominent social class of their congregation, and their husbands were paid accordingly.[41] Jean Boyd Fulton's diaries let us peek into the window of a Maryland parsonage of the 1870s, where life revolved not around the church's efforts at evangelism or social reform, but around its extensive social calendar.[42] Church meetings shifted from homes to church parlors, the sites of sumptuous church suppers and "social teas."

    Women's attention was diverted by the Civil War from reform societies to war service agencies. It seldom returned. When it did, as in the cases of the Presbyterian church woman Grace Hoadley Dodge and the black leaders Lucy Laney, Maggie L. Walker, Janie Porter Barrett, Mary McLeod Bethune, Nannie Burroughs, Charlotte Hawkins Brown, and Jane Hunter, the women chose to build educational, financial, or social insititutions with only a thin lacquer of religion.[43] Affiliative urges among women became predominantly social, giving rise to the women's club movement. Patterns of female patronage likewise took on a different cast. Whereas female philanthropists had earlier become famous for patronizing clergymen and benevolence projects, they were now patrons of the community's social and civic life.[44] The outreach programs that remained were channeled into the home and foreign missions, where women were, as Barbara Welter phrases it, "keeping alive a rhetoric" and "achieving prominence in an institution which was itself declining in prestige."[45] Starting in the late 1860s, the mission movement also retreated from the energetic ecumenical arrangements that had been fired and fueled by a common millennial vision into competitive denominational women's boards.

A notable exception to this trend was the temperance movement, where women could still be found exerting power in the social and political arenas as well as addressing men in public. For Frances E. Willard, whose "unconstrained preference" was to be pastor, the next best thing was the evangelistic work of the WCTU.[46] In early years Willard tried to keep the WCTU centered on a single issue; she had learned well the lesson of concentrated effort, a single cause for a single society, as she told Susan B. Anthony. But before her death Willard pushed the WCTU in the direction of broader reform involvement, much to the dismay of many local leaders and the more conservative national ones. Some local units persistently boiled over into activities for women's suffrage and civic reform, even providing vigorous support for the Progressive movement.

With the more cultured outlook and mannered piety of American churches toward the end of the century and the preoccupation of American middle-class women with culture, there arose a polished, urbane breed of ministers' wives. Although clerical wives displayed literary interests in the earlier period (Harmony Cary Gardner was a frequent contributor to the *Ladies' Repository* and author of ten books),[47] it was only after the Civil War that they took to American cultural and literary life with a passion.

Charlotte Forten Grimké, grandaughter of James Forten and wife of the pastor of Washington's First Presbyterian Church, Francis J. Grimké, best represents this image of the minister's wife as a person of high erudition, culture, and literary attainments. Born in 1837, Grimké began her career as a schoolteacher in Salem, Massachusetts, served as a clerk in the Treasury Department for a few years, and was eventually employed as a teacher by the Freedmen's Aid Society. Her descriptive accounts of the society launched her into national prominence, and her articles and poems began to appear in the *Standard, Atlantic Monthly, Christian Register, Boston Commonwealth,* and *New England Magazine.* She was an accomplished linguist and her translation of a French novel was published by Scribner's in 1869.[48] In December 1878 she married Grimké and tried to impose her decorous values on the parsonage and church. During her husband's seven-year pastorate in Jacksonville, Florida, she taught Sunday school, organized a women's missionary society, and presided at ladies' fundraising meetings. But clearly what interested her most were literary and artistic pursuits, and she lobbied with the bishop in favor of a Literary Society and against inelegant behavior in the pulpit ("Why must these colored ministers scream so?").[49] One can see parallels of her cultural vision in other contemporaries: the popular author Elizabeth Prentiss, a preacher's daughter whose lachrymose image of the minister's wife as a "Daughter of Consolation" spilled over into her sentimental novels; the rigorously intellectual and articulate wife of Lyman Abbott, who edited a column in the *Christian Union* and whose literary and cultural activities kept her secretary almost as busy as her husband's; Rosena Rowe Anderson, a teacher at Dwight Moody's school for girls in Northfield, Massachusetts, principal of New York City's Training School for Christian Workers, and, after her marriage to a Baptist minister and professor at Colgate Theological Seminary, New York's first "college counselor" in connection with the American Baptist women's home and foreign mission societies; and Lucy Drake Osborn, who, even though an invalid, turned her parsonage into a training institute from which missionaries were sent out to India, Africa, and Mexico.[50]

Perhaps the most cogent of all explanations for the decline of women in the ministry has been surprisingly underexploited by historians of American religion. This is the sociosexual explanation. The period from 1880 to 1920 witnessed a profound identity crisis in the American male. Suddenly roused by the sound of woman banging at the door of politics, he awakened to find her already the bastion of society and keeper of the keys to culture. The male reaction was just short of hysterical. Howard Allen Bridgman looked out over a shawled and bonneted congregation one Sunday morning and suffered an anxiety attack. He asked, trying not to panic: Could "saint" by synonymous with "sister"? Had American religion become guilty of sex discrimination? "Have We a Religion for Men?"[51] Nineteenth-century men became aware of something that, as Bari Watkins points out, studies are only beginning to demonstrate: "American women were agents as well as victims in the construction of Victorian culture, which means that men were the victims as well as the agents of women's oppression."[52]

An overwhelming fear of effeminacy and an exaggerated attention to masculinity marked this period in history, which was dominated, some historians believe, by a "virility impulse" and a "masculinity crisis."[53] "The whole generation is womanized," cried Henry James's Basil Ransom in *The Bostonians* (1886); "the masculine tone is passing out of the world." Perceiving threats to masculinity everywhere, men turned in the social order to big sticks, western novels, sports, and war. The military uniform of the Boy Scout movement and the plainer, more virile dress fashions of the 1880s and 1890s reflect both the near-revolutionary impact of modern sports and the stampede away from daintiness. After even their political rallies had been infiltrated by women and children and their rowdy Fourth of July turned into a Sunday school picnic, parade, religious jamboree, and sunrise prayer meeting, men sought to reestablish masculine social rituals. Teddy Roosevelt became a national hero, championing "manly virtues" ("manly" was his favorite adjective), the "strenous life," and the "citizen as soldier" in an age of flabby city living, ragged individualism, and shrewd feminism. The lusty song book of the 1912 Progressive party *Progressive Battle Hymns*, and its muscular motto, "We Stand at Armageddon and Do Battle for the Lord," were only two political formations in the sociosexual warfare that had been waged for decades.

Religious forces were also at work to defeminize the church's constituency and transform this period into an age of aggressive male self-consciousness in religion.[55] Phillips Brooks's success during the Gilded Age in drawing men to his congregation at Trinity Church in Boston was at first an anomaly: he preached a robust gospel and a rugged Christ at a time when, as Ann Douglas has argued, the Bushnellian doctrine of the atonement portrayed God in maternal categories and transformed Jesus into "an example of a quiet and peaceable spirit," in one contemporary's words, "of a becoming modesty and sobriety; just, honest, upright, and sincere, and above all, of a most gracious and benevolent temper and behavior." Brooks's unsentimental, heroic picture of Jesus' "frankness and manliness" pointed the way to numerous imitations—Thomas Hughes's picture of Jesus as a man's man in *The Manliness of Christ*, E. P. Roe's masculine conversion novels, Lew Wallace's epic of heroism *Ben-Hur*, Carl Delos Case's call for a revival of masculine worship in *The Masculine in Religion*, and Harry Emerson Fosdick's sensitive 1913 portrayal of Jesus as the consummation of male and female virtues, whose message was unfortunately reversed by its strapping title, *The Manhood of the Master*.[56] Billy Sunday's husky voice, muscular piety, and platform gymnastics offered a striking contrast to the feminine mannerisms, high-pitched voice, and flowery, teary style of Dwight L. Moody. "It won't save your soul if your wife is a Christian," Sunday thumped, as he thumbed through his Bible picking out passages as he went. "You have got to be something more than a brother-in-law to the church." Individual pastors like E. H. Harriman took to writing inactive male church members personal letters, pleading with them for wide-awake and "whole-souled" involvement in the church to ensure that the children of the parish would not "think it unmanly to attend church and show any interest in religion."[57] The Christian associations (the YM and YWCA), the institutional church with its gyms and bowling alleys, the sermons that embraced the bicycle as "a thoroughly Christian machine" (because it "puts vivacity into a man's religion"), even the Booths' martial Salvation Army and its "agressive Christianity," were efforts to make religion muscular and smash the stereotype that "religious feeling was something peculiar to women and weak men."[58]

It would be careless to call this turn-of-the-century development a masculinization of religion. It was, however, a return of men to the church and the study of the Bible. It was evident in the religious census figures compiled by the Department of Commerce in 1916 that there had been an "advance in the proportion of males in the total membership of all the churches."[59] It was evident in the Baraca and "brotherhood" movements, the ecumenical laymen's missionary and "men and religion" movements, and the general organization of men's and boy's clubs, which spread throughout the churches in startling profusion.[60] The Men's Sunday Club, allegedly the first men's club sponsored by a black church, was started by Reverdy C. Ransom at Chicago's AME Bethel Church in 1896 and soon boasted a membership of over five hundred.[61] "The manliness of Christ" became so metabolized into the living and thinking of early twentieth-century men that clergy found themselves with a men's revival on their hands. The religious spectators had now become the spectacle.

The aggressive re-entry of men into American religious life and their furious bout with effeminacy led to a reassertion of male authority in the home and church and a clamping down on women's more public activities. "I can count the years on my hands," the Washington correspondent Mary Clemmer Ames wrote in 1886, "since I heard a New England pastor's wife, a holy woman, who rose to speak a few words of personal experience in a Sabbath-evening prayer-meeting, silenced by one of her husband's deacons."[62] Women became less visible and public in American popular religious life, and the issue of women's right to speak in church was, if anything, more contentious now than in the antebellum period.[63] It had become mixed up with the sociosexual issue of feminization and the theological issue of biblical authority and higher criticism.

A final and related reason for the loss of this heritage was the decline of itinerancy and the settling of Evangelical clergy in local communities. Emphasis came to be placed less on preaching and revivals and more on pastoral theology and church programming,[64] for which women had been given responsibility in the earlier period while ministers busied themselves with other pursuits. Faced with time on their hands, ministers sought greater control over local church life and thus had to persuade church women in general and their wives in particular to relinquish hold of what had become virtual lay leadership functions.[65] Symbolic of the retrenchment in ministry to women and the ministry of women was the fate of American Protestantism's most popular periodical, *The Ladies' Repository*. Founded by the 1840 General Conference of the Methodist Episcopal church as a means of getting "elegant," "pure," and "chastened" literature, three-quarters of it written by women, into middle- and upper-class homes, the *Ladies' Repository* owed its subscription lists to the Methodist clergy, who by 1866 had raised its circulation to an amazing 34,000. The increasingly strident tone of its feminism, especially evident in the featured digest "Women's Record at Home," and the growing conviction among the denomination's hierarchy that women did not need or want their own periodical, caused clergy to desert the magazine and stop pushing for subscribers. By 1876 the subscription list had fallen to 10,000, making it barely self-supporting and creating a furor at the General Conference over what to do with it. Its editor, a former college president and missionary who had at best a lounging interest in the journal, recommended that it be tenderly euthanized and given a "decent burial." Other voices suggested that the journal's title be taken seriously and a woman editor be elected, and indeed on the first ballot Frances Willard received over a third of the necessary votes. But the overwhelming desire of the clergy was to be done with publishing a magazine for women, and in 1877 a less religious, more cultural replacement called the *National Repository* emerged.[66]

In 1869 James M. Hoppin, professor of homiletics and pastoral theology at Yale, wrote a textbook for ministers that included some comments clearly intended to brake the accelerating locomotion of leadership among ministers' wives. He warned wives against domestic neglect and prodigal involvement in activities that were properly the province of their husbands, and he blew the whistle on ministers who permitted "the parish to command too much of her time and strength."[67] Hoppin talked about the ability of a minister's wife to "make or mar" the minister.[68] The Assistant and the Partner had seen things differently: they defined their role as the making or maring of the gospel.

Notes

ABBREVIATIONS

Chemung County Historical Society, Elmira, New York (CCHS)
  Beecher Collection (BC)
Cincinnati Historical Society (CHS)
Filson Club, Louisville, Kentucky (FC)
Garrett-Evangelical Theological Seminary, Evanston, Illinois (G-ETS)
  William Colbert Papers (WCP)
Library of Congress (LC)
  Titus Coan Papers (TCP)
  Hezekiah Smith Papers (HSP)
  Clarissa Armstrong Papers (CAP)
  John Keep Papers (JKP)
  Blackwell Family Papers (BFP)
    Henry Brown Blackwell
    Lucy Stone
    Antoinette Brown Blackwell
Maryland Historical Society, Baltimore (MHS)
  Graves Family Papers (GFP)
  Jean Boyd Fulton Diaries (JBFD)
  Loosie Bronson Diary (LBD)
  Brune-Randall Collection (B-RC)
  Ridgely-Pue Papers (R-PP)
Moorland-Spingarn Research Center, Washington, D.C. (M-SRC)
  Charlotte Forten Grimké Diary (CFGD)
New York Public Library (NYL)
  Methodist Episcopal Church Records (MR)
  Phoebe Palmer Papers (PPP)
Oberlin College Library, Oberlin, Ohio (OCL)
  Charles G. Finney Papers (FP)
  Dan Beach Bradley Papers (DBP)
  Robert S. Fletcher Papers (RFP)
  George F. Wright Papers (GWP)
  William F. Bohn Papers (WBP)
  Cowles Papers (CP)
Park Church (Elmira, New York) Archives (PCA)
Presbyterian Historical Society, Philadelphia, Pennsylvania (PHS)
Rochester (New York) Public Library (RPL)
Southern Historical Collection, Chapel Hill, North Carolina (SHC)
University of Oregon, Eugene (UO)
  Almira Raymond Letters (ARL)
Vermont Historical Society, Montpelier (VHS)

Introduction

1. The closest things to a history of the minister's wife that we now have are the brief introductory chapters to William Douglas, *Ministers' Wives* (New York: Harper and Row, 1965), pp. 1–7, and Wallace Denton, *The Role of the Minister's Wife* (Philadelphia: Westminster Press, 1962), pp. 1–22. Both are sociopsychological studies aimed at offering guidance to church policymakers and ministers' wives themselves. Margaret H. Watt scans the British scene in *The History of the Parson's Wife* (London: Faber and Faber, 1943). The most sophisticated studies of ministers' wives yet published are Lois A. Boyd's "Presbyterian Ministers' Wives—A Nineteenth-Century Portrait," *Journal of Presbyterian History* 59 (1981): 3–17; Paul Boyer's "Minister's Wife, Widow, Reluctant Feminist: Catherine Marshall in the 1950s," *American Quarterly* 30 (1978): 703–21; Julie Roy Jeffrey, "Ministry through Marriage: Methodist Clergy Wives on the Trans-Mississippi Frontier," in *Women in New Worlds: Historical Perspectives on the Wesleyan Tradition,* Hilah F. Thomas and Rosemary Skinner Keller, ed. (Nashville: Abingdon, 1981), pp. 143–60.

2. William B. Sprague, *A Sermon Preached May 15, 1821, at the Interment of Mrs. Elizabeth Lathrop, Relict of the Rev. Joseph Lathrop* (Springfield, Ill.: A. G. Tannatt, 1821), p. 20.

3. William B. Sprague, *An Address Delivered in the Evangelical Lutheran Ebenezer Church, Albany, on the Occasion of the Funeral of Mrs. Susan C. Pohlman, Wife of Rev. Henry N. Pohlman, Nov. 10, 1863* (Albany: J. Munsell, 1863), pp. 13–18.

4. It has not always been easy to decide where a minister's wife belongs. Peter Cartwright, for example, everybody's favorite Methodist itinerant, paid tribute to his wife of sixty-three years, Frances Gaines, in words that suggest that he subscribed to the Sacrificer ideal: "I am thankful that I have been permitted to associate in the toils of my itinerant life a worthy companion that never hindered me from traveling or preaching, that never scolded me for leaving her destitute and lonesome, but always urged me to do what I thought was my duty" (Peter Cartwright, *Fifty Years as a Presiding Elder,* ed. W. S. Hooper [Cincinnati: Hitchcock and Walden, 1871], p. 210). Yet from other sources we learn that Frances Cartwright joined her husband in seeking out sinners, was independently active in evangelism (Elizabeth A. Roe, *Recollections of Frontier Life* [n.p., n.d.], p. 90), and displayed a jaunty, feisty spirit when she informed her husband in 1840 that she would be attending the annual conference with him. "'You may look for me about Friday.' 'Humph,' said Uncle Peter, 'You need not expect me to look after you if you do come.' 'Thank you, sir,' said she, 'I have a little popularity of my own; I can take care of myself.'" (Chauncey Hobart, *Recollections of My Life: Fifty Years of Itinerancy in the Northwest* [Red Wing: Red Wing Printing Company, 1885], p. 167).

5. Donald G. Mathews, *Religion in the Old South* (Chicago: University of Chicago Press, 1977), p. 102; Paul Boyer, *Urban Masses and Moral Order in America, 1820–1920* (Cambridge, Mass.: Harvard University Press, 1978), p. 1.

6. Frances Trollope, *Domestic Manners of the Americans*, ed. Donald Smalley (New York: Alfred A. Knopf, 1949), p. 75.

7. "A Journal Kept by Mrs. Elizabeth Ford Atkinson Finney during a Visit to England, 1859–60," p. 55, OCL, FP.

8. John M. Williams, "The Beginning," in *The Oberlin Jubilee: 1833– 1883*, ed. W. G. Ballantine and E. J. Goodrich (Oberlin, Ohio: E. J. Goodrich, 1883), p. 83.

9. Lori D. Ginzberg, "Women in an Evangelical Community: Oberlin 1835–1850," *Ohio History* 89 (1980): 85–86.

10. Lawrence J. Friedman, "Racism and Sexism in Antebellum America: The Prudence Crandall Episode Reconsidered," *Societas* 5 (1974): 223-24.

11. John Ffirth, ed., *Experience and Gospel Labors of the Rev. Benjamin Abbott; to Which Is Annexed, a Narrative of His Life and Death* (New York: Carlton and Phillips, 1856), p. 127.

12. Joan Jacobs Brumberg, *Mission for Life: The Story of the Family of Adoniram Judson* (New York: Free Press, 1980), pp. 79–81.

13. Whitney R. Cross, *The Burned-Over District: The Social and Intellectual History of Enthusiastic Religion in Western New York, 1800– 1850* (New York: Harper Torchbooks, 1965), p. 84.

14. Frances Ellen Watkins Harper, "Women's Political Future," in *World's Congress of Representative Women*, ed. May Write Sewall (Chicago: Rand McNally, 1894), p. 433.

15. Mary Schauffler Platt, *The Home with the Open Door* (New York: Student Volunteer Movement, 1920).

16. For a contemporary look at the modern pastor's wife and her quest for self-fulfillment, see Donna Sinclair, *The Pastor's Wife Today* (Nashville: Abingdon, 1981).

Chapter One

1. Daniel Callam, "Clerical Continence in the Fourth Century: Three Papal Decretals," *Theological Studies* 41 (1980): 3–50. The fourth canon of the Council of Gangra in 343 reveals that there were Christians who boycotted the Eucharist when it was administered by married clergymen.

2. John K. Yost, "The Reformation Defense of Clerical Marriage in the Reigns of Henry VIII and Edward VI," *Church History* 50 (1981): 152–53.

3. Kenneth Scott Latourette, *A History of Christianity* (New York Harper, 1953), p. 981.

4. My account of Katherine Luther is drawn from Roland H. Bainton, *Women of the Reformation in Germany and Italy* (Minneapolis: Augsburg, 1971), pp. 23–43; C. V. Eckermann, *Mistress of the Black Cloister: The Story of Kate Luther* (Adelaide: Lutheran Publishing Company, 1976); and Charles Nordhoff, "The Wife of Luther," *Ladies' Repository* 17 (1857): 212–17.

5. Quoted in Richard Stauffer, *The Humanness of John Calvin* (Nashville: Abington, 1971), p. 35.

6. "Calvin's Courtship and Marriage," *Ladies' Repository* 17 (1857): 298.

7. I am dependent here on the treatment of Jasper Ridley, *Thomas Cranmer* (Oxford: Clarendon, 1960), pp. 16–20, 46, 148–55; V. J. K. Brook, *A Life of Archbishop Parker* (Oxford: Clarendon, 1962), pp. 36–37; John Cordy Jeaffreson, *A Book about the Clergy*, 2d. ed., 2 vols. (London: Hurst and Blackett, 1870), 1: 247–86; and Margaret H. Watt, *The History of the Parson's Wife* (London: Faber and Faber, 1943), pp. 7–25. There is some debate about whether Cranmer's marriage took place in 1532 or 1541.

8. George Herbert, "The Parson in His House," in *A Priest to the Temple; or The Country Parson, His Character, and Rule of Holy Life* (London: T. Maxey for T. Garthwait, 1652), reprinted in *The Works of George Herbert*, ed. F. E. Hutchinson, (Oxford: Clarendon Press, 1941), pp. 239–43.

9. Richard Baxter, *Memoirs of Mrs. Margaret Baxter, Daughter of Francis Charlton, Esq., and Wife of Mr. Richard Baxter* . . . 1681; reprinted., (London: Richard Edwards, 1826), pp. 47–49; 51–52, 63, 65, 106–7; Jeaffreson, *Book about the Clergy*, 1: 289–90.

10. Baxter, *Memoirs*, pp. 73, 75, 78.

11. Milton D. Speizman and Jane C. Kronick, "A Seventeenth-Century Quaker Women's Declaration," *Signs* 1 (1975): 231–35; Isabell Ross, *Margaret Fell, Mother of Quakerism* (New York: Longmans, Green, 1949).

12. Amanda Porterfield, *Feminine Spirituality in America: From Sarah Edwards to Martha Graham* (Philadelphia: Temple University Press, 1980), p. 49.

13. Roland Bainton writes, "There were more ministers' wives than ministers in New England"; see "The Office of the Minister's Wife in New England," in *Christian Unity and Religion in New England* (Boston: Beacon Press, 1964), p. 266.

14. *A Priest to the Temple*, p. 260.

15. H. Richard Niebuhr, *The Kingdom of God in America* (Hamden, C.: Shoe String Press, 1956), 91–2.

16. Winthrop S. Hudson, ed., Introduction to Roger Williams, *Experiments of Spiritual Life and Health* (Philadelphia: Westminister Press, 1951), pp. 11, 18; Edwin S. Gaustad, ed., *Baptist Piety: The Last Will and Testimony of Obadiah Holmes* (Grand Rapids, Mich.: Christian University Press, 1978), pp. 93–98.

17. Quoted in G. J. Barker-Benfield, *The Horrors of the Half-Known Life: Male Attitudes toward Women and Sexuality in Nineteenth-Century America* (New York: Harper and Row, 1976), p. 25.

18. David Levin, *Cotton Mather: The Young Life of the Lord's Remembrance, 1663–1703* (Cambridge: Harvard University Press, 1978), pp. 1, 13.

19. Ibid., pp. 128–29, 144, 298. For Cotton Mather's disastrous third marriage, see Robert G. Middlekauff, *The Mathers: Three Generations of Puritan Intellectuals, 1596–1728* (New York: Oxford University Press, 1971), pp. 365–66.

20. Benjamin Franklin summarized his relationship to his wife of almost forty years, Deborah Reed, in just such terms: "She proved a good and faithful helpmate." Quoted in Claude-Anne Lopex and Eugenia W. Herbert, *The Private Franklin: The Man and His Family* (New York: W. W. Norton, 1975), p. 30. See also Abigail Adams's comments in a 5 June 1809 letter to Mrs. Shaw: "I consider it as an indispensable requisite, that every American wife should herself know how to order and regulate her family; how to govern her domestics, and train up her children. For this purpose, the all-wise-Creator made women an help-meet for man, and she who fails in these duties does not answer the end of her creation." In *Letters of Mrs. Adams, the Wife of John Adams* . . . , 2d ed., 2 vol. (Boston: Little, Brown, 1840), 2: 45.

21. William G. McLoughlin, ed., *The Diary of Isaac Backus*, 3 vols. (Providence; R. I.: Brown University Press, 1979), 3: 1535. For the outline of Backus's wedding sermon, see pp. 1538–39.

22. Alvah Hovey, *A Memoir of the Life and Times of the Rev. Isaac Backus* (Boston: Gould and Lincoln, 1859), pp. 81, 307.

23. Barbara Cunningham, "An Eighteenth-Century View of Femininity as seen through the Journals of Henry Melchior Muhlenberg," *Pennsylvania History* 43 (1976): 201.

24. Charles L. Wallis, *Stories on Stone: A Book of American Epitaphs* (New York: Oxford University Press, 1954), p. 94.

25. "She was my pleasing companion," the rector of St. Mary in Woolnoth, London, wrote in his introduction to the volume, "my most affectionate friend, my judicious counsellor. I seldom or ever repented of acting according to her advice. And I seldom acted against it, without being convinced by the events that I was wrong." John Newton, *Letters to a Wife, by the Author of Cardiphonia*, 2 vols. (London: J. Johnson, 1793), 1: xxii. Hezekiah Smith to Hephzibah Smith, 8 June 1776, 27 June 1776, 5 August 1777, 14 July 1780, in LC, HSP. Also see Bunker Gay, *A Discourse in Two Parts, Delivered at Hinsdale, July 29, 1792, and the Sabbath after at Chesterfield, Occasioned by the Death of Mrs. Abigail Gay, Who Departed This Life July 15, 1792* (Greenfield, Mass.: Thomas Dickman, 1792); Joseph Lathrop, *A Funeral Sermon, Deliver'd October 25, 1796, at the Interment of Mrs. Mary Gay, Relict of the Rev. Dr. Gay, Pastor of the First Church in Suffield* (Suffield, Mass: H. and O. Farnsworth, 1797), pp. 19–20. For Ebenezer Parkman's intense feelings toward his wife, which did not surface in his diary until he thought she was dying, see Rose Lockwood, "Birth, Illness and Death in Eighteenth-Century New England," *Journal of Social History* 12 (1978): 121.

26. William Alcott, *The Young Wife; or, Duties of a Woman in the Marriage Relation* (Boston: George W. Lightly, 1837), p. 354.

27. Quoted in Richard L. Bushman, "Jonathan Edwards as Great Man: Identity, Conversion, and Leadership in the Great Awakening," *Soundings* 52 (1969): 18.

28. Quoted in Joseph Tracy, *The Great Awakening: A History of the Revival of Religion in the Time of Edwards and Whitefield* (Boston: Tappan and Dennet, 1842), pp. 226–27.

29. Irene Woodbridge Clark, "A Wifely Estimate of Edwards: An

Unpublished Letter by Edwards's wife," *Congregationalist and Christian World*, 88 (1903): 472–73.

30. Elisabeth D. Dodds, *Marriage to a Difficult Man: The "Uncommon Union" of Jonathan and Sarah Edwards* (Philadelphia: Westminister Press, 1971), pp. 55–65, 91.

31. Quoted in Dodds, *Marriage to a Difficult Man*, p. 87.

32. Bainton, "Office of the Minister's Wife," p. 269.

33. Quoted in Porterfield, *Feminine Spirituality*, p. 46.

34. Quoted in Dodds, *Marriage to a Difficult Man*, p. 96.

35. Porterfield, *Feminine Spirituality*, p. 49.

36. Dodds, *Marriage to a Difficult Man*, pp. 78, 106, 95–106.

37. See N. Ray Hiner, "Preparing for the Harvest: The Concept of New Birth and the Theory of Religious Education on the Eve of the First Awakening," *Fides et Historia* 9 (1976): 8–25.

38. Quoted in Laurie Crumpacker, "Esther Burr's Journal 1754–1757: A Document of Evangelical Sisterhood" (Ph.D. diss., Boston University, 1978), p. 25.

39. Ibid., pp. 143, 206, 188, 27, 30–31; Dodds, *Marriage to a Difficult Man*, p. 186.

40. Crumpacker, "Esther Burr's Journal," p. 1.

41. Ibid., pp. 20–21; Cotton Mather, *Ornaments for the Daughters of Zion* (1692; reprint ed., Delmar, N.Y.: Scholars' Facsimiles and Reprints, 1978).

42. Ibid, pp. 149, 155, 272, 329.

43. William Wale, *Whitefield's Journals, to Which Is Prefixed His "Short Account"*. . . (London: H. J. Drane, n.d.), p. 421; Joshua Huntington, *Memoirs of the Life of Mrs. Abigail Waters* . . . (Boston: Samuel T. Armstrong, 1817), p. 53; Mary Beth Norton, "'My Resting Reaping Times': Sarah Osborn's Defense of Her 'Unfeminine' Activities, 1767," *Signs* 2 (1976): 515–29.

44. Quoted in Crumpacker, "Esther Burr's Journal," p. 16.

Chapter Two

1. Quoted by Richard M. Allen, "Rebellion within the Household: Hans Sach's Conception of Women and Marriage," *Essays in History* 19 (1975): 43.

2. Roland H. Bainton, *Women of the Reformation in Germany and Italy* (Minneapolis: Augsburg 1971), pp. 9–10.

3. In attempting to portray male Puritans as unrepentent misogynists, Koehler forgets that he is a historian and succumbs to the refractory presentism of the psychologist and sociologist. Lyle Koehler, *A Search for Power: The "Weaker Sex" in Seventeenth-Century New England* (Urbana: University of Illinois Press, 1980).

4. Malmsheimer notwithstanding and Ulrich upholding. Laurel Thatcher Ulrich, "Vertuous Woman Found: New England Ministerial Literature, 1668–1735," *American Quarterly* 28 (1976): 20–40, and Lonna M. Malmsheimer, "Daughters of Zion: New England Roots of American Feminism," *New England Quarterly* 50 (1977): 486–87.

5. See Pattie Cowell's Introduction to Cotton Mather's popular conduct manual of 1693, *Ornaments for the Daughters of Zion* (Delmar, N.Y. Scholars' Facsimiles and Reprints, 1978), pp. vi–vii, 46.

6. Roger Thompson, *Women in Stuart England and America: A Comparative Study* (Boston: Routledge and Kegan Paul, 1974); Winthrop S. Hudson, *The Cambridge Connection and the Elizabethan Settlement of 1559* (Durham, N.C.: Duke University Press, 1980), pp. 15, 38 n, 63 n.

7. Margaret W. Masson, "The Typology of the Female as a Model for the Regenerate: Puritan Preaching, 1690–1730," *Signs* 2 (1976): 304–15.

8. Julia Cherry Spruill, *Women's Life and Work in the Southern Colonies* (Chapel Hill: University of North Carolina Press, 1938), pp. 213–14.

9. Carol V. R. George, "Anne Hutchinson and the 'Revolution' Which Never Happened," in *"Remember the Ladies": New Perspectives on Women in American History,* ed. Carol V. R. George (Syracuse: Syracuse University Press, 1975), p. 23.

10. Marlene LeGates, "The Cult of Womanhood in Eighteenth-Century Thought," *Eighteenth Century Studies* 10 (1976): 27.

11. Anne Grant, *Memoirs of an American Lady, with Sketches of Manners and Scenery in America, as They Existed Previous to the Revolution,* 2 vols. (London: Longman, Hurst, Rees and Orme, 1808), 1: 39; Samuel Hopkins, *Memoirs of the Life of Mrs. Sarah Osborn . . . .* (Worcester, Mass.: Leonard Worcester, 1799), and *The Life and Character of Miss Susanna Anthony . . . ,* 2d ed. (Portland, Me.: Lyman, Hall, 1810).

12. Carl N. Degler, *At Odds: Women and the Family in America from the Revolution to the Present* (New York: Oxford University Press, 1980); Mary Beth Norton, *Liberty's Daughters: The Revolutionary Experience of American Women, 1750–1800* (Boston: Little, Brown, 1980).

13. Arthur Darby Nock, *Conversion* (New York: Oxford University Press, 1933).

14. Barbara Sicherman has called the doctrine of the spheres "a nineteenth-century paradox" in her review essay, "American History," *Signs* 1 (1975): 470.

15. Jean Jacques Rousseau, "A Discourse on the Origin of Inequality," in *The Social Contract and Discourses*, trans. G. D. H. Cole (New York: E. P. Dutton, 1950), p. 187.

16. William Greenleaf Eliot, *Lectures to Young Women*, 3d ed. (Boston: Crosby, Nichols, 1854; micropublished ed., New Haven, Conn. Research Publications, 1975), p. 72.

17. See Beecher's address before the eleventh National Woman's Rights Convention, 10 May 1866, in *Speeches of George William Curtis, Henry Ward Beecher* (New York: National American Women Suffrage Association, 1898), p. 82; Virginia (Randolph) Cary, *Letters on Female Character Addressed to a Young Lady on the Death of Her Mother* (Richmond, Va.: Waiks, 1828).

18. Jerald Brauer, "Puritanism, Revivalism, and the Revolution," in *Religion and the American Revolution*, ed. Jerald Brauer (Philadelphia: Fortress Press, 1976), pp. 1–27.

19. This story crops up in many places. See, e.g., Samuel Irenaeus Prince, *The Power of Prayer, Illustrated in the Wonderful Displays of Divine Grace at the Fulton Street and Other Meetings in New York and Elsewhere, in 1857 and 1858* (New York: Charles Scribner, 1859), pp. 139–40, and (Nashville) *Christian Advocate* 22 (2 September 1858).

20. Catharine E. Beecher and H. B. Stowe, *The American Woman's Home, or Principles of Domestic Science: Being a Guide to the Formation and Maintenance of Economical, Healthful, Beautiful, and Christian Homes* (New York: J. B. Ford, 1870); Clifford E. Clark, Jr., "Domestic Architecture as an Index to Social History: The Romantic Revival and the Cult of Domesticity in America, 1840–1870," *Journal of Interdisciplinary History* 7 (1976): 42, 44; E. W. Hooper, *Address to Christian Parents of the Churches in Vermont* (n.p., n.d.), p. 14. For the change that occurred between the beginning of the century, when the responsibility for religious instruction in the home was assumed to be the man's, and mid-century, when it was delegated to the woman, contrast James Hall, *National Virtue and Vice Contrasted . . .* (Raleigh, N.C.: E. M. Boyland, 1870), pp. 6–7, and Rufus W. Bailey, *Domestic Duties; or, The Family a Nursery for Earth and Heaven* (Philadelphia: Presbyterian Board of Publication, n.d.), p. 65.

21. Carl N. Degler, *At Odds*, p. 298. For a representative nineteenth-century statement of this argument, see N. S. S. Beman, *The Claims of Jesus Christ on Young Women: A Discourse Delivered in the First Presbyterian Church, Troy, November 21, 1841* (Lowell: A. Upton, 1842).

22. Mary P. Ryan, "A Women's Awakening: Evangelical Religion and the Families of Utica, New York, 1800–1840," *American Quarterly* 30 (1978): 623.

23. Lydia Keep formed the reading society after convincing her indignant husband that it was a better approach than denouncing the youth and their adolescent rebellion from the pulpit. See "Autobiography of the Rev. John Keep of Blandford, Massachusetts," typescript copy in LC, JKP.

24. *Woman's Mission in the Christian Church* (Philadelphia: King and Baird, 1864), pp. 2, 25–29.

25. *The Revivalist: Exclusively Devoted to the Revival and Extension of Evangelical Religion* (London: Simpkin and Marshall, 1832), p. 197.

26. Ann Douglas's discovery of an alliance between women and the liberal clergy in *The Feminization of American Culture* (New York: Alfred A. Knopf, 1977) is eclipsed in historical importance by Sandra S. Sizer's elaboration of the alliance between women and the Evangelical clergy, which she calls "evangelical domesticity," in *Gospel Hymns and Social Religion: The Rhetoric of Nineteenth-Century Revivalism* (Philadelphia: Temple University Press, 1978).

27. Eliot, *Lectures to Young Women*, pp. 33–82.

28. Nathan S. S. Beman, *The Intellectual Position of Our Country: An Introductory Lecture Delivered before the Young Men's Association for Mutual Improvement, in the City of Troy, December 10th, 1839* (Troy: N. Tuttle, 1839), p. 6.

29. "Women's Mission," *Millennial Harbinger* 6 (1856): 466.

30. Caroline Tenney Keith wrote to her brother in 1849, "Indeed, the greatest trial of my life has been to content myself with the sphere of a woman. Her dependence—oh! it is excruciating and yet necessary." Keith also expressed her frustration at not being able to go into the ministry. "Oh, if I were a man! I do not suppose I should do great things, but I would preach the unsearchable riches of Christ." William C. Tenney, ed., *Memoirs of Mrs. Caroline Keith, Missionary of the Protestant Episcopal Church to China* (New York: D. Appleton, 1869), pp. 63, 76. See also Lucretia Mott's comment after listening to a man who waxed enthusiastic about the moral superiority of woman: "Woman is now sufficiently developed to prefer justice to compliment." Quoted in Elizabeth Cady Stanton, Susan B. Anthony, and Matilda Joslyn Gage, *The History of Woman Suffrage*, 6 vols. (New York: Fowler and Wells, 1881–1922), 1: 80.

31. Florence Howe Hall, *Julia Ward Howe and the Woman Suffrage Movement: A Selection from her Speeches and Essays, with Introduction and Notes by Her Daughter* (Boston: Dana Ester, 1913; reprint ed., New York: Arno Press and the New York Times, 1969).

32. "A Tilt at the Woman's Question," *Harper's New Monthly Magazine* 26 (1863): 350–56.

33. *Ladies' Repository* 31 (1871): 213, 35 (1876): 284; Frances E. Willard, *Women in the Pulpit* (Boston: D. Lothrop, 1888), pp. 39, 63–65; Eliza Bisbee Duffey, *The Relations of the Sexes* (New York: Estill, 1876), p. 15. The Phillips quotation can be found in *Speeches on Rights of Women* (Philadelphia: Alfred J. Ferris, 1898), p. 62; the Gilman quotation can be found in *His Religion and Hers: A Study of the Faith of Our Fathers and the Work of Our Mothers* (New York: Century, 1923), pp. 55–56. For an Evangelical leader who advocated giving women the ballot for millennial reasons, see Clarence T. Wilson, *Matthew Simpson: Patriot, Preacher, Prophet* (New York: Methodist Book Concern, 1929), p. 77. The most thorough treatment of this thesis can be found in Leo Miller, *Woman and the Divine Republic* (Buffalo: Haas and Nauert, 1874).

34. Richard D. Shiels, "The Feminization of American Congregationalism, 1730–1835," *American Quarterly* 33 (1981): 46–62.

35. Mather, *Ornaments*, pp. 10–11; Cedric B. Cowing, "Sex and Preaching in the Great Awakening," *American Quarterly* 20 (1968): 629; William Lumpkin, "The Role of Women in Eighteenth-Century Virginia Baptist Life," *Baptist History and Heritage* 8 (1973): 160–61; Douglas, *Feminization of American Culture*, pp. 98–99; Timothy Dwight, *Travels in New England and New York*, 4 vols., ed. Barbara Miller Solomon (Cambridge, Mass.: Belknap Press of Harvard University Press, 1969), 4: 335; Donald G. Mathews, *Religion in the Old South* (Chicago: University of Chicago Press, 1977), pp. 47–48. See also Carroll Smith-Rosenberg, "The New Woman and the New History," *Feminist Studies* 3 (1975): 189.

36. Shiels, "Feminization of American Congregationalism," p. 49.

37. James Stuart, *Three Years in North America*, 2 vols. (New York: J. and J. Harper 1833), 2: 281; *Christian Repository* 2 (1823): 156, as quoted in Keith Melder, "Ladies Bountiful: Organized Women's Benevolence in

Early Nineteenth-Century America," *New York History* 48 (1967): 240; Terry David Bilhartz, "Urban Religion and the Second Great Awakening: A Religious History of Baltimore, Maryland, 1790–1830" (Ph.D. diss., George Washington University, 1979), pp. 62–63; Douglas, *Feminization of American Culture*, pp. 98–99. Another variable to which attention must be paid in future constituency studies is the proportion of black females to males. George Lewis, visiting in the mid-1840s a Virginia Baptist church where one-third of the membership was black and two-thirds white, observed that two-thirds of the black members of the church were female; see George Lewis, *Impressions of America and the American Churches . . .* (Edinburgh: W. P. Kennedy 1787), p. 67.

38. *Parish Statistics of the Church of the Ascension, New York* (New York: Baker, Godwin, 1851), p. 71; *Parish Statistics of the Church of the Ascension, New York* (New York: A. Cunningham, 1852), p. 13; *Parish Statistics of the Church of the Ascension, New York* (New York: J. A. Gray, 1854), p. 13. *Parish Statistics of the Church of the Ascension, New York* (New York: J. S. Gray, 1856), p. 14.

39. George Coles, *Heroines of Methodism; or, Pen and Ink Sketches of the Mothers and Daughters of the Church* (New York: Carlton and Porter, 1857), p. 181; Henry B. Blackwell, "Christianity and Woman Suffrage," *Woman's Journal* 9 (1878): 268; Willard, *Women in the Pulpit*, pp. 25–26; James Barlow Simmons, *Women's Bible Bands: An Address Delivered before the American Baptist Publication Society at the Sixty-Fourth Anniversary, May, 1888, in the City of Washington, D.C.* (Philadelphia: American Baptist Publication Society, 1888), p. 9; B. T. Roberts, *Ordaining Women* (Rochester, N. Y.: Earnest Christian Publishing Office, 1891), p. 112; T. W. Higginson, "The Religious Weakness of Women," *Woman's Journal* 8 (1877): 113; *Brother Mason, the Circuit Rider; or, Ten Years a Methodist Preacher* (Cincinnati: H. N. Rulison, 1858), p. 232; Peter Cartwright, *Fifty Years as a Presiding Elder*, ed. W. S. Hooper (Cincinnati: Hitchcock and Walden, 1871), p. 235; *Journal of the General Conference of the Methodist Episcopal Church, Volume Three, 1848–56* (New York: Carlton and Phillips, 1856), p. 60. The only evidence I have been able to discover that would suggest that males were present in greater numbers than heretofore thought is Edward Hungerford, *A Report on the Moral and Religious Condition of the Community, in the City of Burlington, Vermont* (Burlington: n.p., 1867), as quoted in Lewis S. Feuer and Mervyn W. Perrine, "Religion in a Northern Vermont Town: A Cross-Century Comparative Study," *Journal for the Scientific Study of Religion* 5 (1966): 369. Hungerford took a tally of church attendance at each Burlington church on Sunday morning, 3 March 1867, and found that 44 percent of those present at the Congregational churches were males, 49 percent of the Baptists, 61 percent of the Methodists, 50 percent of the Episcopalians, and 42 percent of the Unitarians. All totaled, Burlington Protestant females were in the ascendancy only by a ratio of 55 to 45.

40. Cowing, "Sex and Preaching," pp. 629–31; Elisabeth D. Dodds, *Marriage to a Difficult Man: The "Uncommon Union" of Jonathan and Sarah Edwards* (Philadelphia: Westminster Press, 1971), p. 74; James

Walsh, "The Great Awakening in the First Congregational Church of Wood-bury, Connecticut," *William and Mary Quarterly* 28 (1871): 544; Ryan, "A Women's Awakening," pp. 603–4; "Revivals of Religion," *American Baptist Magazine and Missionary Intelligencer* 11 (1831): 277–78; Anne C. Love-land, "Presbyterians and Revivalism in the Old South," *Journal of Presbyterian History* 57 (1979): 45; Ruth Ramble, "Facts and Fancies of Life in the Old Dominion," *Ladies' Repository* 35 (1875): 46.

41. Mather, *Ornaments*, p. 48; Cowing, "Sex and Preaching," p. 629.

42. Masson, "Typology of the Female," pp. 304–15.

43. Frances Wright, *Course of Popular Lectures, with Three Addresses, on Various Public Occasions, and a Reply to the Charges against the French Reforms of 1789* (London: James Watson, 1834; reprint ed., New York: Arno Press, 1972), pp. vi–vii.

44. Margaret Fuller Ossoli, *Woman in the Nineteenth Century, and Kindred Papers Relating to the Sphere, Condition, and Duties of Women*, ed. Arthur B. Fuller (Boston: John P. Jewett, 1855; reprint ed., New York: Source Book Press, n.d.), p. 35.

45. Mathews, *Religion in the Old South*, pp. 109–10.

46. Nancy F. Cott, "Young Women in the Second Great Awakening in New England," *Feminist Studies* 3 (1975): 15–29.

47. The classic statement of this position is Barbara Welter, "The Cult of True Womanhood: 1820–1860," reprinted in *American Family in Social-Historical Perspective*, ed. Michael Gordon (New York: St. Martin's Press, 1973), pp. 224–50.

48. Ryan, "A Women's Awakening," p. 604.

49. Hazard's home was a haven for many women who wanted to avoid the ceremony of "churching" after childbirth. See Margaret McLaren Cook, "Dorothy Hazard," in *Great Baptist Women by Baptist Women*, ed. A. S. Clement (London: Carey Kings Gate Press, 1955), pp. 9–13, and Claire Cross, "'He-Goats before the Flocks': A Note on the Part Played by Women in the Founding of Some Civil War Churches," in *Popular Belief and Practices*, ed. G. J. Cuming and Derek Baker (Cambridge: Cambridge University Press, 1972), pp. 195–202.

50. Roger Williams, *Experiments of Spiritual Life and Health*, ed. Winthrop Hudson (Philadelphia: Westminster Press, 1951), p. 16; Edwin S. Gaustad, ed., *Baptist Piety: The Last Will and Testimony of Obadiah Holmes* (Grand Rapids, Mich.: Christian University Press, 1978), p. 93.

51. Bailey, *Domestic Duties*, p. 41.

52. Quoted in Miriam Gurko, *The Ladies of Seneca Falls: The Birth of the Woman's Rights Movement* (New York: Macmillan, 1974), pp. 9–10.

53. Isaac Backus, *A History of New England*, ed. David Weston, 2d ed., 2 vols. (Newton, Mass.: Backus Historical Society, 1871), 2: 490.

54. Bailey, *Domestic Duties*, pp. 37–39. See also Bailey's *The Family Preacher; or, Domestic Duties Illustrated and Enforced in Eight Discourses* (New York: John S. Taylor, 1837), pp. 41–45; and Catherine L. Adams, *Daily Duties Inculcated in a Series of Letters, Addressed to the Wife of a Clergyman* (Boston: Crocker and Brewster, 1835), pp. 37–41.

55. Mathew, *Religion in the Old South*, pp. 103–4.

56. Martha Tomhave Blauvelt, "Women and Revivalism," in *Women and Religion in America: The Nineteenth Century*, ed. Rosemary Ruether and Rosemary Keller, 2 vols. (San Francisco: Harper and Row, 1981), 1:5.

57. Fredrick A. Norwood, ed., *The Doctrine and Discipline of the Methodist Episcopal Church, in America; with Explanatory Notes, by Thomas Coke and Francis Asbury*, 10th ed. (Philadelphia: Henry Tuckards, 1798; facsimile ed., Rutland: Academy Books, 1979), pp. 156–57.

58. See Peggy Dow, *Vicissitudes; or, the Journey of Life* in *History of Cosmopolite; or, The Four Volumes of Lurenzo Dow's Journal Concentrated in One . . .* , 3d ed. rev. (Wheeling, Va: Joshua Martin, 1848), p. 632. Benjamin St. James Fry, *The Life of Robert R. Roberts, One of the Bishops of the Methodist Episcopal Church* (New York: Carlton and Porter, 1856), p. 14.

59. Elizabeth A. Roe, *Recollections of Frontier Life* (n.p., n.d.), pp. 21, 23, 25–27, 69.

60. See Daniel Wise, *Sketches and Anecdotes of American Methodists of "The Days That Are No More" : Designed for Boys and Girls* (New York: Phillips and Hunt, 1883), pp. 84, 88–89, 94–100.

61. Mary B. Allen King, *Looking Backward; or, Memories of the Past* (New York: Anson D. F. Randolph, 1870), pp. 141–42.

62. P. H. Fowler, *Historical Sketch of Presbyterianism within the Bounds of the Synod of Central New York* (Utica, N.Y.: Curtiss and Childs, 1877), 722–23.

63. Barbara Leslie Epstein, *The Politics of Domesticity: Women, Evangelism, and Temperance in Nineteenth-Century America* (Middletown, C.: Wesleyan University Press, 1981), 14.

64. James Wood, *Directions and Cautions Addressed to the Class Leaders, in the Methodist Connection; and Designed to Shew the Nature of Their Office, and the Necessity of Their Being Faithful in the Discharge of Their Duty* (London: Conference Office, 1803), pp. 20–21.

65. The story of the wife, persecuted and beaten because of her religious faith, only to win over her husband in the end, was a common theme in Evangelical circles. See Coles, *Heroines of Methodism, pp. 160–66; John Ffirth, ed., Experience and Gospel Labors of the Rev. Benjamin Abbott; to Which is Annexed, a Narrative of His Life and Death* (New York: Carlton and Phillips, 1854), p. 48; Maxwell Gaddis, *Brief Recollections of the Late Rev. George Walker* (Cincinnati: Swormstedt and Poe, 1857), p. 62; James B. Finley, *Sketches of Western Methodism; Biographical, Historical and Miscellaneous, Illustrative of Pioneer Life*, ed. W. P. Strickland (Cincinnati: Methodist Book Concern, 1857), pp. 518–22.

66. See H. L. Chapman, *Memoirs of an Itinerant* (n.p., n.d.), p. 32; James W. Alexander, *The Life of Archibald Alexander* (New York: Charles Scribner, 1854), pp. 116–17; George Brown, *Recollections of Itinerant Life; Including Early Reminiscences*, 3d. ed. (Cincinnati: R. W. Carroll, 1866), p. 82.

67. Quoted in Paul E. Johnson, *A Shopkeeper's Millennium: Society and Revivals in Rochester, New York, 1815–1837* (New York: Hill and Wang, 1978), pp. 19, 108.

68. *Savannah Daily Republican*, 13 October 1858.
69. Frances Trollope, *Domestic Manners of the Americans*, ed. Donald Smalley (New York: Alfred A. Knopf, 1949), pp. 173–75; Whitney R. Cross, *The Burned-Over District: The Social and Intellectual History of Enthusiastic Religion in Western New York* (New York: Harper Torchbooks, 1965), p. 187. For a variety of literary treatments of the sexual dimension of the pastor-parishioner relationship, see Harriet Beecher Stowe, *The Minister's Wooing* (1859); Margaret Deland, *John Ward, Preacher* (Boston: Houghton Mifflin, 1888); and Rose Terry Cook, *Steadfast: The Story of the Saint and the Sinner* (Boston: Ticknor, 1889). It became part of the scandal of the day with Catharine E. Beecher's expose, *Truth Stranger Than Fiction . . .* (Boston: Phillips, Sampson, 1850). The only minister's wife to address the issue directly was the witty, irreverent, erudite Corra Harris; see *A Circuit Rider's Wife* (Philadelphia: Henry Altemus, 1910), pp. 162–65, where she describes the various forms of seduction and concludes that "spiritual invalids" who are "forever wanting to consult the pastor between times about their spiritual symptoms" most likely "sustained the same relation to their souls that young and playful kittens do to their tails. . . . But the most dangerous of them all is the one who refuses to take up her bed and walk spiritually and who wants the preacher to assist her every step. . . . This is why, when we hear of a minister who has disgraced himself with some female member of his flock, my sympathies are all with the preacher" (pp. 161–62). Because of their emotional, demonstrative modes of worship, revival services were especially dangerous for some: "I have seldom seen a preacher of respectability join in these night revellings; it is generally conducted by the ignorant understrappers, who know of nothing but jumping, hallooing, and squeezing, and the freedom they take on such occasions with the young female converts." Quoted by Bilhartz, "Urban Religion and the Second Great Awakening," p. 161.

Chapter Three

1. Peggy Dow, *Vicissitudes; or, the Journey of Life* in *History of Cosmopolite; or, The Four Volumes of Lorenzo Dow's Journal Concentrated in One . . .*, 3d. ed. rev. (Wheeling, Va.: Joshua Martin, 1848), pp. 609–10. For Lorenzo's own account of his marriage, see pp. 209–12. For Lorenzo's appearance, see George Peck, *Early Methodism within the Bounds of the Old Genesee Conference from 1788 to 1828; or, The First Forty Years of Wesleyan Evangelism in Northern Pennsylvania, Central Western New York and Canada* (New York: Carlton and Porter, 1860), pp. 198–203; Judge R. C. Ewing, *Historical Memoirs, Containing a Brief History of the Cumberland Presbyterian Church in Missouri, and Biographical Sketches of a Number of Those Ministers Who Contributed to the Organization and the Establishment of That Church, in the Country West of the Mississippi River* (Nashville: Cumberland Presbyterian Board of Publication, 1874), p. 154; Charles Coleman Sellers, *Lorenzo Dow: The Bearer of the Word* (New York: Monton, Balch, 1928), p. 148; Marion Plyler and Alva W. Plyler, *Men of the Burning Heart: Ivey—Dow—Doub* (Raleigh, N.C.: Commercial Printing Company, 1918), pp. 96–97.

2. For Dow's defense of ministerial marriages, see his "Reflections on the Important Subject of Matrimony," in *History of Cosmopolite*, pp. 399–418: "When I hear persons who are married trying to dissuade others from marrying, I infer one of two things; that they are either unhappy in their marriage, else they enjoy a blessing which they do not wish others to partake of" (p. 400).

3. George Peck, *Early Methodism*, p. 198. For an example of Dow's extended influence, see Chauncey Hobard, *Recollections of My Life: Fifty Years of Itinerancy in the Northwest* (Red Wing: Red Wing Printing Company, 1885), p. 37.

4. Thomas M. Finney, *The Life and Labors of Enoch Mather Marvin, Late Bishop of the Methodist Episcopal Church, South* (St Louis, Mo.: James H. Chambers, 1880), p. 157.

5. Robert J. Lowenberg, *Equality on the Oregon Frontier: Jason Lee and the Methodist Mission, 1834–43* (Seattle: University of Washington Press, 1976), pp. 112–13. The threatening passions awakened in Charles Wesley by Sarah Gwynne, whom he would eventually marry, inspired the following stanza in an anguished 1748–49 hymn:

> Keep from me thy loveliest Creature,
>   Till I prove
>   Jesus' Love
> Infinitely sweeter.

See Frank Baker, ed., *Representative Verse of Charles Wesley* (Nashville: Abingdon, 1962), p. 265. I thank Rev. Hallock Mohler for pointing out this reference to me.

6. Ewing, *Historical Memoirs*, p. 210. Margaret Ewing, wife of a Cumberland Presbyterian itinerant, also stressed the evils of early marriage among preachers. See *Aunt Peggy: Being a Memoir of Mrs. Margaret Davidson Ewing, Wife of the Late Rev. Finis Ewing, by One of Her Sons* (Nashville: Cumberland Presbyterian Board of Publication, 1873), p. 138.

7. *Autobiography of Rev. Tobias Spicer, Containing Incidents and Observations; Also, Some Account of His Visit to England* (New York: Lane and Scott, 1852), p. 28. The Ohio Conference from the mid-1830s to the 1850s discontinued young men who married within two years of their admission to conference. James B. Finley, *Sketches of Western Methodism; Biographical, Historical and Miscellaneous, Illustrative of Pioneer Life*, ed. W. P. Strickland (Cincinnati: Methodist Book Concern, 1857), p. 181.

8. Minton Thrift, *Memoir of the Rev. Jesse Lee; with Extracts from His Journals* (New York: D. Bangs and T. Mason, 1823; reprint ed., New York: Arno Press and the New York Times, 1969), p. 40; William Larkin Duren, *The Top Sergeant of the Pioneers: The Story of a Lifelong Battle for an Ideal* (Emory University, Ga.: Banner Press, 1930), p. 59.

9. O. P. Fitzgerald, *Sunset Views* (Nashville: Publishing House of the M. E. Church, South, 1906), p. 44.

10. John Burgess, *Pleasant Recollections of Characters and Works of Nobel Men, with Old Scenes and Merry Times of Long, Long Ago* (Cincinnati:

Cranston and Stowe, 1887), p. 355; George Brown, *Recollections of Itinerant Life, Including Early Reminiscences* (Cincinnati: R. W. Carroll, 1868), pp. 109–10; A. Q. Field, *Worthies and Workers, Both Minister and Laymen, of the Rock River Conference* (Cincinnati: Cranston and Curtiss, 1896), p. 40.

11. Peck, *Early Methodism*, p. 340, reprint of diary entry for 25 January 1804. For this same sentiment at work in the Cumberland Presbyterian church—"The man who marries a wife, and then deserts the pulpit, had better never entered it"—see Ewing, *Historical Memoirs*, p. 120. For the Cumberland Presbyterian church's problem with ministers who located as soon as they married, see Richard Beard, *Brief Biographical Sketches of Some of the Early Ministers of the Cumberland Presbyterian Church* (Nashville: Cumberland Presbyterian Board of Publication, 1874), pp. 266–76.

12. H. M. Eaton, *The Itinerant's Wife: Her Qualifications, Duties, Trials and Rewards* (New York: Lane and Scott, 1851; micropublished ed., New Haven: Research Publications, 1975), p. 64.

13. O. P. Fitzgerald, *John B. McFerrin: A Biography* (Nashville: Publishing House of the M. E. Church, South, 1888), pp. 104–5.

14. Samuel Ayres, *Methodist Heroes of Other Days* (New York: Methodist Book Concern, 1916), p. 30.

15. "Address of the Bishops," in *Journal of the General Conference of the Methodist Episcopal Church, Held in the City of New York, 1844* (New York: Carlton and Phillips, 1856), pp. 158–60. The solution proposed by the bishops was to increase the probationary period to four years.

16. James O. Andrew, *Miscellanies, Comprising Letters, Essays, and Addresses to Which Is Added a Biographical Sketch of Mrs. Ann Amelia Andrew* (Louisville: Morton and Griswold, 1854), pp. 339–52. For his wife, see pp. 371–95.

17. J. Marring Potts et al., eds., *The Journal and Letters of Francis Asbury*, 3 vols. (Nashville: Abingdon Press, 1958), 3: 278.

18. Julie Roy Jeffrey, "Ministry through Marriage: Methodist Clergy Wives on the Trans-Mississippi Frontier," in *Women in New Worlds: Historical Perspectives on the Wesleyan Tradition*, ed. Hilah F. Thomas and Rosemary Skinner Keller (Nashville: Abingdon, 1981), p. 143.

19. See Jennie F. Willing, "A Wife for Our Minister," *Ladies' Repository* 24 (1864): 105–8. By 1860 three-fourths of the Methodist clergy would be married. See (Nashville) *Christian Advocate* 23 (20 January 1859).

20. Frank Milton Bristol, *The Life of Chaplain McCabe; Bishop of the Methodist Episcopal Church* (New York: Fleming H. Revell, n.d.), p. 68.

21. Benjamin Brawley, "Lorenzo Dow," *Journal of Negro History* 1 (1916): 265.

22. For accounts of frontier women see June Socher, "Frontier Women: A Model for All Women?" *South Dakota History* 7 (1976): 36–56; Glenda Riley, "Women Pioneers in Iowa," *Palimpsest* 57 (1976): 34–53; Glenda Riley, "Women in the West," *Journal of American Culture* 3 (1980): 311–29; Barbara Meldrum, "Images of Women in Western American Literature," *Midwest Quarterly* 17 (1976): 252–67.

23. Dow, *History of Cosmopolite*, p. 241.

24. John Kent, *Holding the Fort: Studies in Victorian Revivalism* (London: Epworth Press, 1978), p. 57.

25. Dow, *History of Cosmopolite*, pp. 671, 79, 84, 90.

26. William Colbert to Elizabeth Colbert, 7 June 1805, G-ETS, WCP.

27. Peggy Dow, *A Collection of Poetry* (Philadelphia: Griggs and Dickinson, 1815); *A Collection of Camp Meeting Hymns,* 2d ed. (Philadelphia: D. Dickinson, 1816); *A Collection of Hymns,* 2d ed. (Montpelier, Vt.: E. P. Walton, 1822).

28. See William Colbert's gentle, moving account of his courtship of Elizabeth Stroud in his undated Journal, pp. 1–19, G-ETS, WCP.

29. Dow, *History of Cosmopolite,* p. 621.

30. Beard, *Brief Biographical Sketches,* p. 73.

31. Dow, *History of Cosmopolite,* p. 211; see also p. 298.

32. Ibid., p. 619.

33. Elizabeth Colbert to William Colbert, 20 March 1805, G-ETS, WCP.

34. Dow, *History of Cosmopolite,* p. 665.

35. Ibid., p. 655.

36. Kent, *Holding the Fort,* pp. 11, 38–70.

37. Sellers, *Lorenzo Dow,* p. 190.

38. Ibid., p. 192.

39. Ibid., pp. 193–95.

40. Accounts of Dow's second marriage proposal are found in Sellers, *Lorenzo Dow,* pp. 197–99. My only source for Dow's second marriage is the undocumented material on pp. 197–263. The best supporting evidence I have been able to produce is an editorial notation that Dow's second wife lived in the vicinity of New London, Connecticut, in *The Eccentric Preacher; or, a Sketch of the Life of the Celebrated Lorenzo Dow, Abridged from His Journal, and Containing the Most Interesting Facts in His Experiences . . .* (Lowell: E. A. Rice, 1841).

41. It was quite common, however, for circuit riders to double as physicians, since they were the most educated and informed people frontier folk were likely to meet. See Finley, *Sketches of Western Methodism,* pp. 248, 296.

42. Sellers, *Lorenzo Dow,* p. 236.

43. Finney, *Life and Labors of Enoch Mather Marvin,* pp. 190–91.

44. See, as an example, the *American Baptist Magazine and Missionary Intelligencer* 1 (1818): 430–31; 2 (1819): 188–90; 2 (1819): 230–31; and 2 (1820): 384.

45. Daniel Wise, *Bridal Greetings: A Marriage Gift, in Which the Mutual Duties of Husband and Wife Are Familiarly Illustrated and Enforced* (New York: Carlton and Phillips, 1852), p. 135. Emphasis in original.

46. Ibid., p. 141. Emphasis in original.

47. Heman Bangs, *Autobiography and Journal of Rev. Heman Bangs, with an Introduction by Rev. Bishop Janes, D.D.,* ed Bangs's daughters (New York: N. Tibbals and Son, 1872), p. 91, and Appendix, p. 13.

48. Beard, *Brief Biographical Sketches,* p. 37. For other examples see Milton Bird, *The Life of Rev. Alexander Chapman* (Nashville: W. E. Dun-

away, 1872), pp. 52, 163; John Carroll, ed., *"Father Corson"; or, The Old Style Canadian Itinerant, . . .* (Toronto: Rev. Samuel Rose, D.D., at the Methodist Book Room, 1879), p. 78; Bangs, *Autobiography*, p. 30; Horace M. DuBose, *Life and Memories of Rev. J. D. Barbee* (Nashville: Smith and Lamar, 1906), p. 108.

49. Benjamin St. James Fry, *The Life of Robert R. Roberts, One of the Bishops of the Methodist Episcopal Church* (New York: Carlton and Porter, 1856), pp. 38–39, 77.

50. John A. Williams, *Life of Elder John Smith . . .* (Cincinnati: R. W. Carroll, 1870), pp. 237–38.

51. Harriet Beecher Stowe, "The Minister's Housekeeper," in *Native American Humor (1800–1900)*, ed. Walter Blair (New York: American Book Company, 1937), p. 492.

52. Barbara Cunningham, "An Eighteenth-Century View of Femininity as Seen through the Journals of Henry Melchior Muhlenberg," *Pennsylvania History* 43 (1976): 210–11.

53. Elijah Woolsey, *The Supernumerary; or, Lights and Shadows of Itinerancy*, comp. George Coles (New York: Lane and Scott, 1852), pp. 86, 90.

54. Shirley M. Souther, comp., *A History of the Methodist Episcopal Church, Hingham, Massachusetts, 1828–1928* (n.p., 1928), no pagination.

55. Corra Harris, *A Circuit Rider's Wife* (Philadelphia: Henry Altemus, 1910), p. 65.

56. William Henry Milburn, *The Pioneers, Preachers and People of the Mississippi Valley* (New York: Derby and Jackson, 1860), p. 378.

57. John Carroll, *Case and His Contemporaries; or, The Canadian Itinerant's Memorial, . . .* 5 vols. (Toronto: Samuel Rose, 1867–1877), 5: 182.

58. Quoted in John P. Lockwood, *The Western Pioneers; or, Memorials of the Lives and Labours of the Rev. Richard Boardman and the Rev. Joseph Pilmoor, the First Preachers Appointed by John Wesley to Labour in North America* (London: Wesleyan Conference Office, 1881), p. 95.

59. Cited in Almer Pennewell, *A Voice in the Wilderness: Jesse Walker, "The Daniel Boone of Methodism"* (Nashville: Parthenon Press, n.d.), pp. 28–29.

60. Peter Cartwright, *Fifty Years as a Presiding Elder*, ed. W. S. Hooper (Cincinnati: Hitchcock and Walden, 1871), p. 210.

61. Nehemiah Curnock, ed., *The Journal of the Rev. John Wesley . . ,* 8 vols. (London: R. Culley, 1909–16), 3: 517. For English examples of Wesleyan preachers following in the footsteps of their founder, see Isabel Rivers, "'Strangers and Pilgrims': Sources and Patterns of Methodist Narrative," in *Augustan Worlds: New Essays in Eighteenth Century Literature*, ed. J. C. Hilson, M. M. B. Jones, and J. R. Watson (New York: Barnes and Nobel, 1978), pp. 198–99.

62. Horace M. DuBose, *Life of Joshua Soule* (Nashville: Publishing House of the M. E. Church, South, 1911), pp. 59, 275.

63. See for example J. J. Fleharty, *Glimpses of the Life of Rev. A. E. Phelps . . .* (Cincinnati: Hitchcock and Walden, 1878), p. 132; John Ellis

Edwards, *Life of Rev. John Wesley Childs: For Twenty-Three Years an Itinerant Methodist Minister* (Richmond, Va.: John Early, 1852), p. 182.

64. *Methodist Heroes of Other Days*, p. 30.

65. Bangs, *Autobiography*, pp. 49, 160. For the leaving of seriously ill children, see D. Gregory Claiborne Butts, *From Saddle to City by Buggy, Boat, and Railway* (Hilton Village, Va.: n.p., 1922), pp. 72–73.

66. John L. Dyer, *The Snow-Shoe Itinerant* (Cincinnati: Cranston and Stowe, 1890), p. 75.

67. Mary Kelley, "A Woman Alone: Catharine Maria Sedgwick's Spinsterhood in Nineteenth-Century America," *New England Quarterly* 51 (1978): 213.

68. Warren A. Candler, *Life of Thomas Coke* (Nashville: Publishing House of the M. E. church, South, 1923), p. 259.

69. Wesley's response to a man desirous of entering the Wesleyan itinerancy but married to an unsupportive woman was significant: "My Dear Brother, —When a preacher travels without his wife, he is exposed to innumerable temptations. And you cannot travel with your wife till she is so changed as to ordain the gospel. It seems, therefore, all you can do at present is to act as a local preacher." John Telford, ed., *The Letters of the Rev. John Wesley*, 8 vols. (London: Epworth Press, 1931), 3: 116.

70. Julia C. Bonham, "Feminist and Victorian: The Paradox of the American Seafaring Woman of the Nineteenth Century," *American Neptune* 37 (1977): 203–18. For the piercing loneliness of the minister's wife, see as examples Mrs. H. A. Terwilligar Sharpe, *Reminiscences of a Minister's Daughter, Wife of a Widow* (Seymour, Conn.: n.p., 1911), p. 211; Bangs, *Autobiography*, Appendix, p. 13.

71. Andrew, *Miscellanies*, pp. 375–76; Rodney Cline, *Asbury Wilkinson: Pioneer Preacher* (New York: Vantage Press, 1956), p. 33.

72. Elnathan C. Gavitt, *Crumbs from My Saddle Bags; or, Reminiscences of Pioneer Life and Biographical Sketches* (Toledo: Blade Printing and Paper Company, 1884), p. 108.

73. Carroll, *Case and Contemporaries*, 1: 124–25.

74. Helen R. Cutler, *Jottings from Life; or, Passages from the Diary of an Itinerant's Wife* (Cincinnati Poe and Hitchcock, 1866), p. 22.

75. The reluctance of Marmaduke Gwynne of South Wales to consent to Charles Wesley's courtship of his daughter Sarah because of Charles's uncertain financial prospects was a foreshadowing of things to come. George Coles, *Heroines of Methodism; or Pen and Ink Sketches of the Mothers and Daughters of the Church* (New York: Carlton and Porter, 1857), pp. 33–36; Baker, *Representative Verse of Charles Wesley*, p. 264.

76. Cutler, *Jottings from Life*, pp. 12–15. Harriet Porter countered her parents' opposition to a marriage proposal from the newly widowed but always impoverished Lyman with the significant argument that the marriage would spell her admission into a wider field of usefulness; see Marie Caskey, *Chariot of Fire: Religion and the Beecher Family* (New Haven: Yale University Press, 1978), p. 11.

77. William Henry Milburn, *Ten Years of Preacher-Life: Chapters from an Autobiography* (New York: Derby and Jackson, 1859), p. 83.

78. Reverdy C. Ransom, *The Pilgrimage of Harriet Ransom's Son* (Nashville: Sunday School Union, n.d.), p. 45.

79. Elizabeth A. Roe, *Recollections of Frontier Life* (n.p., n.d.), p. 95.

80. Sharpe, *Reminiscences of a Minister's Daughter*, pp. 3–4.

81. Ebenezer Francis Newell, *Life and Observations of Rev. E. F. Newell, Who Has Been More Than Forty Years an Itinerant Minister in the Methodist Episcopal Church, New England Conference* (Worcester, Mass.: C. W. Ainsworth, 1847), pp. 138–40, 149, 160, 184, 200, 246.

82. Harris, *Circuit Rider's Wife*, p. 12.

83. Paulina Bascom Williams, Diary, 27 August 1830, VHS.

84. Jeffrey, "Ministry through Marriage," pp. 143–60.

85. Catherine L. Adams, *Daily Duties Inculcated in a Series of Letters, Addressed to the Wife of a Clergyman* (Boston: Crocker and Brewster 1835), p. 164.

86. Paulina Bascom Williams, Diary, 20 March 1830.

87. Ibid., 3 May 1830.

88. Ibid., 6 June 1830.

89. Ibid., 8 September 1830. "'Tis hard to try to do well, and then be ill spoken of. I have fact misrepresented and motives maligned."

90. Ibid., 1 May 1831.

91. Ibid., 14 October 1831.

92. Ibid., 14 October, 20 November 1831.

93. Ibid., 6 December 1831.

94. Ibid., 10 September, 8 June 1832.

95. *Memoirs of the Late Mrs. Susan Huntington, of Boston, Massachusetts, Consisting Principally of Extracts from Her Journals and Letters;* . . . (Edinburgh: Waugh and Innes, 1828), pp. 48–49.

96. Ibid., p. 117.

97. [Josephus Brockway?], *Brief Account of the Origin and Progress of the Divisions in the First Presbyterian Church in the City of Troy, Containing, Also, Strictures upon the New Doctrines Preached by the Rev. C. G. Finney and N. S. S. Beman, with a Summary Relation of the Trial of the Latter before the Troy Presbytery, by a Member of the Late Church and Congregation* (Troy: Tuttle and Richards, 1827), pp. 9, 31, 32; Owen Peterson, "Nathan S. S. Beman at Mt. Zion," *Georgia Historical Quarterly* 49 (1965): 168–69.

98. Eunice White Bullard Beecher, *From Dawn to Daylight; or, The Simple Story of a Western Home, by a Minister's Wife* (New York: Derby and Jackson, 1859; micropublished ed., New Haven: Research Publications, 1975), pp. 40, 58, 59, 60, 100, 184; Jane Shaffer Elsmere, *Henry Ward Beecher: The Indiana Years, 1837–1847* (Indianapolis: Indiana Historical Society, 1973), pp. 22, 65, 166, 294.

99. Cutler, *Jottings from Life*, p. 296.

100. Adams, *Daily Duties*, p. iii.

101. Cutler, *Jottings from Life*, pp. 40, 41–42, 53–54.

102. Ibid., pp. 87, 104–6, 108.

103. George Leon Walker, "Ministers and Their Households," *Congregational Quarterly* 6 (1864): 346.

104. *A Plea for the Ministers of the Gospel, Offered to the Consideration of the People of New England, Being an Exposition of Galatians VI.6* (Boston: B. Green, 1706), p. 11.

105. James W. Schmotter, "The Irony of Clerical Professionalism: New England's Congregational Ministers and the Great Awakening," *American Quarterly* 31 (1979): 151, 155–56, 159–60.

106. Quoted in Niels Henry Sonne, *Liberal Kentucky: 1780–1828* (New York: Columbia University Press, 1939), p. 7, n. 24. For the story of another minister who "struck," see Sharpe, *Reminiscences of a Minister's Daughter*, p. 22.

107. William R. Weeks, *Withholding a Suitable Support from the Ministers of Religion, is Robbing God: A Sermon Preached to the Presbyterian Congregation in Plattsburgh, New York, September 26, 1813* (Albany: n.p., 1814). See also *Watchman of the South*, 8 (26 December 1844): 73.

108. Finney's motto was reported by Antoinette Brown Blackwell to Lucy Stone according to "Antoinette Brown Blackwell: the First Woman Minister," ed. Claude U. Gilson, p. 17. Typescript in OCL, RFP. See also Charles G. Finney to Henry Cowles, 8 February 1847, OCL, CP.

109. The quotation is taken from Stephen Chapin, "Reciprocal Duties at Pastoral Churches," *Baptist Preacher* 1 (1827): 12. See also William Wilson Manross, *The Episcopal Church in the United States, 1800–1840: A Study in Church Life* (New York: Columbia University Press, 1938), pp. 98–101; Reba Carolyn Strickland, *Religion in the State of Georgia in the Eighteenth Century* (New York: Columbia University Press, 1939), p. 171.

110. George Lewis, *Impressions of America and the American Churches* . . . (Edinburgh: W. P. Kennedy, 1845), pp. 54–55.

111. Joel Parker, J. W. C. Bliss, and William Green, Jr., to Charles G. Finney, 1 June 1832, OCL, FP. In the rural community of Ogdensburg, New York, the Pesbyterian pastor was receiving $400 in 1828. See Joab Seeley to Charles G. Finney, 2 April 1828, OCL, FP.

112. John M. Carpenter, *A Sermon, on Behalf of the Widows' Fund Delivered before the New Jersey Association* . . . (Philadelphia: King and Baird, 1845), p. 15; Stephen Parks, *Troy Conference Miscellany, Containing a Historical Sketch of Methodism within the Bounds of the Troy Conference* (Albany: J. Lord, 1854); p. 68.

113. John Henry Hopkins, *The American Citizen* (n.p., 1857), p. 267. For estimates that put the average clerical salaries at just under $500 in 1860, see the *Presbyterian* 31 (18 July 1861); "Ministers' Sons and Daughters," *Christian Instructor* 15 (1859): 262, and and the (Nashville) *Christian Advocate* 22 (23 December 1858). Terry David Bilhartz's thorough study of clerical salaries in Baltimore during the Second Great Awakening reveals surprisingly high stipends for the Episcopalian, Presbyterian, and Unitarian clergy. See "Urban Religion and the Second Great Awakening: A Religious History of Baltimore, Maryland, 1790–1830" (Ph.D. diss., George Washington University, 1979), pp. 109–15.

114. Lewis, *Impressions,* pp. 210–17. According to the statistical charts reproduced in James J. Barclay, *An Address Delivered at the Organization of the Normal School on Thursday, the Thirteenth of January, 1848*

(Philadelphia: n.p., 1848), p. 8, the average male public school teacher's salary in 1847 was $191.40 in New York and $185.00 in Ohio. The highest salaries were paid in Massachusetts, where male public school teachers averaged $294.12 in 1847.

115. Perry J. Stackhouse, *Chicago and the Baptists: A Century of Progress* (Chicago: University of Chicago Press, 1933), p. xiv.

116. Stuart Clarke Henry, *George Whitefield, Wayfaring Witness* (New York: Abingdon Press, 1957), p. 52.

117. Quoted by Don W. Holter in "Some Changes Related to the Ordained Ministry in the History of American Methodism," *Methodist History: A. M. E. Zion Quarterly Review News Bulletin* (April 1975): 180.

118. B. M. Drake, *A Sketch of the Life of Rev. Elijah Steele . . .* (Cincinnati: R. P. Thompson, 1843), p. 95.

119. "A Wife for an Itinerant," *Ladies' Repository* 7 (1847): 103. Some itinerants who did manage to marry wealthy women were Bishop Thomas Coke, Hope Hull (Asbury's traveling companion), and George Pickering; see Ayres, *Methodist Heroes of Other Days*, p. 350, and Candler, *Life of Thomas Coke*, p. 258. The search for women of means as wives of clergy was not limited to Methodists. A Rochester Presbyterian minister, William Wisner, who wrote to Finney asking for help in finding a wife for his minister son, accented five desirable characteristics: ardent piety, good sense, decent education, kind disposition, and a good if not handsome appearance; the ideal candidate would be "so well off as to property, that she will have the means of supporting herself if she should in the Providence of God be left a minister's widow." William Wisner to Charles G. Finney, 14 January 1833, OCL, FP.

120. Achille Murat, *A Moral and Political Sketch of the United States of North America* (London: E. Wilson, 1833), p. 131.

121. Richard M. Cameron, *Methodism and Society in Historical Perspective* (New York: Abingdon, 1961), p. 102.

122. Brown, *Recollections of Itinerant Life*, p. 190. Likewise there were cases of congregations refusing to pay their pastor what the *Discipline* allowed his wife because she already was earning an income by teaching. See Ann J. Marshall, *The Autobiography of Mrs. A. J. Marshall, Age 84 Years* (Pine Bluff, Ark.: Adams-Wilson, 1897), p. 84.

123. *Journal of General Conference, 1796–1836* (New York: Carlton and Phillips, 1855), 1: 29, 37–38, 485.

124. Guerdon Gates, "Record Book: 1824–1858;" Thomas Horace Cleland, "Memorandum Books," FC. In the Methodist tradition such money gifts as wedding fees were at first forbidden, following Wesley's dictum "Let there be no pretence to say we grow rich by the Gospel." Soon Methodists allowed their preachers to accept fees provided they were deducted from the designated annual allowance. By 1800 preachers could keep wedding fees without any accounting, and this income provided for ministers' wives (in all traditions) funds necessary to keep the household going. One itinerant who received $2.00 for a wedding in 1828 performed 979 weddings during his career (Gavitt, *Crumbs from My Saddle Bags*, p. 75). For larger fees, see Burgess, *Pleasant Recollections*, p. 345, and John Wesley Carhart, *Four*

Years on Wheels; or, Life as a Presiding Elder (Oshkosh, Wisc. Allen and Hicks, 1880), p. 70. See also Cameron, *Methodism and Society*, pp. 102–3; Thrift, *Memoir of the Rev. Jesse Lee*, p. 100; and *Journal of the General Conference*, 1: 94.

125. Elisabeth D. Dodds, *Marriage to a Difficult Man: The "Uncommon Union" of Jonathan and Sarah Edwards* (Philadelphia: Westminister Press, 1971), pp. 88, 90. James W. Schmotter's contention that supplemental salary settlements had declined by 1740 does not seem to hold true for the rest of the century; see "Irony of Clerical Professionalism;" pp. 159–60.

126. Cartwright, *Fifty Years as a Presiding Elder*, pp. 210, 42, 63. For another example, see Brown, *Recollections of Itinerant Life,* p. 110. For Presbyterian delinquency, see P. H. Fowler, *Historical Sketch of Presbyterianism within the Bounds of the Synod of Central New York* (Utica, N.Y.: Curtiss and Childs, 1877), p. 116; *Watchman of the South*, 3 (12 March 1840), p. 114.

127. The prominent minister Robert Baird wrote an introduction to L. K. Langsworth, *A Practical Treatise on the Hive and Honey-Bee*, 3d ed. (New York: C. M. Saxton, 1862), pp. iv–v, announcing to clergymen that the author had given them free use of his invention.

128. For wives taking on boarders, see, for example, Marilla Marks to Charles G. Finney, 7 April 1845, OCL, FP.

129. Harris, *Circuit Rider's Wife*, p. 115.

130. J. E. Godbey, *Lights and Shadows of Seventy Years* (St. Louis: Nixon-Jones, 1913), p. 2.

131. Bernard A. Weisberger, *They Gathered at the River: The Story of the Great Revivalists and Their Impact upon Religion in America* (Boston: Little, Brown, 1958), pp. 72, 30; Caskey, *Chariot of Fire*, pp. 7, 9.

132. See Sue F. Dromgoole Mooney, *My Moving Tent* (Nashville: Publishing House of the Methodist Episcopal church, South, 1903), pp. 203–4.

133. R. K. Brown, *Life of Mrs. M. L. Kelley* (n.p., 1889), p. 51; William Lumpkin, "The Role of Women in Eighteenth-Century Virginia Baptist Life," *Baptist History and Heritage* 8 (1973): 162; Ayers, *Methodist Heroes of Other Days*, p. 27; Roland H. Bainton, "The Office of the Minister's Wife in New England," in *Christian Unity and Religion in New England* (Boston: Beacon Press, 1964), p. 268.

134. Adams, *Daily Duties*, p. 19.

135. In one case the entire donation party consisted of the passing of a hat around the parsonage one evening to help pay the pastor's salary; see *Autobiography with Letters, Poems and Papers of Permelia Ann Post with Poems and Diary of Rev. Woodruff Post*, 2d ed. (Olean, N.Y.: n.p., 1902), p. 57.

136. Cutler, *Jottings from Life*, p. 102.

137. F. A. Cole to Lydia Finney, 22 January, 21 April 1847, OCL, FP. For detailed descriptions of donation parties, see Ellen Roberts to Aunt Lydia, 21 February 1850, in Benson Howard Roberts, *Benjamin Titus Roberts* (North Chili, N.Y.: "Earnest Christian Publishing Office," 1900), pp. 47–48; *Autobiography of Rev. Tobias Spencer, Containing Incidents and*

Observations; also Some Account of his Visit to England (New York: Lane and Scott, 1852), p. 75; (Nashville) *Christian Advocate* 23 (3 March 1859); *Rochester Union and Advertiser* 12 February 1863; Harris, *Circuit Rider's Wife*, pp. 23–24; Beecher, *From Dawn to Daylight*, pp. 202–29; Jay Benson Hamilton, *From the Pulpit to the Poor-House and Other Romances of the Methodist Itinerancy* (New York: Hunt and Eaton, 1892), pp. 21–26; and *Christian Intelligencer*, 65 (1894): 811. For a highly critical assessment of donation visits, see the *Ladies' Repository* 31 (1871): 140–42. For a laudatory appraisal, see the *Presbyterian* 18 (1 January 1848), p. 2.

138. Emma Smith Brown to Fidelia C. Coan, 8 February 1836, LC, TCP.

Chapter Four

1. *Reminiscences of Rev. Charles G. Finney: Speeches and Sketches at the Gathering of His Friends and Pupils, in Oberlin, July 28, 1876* (Oberlin: E. J. Goodrich, 1876), p. 32.

2. As quoted by Alice Welch Cowles in "Miscellaneous Addresses." Typescript in OCL, RFP.

3. P. H. Fowler, *Historical Sketch of Presbyterianism within the Bounds of the Synod of Central New York* (Utica, N.Y.: Curtiss and Childs, 1877), p. 720. See also Alexander Campbell, *Memoirs of Elder Thomas Campbell, Together with a Brief Memoir of Mrs. Jane Campbell* (Cincinnati: H. S. Bosworth, 1861), p. 310.

4. Mrs. H. C. Gardner, *Ellinor Grey; or, The Sunday School Class at Trimble Hollow* (New York: Carlton and Porter, 1858), pp. 10–11; *Miss Carroll's School* (New York: Carlton and Porter, 1868), p. 10. For further unabashed advocacy of "masculine" traits, see Joshua Priestly, *True Womanhood: Memorials of Eliza Hessel*, 2d ed. (London: Hamilton, Adams, 1859), p. 29.

5. Catherine L. Adams, *Daily Duties Inculcated in a Series of Letters, Addressed to the Wife of a Clergyman* (Boston: Crocker and Brewster, 1835), pp. 37–41. This accent can be seen also in H. M. Eaton's requirement that the minister's wife "be able to form opinions for herself." See *The Itinerant's Wife: Her Qualifications, Duties, Trials and Rewards* (New York: Lane and Scott, 1851; micropublished ed., New Haven: Research Publications, 1975), p. 13.

6. As quoted by Alice Welch Cowles in "Miscellaneous Addresses."

7. Charles G. Finney, "Last Sickness and Death of Mrs. Finney," *Oberlin Evangelist* (5 January 1848): 3. Finney's personal grief at Lydia's death should in no way be slighted. The depth of his love and the quality of his tenderness are revealed in an unpublished portion of his memoirs. The night before he was to leave for England in late 1847, Lydia began coughing blood and could not not sit up. As Finney held her in his arms, he watched in agonizing helplessness as the life drained out of her until she almost died. After this consumptive episode, Finney canceled his trip and "gave myself up to nursing her." For the next two years, he restricted himself to laboring for revivals in Oberlin and Michigan. While Finney himself was involved in a life-and-death struggle with typhus, Lydia was succumbing to consumption

and finally died "about the middle of December" in 1847. See Garth Rosell and Richard Dupuis, eds., *The Memoirs of Charles G. Finney* (Grand Rapids: Zondervan Press, forthcoming), chap. 28.

8. Mrs. W. W. Scott, "The Model Woman: First Paper," *Ladies' Repository* 34 (1874): 350. See also the "Second Paper" in the next issue of the same volume, pp. 432–33.

9. Winthrop S. Hudson, *Religion in America*, 2d ed. (New York: Charles Scribner's Sons, 1973), p. 179; *American Protestantism* (Chicago: University of Chicago Press, 1961), pp. 71–74, 99–104. For a critique of William G. McLoughlin's classic treatment of revivalism and his failure to apreciate the Methodist and Baptist antecedents of Finney, see John Kent, *Holding the Fort: Studies in Victorian Revivalism* (London: Epworth Press, 1978), pp. 23–25.

10. Keith Melder, "Ladies Bountiful: Organized Women's Benevolence in Early Nineteenth-Century America," *New York History* 48 (1967): 231–34.

11. Robert Wearmouth, *Methodism and the Common People of the Eighteenth Century* (London: Epworth Press, 1945), p. 223.

12. Howard Alexander Morrison, "The Finney Takeover of the Second Great Awakening during the Oneida Revivals of 1825–27," *New York History* 59 (1978): 33. See also my "Views of Man Inherent in New Measures Revivalism," *Church History* 45 (1976): 211–12, n. 39.

13. For samples of the evidence, which abounds, see Stephen Parks, *Troy Conference Miscellany* (Albany: J. Lord, 1854), p. 46; George Coles, *Heroines of Methodism; or, Pen and Ink Sketches of the Mothers and Daughters of the Church* (New York: Carlton and Porter, 1857), pp. 190–91, 194–95.

14. Mr. and Miss Martin, *Heroines of Early Methodism* (Nashville: Publishing House of the Methodist Episcopal Church, South, Sunday School Department, n.d.); O. P. Fitzgerald, *Centenary Cameos* (Nashville: Barbee and Smith, 1893), pp. 53–56, 75–80, 94–101, 111–19, 145–52.

15. Fredrick E. Maser has pointed to the crying need in particular for a better understanding of Wesley's relationship with his mother in "The Unknown John Wesley," *Drew Gateway* 49 (Winter 1978): 3.

16. This is a familiar theme in later nineteenth-century Methodist circles. "Christianity created a new sphere for woman," John Wesley Buoy remarked before a YWCA assembly in 1891, "and Methodism is the only Church which perfectly fills it." See Buoy's *Representative Women of Methodism* (New York: Hunt and Eaton, 1893), p. 21.

17. See the first biography of Susanna, John Kirk, *The Mother of the Wesleys: A Biography*, 2d ed. (London: Henry James Tresidder, 1864), p. 137, and W. H. Withrow, *Makers of Methodism* (New York: Eaton and Mains, 1898), p. 32.

18. Buoy, *Representative Women of Methodism*, p. 259.

19. Ibid.

20. Ibid., pp. 38–40.

21. See Wesley's letters to Sarah Crosby in 1761 and in 1769 in John Telford, ed., *The Letters of the Rev. John Wesley*, 8 vols. (London: Epworth

Press, 1931), 4: 33, 132–33; 5: 257, 130–31; Abel Stevens, *The Women of Methodism: Its Three Foundresses, Susanna Wesley, the Countess of Huntingdon, and Barbara Heck, with Sketches of Their Female Associates and Successors in the Early History of the Denomination* (New York: Carlton and Porter, 1866), p. 105; Luke Tyerman, *The Life and Times of the Rev. John Wesley, M.A. Founder of the Methodists*, 3 vols. (London: Hodder and Stoughton, 1872–75), 2: 398.

22. John Wesley to Mary Bosanquet, 13 June 1771, in Telford, *Letters of Wesley*, 5: 257.

23. Quoted in Leslie F. Church, *More about the Early Methodist People* (London: Epworth Press, 1949), p. 145.

24. Telford, *Letters of Wesley*, 5: 257.

25. Earl Kent Brown, "Women of the Word," *Women in New Worlds: Historical Perspectives on the Wesleyan Tradition*, ed. in Hilah F. Thomas and Rosemary Skinner Keller (Nashville: Abingdon, 1981), p. 70. For another treatment of early Methodist women in England, see Maldwyn Edwards, *My Dear Sister: The Story of John Wesley and the Women in His Life* (Manchester: Penwick, 1980).

26. Thomas M. Morrow, *Early Methodist Women* (London: Epworth Press, 1967), pp. 106–19.

27. See pp. 27–39, ibid., and Thomas Walter Laquerer, *Religion and Respectability: Sunday Schools and Working Class Culture, 1780–1850* (New Haven: Yale University Press, 1976), pp. 21–25.

28. Samuel J. Rogal, "John Wesley's Women," *Eighteenth-Century Life* 1 (1974): 8–10; "'The Elder unto the Well-Beloved': The Letters of John Wesley," *Journal of Religious Studies* 7 (1979): 82–83.

29. Albert B. Lawson, "Appendix 1: Wesley and the Ministry of Women," in *John Wesley and the Christian Ministry: The Sources and Development of His Opinion and Practice* (London: S.P.C.K., 1963), pp. 176–81; Leslie F. Church, "Women Preachers," in *More about the Early Methodist People*, pp. 136–76.

30. Earl Kent Brown, "Women in Church History: Stereotypes, Archetypes and Operational Modalities," *Methodist History* 18 (1980): 130; Stevens, *Women of Methodism*, pp. 113–23; Helen C. Knight, comp., *Lady Huntington and Her Friends; or, The Revival of the work of God in the Days of Wesley, Whitefield, Romaine, Venn, and Others in the Last Century* (New York: American Tract Society, 1853).

31. Quoted in Stevens, *Women of Methodism*, p. 123.

32. Ibid., p. 118. Taken from a manuscript written by Wesley, "Narrative of a Remarkable Transaction," now held in the British Museum.

33. Stevens, *Women of Methodism*, pp. 123–4.

34. Morrow, *Early Methodist Women*, p. 49.

35. Ibid., pp. 64–65, 98; Coles, *Heroines of Methodism*, 255–61; Samuel Burder, *Memoirs of Eminently Pious Women*, (Philadelphia: J. J. Woodward, 1834), pp. 705–12; Henry Moore, comp., *The Life of Mrs. Mary Fletcher . . .* (New York: Hunt and Eaton, n.d.), pp. 47, 51, 74–77, 134, 172.

36. Coles, *Heroines of Methodism*, p. 286; Church, *More about the Early Methodist People*, p. 138; Stevens, *Women of Methodism*, pp. 55–56.

37. Mary Fletcher and Lady Maxwell served as heroic models for Harriet Livermore and Jarena Lee. Harriet Livermore, *A Narration of Religious Experience, in Twelve Letters* (Concord: Jacob B. Moore, 1826), pp. 17, 231–32; Jarena Lee, *Religious Experience and Journal of Mrs. Jarena Lee, Giving an Account of Her Call to Preach the Gospel* (Philadelphia: privately published, 1849), p. 38.

38. Nathan Bangs, "Influence of Female Character," *Ladies' Repository* 8 (1848): 144. See also Stevens, *Women of Methodism*, p. 98.

39. *An Account of the Experience of Mrs. Hester Anne Rogers, Written by Herself* . . . (New York: Sand D. A. Forbes, 1830), p. 187.

40. Fitzgerald, *Centenary Cameos*, pp. 94–101.

41. Wesley F. Swift, "The Women Itinerant Preachers of Early Methodism," in *Proceedings of the Wesley Society*, vol. 28 (Liverpool: C. Tinkling, 1951–52), pp. 90–92; J. Holland Brown, *Memoir of Charlotte Sophia Berger, of Suffron-Walden* (London: E. Marlborough, 1879), p. 25.

42. Stevens, *Women of Methodism*, pp. 130–32.

43. Jonathan K. Peck, *Luther Peck and His Five Sons* (New York: Eaton and Mains, 1897), p. 35. The five Methodist itinerants were Luther H., George, Andrew, William, and Bishop Jesse T. Peck.

44. Winthrop S. Hudson, "The Methodist Age in America," *Methodist History* 12 (1974): 3–15.

45. Charles W. Ferguson, *Organizing to Beat the Devil: Methodists and the Making of America* (Garden City, N.Y.: Doubleday, 1971).

46. Finney left Whitestown for Evans Mills with the intention of sending for Lydia after he had found accommodations for her. But his energies were so absorbed in revivalism that he forgot about his new wife. See Bernard Weisberger, *They Gathered at the River: The Story of the Great Revivalists and Their Impact upon Religion in America* (Boston: Little, Brown, 1958), p. 98.

47. Charles G. Finney, "Last Sickness and Death of Mrs. Finney," *Oberlin Evangelist* (5 January 1848): 3.

48. See, for example, E. W. Gilbert to Charles G. Finney, 19 October 1827; Zephaniah Platt to Charles G. Finney, 10 March 1828; W. Stafford to Charles G. Finney, 12 June 1828. OCL, FP.

49. Helen Platt to Lydia Finney, 22 February 1828, OCL, FP.

50. Amey was the first wife of Orange Scott, one of the founders of the Wesleyan Methodist Connection. *Memoirs of Amey Scott: Written by Herself* (New York: Orange Scott, 1846), pp. 33, 39.

51. Daniel T. Rodgers, *The Work Ethic in Industrial America, 1850–1920* (Chicago: University of Chicago Press, 1978), p. 10.

52. Timothy Dwight, *Theology, Explained and Defended* . . . 5 vols. (Middletown, Connecticut: Clark and Lyman, 1818–1819), 3: 454; Hudson, "The Methodist Age in America," pp. 3–15.

53. Charles Finney, "Occasional Lectures," OCL, FP.

54. Ian Bradley, *Call to Seriousness: The Evangelical Impact on the Victorians* (New York: Macmillan, 1976), p. 25. Anne C. Loveland and Donald G. Mathews have pointed to the importance of the doctrine of usefulness for southern Evangelical clergy and women, respectively, in

Southern Evangelicals and the Social Order, 1800–1860 (Baton Rouge: Louisiana State University Press, 1980), 160–61, 173 and *Religion in the Old South* (Chicago: University of Chicago Press, 1977), 114–16.

55. William B. Sprague, *A Sermon Addresed to the Second Presbyterian Congregation, Albany, Sabbath Morning, March 14, 1858, on Occasion of the Death of Mrs. Alexander Marvin* (Albany: Van Benthuysen, 1858), p. 4.

56. Ann D. Gordon and Mari Jo Buhle, "Sex and Class in Colonial and Nineteenth-Century America," in *Liberating Women's History: Theoretical and Critical Essays,* ed. Berenice A. Carroll (Urbana: University of Illinois Press, 1976), pp. 284–85.

57. *Sumter Democrat,* 18 September 1852.

58. Joseph F. Kett, *Rites of Passage: Adolescence in America, 1790 to the Present* (New York: Basic Books, 1977), p. 75.

59. *Memoirs of Mrs. Eleanor Emerson, Containing a Brief Sketch of Her Life, with Some of Her Writings . . . ,* 2d ed. (Boston: Lincoln and Edmonds, 1809), p. 48.

60. Charles Betts Galloway, *The Editor Bishop; Linus Parker, His Life and Writings* (Nashville: Southern Methodist Publishing House, 1886), p. 307. The coincidence (and sometimes confusion) of conversion and the call to the ministry among virtually all the nineteenth-century clergy needs to be interpreted within this context of conversion as a vocational decision, as Winthrop S. Hudson has pointed out in personal correspondence with the author, 29 August 1976. For the relationship between conversion and calling, see Loveland, *Southern Evangelicals and the Social Order,* pp. 16–18; Donald M. Scott, *From Office to Profession: The New England Ministry, 1750–1850* (University of Pennsylvania Press, 1978), 84–5.

61. Rodgers, *Work Ethic in Industrial America,* p. 131.

62. A. A. Norton to Lydia Finney, 23 October 1826, OCL, FP.

63. Adams, *Daily Duties,* p. 24.

64. Rufus Anderson, *An Address Delivered in South Hadley, Massachusetts, July 24, 1899, at the Second Anniversary of the Mt. Holyoke Female Seminary* (Boston: Perkins and Marvin, 1839), p. 3; Lucy Stone, "Oberlin and Women," in *The Oberlin Jubilee: 1833–1883,* ed. William G. Ballantine and E. J. Goodrich (Oberlin: E. J. Goodrich, 1883), p. 313.

65. Anderson, *Address,* pp. 6–8.

66. David Rennie-Massey, "The Coming of Women's Sphere to the West: A Look at Narcissa Whitman, Frontier Missionary," unpublished manuscript, p. 3.

67. Samuel W. May to Lydia Finney, 8 October 1828; Charles G. Finney to Helen Finney Cochran, 8 May 1846. OCL, FP. For an example of one of the countless Evangelical women who, after reading Harriet Newell's memoirs, desired to be like her, see Andrew Manship, *Cherished Memories of Rebecca Ann Manship* (Philadelphia: Philadelphia Conference Tract Society, 1859), p. 16.

68. Emile Royce Bradley, Diary, 1 July 1832, OCL, DBP; Laura Fish (Judd) to Charles G. Finney, 6 July 1826, and to Lydia Finney, 6 August 1826, OCL, FP.

69. James A. Martling, *Poems of Home and Country* (Boston: James H. Earle, 1885), p. 22.

70. *Autobiography with Letters, Poems and Papers of Permelia Ann Post, with Poems and Diary of Rev. Woodruff Post*, 2d ed. (Olean, N.Y.; n.p., 1902), pp. 7, 14, 22, 25, 35, 96.

71. Eloise Miles Abbott, *Personal Sketches and Recollections; in a Series of Familiar Letters to a Friend, and Miscellaneous Essays* (Boston: Abel Tompkins, 1861; micropublished ed., New Haven: Research Publications, 1975), p. 111; Corra Harris, *A Circuit Rider's Wife* (Philadelphia: Henry Altemus, 1910), p. 16.

72. Thomas W. Tucker, ed., *Itinerant Preaching in the Early Days of Methodism, by a Pioneer Preacher's Wife* (Boston: B. B. Russell, 1872), pp. 34–36, 128.

73. Ann J. Marshall, *The Autobiography of Mrs. A. J. Marshall, Age, 84 Years* (Pine Bluff, Ark.: Adams-Wilson, 1897), pp. 67–68.

74. Sue F. Dromgoole Mooney, *My Moving Tent* (Nashville: Publishing House of the Methodist Episcopal Church, South, 1903), pp. 55, 74.

75. William Wisner to Charles G. Finney, 14 January 1833; Eliza Wheaton to Lydia Finney, 17 August 1828; Samuel W. May to Lydia Finney, 8 October 1828; Milton Brayton to Charles G. Finney, 27 May 1829. OCL, FP. Part of the Finney legend that still circulates at Oberlin today is the story about how Finney's daughter Julia came to marry a minister, James Monroe. After the death of his first wife, Monroe, whom Finney would never forgive for his later abandonment of the ministry for politics, solicited Finney's opinion of the qualifications of a certain lady for the role of minister's wife. Finney is supposed to have pooh-poohed Monroe's selection and suggested Julia instead. See Charles G. Finney to Dolson Cox, 2 September 1871, OCL, FP.

76. Anne Tuttle Bullard, *The Wife for a Missionary* (Cincinnati: Truman, Smith, 1834), p. 137.

77. Rhoda C. Churchill to Charles G. Finney, 15 March 1828; Roxanna Crosby to Lydia Finney, 12 September 1835; Almeda E. Clark to Lydia Finney, 8 October 1846, OCL, FP.

78. Sarah T. Seward to Lydia Finney, 21 November 1831, 4 December 1833, and 9 March 1835, OCL, FP. Since she could not become a missionary, she made her presence felt in the mission field by supporting one.

79. See the entries of Charles and Lydia Finney and Daniel Nash in Sarah T. Seward's Album, a repository of messages, mementos, poems, and good wishes from her friends. The manuscript copy is in RPL.

80. Richard Knill, *The Missionary's Wife; or, A Brief Account of Mrs. Loveless, of Madras, the First American Missionary to Foreign Lands* (Philadelphia: Presbyterian Board of Publication, 1839), p. 5.

81. See for example Gardner, *Miss Carroll's School*, pp. 174 and passim.

82. Catharine Beecher to Mrs. J. K. Polk, undated letter, NYL, MR, PPP.

83. Israel P. Warren, *The Sisters: A Memoir of Elizabeth K., Abbie A., and Sarah F. Dickerman* (Boston: American Tract Society, 1859), pp. 24, 52–55, 139, 166, 170–71, 174–77, 182; *The Revivalist: Exclusively Devoted to the Revival and Extension of Evangelical Religion* (London: Simpkin and Marshall, 1832), pp. 102–3; Keith E. Melder, *Beginnings of Sisterhood: The American Woman's Rights Movement, 1800–1850* (New York: Schocken, 1977), p. 37.

84. Laura Fish Judd to Lydia Finney, 10 December 1832; A. and S. A. Bushnell to Charles G. Finney, 31 January 1848, OCL, FP.

85. Almira Seldon to Lydia Finney, 5 June 1826, OCL, FP.

86. Sophia Royce to Lydia Finney, 6 August 1826; Sarah and Cynthia Brayton to Lydia Finney, 14 August 1826; R. C. Churchill to Lydia Finney, 3 December 1827; Eliza Wheaton to Lydia Finney, 17 August 1828, OCL, FP.

87. Frances J. Hosford, "Things Old and New: 'Those Horrid Men,'" *Oberlin Alumni Magazine* 24 (December 1927): 10; "The Pioneer Women of Oberlin College," *Oberlin Alumni Magazine* 23 (November 1926): 16–18. Caroline Rudd married Oberlin's professor of music George N. Allen, Mary Hosford married Rev. Caleb E. Fisher, and Elizabeth Prall married an Oberlin student, William D. Russell. See Sarah C. Little, "Oberlin and the Education of Women," in Ballantine and Goodrich, *Jubilee: 1833–1883*, p. 150.

88. Hosford, "Things Old and New," p. 11.

89. Alice Welch Cowles to Henry Cowles, 2 January 1838. Typescript copy in OCL, RFP. Arabella Cook to Lydia Finney, 2 April 1844, and Emily S. Bartlett to Lydia Finney, 27 April 1846, OCL, FP. Delavan L. Leonard, *The Story of Oberlin* (Boston: Pilgrim Press, 1898); "Antoinette L. Brown Blackwell's Reminiscences: Notes Taken by Alice Stone Blackwell, August 19, 1903." Typescript in OCL, RFP.

90. Cited by Helene E. Roberts, "'The Exquisite Slave': The Role of Clothes in the Making of the Victorian Home," *Signs* 2 (1977): 555.

91. "An Essay on Dress," *American Baptist Magazine and Missionary Intelligencer* 1 (1817): 57.

92. See as an early example *A Treatise on Dress Intended as a Friendly and Seasonable Warning to the Daughters of America* (New Haven: Thomas and Samuel Green, 1783); also William Greenleaf Eliot, *Lectures to Young Women*, 3d ed. (Boston: Crosby, Nichols, 1854; micropublished ed., New Haven: Research Publications, 1975), pp. 145–54.

93. *The Doctrines and Discipline of the Methodist Episcopal Church* (New York: Lane and Scott, 1850), p. 81; John Carroll, ed., *"Father Corson"; or, The Old Style Canadian Itinerant* (Toronto: Rev. Samuel Rose, D.D., at the Methodist Book Room, 1879), pp. 216–17; Edward W. Hooker, *Memoir of Mrs. Sarah Lanman Smith, Late of the Mission in Syria, under the Direction of the American Board of Commissioners for Foreign Missions,* (Boston: Perkins and Marvin, 1840), p. 68; W. P. Strickland, ed., *Autobiography of Rev. James B. Finley; or, Pioneer Life in the West* (Cincinnati: Jennings and Graham, 1905), p. 98.

94. Adams, *Daily Duties*, p. 22.

95. *Ladies' Repository* 31 (1871): 236.

96. Adams, *Daily Duties*, p. 21.

97. George Lewis, *Impressions of America and the American Churches* . . . (Edinburgh: W. P. Kennedy, 1845), pp. 27–28.

98. Missionary wives were a prominent exception to this statement, for their aesthetic was most often one of "rigid simplicity." See Susan Adeline Beers House, *A Life for the Balkans: The Story of John Henry House of the American Farm School, Thessaloniki, Greece* . . . (New York: Fleming H. Revell, 1939), p. 42.

99. Scott, *Memoirs*, pp. 4, 29, 34, 39.

100. Carroll, *"Father Corson,"* p. 214.

101. John Burgess, *Pleasant Recollections of Characters and Works of Noble Men, with Old Scenes and Merry Times of Long, Long Ago* (Cincinnati: Cranston and Stowe, 1887), pp. 168, 341, 342.

102. Daniel Parish Kidder, *The Christian Pastorate: Its Character, Responsibilities, and Duties* (Cincinnati: Hitchcock and Walden, 1871), p. 253.

103. Adams, *Daily Duties*, p. 140.

104. Ibid, p. 142.

105. Ibid., p. 14.

106. Ibid., p. 16.

107. Ibid., pp. 26–28.

108. Ibid., p. 45.

109. Ibid., p. 132.

110. Ibid., pp. 127, 98. One minister's wife described this condition as being "religiously dissipated." See Lot Jones, *Memoir of Mrs. Sarah Louisa Taylor; or, An Illustration of the Work of the Holy Spirit, in Awakening, Renewing, and Sanctifying the Heart*, 4th ed. (New York: John S. Taylor, 1843), pp. 112–13.

111. Phoebe Palmer, "The Minister's Wife," in *Incidental Illustrations of the Economy of Salvation, Its Doctrines and Duties* (Boston: H. V. Degan, 1859), pp. 281.

112. Eaton, *The Itinerant's Wife*, pp. 54–55. The first publication in English intended as a handbook for the wives of clergy was the *Hints for a Clergyman's Wife; or, Female Parochial Duties* (London: Holdworth and Ball, 1832).

113. See, e.g., *The Doctrines and Discipline of the Methodist Episcopal Church* (New York: B. Waughard T. Mason, 1832), 87. From 1810 to 1824 the *Discipline* even prohibited traveling preachers from publishing anything without the permission of the conference. For the work of the stationing committee, see Carroll, *"Father Corson,"* pp. 120–21, 216. The rule requiring consultation with one's peers when planning matrimony remained in the *Discipline* until 1928.

114. Eaton, *The Itinerant's Wife*, pp. 13, 19, 20, 27, 28.

115. Ibid., pp. 34, 36, 50–53.

116. Enoch Pond isolates three types of visitation is his textbook for New England Congregational seminarians, *Lectures on Pastoral Theology* (Boston: Draper and Halliday, 1867), pp. 56–57, 66, 73.

117. Francis Wayland, *Letters on the Ministry of the Gospel* (Boston: Gould and Lincoln, 1863), p. 145.

118. Robert G. Middlekauff, *The Mathers: Three Generations of Puritan Intellectuals, 1596–1728* (New York: Oxford University Press, 1971), p. 88.

119. Ronald Wilson Long, "Religious Revivalism in the Carolinas and Georgia, 1740–1805" (Ph.D. diss. University of Georgia, 1968), p. 22.

120. A. D. Field, "An Essay on Preaching," *Ladies' Repository* 24 (1864): 101. It is true that some Methodists, including the rough-and-tumble Peter Cartwright, lamented the decline in home visitation, and there was an effort at the 1848 General Conference to promote pastoral visitation by requiring preachers to report on the number of calls they made during the year, but this had the effect of accelerating the move toward briefer, more pleasurable, less strenuous "social calls" that enabled John Carhart to brag about having made over seven hundred pastoral visits in one year. See Peter Cartwright, *Fifty years as a Presiding Elder*, ed. W. S. Hooper (Cincinnati: Hitchcock and Walden, 1871), p. 277; *Journal of the General Conference of the Methodist Episcopal Church, Volume III, 1848–56* (New York: Carlton and Phillips, 1856), p. 27; John Wesley Carhart, *Four Years on Wheels; or, Life as a Presiding Elder* (Oshkosh, Wis.: Allen and Hicks, 1880), p. 191.

121. Clifford Clark, Jr., *Henry Ward Beecher: Spokesman for a Middle-Class America* (Urbana: University of Illinois Press, 1978), p. 2.

122. William S. Plumer, *Hints and Helps in Pastoral Theology* (New York: Harper and Brothers, 1874), p. 258. Plumer's priorities in visitation were the sick, aged, or shut-ins, youth, and domestics. See also Pond, *Lectures on Pastoral Theology.*

123. Lewis, *Impressions*, pp. 36–37.

124. For England, see George Herbert, *A Priest to the Temple; or, The Country Parson, His Character, and Rule of Holy Life* (London: T. Maxey for T. Garthwait, 1652). Reprinted in *The Works of George Herbert*, ed. F. E. Hutchinson, (Oxford: Clarendon Press, 1941), p. 239; and Peter C. Hammond, *The Parson and the Victorian Parish* (London: Hodder and Stoughton, 1977), pp. 132–51. Whatever demand for "social visitation" there was seems to have come primarily from the South. See James W. Alexander, *The Life of Archibald Alexander* (New York: Charles Scribner, 1854), p. 169.

125. Kirk, *The Mother of the Wesleys*, p. 111.

126. George Whitefield, *The Works of Reverend George Whitefield . . .* 6 vols. (London: Edward and Charles Dilly, 1771–2), 1: 44. For Watts, see Plumer, *Hints and Helps in Pastoral Theology*, p. 258.

127. *Oberlin Evangelist* 1 (9 October 1839): 174.

128. *Digest of the Principal Acts and Deliverances of the General Assembly of the United Presbyterian Church of North America from 1859 to 1902*, 3d ed. (Pittsburgh: United Presbyterian Board of the Publication, 1903), 64; *Watchman of the South*, 5 (1842): 113.

129. George Peck, *Early Methodism within the Bounds of the Old Genesee Conference from 1788 to 1828; or, The First Forty Years of Weslyan Evangelism in Northern Pennsylvania, Central Western New York and Canada* (New York: Carlton and Porter, 1860), p. 349; see also John Carr,

Early Times in Middle Tennessee (Nashville: E. Stevenson and F. A. Owen, 1857), p. 184; Lewis, *Impressions*, pp. 36–37; Burgess, *Pleasant Recollections*, p. 340; John L. Dyer, *The Snow-Shoe Itinerant* (Cincinnati: Cranston and Stowe, 1890), p. 64.

130. William C. Chapin to Charles G. Finney, 6 February 1851, OCL, FP; Jones, *Memoir of Mrs. Sarah Lousia Taylor*, p. 62.

131. Finney's daughter recalled, "He never made social visits, he never went out to dine or take tea with a neighbor." Helen Finney Cox, "Charles Finney," in *Lives of the Leaders of Our Church Universal . . .* , ed. Ferdinand Piper (Philadelphia: Presbyterian Board of Publication, 1879), p. 739.

132. *Oberlin Evangelist* 2 (20 May 1840): 84. These "inquiry meetings" lost nothing of their inquisitory nature in the transition. "See that young woman. O how much she needs to have a plain, and searching, and personal conversation with her pastor. How much she needs to be told what will be the result of her affectation, gay dressing, tight lacing, and the thousand foolish and Spirit-grieving things in which young women are apt to indulge." "Male heads of families," Finney believed, "ought to feel and we ought to feel, as if it was our business, to inquire affectionately and particularly into all their habits in the relations they sustain to their families, to the Church, and to the world; to ascertain on what principles they conduct their business, . . . what their political principles, in reference to party strifes and party questions, are; whether or not, they are aspiring to office, or whether they are cleaving to a party, without regard to principle; in what manner they demean themselves toward those who are in their employment. . . . In short, it seems to me, that we are to interest ourselves in whatever interests them, and interests Zion; and to watch over, and warn, and reprove, and encourage, and instruct them, in regard to every thing that has a bearing upon their spiritual interests."

133. "But may not women as well as men bear a part of this horrible service? Undoubtedly they may; nay, they ought—it is meet, right, and their bounden duty. . . . Indeed it has long passed for a maxim with many that 'women are only to be seen; not heard.' . . . Yield not to that vile bondage any longer. You, as well as men, are rational creatures. You, like them, were made in the image of God; you are equally candidates for immorality. You too are called of God, as you have time, to 'do good unto all men.' Be 'not disobedient to the heavenly calling.'" John Wesley, "On Visiting the Sick," in *The Works of the Rev. John Wesley . . .* , ed. John Emory, 7 vols. 3d ed. (Cincinnati: Cranston and Stowe, 189–?), 2: 329–36.

134. Elizabeth A. Roe, *Recollections of Frontier Life* (n.p., n.d.), pp. 50–51.

135. *Memorial Offering to the Late Mrs. Mary G. Harley, of Barnwell South Carolina, by Rev. M. R. Suares, of Barnwell, South Carolina* (Columbia, S.C.: Charles A. Calvo, Jr., 1883); Manross, *Episcopal Church in the United States*, p. 191.

136. John Atkinson, *The Class Leader: His Work and How to Do It* (New York: Nelson and Phillips, 1875), pp. 110–11; John Miley, *Treatise on*

Class Meetings (Cincinnati: Poe and Hitchcock, 1866), p. 216; Mary Weems Chapman, *Mother Cobb; or, Sixty Years Walk with God* (Chicago: T. B. Arnold, 1896), p. 19.

137. S. B. Halliday, *Winning Souls: Sketches and Incidents during Forty Years of Pastoral Work* (New York: J. B. Ford, 1873), p. 32.

138. J. H. Potts, "Ladies' and Pastors' Christian Union," *Ladies' Repository* 36 (1876): 392–95; Fowler, *Historical Sketch of Presbyterianism*, p. 719. Areas of assistance outlined by the organization included calling on new residents, the unchurched, the sick, distributing food and tracts, recruiting teachers for Sunday school, counseling at revival meetings, teaching, and handling the "temporal affairs" of the church.

139. *New England Conference Journal* (n.p. 1910), 46–47.

140. William C. Beecher and Samuel Scoville, assisted by Mrs. Henry Ward Beecher, *A Biography of Rev. Henry Ward Beecher* (New York: Charles L. Webster, 1880), p. 158.

141. One of the earliest instructions given to clerical wives called for the "caring and healing of all wounds and sores with her own hands." See Herbert, *A Priest to the Temple*, p. 247.

142. Harris, *Circuit Rider's Wife*, pp. 71–75.

143. Eaton, *The Itinerant's Wife*, p. 50; Adams, *Daily Duties*, pp. 44–46, 112, 124; "A Wife for an Itinerant," *Ladies' Repository* (1847): 102.

144. For a Methodist example, see Scott, *Memoirs*, p. 26; for a Presbyterian one, see Rev. Joseph Sanderson, *In Memory of a Beloved Wife: October 6, 1864* (n.p., n.d.), pp. 12–13.

145. Arria S. Huntington, *Memoir and Letters of Frederic Dan Huntington, First Bishop of Central New York* (Boston: Houghton, Mifflin, 1906), p. 90.

146. Paul E. Johnson, *A Shopkeeper's Millennium: Society and Revivals in Rochester, New York, 1815–1837* (New York: Hill and Wang, 1978), pp. 98–99.

147. See Herman Norton to Charles G. Finney, 12 November 1830, OCL, FP.

148. Daniel Wise, *Sketches and Anecdotes of American Methodists of "The Days That Are No More": Designed for Boys and Girls* (New York: Phillips and Hunt, 1883), pp. 153–57.

149. Frank A. Sickels, *Fifty Years of the Young Men's Christian Association of Buffalo* (Buffalo: The Association, 1902), p. 25.

150. Adams, *Daily Duties*, pp. 19, 69; Eaton, *The Itinerant's Wife*, p. 53.

151. Rodgers, *Work Ethic in Industrial America*, pp. 184–86.

152. *The Evils Suffered by American Women and American Children: The Causes and the Remedy, Presented in an Address by Miss Catharine E. Beecher, to Meetings of Ladies in Cincinnati, Washington, Baltimore, Philadelphia, New York and Other Cities; Also An Address to the Protestant Clergy of the United States* (New York: Harper and Brothers, 1846); *New York Evangelist* (17 May 1849): 77. For Evangelical sensitivity to this issue,

see "Duties to Domestics," *Oberlin Evangelist* 3 (14 April 1841): 64 and (28 April 1841): 72. By the census of 1870, 9 percent of American women worked as domestics. *Woman's Journal* 9 (1878): 220.

153. Kirk, *The Mother of the Wesleys*, p. 137. For an eighteenth-century American example, see the 27 June 1776 letter of Hezekiah Smith, a chaplain in the Fourth Continental Infantry during the Revolution, to his wife, Hephzibah, in Haverhill, Massachusetts: "Pray procure some good help to be with you, and don't oppose yourself to any unnecessary hardships." LC, HSP.

154. For evidence of churches underwriting the cost of boarding a domestic, see Chapman, *Memoirs of an Itinerant*, p. 164, and G. W. Musgrave, *The Polity of the Methodist Episcopal Church in the United States: Being an Exposure* (Baltimore: Richard J. Matchett, 1843), p. 153. For the hiring of domestics by the pastor's family itself, see the *American Baptist Magazine and Missionary Intelligencer* 2 (1819): 231; Tucker, *Itinerant Preaching in the Early Days of Methodism*, p. 135; *Memoirs of the Late Mrs. Susan Huntington, of Boston, Massachusetts . . .* (Edinburgh: Waugh and Innes, 1828), p. 65; Heman Bangs, *Autobiography and Journal of Rev. Heman Bangs, with an Introduction by Rev. Bishop Janes, D.D.*, ed. Bangs's daughters (New York: N. Tibbals and Son, 1872), p. 160; *Aunt Peggy: Being a Memoir of Mrs. Margaret Davidson Ewing, Wife of the Late Rev. Finis Ewing, by One of Her Sons* (Nashville: Cumberland Presbyterian Board of Publication, 1873), p. 32; *Memorabilia of George B. Cheever, Late Pastor of the Church of the Puritans, Union Square, New York, and of his Wife Elizabeth Whetmore Cheever* (New York: Fleming H. Revell, 1890), p. 36; Camilla Sanderson, *John Sanderson the First; or, A Pioneer Preacher at Home* (Toronto: William Briggs, 1910), pp. 55–56; Mrs. H. A. Terwilligar Sharpe, *Reminiscences of a Minister's Daughter, Wife of a Widow* (Seymour, Conn.: n.p., 1911), p. 33; Emma Freeland Shay, *Mariet Hardy Freeland: A Faithful Witness*, 3d ed. (Winona Lake, Ind.: Woman's Missionary Society of the Free Methodist Church, 1937).

155. C. C. Copeland to Lydia Finney, 13 August 1846, OCL, FP.

156. S. R. Ingraham to Lydia Finney, 16 January 1847; C. D. Martin to Charles G. Finney, 15 April 1847; Charles G. Finney to Julia Finney, 23 January 1858; Elizabeth Finney to Mr. and Mrs. Lawson, 12 January 1860; Charles G. Finney to Julia Finney, 15 February 1863; Charles G. Finney to "My Dear Children," 15 May 1869, OCL, FP. Finney insisted that his children not do without servants, once even volunteering to pay for one himself. See Frances J. Hosford, "Finney and His Children," *Oberlin Alumni Magazine* 30 (1934): 301.

157. William A. Alcott, *The Young Wife; or, Duties of a Woman in the Marriage Relation* (Boston: George W. Lightly, 1837), pp. 181–82, 154. For the assumption that most middle-class marriages included domestics, see Daniel Wise, *Bridal Greetings: A Marriage Gift, in Which the Mutual Duties of Husband and Wife Are Familiarly Illustrated and Enforced* (New York: Carlton and Phillips, 1852), pp. 140–60; and Rufus W. Bailey, *Domestic Duties; or, The Family a Nursery for Earth and Heaven* (Philadelphia: Presbyterian Board of Publication, n.d.), passim.

158. Adams, *Daily Duties*, pp. iv, 147–52; Emily S. Bartlett to Lydia Finney, 27 April 1846, OCL, FP.

159. John H. Rice to Jane I. White, 13 February 1828, reprinted as "Hints to a Minister's Wife," *Presbyterian Magazine* 5 (1855): 504–6.

160. "A Minister's Wife," *Presbyterian* 16 (10 January 1846): 8.

161. "Ministers' Wives," *Christian Instructor* 15 (1859): 182.

Chapter Five

1. W. H. Ryder, of Andover, Massachusetts, recollects this remark in a 10 April 1890 letter to G. F. Wright, OCL, GWP.

2. See Helen Finney Cox's account of her father's life in *Lives of the Leaders of Our Church Universal . . .* , ed. Ferdinand Piper (Philadelphia: Presbyterian Board of Publication, 1879), pp. 730–40.

3. Charles G. Finney, "Last Sickness and Death of Mrs. Finney," *Oberlin Evangelist* (5 January 1848): 3.

4. Anne C. Loveland, "Presbyterians and Revivalism in the Old South," *Journal of Presbyterian History* 57 (1979): 41.

5. Celia R. Ladd, *Personal Recollections of President Finney* (Spring Arbor: n.p., n.d.), p. 9.

6. Helen Finney Cox to G. F. Wright, 17 October 1889, OCL, GWP.

7. Sarah T. Seward, Album, RPL; Ladd, *Personal Recollections*, p. 9; J. H. McIlvaine to G. F. Wright, 4 May 1890, OCL, GWP.

8. Nancy F. Cott, *The Bonds of Womanhood: "Woman's Sphere" in New England, 1780–1835* (New Haven: Yale University Press, 1977), p. 142.

9. Sandra S. Sizer, *Gospel Hymns and Social Religion: The Rhetoric of Nineteenth-Century Revivalism* (Philadelphia: Temple University Press, 1978), pp. 50–82.

10. Elmer T. Clark et al., eds., *The Journal and Letters of Francis Asbury*, 3 vols. (Nashville: Abingdon, 1958), 1: xii, 3: 140; Ezra Squier Tipple, *Francis Asbury: The Prophet of the Long Road* (New York: Methodist Book Concern, 1916), pp. 50–51.

11. See for example "Rhoda's" letter to *The Revivalist: Exclusively Devoted to the Revival and Extension of Evangelical Religion* (London: Simpkin and Marshall, 1832), pp. 171–72.

12. Julia Frances Tracy to Lydia Finney, 27 August 1827, OCL, FP.

13. Stephen W. Burritt to Charles G. Finney, 26 April 1827, OCL, FP.

14. Florence Hayes, *Daughters of Dorcas* (New York: Board of National Missions, 1952), pp. 23–24.

15. Sarah R. Ingraham, *Walks of Usefulness among the Sinning and the Sorrowing; or, Reminiscences of the Life Work of Margaret Barritt Prior*, 17th ed. (New York: American Female Guardian Society, 1859), p. 46.

16. Emilie Royce Bradley, Diary, 26 June 1831, OCL, DBP.

17. See for example *Memoirs of Amey Scott: Written by Herself* (New York: Orange Scott, 1846), p. 34; "Memoirs of Mrs. Sally Phippen," *American Baptist Magazine and Missionary Intelligencer* 1 (1818): 315–16.

18. William Green, Jr., and Mrs. H. C. Green to Charles G. Finney, 26 June 1833, OCL, FP.

19. Mary Ann and C. S. Andrews to Lydia Finney, 9 August 1826, OCL, FP. The only reference to an exclusively male prayer meeting I have been able to locate in the Finney correspondence is in a letter from Catherine N. Knowles to Charles G. Finney, 13 January 1831, OCL, FP.

20. Jesse Lee, *A Short Account of the Life and Death of the Rev. John Lee, a Methodist Minister in the United States of America* (Baltimore: John West Butler, 1805), pp. 16–17.

21. David O. Mears, *Life of Edward Norris Kirk* (Boston: Lockwood, Brooks, 1878), p. 51; Austin Phelps, *Women's Prayer-Meetings* (Boston: Congregational Publishing Society, 1877), pp. 3–5.

22. Stephen W. Burritt to Charles G. Finney, 2 April 1827, OCL, FP. For an example of how female prayer meetings served as a trigger of revivals, see the account of the first big revival in Ithaca, New York, in Charles D. Burritt, *Methodism in Ithaca* (Ithaca: Andrus, Gautlett, 1852), p. 67; and in *The Revivalist*, pp. 119–24, 171–72.

23. See for example Helen Platt to Lydia Finney, 23 April 1827, OCL, FP.

24. Henrietta Platt to Lydia Finney, 26 December 1827, January 1827. Laments were not confined to Lydia's vacated leadership of prayer meetings. A maternal association crumbled after her departure at the conclusion of Finney's Rochester revival; see letter from Mrs. M. L. Mathews to Lydia Finney, 16 May 1831, OCL, FP.

25. Ellen M. and Elizabeth Knight to Lydia Finney, 8 September 1829, OCL, FP.

26. William Green, Jr., and Mrs. H. C. Green to Lydia Finney, 9 July 1833; Juliet Pardee to Lydia Finney, 17 January 1828; Cynthia Brayton to Lydia Finney, 22 March 1828; M. J. Cushman to Lydia Finney, 9 March 1830. OCL, FP.

27. N. Royce to Lydia Finney, 23 May 1841; Susan P. Farnen to Lydia Finney, 8 April 1840; George Cheever to Charles G. Finney, 29 May 1858. Lydia's father and sister, Samuel and Susan Andrews, wrote to the Finneys on 10 May 1840 and confessed, "We take the *[Oberlin] Evangelist* and think it an excellent paper—so far as we can understand it. You must attribute it to my ignorance or whatever else you please but the doctrine of sanctification is but a very little plainer to my mind than before." OCL, FP.

28. Lewis Tappan to Lydia Finney, 18 July 1834, OCL, FP.

29. Catherine Huntington to Lydia Finney, 19 November 1829, OCL, FP.

30. Lydia M. Gilbert to Lydia Finney, 19 October 1827. See also Eliza T. Mitchell to Lydia Finney, 6 August 1826; Helen Platt to Lydia Finney, 17 December 1827; Arabella Cook to Lydia Finney, 2 April 1844; Catherine Huntington to Lydia Finney, 15 September 1829. OCL, FP.

31. A. A. Flint to Lydia Finney, 18 July 1826; Sarah Brayton to Lydia Finney, February 1828; Adeline J. Rockwell to Lydia Finney, 4 December 1830; Henrietta Platt to Lydia Finney, 25 April 1828; Sarah Seward to Lydia Finney, 15 March 1828. OCL, FP.

32. See for example Amelia A. Norton to Lydia Finney, 8 March, 4

July 1829, 2 July 1830; Ann F. Cole to Lydia Finney, 26 November 1844. OCL, FP.

33. Quoted in Anna Mary Dunton, "The New Lebanon Society and the Charles Finney Saga," unpublished manuscript, p. 4; Silas Churchill to Charles G. Finney, 8 March, 6 April, 10 July 1827, OCL, FP. For earlier controversy over public prayer by women, see George Keely, *The Nature and Order of a Gospel Church* . . . (Haverhill: P. N. Green, 1819), p. 23.

34. *Personal Reminiscences of the Life and Times of Gardiner Spring* . . . , 2 vols. (New York: Charles Scribner, 1866), 1: 182, 2: 81.

35. Sizer, *Gospel Hymns and Social Religion*, p. 52.

36. Asahel Nettleton to John Frost, 15 February 1827, OCL, FP.

37. Timothy Dwight to Charles G. Finney, March 1831; John Frost to Charles G. Finney, 21 April 1827; George W. Gale to Charles G. Finney, 11 March 1827. OCL, FP. *Pastoral Letter of the Ministers of the Oneida Association, to the Churches under Their Care, on the Subject of Revivals of Religion* (Utica, N.Y.: Arial Works, 1827), p. 16; Presbyterian Church of the U.S., *Minutes of the General Assembly of the Presbyterian Church in the United States of America from A.D. 1821 to A.D. 1835 Inclusive* (Philadelphia: Presbyterian Board of the Publications, n.d.), pp. 378–79.

38. Isaac Backus, *A History of New England*, ed. David Weston, 2d ed. 2 vols. (Newton, Mass.: Backus Historical Society, 1871), 1: 365.

39. James B. Taylor, *Virginia Baptist Ministers*, 2d ed. (Richmond, Va.: n.p., 1838), p. 20; William Lumpkin, "The Role of Women in Eighteenth-Century Virginia Baptist Life," *Baptist History and Heritage* 8 (1973): 163–64.

40. William G. McLoughlin, ed., *The Diary of Isaac Backus*, 3 vols. (Providence, R.I.: Brown University Press, 1979), 1: 90, 91, n. 1. For a revealing step in this direction, see Lumpkin, "The Role of Women," pp. 164–67.

41. Earl Kent Brown, "Women of the Word," in *Women in New Worlds: Historical Perspectives on the Wesleyan Tradition*, ed. Hilah F. Thomas and Rosemary Skinner Keller, (Nashville: Abingdon, 1981), p. 71.

42. Stephen Parks, *Troy Conference Miscellany, Containing a Historical Sketch of Methodism within the Bounds of the Troy Conference* (Albany: J. Lord, 1854), p. 46; Elizabeth A. Roe, *Recollections of Frontier Life* (n.p., n.d.), p. 52; Benjamin St. James Fry, *The Life of Robert R. Roberts, One of the Bishops of the Methodist Episcopal Church* (New York: Carlton and Porter, 1856), p. 15; John Burgess, *Pleasant Recollections of Characters and Works of Nobel Men, with Old Scenes and Merry Times of Long, Long Ago* (Cincinnati: Cranston and Stowe, 1887), pp. 259–63; Milton Bird, *The Life of Rev. Alexander Chapman* (Nashville: W. E. Dunaway, 1872), p. 162; Thomas W. Tucker, ed., *Itinerant Preaching in the Early Days of Methodism, by a Pioneer Preacher's Wife* (Boston: B. B. Russell, 1872), pp. 132–52.

43. John Weiss, *Life and Correspondence of Theodore Parker*, 2 vols. (New York: D. Appleton, 1864), 1: 93.

44. A. P. Mead, *Mana in the Wilderness; or, The Grove and Its Altar, Offerings, and Thrilling Incidents, Containing a History of the Origin and*

Rise of Camp Meetings, and a Defense of This Remarkable Means of Grace . . . , 3d ed.: (Philadelphia: Perkinpine and Higgins, 1860), pp. 240–41. Emphasis in original.

45. George Peck, *Early Methodism within the Bounds of the Old Genesee Conference from 1788 to 1828; or, The First Forty Years of Wesleyan Evangelism in Northern Pennsylvania, Central and Western New York and Canada* (New York: Carlton and Porter, 1860), p. 208.

46. In the early 1820s Princeton theology students formed two "bands," modeled after Wesley's small-group pattern, which sparked a revival on campus, Mears, *Life of Edward Norris Kirk*, pp. 30–31.

47. John Atkinson, *The Class Leader: His Work and How To Do It* (New York: Nelson and Phillips, 1875), p. 335; Mary Boardman, *Life and Labours of the Rev. W. E. Boardman* (New York: D. Appleton, 1889), pp. 40, 52, 50.

48. E. S. Jones, *Address to Class Leaders* (New York: Carlton and Lanahan, 1868), p. 29.

49. P. C. Headley, *Evangelists in the Church from Philip, A.D. 35, to Moody and Sanby, A.D. 1875* (Boston: Henry Hoyt, 1875), pp. 394, 395. See also *Life Sketches: Ancestry, Early Life, Christian Experience, and Extensive Labors, of Elder James White, and His Wife, Mrs. Ellen G. White* (Battle Creek, Mich.: Seventh-Day Adventist Publishing Company, 1880), pp. 164–65.

50. Ebenezer Francis Newell, *Life and Observation of Rev. E. F. Newell, Who Has Been More Than Forty Years an Itinerant Minister in the Methodist Episcopal Church, New England Conference* (Worchester, Mass.: C. W. Ainsworth, 1847), pp. 138–140, 149, 160, 184.

51. *The New Jersey Conference Memorial* . . . (Philadelphia: Perkinpine and Higgins, 1865), p. 91.

52. Quoted in *Methodism in Arkansas, 1816–1956* (Little Rock: Joint Committee for the History of Arkansas Methodism, 1976), p. 351.

53. George Brown, *The Lady Preacher: or, The Life and Labors of Mrs. Hannah Reeves, Late Wife of the Rev. William Reeves, D.D., of the Methodist Church* (Philadelphia: Daughaday and Becker, 1870).

54. Scott, *Memoirs*, pp. 67, 69.

55. For the Bangs family see John Carroll, ed., *"Father Corson"; or, The Old Style Canadian Itinerant.* . . . (Toronto: Rev. Samuel Rose, D.D., at the Methodist Book Room, 1879), pp. 10, 215; John Carroll, *Case and His Contemporaries; or, the Canadian Itinerant's Memorial* . . . , 5 vols. (Toronto: Samuel Rose, 1867–1877), 1: 224. For Evans see Jualynne Dodson, "Nineteenth Century A. M. E. Preaching Women," in Thomas and Keller, *Women in New Worlds*, p. 279.

56. P. H. Fowler, *Historical Sketch of Presbyterianism within the Bounds of the Synod of Central New York* (Utica, N.Y.: Curtiss and Childs, 1877), pp. 279–80; William G. McLoughlin, *Modern Revivalism: Charles Grandison Finney to Billy Graham* (New York: Ronald Press, 1959), pp. 133–57; Mary Clemmer (Ames), *Memorial Sketch of Elizabeth Emerson Atwater, Written for Her Friends* (Buffalo: Courier, 1879), p. 60; Headley, *Evangelists in the Church*, pp. 280, 283–87; Mary B. Allen King, *Looking*

Backward; or, Memories of the Past (New York: Anson D. F. Randolph, 1870), pp. 141–42.

57. See for example Julie Roy Jeffrey, *Frontier Women: The Trans-Mississippi West, 1840–1880* (New York: Hill and Wang, 1979), pp. 93, 97.

58. Horace McGuire, "Historical Sketch Read at the 100th Anniversary of the Formation of School District No. 6 in Brighton, Known as the Allen's Creek School," p. 2. Transcript in RPL.

59. William Martain Ferguson, *Methodism in Washington, District of Columbia* (Baltimore: Methodist Episcopal Book Depository, 1892), p. 62; Maxwell Gaddis, *Brief Recollections of the Late Rev. George Walker* (Cincinnati: Swormstedt and Poe, 1857), p. 76.

60. Jarena Lee, *Religious Experience and Journal of Mrs. Jarena Lee, Giving an Account of Her Call to Preach the Gospell* (Philadelphia: privately published, 1849), p. 5.

61. Gilbert Haven and Thomas Russell, *Father Taylor, the Sailor Preacher* (Boston: B. B. Russell, 1872), pp. 13, 14, 63, 71–78, 89, 327, 372–73.

62. See as an example Miriam Gurko, *The Ladies of Seneca Falls: The Birth of the Woman's Rights Movement* (New York: Macmillan, 1974), p. 335.

63. Nancy Towle, *Vicissitudes Illustrated in the Experience of Nancy Towle, in Europe and America*, 2d ed. (Portsmouth, N.H.: John Caldwell, 1833), p. 53.

64. Catherine S. Lawrence, *Autobiography. Sketch of Life and Labors of Miss Catherine S. Lawrence. . .* (Albany, N.Y.: Amasa J. Parker, Weed, Parsons, 1893), p. 17.

65. Stephen Peet to Milton Badger, 24 February 1825, PHS. Peet goes on to observe that "the practice has subsided," but he reveals that "under the circumstances" the best strategy had been one of tolerating the popular practice. Those who attacked it openly found themselves the objects of hostility and prejudice.

66. C. A. Burdick, ed., *Autobiography of Rev. Alexander Campbell* (Watertown, N.Y.: Post Printing House, 1883), pp. 46–47; *Living Life; or, Autobiography of Rev. Emerson Andrews, Evangelist* (Boston: James H. Earle, 1872), p. 36.

67. See the account of Aikins's Utica church in *A Narrative of the Revival of Religion in the County of Oneida, Particularly in the Bounds of the Presbytery of Oneida, in the Year of 1826* (Utica, N.Y.: Hastings and Tracy, 1826), p. 26. For Brown see Frances J. Hosford, "The Pioneer Women of Oberlin College: Antoinette Brown Blackwell," *Oberlin Alumni Magazine* 23 (1927): 7.

68. Theodore Weld to Angelina and Sarah Grimké, 26 August 1837, in *Letters of Theodore Dwight Weld, Angelina Grimké Weld and Sarah Grimké 1822–44*, Gilbert H. Barnes and Dwight L. Dumond, (New York: 2 vols. D. Appleton-Century Crofts, 1934; reprint ed., Gloucester, Mass.: Peter Smith, 1965), 1: 433; Whitney R. Cross, *The Burned-Over District: The Social and Intellectual History of Enthusiatic Religion in Western New York* (New York: Harper Torchbooks, 1965), p. 177.

69. Clifford M. Drury, *Marcus and Narcissa Whitman and the Opening of Old Oregon*, 2 vols. (Glendale, Cal.: Arthur H. Clark 1973), 1: 333.

70. Lucy Drake Osborn, *Heavenly Pearls Set in a Life: A Record of Experiences and Labors in America, India and Australia* (New York: Fleming H. Revell, 1893), pp. 20, 64–77, 95.

71. "Ought Women to Pray and Speak in Public and Promiscuous Assemblies?" *Presbyterian* 32 (1862): 125.

72. Quoted in Sizer, *Gospel Hymns and Social Religion*, p. 62.

73. For an interesting editorial on the "Impropriety of Long Prayers," which reviewed the fifty-five prayers recorded in the Bible (exclusive of the Psalms) and discovered that the longest took eight to ten minutes to recite, and thirty-nine took from one minute to two seconds, see the *American Baptist Magazine and Missionary Intelligencer* 1 (1818): 399–401.

74. Parsons Cook, *Female Preaching, Unlawful and Inexpedient: A Sermon* (Lynn: James R. Newell, 1837), p. 2.

75. Ibid., pp. 4, 7, 10–15.

76. Ibid., pp. 9, 14–15, 16, 18.

77. Mary J. Wilber, "Address on Home Missions," in *Circular of the Cincinnati Ladies' Home Missionary Society of the Methodist Episcopal Church; Also, An Address on Home Missions, by Mrs. Mary C. Wilber* (Cincinnati: Methodist Book Corner, 1854), p. 9.

78. Towle, *Vicissitudes*, p. 27; Deborah Peirce, *A Spiritual Vindication of Female Preaching, Prophesying, or Exhortation* (Carmel, N.H.: E. Burroughs, n.d.), pp. 11–12; Lee, *Religious Experience and Journal*, p. 12.

79. This issue is discussed by the editor, W. K. Pendelton, in "Shall Women Pray or Exhort in Public," *Millennial Harbinger* 7 (1864): 325–33. See also the response of R. Faurot in the following issue, pp. 370–71.

80. Presbyterian Church in the U.S., *General Assembly Minutes, 1832*, pp. 378–79. As Janet Harbison Penfield has shown in "Women in the Presbyterian Church—An Historical Overview," *Journal of Presbyterian History*, 55 (1977), p. 110, this issue was still being debated into the second half of the nineteenth century, with the same results: "If they will exercise their gifts publicly, let them have prayer meetings." Not until after World War I did the General Assembly allow women to preside over its meetings.

81. Green's discourse is quoted in Hayes, *Daughters of Dorcas*, p. 27.

82. *Woman's Journal* 9 (1877): 100.

83. Claude U. Gilson, ed., "Antoinette Brown Blackwell: The First Woman Minister." Typescript in OCL, RFP. See also George W. Gale's report to Finney about the Oneida Presbytery proceedings and its judgment that female prayers "should be ordinarily confined to social circles, which you know with few exceptions they have been with us." John Frost to Charles G. Finney, 22 March 1827, OCL, FP.

84. See Sarah C. Little, "Oberlin and the Education of Women," and Lucy Stone, "Oberlin and Women," in *The Oberlin Jubilee: 1833–1883*, ed. W. G. Ballantine and E. J. Goodrich (Oberlin: E. J. Goodrich, 1883), pp. 150–51 and 316–17; Delavan L. Leonard, *The Story of Oberlin* (Boston: Pilgrim Press, 1898), p. 173.

85. Flora Bridges speculates that this may have afforded the inspiration for the formation of the Ladies' Literary Society, the oldest women's

literary society in America. See "Antoinette Brown Blackwell," *Oberlin Alumni Magazine* 5 (1909): 204.

86. Gilson, "Blackwell," p. 5.

87. Quoted in Robert S. Fletcher, A *History of Oberlin College from Its Foundation through the Civil War*, 2 vols. (Oberlin: Oberlin College, 1943), 1: 292.

88. Gilson, "Blackwell," p. 12.

89. Ibid., p. 8; Lillian F. O'Connor, "Excerpts from 'Lucy Stone's Preparation for Public Speaking.'" Typescript in LC, BFP (Lucy Stone Papers). For Thome's feminist inclinations, see his *Address to the Females of Ohio, Delivered at the State Anti-Slavery Anniversary* (Cincinnati: Ohio Anti-Slavery Society, 1836); Fletcher, *History of Oberlin*, 1: 294.

90. Fletcher, *History of Oberlin*, 1: 291, 339.

91. Gilson, "Blackwell," p. 11; Antoinette Brown to Lucy Stone, 1848, pp. 19–20, in Claude U. Gilson, ed., "Letters of Antoinette Brown Blackwell," OCL, RFP.

92. Antoinette Brown to Gerritt Smith, 26 December 1851, OCL, RFP.

93. Leonard I. Sweet, "Views of Man Inherent in New Measures Revivalism," *Church History* 45 (1976): 206–21.

94. Theodore Weld to Angelina and Sarah Grimké, 26 August 1837, in Barnes and Dumond, *Letters of Theodore Dwight Weld, Angelina Grimké Weld and Sarah Grimké*, 1: 432.

95. E. P. Barrows to Finney, 19 February 1831, OCL, FP.

96. Finney, "Last Sickness and Death," *Oberlin Evangelist* (5 January 1848): 3.

97. Lydia M. Gilbert to Lydia Finney, February 1828, OCL, FP; *Memoirs of Rev. Charles G. Finney* (New York: A. S. Barnes, 1876), pp. 234–38.

98. W. Emerson Wilson, ed., *Diaries of Phoebe George Bradford, 1832–1839* (Wilmington, Del.: Historical Society of Delaware, 1976), p. 5.

99. C. J. and N. Andrews to Mr. and Mrs. Finney, 6 August 1827, OCL, FP.

100. Mrs. L. Lansing to Lydia Finney, 10 November 1826; John P. Cushman to Charles G. Finney, 4 November 1826; Mrs. M. S. Wright to Lydia Finney, 28 February 1828, OCL, FP.

101. Lydia M. Gilbert to Lydia Finney, February 1828; Amelia Norton to Lydia Finney, 1 January, 20 February 1828, OCL, FP.

102. James Buchan to Charles G. Finney, 16 November 1830, OCL, FP.

103. Miss Miller and Nancy Norman were a pair, for example, as were Rebecca Jackson and Rebecca Perot, and Nancy Towle traveled with Martha Spalding, Elizabeth Venner, and Thomasine O'Bryan She ended up traveling without an associate because, she wrote, "I can seldom find a female that has courage sufficient—or, if she has that qualification, she has not grace proportionate." *Vicissitudes*, p. 251.

104. For Olney see *New York Daily Tribune*, 13, 17, 26, 29 March 1858. There is no record of her book *Christian Experiences of Harriet Olney* (New York: n.p., 1858) except the advertisement in the 18 March 1858 issue

of the *Tribune*. The Library of Congress, the only known location for her other book, *The Old Way of Holiness* (New York: n.p., 1857), reports its copy missing.

105. Burritt, *Methodism in Ithaca*, pp. 101, 104, 127. Towle's own account of the incident is found in her *Vicissitudes*, pp. 165–66. For the English counterpart to this belief that female public speaking was permissible so long as it was not preaching, see John Kirk, *The Mother of the Wesleys: A Biography*, 2d ed. (London: Henry James Tresidder, 1864), pp. 262–63.

106. As quoted in a 1610 sermon by John Robinson, reproduced in Backus, *History of New England*, 1: 15.

107. Reported in *Ladies' Repository* 35 (1875): 267.

108. George Coles, *Heroines of Methodism; or, Pen and Ink Sketches of the Mothers and Daughters of the Church* (New York: Carlton and Porter, 1857), pp. 194–95.

109. Jeffrey, *Frontier Women*, p. 97; Lee, *Religious Experiences and Journal*, p. 67; Towle, *Vicissitudes*, p. 36.

110. Mary Clemmer Ames, *Ten Years in Washington: Life and Scenes in the National Capital, as a Woman Sees Them* (Cincinnati: Queen City, 1874), p. 61.

111. W. T. Livermore, *Harriet Livermore, the "Pilgrim Stranger"* (Hartford, Conn.: Case, Lockwood and Brainard, 1884), pp. 17, 82, 82, 151, 153, 155.

112. James B. Finley, *Sketches of Western Methodism: Biographical, Historical and Miscellaneous, Illustrative of Pioneer Life*, ed. W. P. Strickland (Cincinnati: Methodist Book Concern, 1855), pp. 194–95.

113. John A. Williams, *Life of Elder John Smith . . .* (Cincinnati: R. W. Carroll, 1870), pp. 240–41.

114. Towle, *Vicissitudes*, p. 33.

115. Lee, *Religious Experiences and Journal*, p. 17.

116. Leonard I. Sweet, "Millennialism in America: Recent Studies," *Theological Studies* 40 (1979): 510–31.

117. Peirce, *A Scriptural Vindication*, p. 3, passim; *Life Sketches of Elder James White and Ellen G. White*, p. 169.

118. It is somewhat ironic to find the unmarried and stoutly nonconformist preacher Harriet Livermore touted as a model of courage in Pliny DeKalb's rhapsodic celebration of woman as wife and helpmeet, *The American Wife: An Offering to Worth and Loveliness* (Philadelphia: C. W. Murray, 1844), pp. 12–14.

119. Harriet Livermore, *A Testimony for the Times* (New York: Piercy and Reed, 1843), pp. v, viii, xiii, 26; *The Harp of Israel, to Meet the Loud Echo in the Wilds of America* (Philadelphia: J. Rabestraw, 1835), pp. 4, 7, 11, 173–80. I have only been able to locate the fourth issue of *Millennial Tidings* (Philadelphia: privately published, 1839), pp. 1–7.

120. Phoebe Palmer, *The Promise of the Father; or, A Neglected Specialty of the Last Days* (Boston: H. V. Degan, 1859); Catherine Booth, *Female Ministry: Woman's Right to Preach the Gospel* (London: Morgan

and Chase, 1895). For a discussion of the debate, see Olive Anderson, "Women Preachers in Mid-Victorian Britain: Some Reflections on Feminism, Popular Religion and Social Change," *Historical Journal* 13 (1969): 480–81. The "last days" defense of Palmer's preaching was also used by Robert Young to justify the patronage of her ministry by Wesleyan clergy in northern England. See *Prophesying of Women* (Newcastle on Tyne: R. Curtiss, 1859), pp. 2–8.

121. Zilpha Elaw, *Memoirs of the Life, Religious Experience, Ministerial Travels and Labours, of Mrs. Zilpha Elaw, an American Female of Colour, Together with Some Account of the Great Religious Revivals in America* (London: privately published, 1846), p. 114; see also "Elizabeth," *A Colored Minister of the Gospel, Born in Slavery* (Philadelphia: Tract Association of Friends, 1889), p. 11.

122. Peirce, *A Scriptural Vindiction*, p. 20.

123. Arabel W. Alexander, *Life and Work of Lucinda B. Helm, Founder of the Woman's Home Mission Society of the Methodist Episcopal Church, South*, 3d ed. (Nashville: Publishing House of the Methodist Episcopal Church, South, 1904), p. 39.

124. Angelina Grimké, *Letters to Catharine Beecher, in Reply to an Essay on Slavery and Abolitionism, Addressed to A. E. Grimké* (Boston: Isaac Knapp, 1838; reprint ed., New York: Arno Press and the New York Times, 1969), pp. 188–89.

125. Quoted in Ernest R. Sandeen, *The Roots of Fundamentalism: British and American Millennialism, 1800–1930* (Chicago: University of Chicago Press, 1970), p. 49.

126. Finney believed that if Evangelicals "were united all over the world the Millennium might be brought about in three months." Quoted in Paul E. Johnson, *A Shopkeeper's Millennium: Society and Revivals in Rochester, New York, 1815–1837* (New York: Hill and Wang, 1978), p. 109.

127. Towle, *Vicissitudes*, p. 16.

128. Anderson, "Women Preachers in Mid-Victorian Britain," p. 475.

129. Towle, *Vicissitudes*, pp. 98, 253; Lee, *Religious Experience and Journal*, p. 61.

130. Lucille Sider Dayton and Donald W. Dayton, "'Your Daughters Shall Prophesy': Feminism in the Holiness Movement," *Methodist History* 14 (1976): 67–92; Nancy Hardesty, "Your Daughters Shall Prophesy: Revivalism and Feminism in the Age of Finney" (Ph.D. diss., University of California, 1976); Timothy L. Smith, "Righteousness and Hope: Christian Holiness and the Millennial Vision in America, 1800–1900," *American Quarterly* 31 (1979): 21–45; Anderson, "Women Preachers in Mid-Victorian Britain," p. 477.

131. Osborn, *Heavenly Pearls*, pp. 66–67, 70–71.

132. Jean McMahon Humez, "Introduction," in *Gifts of Power: The Writings of Rebecca Jackson, Black Visionary, Shaker Eldress*, ed. Jean McMahon Humez (n.p.: University of Massachusetts Press, 1981), 4–7.

133. Quoted in Rosemary Radford Ruether and Eleanor McLaughlin,

eds., *Women of Spirit* (New York: Simon and Schuster, 1979), p. 232. Emphasis in original. In 1865 the Palmers purchased the magazine, then called the *Guide to Holiness*, and Phoebe became its editor.

134. Phoebe Palmer, *Pioneer Experiences; or, The Gift of Power Received by Faith* (New York: W.C. Palmer, Jr., 1868), p. 74.

135. Melinda Hamline to Phoebe Palmer, 2 November 1847, NYL, MR, PPP.

136. G. Boynton, *Sanctification Practical: A Book for the Times* (New York: Foster and Palmer, 1867), p. 65.

137. Such revival teams included Ellen Lois and Rev. B. T. Roberts, Martha B. and Rev. E. P. Hart, Minerva and Rev. William Cooley, Delia Jeffres and Rev. T. B. Cotton, Janet and Rev. J. D. Osmun, Mariet Hardy and Rev. LaDue, and Rev. and Mrs. Joseph McCreery. These women preached from a tent, exhorted, led the singing, presided at class meetings, conducted altar calls, taught Sunday school, visited, organized mothers' meetings, and served in temperance, antislavery, and other reform societies. At their fiftieth wedding aniversary, Jonathan Freeland toasted his wife's ministry in the following terms: "Any success I may have had in the work of saving souls and building up the church in that holiness without which no man shall see the Lord, has been realized largely as the result of your able and constant cooperation in all departments." Emma Freeland Shay, *Mariet Hardy Freeland: A Faithful Witness*, 3d ed. (Winona Lake, Ind.: Woman's Missionary Society of the Free Methodist Church, 1937), pp. 106–8, 112–13, 119, 207. For another example of how holiness doctrine spurred women to take advantage of more freedom, see Austin A. Phelps, *The Life of Mrs. Fanny L. Bartlett, Consort of the Late Dr. Oliver C. Bartlett . . .* (Boston: H. V. Degen, 1860).

138. B. T. Roberts, "The Right of Women to Preach the Gospel," in *Ordaining Women* (Rochester, N.Y.: "Earnest Christian" Publishing House, 1891).

139. Melissa Booth Carter, *Beulah Land: An Autobiography* (Boston: James H. Earle, 1888), pp. 83–84. For Roberts's difficulties with his church, see John Wesley Howell, "'When Called of God and Duly Qualified': Issues Surrounding Women in the Ordained and Pastoral Ministry in the Free Methodist Church of North America," unpublished manuscript, 1981, p. 26.

140. Shay, *Freeland*, p. 189; Benson Howard Roberts, *Benjamin Titus Roberts: A Biography* (North Chili, N.Y.: "Earnest Christian" Publishing House, 1900), p. 530.

141. Lee, *Religious Experience and Journal*, p. 11.

142. Ibid., passim.

143. *Sketches and Incidents; or, A Budget from the Saddle-Bags of a Superannuated Itinerant*, 2 vols. (New York: Carlton and Phillips, 1853), 2: 16–17.

144. Elaw, *Memoirs*, p. 48.

145. Ibid., pp. 26, 78, 83, passim.

146. Elizabeth, *A Colored Minister of the Gospel*, p. 13.

147. Harriet Livermore, *A Narration of Religious Experience, in*

Twelve Letters (Concord: Jacob B. Moore, 1826), pp. 14, 146, 156, 160, 243, 260.

148. Ibid., pp. 13, 15–16, 270, 276.

149. Ibid., 103, 161.

150. Towle, *Vicissitudes*, 175–78. For Towle's refusal to accept some letters of recommendation from clergymen, see p. 35. For a complete text of another letter of introduction, see Carter, *Beulah Land*, pp. 187–89. Richard Kern's biography of John Winebrenner is strangely silent about his endorsement of women preachers, although Winebrenner's serving as an agent for Dow's medicinal syrup is mentioned. *John Winebrenner: Nineteenth-Century Reformer* (Harrisburg, Pa.: Central Publishing House, 1974), p. 183.

151. Horace Bushnell, *Women's Suffrage: The Reform against Nature* New York: Charles Scribner, 1870).

152. Cited by Annis Ford Eastman, "Woman in Church and State," a pamphlet reprinted from the *Elmira Daily Advertiser*, 4 February 1903, pp. 10–11.

153. The Garfield quotation is found in William C. Ringenberg, "Preacher in the White House," *Christian Herald* 103 (1980): 80.

154. Lee, *Religious Experience and Journal*, p. 67; Livermore, *Narration*, p. 213; W. P. Strickland, ed., *Autobiography of Rev. James B. Finley* (Cincinnati: Jennings and Graham, 1905), pp. 286–86; Corra Harris, *A Circuit Rider's Wife* (Philadelphia: Henry Altemus, 1919), p. 36; Towle, *Vicissitudes*, pp. 36, 93, 102, 106, 145, 157, 167, 175, 182–83.

155. Towle, *Vicissitudes*, pp. 159–60.

156. The entire Miller episode is derived from the account by George Brown, *Recollections of Itinerant Life, Including Early Reminiscences* (Cincinnati: R. W. Carroll, 1866), pp. 183–89.

157. Coles, *Heroines of Methodism*, p. 13; Shay, *Freeland*, pp. 41, 48, 62. The praying women of the postbellum years were more inclined to wait deferentially for clergymen to call upon them to pray publicly than their gifted sisters of the early nineteenth century had been. See Mrs. H. A. Terwillingar Sharpe, *Reminiscences of a Minister's Daughter, Wife of a Widow* (Seymour, Conn.: n.p., 1911), p. 4.

158. Three years later Frances Willard did arrange to address Chautauquans of both sexes. See Anne M. Boylan, "Evangelical Womanhood in the Nineteenth Century: The Role of Women in Sunday Schools," *Feminist Studies* 4 (1978): 73.

159. Livermore, *Narration*, p. 270.

160. Lee, *Religious Experience and Journal*, pp. 4–6; Peirce, *A Scriptural Vindication*, pp. 2–3.

Chapter Six

1. For the 1800s as the "Woman's Century," see William Hepworth Dixon, *New America* (Philadelphia: J. B. Lippincott, 1867), p. 293; Florence Hayes, *Daughters of Dorcas* (New York: Board of National Missions, 1952), p. 39. For the 1800s as a "Practical Age," see *Personal Reminiscences of the*

Life and Times of Gardiner Spring. . . , 2 vols. (New York: Charles Scribner, 1866), 2: 272–74; Stephen Colwell, *New Themes for the Protestant Clergy: Creeds without Charity, Theology without Humanity, Protestantism without Christianity* (Philadelphia: Lippincott, Grambo, 1851; reprint ed., New York: Arno Press and the New York Times, 1969), pp. 180–81. The theme of "Practical Christianity" (it was assumed that everyone would read the term as "Practical Protestantism"), elaborated first by Hannah More in her *Practical Piety; or, The Influence of the Religion of the Heart on the Conduct of the Life* (New York: American Tract Society, 1811?), even spawned a Roman Catholic equivalent in 1882, when the Knights of Columbus society was organized to develop "practical Catholicity" among its members.

2. Emily Faithfull, *Three Visits to America* (New York: Fowler and Wells, 1884), p. vii; Thomas Wentworth Higginson, *Women and the Alphabet: A Series of Essays* (1881; reprint ed., Boston and New York: Houghton, Mifflin, 1900), pp. 5–6. For one of the women who plowed the back forty in the untilled field of American religious history, see Hannah Adams, *Alphabetical Compendium of the Various Sects . . . From the Beginning of the Christian Era to the Present Day* (Boston: B. Edes and Sons, 1784); Hannah Adams, *A View of Religion in Two Parts: Part I, Containing an Alphabetical Compendium of the Various Religious Denominations, Which Have Appeared in the World, from the Beginning of the Christian Era to the Present Day; Part II, Containing a Brief Account of the Different Schemes of Religion Now Embraced among Mankind,* 3d ed. (Boston: Manning and Loring, 1801); and *A Memoir of Miss Hannah Adams, Written by Herself with Additional Notices by a Friend* (Boston: Gray and Bowen, 1832).

3. Eleanor Flexner, *Century of Struggle: The Woman's Rights Movement in the United States* (Cambridge: Harvard University Press, 1959); Aileen Kraditor, *The Ideas of the Woman Suffrage Movement, 1890–1920* (Garden City, N.Y.: Anchor Books, 1971); Gerda Lerner, "Women's Rights and American Feminism," *American Scholar* 40 (1971): 235–48; William O'Neill, *Everyone Was Brave: The Rise and Fall of Feminism in America* (Chicago: Quadrangle, 1969); Andrew Sinclair, *The Better Half: The Emancipation of the American Woman* (New York: Harper and Row, 1965); Alan P. Grimes, *The Puritan Ethic and Woman Suffrage* (New York: Oxford University Press, 1967).

4. Janet Todd, *Women's Friendship in Literature* (New York: Columbia University Press, 1979); Carroll Smith-Rosenberg, "The Female World of Love and Ritual: Relations between Women in Nineteenth-Century America," *Signs* 1 (1975): 1–29.

5. F. W. B. Bullock, *Voluntary Religious Societies, 1520–1799* (St. Leonards on Sea: Budd and Gillatt, 1963), pp. 157, 254.

6. Higginson, *Women* pp. 118–19; "Women's Record at Home," *Ladies' Repository* 36 (1876): 172.

7. Gregory H. Singleton, "Protestant Voluntary Organizations and the Shaping of Victorian America," *American Quarterly* 27 (1975): 549–62; Don H. Doyle, "The Social Functions of Voluntary Associations in a Nineteenth-Century American Town," *Social Science History* 1 (1977): 333–55; Walter

S. Glazer, "Participation and Power: Voluntary Associations and the Functional Organization of Cincinnati in 1840," *Historical Methods Newsletter* 5 (1972): 151–68.

8. Donald G. Mathews, "The Second Great Awakening as an Organizing Process," *American Quarterly* 21 (1969): 23–43.

9. Frances Trollope, *Domestic Manners of the Americans*, ed. Donald Smalley (New York: Alfred A. Knopf, 1949), p. 275; Harriet Martineau, *Society in America*, ed. Seymour Martin Lipset (Garden City, N.Y.: Anchor, 1962), p. 342–43; William M. Clements, "Five British Travelers and Religion in Nineteenth-Century America," *Research Studies* 46 (1978): 44–49.

10. Jean P. Jordan, "Women Merchants in Colonial New York," *New York History* 58 (1977): 412–39.

11. Joshua Priestly, *True Womanhood, Memorials of Eliza Hessel*, 2d ed. (London: Hamilton, Adams, 1859), pp. 172, 244–46; Edward W. Hooker, *Memoir of Mrs. Sarah Lanman Smith, Late of the Mission in Syria, under the Direction of the American Board of Commissioners for Foreign Missions*, 2d ed. (Boston: Perkins and Marvin, 1840), pp. 118–20; *An Account of the Experiences of Mrs. Hester Anne Rogers, Written by Herself . . .* (New York: S. and D. A. Forbes, 1830), pp. 67–68, 95; Abel Stevens, *The Women of Methodism: Its Three Foundresses, Susanna Wesley, the Countess of Huntingdon, and Barbara Heck, with Sketches of Their Female Associates and Successors in the Early History of the Denomination* (New York: Carlton and Porter, 1866), p. 181; Eunice White Bullard Beecher, *From Dawn to Daylight; or, The Simple Story of a Western Home, by a Minister's Wife* (New York: Derby and Jackson, 1859; micropublished ed., New Haven: Research Publications, 1975); Kitty to Francais W. Collins, 28 February 18—, David Hedden Letters, FC. For the commonness of depression among the clergy, see Jesse Lee, *A Short Account of the Life and Death of the Rev. John Lee, a Methodist Minister in the United States of America* (Baltimore: John West Butler, 1805), p. 81.

12. Keith E. Melder, *Beginnings of Sisterhood: The American Woman's Rights Movement, 1800–1850* (New York: Schocken, 1977), p. 39; Hayes, *Daughters of Dorcas*, p. 7.

13. See Elizabeth Fry, *The Christian Philanthropist* (Philadelphia: American Sunday School Union, 1851), a book sanctioned unanimously by the ASSU's Committee of Publication, which consisted of fourteen delegates from the Baptist, Methodist, Episcopal, Congregational, Presbyterian, Lutheran, and Reformed Dutch churches; *The New York Missionary Magazine and Repository of Religious Intelligence, for the Year 1801*, 2 vols. (New York: Cornelius Davis, 1801), 2: 426–42; Harriet Martineau, *Society in America*, 2d ed., 3 vols. (London: Saunders and Oxley, 1837), 2: 219.

14. Warren Fay, *The Obligations of Christians to the Heathen World: A Sermon Delivered at the Old South Church in Boston, before the Auxiliary Foreign Mission Society of Boston and Vicinity, at Their Annual Meeting, January 3, 1825* (Boston: Crocker and Brewster, 1825).

15. Keith Melder, "Ladies Bountiful: Organized Women's Benevolence in Early Nineteenth-Century America," *New York History* 48 (1967): 243.

16. Ibid., p. 232.

17. The New York Missionary Magazine, pp. 261–68, 379–85; Hayes, Daughters of Dorcas, pp. 8–9; R. Pierce Beaver, American Protestant Women in World Mission: History of the First Feminist Movement in North America, (1968; Grand Rapids, Mich: William B. Eerdmans, n.d.), pp. 13–35.

18. Page Putnam Miller, "The Evolving Role of Women in the Presbyterian Church in the Early Nineteenth Century" (Ph.D. diss. University of Maryland, 1979), p. 143; American Baptist Magazine 1 (1818): 466–67; Daniel Huntington, A Discourse Delivered at Braintree, on Thursday, April 9, 1818, at the Funeral of Mrs. Sarah Storrs, Wife of the Rev. Richard Storrs (Boston: Nathaniel Willis, 1818), p. 20; Nancy F. Cott, The Bonds of Womanhood: "Woman's Sphere" in New England 1780–1835 (New Haven: Yale University Press, 1977), pp. 131–32; Eleanor P. Copeland, "James Hoge, Pioneer Ohio Preachers, II, " Journal of the Presbyterian Historical Society 36 (1958): 262; J. B. Simmons, Women's Bible Bands . . . (Philadelphia: American Baptist Publication Society, 1888) p. 5; Bishop L. J. Coppin, Unwritten History (Philadelphia: A. M. E. Book Concern, 1919), p. 357–58.

19. History of the Women's Home Missionary Society of the First Presbyterian Church of Batavia, New York, 1837–1937 (Batavia: Fix Printing Co., n.d.), pp. 6–7, 14.

20. This observation applies mainly to Baptists and Methodists, who moved more frequently than clergymen in other traditions. See, for example, Thomas W. Tucker, ed., Itinerant Preaching in the Early Days of Methodism, by a Pioneer Preachers' Wife (Boston: B. B. Russell, 1872), pp. 98, 133.

21. For a very helpful listing of Presbyterian societies, see Hayes, Daughters of Dorcas, pp. 141–58; see also Mary F. Kihlstrom, "The Morristown Female Charitable Society," Journal of Presbyterian History 58 (1980): 255–72. For Baptist societies, see the American Baptist Magazine and Missionary Intelligencer 1 (1817): 31–35, 116–17, 2 (1819): 32–33, 226–27; Leo Taylor Crismon, ed., Baptists in Kentucky, 1776–1976: A Bicentennial Volume (Middletown, Ky.: Kentucky Baptist Convention, 1975), p. 82; Mrs. T. Seymore Scott, "The Dorcas Society," in History of the First Baptist Church of Philadelphia, ed. William Williams Keen (n.p. 1889), pp. 315–22. For the Episcopalians, see William Wilson Manross, The Episcopal Church in the United States, 1800–1840: A Study in Church Life (New York: Columbia University Press, 1938), pp. 217–20. For the Methodists see for example Andrew Carroll, Moral and Religious Sketches and Collections, with Incidents of Ten Years' Itinerancy in the West (Cincinnati: Methodist Book Concern, 1857), 204; Heman Bangs, Autobiography and Journal of Rev. Heman Bangs, with an Introduction by Rev. Bishop Janes, D.D., ed. Bangs's daughters (New York: N. Tibbals and Son, 1872), pp. 51–63.

22. Ellen DuBois, "Women's Rights and Abolition: The Nature of the Connection," in Antislavery Reconsidered: New Perspectives on the Abolitionists, ed. Lewis Perry and Michael Fellman (Baton Rouge: Louisiana State University Press, 1979), pp. 238–40.

23. O'Neil, *Everyone Was Brave*; Melder, *Beginnings of Sisterhood*; Cott, *Bonds of Womanhood*; Ronald W. Hogeland, "Charles Hodge, the Association of Gentlemen and Ornamental Womanhood: 1825–1855," *Journal of Presbyterian History* 13 (1975): 242–43. For Archibald Alexander's wife, see James W. Alexander, *The Life of Archibald Alexander* (New York: Charles Scribner, 1854), pp. 527–29.

24. Lucy Stone, "Work by Women in the Churches," *Woman's Journal* 9 (1877): 132.

25. See as an example the wife of Steubenville, Ohio's Presbyterian minister, as outlined in A. M. Reid, *Biographical Sketch of Mrs. Hetty Elizabeth Beatty* (New York: J. J. Little, 1883), p. 119.

26. Almira Raymond to Parents, 3 September 1840, 7 March 1842, UO, ARL. It is likely that Raymond is the student Mary B. Allen King refers to in her *Looking Backward; or, Memories of the Past* (New York: Anson D. F. Randolph, 1870), p. 139.

27. *The New York Missionary Magazine*, 2: 383.

28. Hayes, *Daughters of Dorcas*, p. 9.

29. *American Baptist Magazine* 2 (1919): 32.

30. *The First Annual Report of the Illinois Baptist Female Society, Which Was Formed in Alton County, February 17, 1841* (Belleville, Ill.: P. B. Fouke, 1842), pp. 3, 7–9.

31. Ibid., pp. 14–15.

32. Lucy Scaman Bainbridge, *Round the World Letters* (Boston: D. Lothrop, 1882), p. 37; Kathryn Kish Sklar, *Catharine Beecher: A Study in American Domesticity* (New Haven: Yale University Press, 1973), p. 175.

33. Quoted in Hayes, *Daughters of Dorcas*, p. 37. See also *American Baptist Magazine* 1 (1817): 69–70.

34. Anne Firor Scott, "What, Then, is the American: This New Woman," *Journal of American History* 65 (1978): 693; Sarah Seward to Lydia Finney, 3 May 1828, OCL, FP.

35. Cott, *Bonds of Womanhood*; Anne M. Boylan, "Evangelical Womanhood in the Nineteenth Century: The Role of Women in Sunday Schools," *Feminist Studies* 4 (1978): 62–80.

36. Hayes, *Daughters of Dorcas*, pp. 15–16. Many of the early Presbyterian Female Cent Societies devoted themselves at least in part to "the care of the Theological Seminary at Princeton."

37. Ibid., pp. 8–9.

38. Shirley Cartwright, "'Blessed Drudgery': Womanly Virtue and Nineteenth-Century Organizations" (Ph.D. diss. University of California, Davis, 1977), p. 11. See also the *New York Evangelist* (7 June 1849): 92.

39. Hayes, *Daughters of Dorcas*, p. 17; *Report of the Proceedings of the Congregational and Presbyterian Female Association, for Assisting in the Education of Pious Youth for the Gospel Ministry, from March 1819, to December 1822* (Charleston, S.C.: William Riley, 1823), p. 7.

40. Frederick A. Agar, *"Help Those Women": A Manual for Women Church Workers* (New York: Fleming H. Revell, 1917), p. 11.

41. Trollope, *Domestic Manners*, pp. 280–82.

42. Joanna Bethune, ed., *The Power of Faith, Exemplified in the Life*

and Writings of the Late Mrs. Isabella Graham: A New Edition (New York: American Tract Society, 1843), pp. 129–31, 143–44, 228, 234, 242, 277.

43. Kihlstrom, "Morristown Female Charitable Society," p. 258.

44. Mary P. Ryan has suggested that by the 1830s women's voluntary associations had undergone a "leveling" process and lost their "condescending manners." See "The Power of Women's Networks: A Case Study of Female Moral Reform in Antebellum America," *Feminist Studies* 5 (1979): 66–86. I have been unable to corroborate this observation. For a typically lachrymose story of patronizing charity, see Mrs. V. McConaughy, *The Widow's Sewing Machine; or, What A Helping Hand Did for a Poor Family* (New York: Carlton and Porter, 1862).

45. The constitution of Cincinnati's Dorcas Society forbade its thirteen managers to give out relief unless they visited the family first. "Constitution of the Dorcas Society of Cincinnati," p. 4; "Proceedings of the Managers of the Dorcas Society of Cincinnati from December 30th 1816 until June 30th 1817." Both in CHS. The Rochester Female Charitable Society was probably not the "only relief organization in Rochester," as Paul E. Johnson says in *A Shopkeeper's Millennium: Society and Revivals in Rochester, New York, 1815–1837* (New York: Hill and Wang, 1978), p. 118; on 13 November 1833 some black women, after being addressed by David Ruggles, formed the "Ladies' Literary and Dorcas Society of Rochester" to clothe the poor, encourage mothers to send their children to infant, sabbath, and public schools, and promote Prudence Crandall's school in Canterbury, Connecticut. See the *Emancipator: A Journal of Public Morals* 2 (21 January 1834). For other black women's societies, see the *Weekly Advocate* (11 February 1837). In 1827 the married women of St. Luke's Episcopal Church founded the Female Benevolent and Auxiliary Missionary Society, and the unmarried ones formed the Young Ladies' Benevolent and Reading Society. See Henry Anstice, *Annuals of St. Luke's Church, Rochester, New York . . .* (Rochester: Scrantom, Wetmore, 1883), pp. 25, 27.

46. A. E. Safford, *A Memoir of Daniel Safford, by His Wife* (Boston: American Tract Society, 1861), p. 162.

47. Mary Ryan, "Power of Women's Networks," pp. 66–85.

48. Huntington was a life member of the Female Orphan Society, the Female Fragment Society, and the Female Bible Society, a life member and director of the Carbon Society and the Female Society of Boston and Vicinity for the Promotion of Cristianity among the Jews, a life member and vice president of the Graham Society, and a supporter of the Widows' Society, the Boston Female Education Society, the Boston Female Tract Society, and the Boston Maternal Association. See *Memoirs of Mrs. Susan Huntington, of Boston, Massachusetts* (Edinburgh: Waugh and Innes, 1828), pp. 138–41. In 1819 Hannah Kinney was the first directress of the Cincinnati Dorcas Society and president of the Female Bible Society and the Female Association for the Benefit of Africans. See *Extracts from the Reports of the Dorcas Society of Cincinnati, for the Years 1817, 1818, 1819* (n.p.: n.d.), p. 7.

49. For David Schuyler's blistering critique of Ann Douglas's *The*

Feminization of American Culture (New York: Alfred A. Knopf, 1977), see "Inventing a Feminine Past," *New England Quarterly* 51 (1978): 291–308.

50. Hayes, *Daughters of Dorcas*, pp. 13–14; *History of the Women's Home Missionary Society, Batavia*, pp. 10–11, 13; William Martain Ferguson, *Methodism in Washington, District of Columbia* (Baltimore: Methodist Episcopal Book Depository, 1892), p. 99; *New York Evangelist*, (7 June 1849): 90; Bangs, *Autobiography*, p. 269.

51. J. E. Godbey, *Lights and Shadows of Seventy Years* (St. Louis: Nixon-Jones, 1913), pp. 160–70.

52. Some of these tracts were commissioned by Graham herself. Bethune, *The Power of Faith*, p. 242.

53. Hayes, *Daughters of Dorcas*, pp. 8, 24–25.

54. John Stevens Cabot Abbott, *The Mother at Home; or, The Principles of Maternal Duty Familiarly Illustrated* (New York: American Tract Society, 1833), p. 107; William A. Alcott, *Gift Book for Young Ladies; or, Familiar Letters on the Acquaintances, Male and Female, Employments, Friendships, etc.* (Buffalo: G. H. Derby, 1852), pp. 255, 264.

55. Hayes, *Daughters of Dorcas*, pp. 8, 9; Melder, "Ladies Bountiful," p. 235.

56. *The Eighth Annual Report of the Society for the Education of Pious Young Men for the Ministry of the Protestant Episcopal Church* (Washington, D.C.: James C. Dunn, 1825), pp. 10–18, 27.

57. *Extracts from the Minutes of the General Assembly of the Presbyterian Church in the U.S.A.*, 2 vols. (Philadelphia: n.p., 1811), 2: 310, 483; Hayes, *Daughters of Dorcas*, pp. 18, 19; Janet Harbison Penfield, "Women in the Presbyterian Church—An Historical Overview," *Journal of Presbyterian History* 55 (1977): 108–9.

58. S. D. Alexander, *The Presbytery of New York, 1738–1888* (New York: Anson D. F. Randolph, n.d.), pp. 64–65; Kihlstrom, "Morristown Female Charitable Society," p. 267.

59. The six sources of funds for the American Education Society were (1) occasional contributions, (2) female charitable societies, (3) minor auxiliary societies, (4) district auxiliary societies, (5) annual subscriptions of members, and (6) life memberships. Of contributors identifiable by sex, 46 percent were women in 1815–1818, 81 percent in 1819–1820, and 68 percent in 1822–23. Female charitable societies, which were, of course, 100 percent female, were encouraged to accept the goal of $13.00 per member per year, since it was figured that each member could earn with her needle .25 in the one afternoon donated each week. The majority of minor auxiliary societies were women's societies. Some required an annual membership fee; other, segregated by marital status or age, required a gift of productive labor. It is unclear just how many district auxiliary societies were female. Roughly 80 percent of the annual subscriptions to the American Education Society from 1815 to 1825 were from men. Life memberships ($40.00 for clergymen, $100.00 for lay people) were most often presented to ministers by the women of their parishes. Half of the ministers who became life members in 1818 received their memberships from female parishioners and women's

societies; by 1820 this figure had climbed to at least 80 percent. My statistics are culled from the *Third Report of the Directors of the American Society for Educating Pious Youth for the Gospel Ministry, September 30, 1818* (Andover: Flagg and Gould, 1818); *Fifth Report of the Directors of the American Education Society, October 4, 1820* (Andover: Flagg and Gould, 1820): and *Ninth Annual Report of the Directors of the American Education Society, September 29, 1824* (Boston: Crocker and Brewster, 1824). For the Presbyterian Education Society, which merged in 1827 with the American Education Society to become the Presbyterian Branch of the American Education Society, see the *Seventh Annual Report of the Board of Directors of the Presbyterian Education Society, May 12, 1825* (New York: J. Seymour, 1825).

60. Donald G. Mathews, *Religion in the Old South* (Chicago: University of Chicago Press, 1977), p. 110.

61. *Report of the Directresses of the Congregational and Presbyterian Female Association, for Assisting in the Education of Pious Youth for the Gospel Ministry* (Charleston, S.C.: T. B. Stephens, 1819), pp. 3–5; *Report of the Congregational and Presbyterian Female Association for Assisting in the Education of Pious Youth*, pp. 6, 5.

62. Crismon, *Baptists in Kentucky*, pp. 82–83.

63. Robert S. Fletcher calls 1835 Oberlin's "great organizing year"; it witnessed the establishment of the Oberlin Maternal Association, the Oberlin Female Society, the Oberlin Anti-Slavery Society, the Obedin Female Anti-Slavery Society, the Female Society of Oberlin for the Promotion of Health, and the Oberlin Female Moral Reform Society. "Distaff and Gavel: Women's Organizations in Early Oberlin," *Oberlin Alumni Magazine* 36 (April 1940): 4–5, 19.

64. See 12 June 1834 letter from Emily Louisa (Seely?) to Lydia Finney, who was staying at Whitesborough while Finney was away on a Mediterranean cruise intended to alleviate his nagging throat problems. OCL, FP.

65. Julie Roy Jeffrey, "Ministry through Marriage: Methodist Clergy Wives on the Trans-Mississippi Frontier," in *Historical Perspectives on the Wesleyan Tradition*, ed. Hilah F. Thomas and Rosemary Skinner Keller (Nashville: Abingdon, 1981), p. 156.

66. Quoted by Dean May and Maris A. Vinovskis, "A Ray of Millennial Light: Early Education and Social Reform in the Infant School Movement in Massachusetts, 1826–1840," in *Family and Kin in American Urban Communities, 1700–1940*, ed. Tamara K. Hareven (New York: New View Points, 1977), pp. 62–99.

67. Amelia A. Norton to Lydia Finney, 2 July 1830; Elijah and Mary Deckart to Mr. and Mrs. Finney, 2 November 1829; Maria J. Cushman to Lydia Finney, 27 May 1828, 29 January 1829; Mrs. C. A. Ely to Lydia Finney, 20 June 1832; and E. B. Woodbury to Lydia Finney, 9 January 1830. OCL, FP.

68. Oberlin Maternal Association Minutes, Constitution of the Maternal Society of Oberlin, vol. 1, OCL.

69. See Lydia's obituary, written by A. A. Thome, recording secretary for the Oberlin Maternal Association, as part of her annual report for 1848 in the Oberlin Maternal Association Minutes, vol. 2, OCL. See also the 1843 Annual Report in the Second volume of the Minutes.

70. Mary S. Whitney, "Oberlin Thirty Years Ago: Some Reminiscences" (1890), p. 6, OCL, RFP.

71. *Mother's Magazine* 1 (January 1833).

72. Mathews, *Religion in the Old South*, pp. 99–100.

73. Mrs. M. L. Hastings to Lydia Finney, 5 September 1846, OCL, FP. For a rare eyewitness account of a maternal association's activities, see Rebecca Gifford's letter to the *American Baptist Magazine* 7 (1827): 123–24, and the Hudson Baptist Maternal Society's annual report in the same issue; see also Nehemiah Adams, *Bertha and Her Baptism* (Boston: S. K. Whipple, 1857), chap. 10.

74. Oberlin Maternal Association Minutes, vol. 2, Annual Report, 1842, 1843, OCL.

75. Oberlin Maternal Association Minutes, vol. 2, Annual Report, 1842, OCL.

76. Lydia Finney to William and Helen Cochran, 8 May 1846, OCL, FP. For the checkered career of William Cochran, see Robert S. Fletcher, *A History of Oberlin College from Its Foundation through the Civil War*, 2 vols. (Oberlin: Oberlin College, 1943), 1: 126, 311, 418, 444–45, 474; 2: 690–91.

77. Charles G. Finney, "Last Sickness and Death of Mrs. Finney," *Oberlin Evangelist*, (5 January 1848): 3; Oberlin Maternal Association Minutes, vol. 2, Annual Report, 1848, OCL.

78. Lydia Finney to Helen, Charles, Julia, and Norton, 19 July 1842, OCL, FP.

79. *The Son Unguided, His Mother's Shame, and the Social Position and Culture Due to Woman: Two Addresses before the Maternal Association of the Amity St. Baptist Church, New York, at Their Annual Meetings in 1845 and 1846* (New York: John Gray, 1847).

80. Cott, *Bonds of Womanhood*, p. 150.

81. See the advertisement of Hastings, *The Mother's Hymn Book* (New York: Myron Finch, n.d.), in the *New York Evangelist* (14 June 1849): 95; Mrs. C. L. Brown to Lydia Finney, 12 June 1834, OCL, FP.

82. *Oberlin Evangelist* (7 May 1851). It is not accidental that the growth of maternal associations paralleled a growing clerical guilt over their pulpit neglect of children and a rise in the publication of books of sermons for children. See for example E. W. Hooker, et al., *Address to Christian Parents of the Church in Vermont* (n.p., 1833), pp. 32–33; *Sermons to Children, Preached in the Chapel of the New York Protestant Episcopal Public School, in 1827–8*, 4 vols. (New York: General Protestant Episcopal Sunday School Union, 1833); Abbott, *Mother at Home*, p. 155.

83. Oberlin Maternal Association Minutes, Constitution, vol. 1, OCL; Joseph F. Kett, *Rites of Passage: Adolescence in America, 1790 to the Present* (New York: Basic Books, 1977), p. 16; Cott, *Bonds of Womanhood*, p. 150.

84. Ann D. Gordon and Mari Jo Buhle, "Sex and Class in Colonial and Nineteenth-Century American," in *Liberating Women's History: Theoretical and Critical Essays*, (Urbana: University of Illinois Press, 1976), p. 285; Oberlin Maternal Association Minutes, vol. 1, 3 August 1836; vol. 2, Annual Report, 1841, OCL.

85. Compare the 1835 Constitution of the Oberlin Maternal Association Minutes, vol. 1, OCL, with the amended Constitution as it was printed in the *Oberlin Evangelist* 2 (29 July 1840).

86. Oberlin Maternal Association Minutes, vol. 2, November 1847, OCL.

87. Amelia Ann Norton to Lydia Finney, 2 November 1830; Anson G. Phelps to Charles G. Finney, 29 November 1830. OCL, FP. David Stuart Dodge, comp. and ed., *Memorials of William E. Dodge* (New York: Anson D. F. Randolph, 1887), p. 199.

88. Oberlin Maternal Association Minutes, vol. 2, Annual Report, 1848, OCL.

89. Ibid., vol. 1, "Annual Report," 1837; Amelia Ann Norton to Lydia Finney, 2 November 1830, OCL, FP. A mandatory donation of six cents a month for the purchase of books for the association's library was made optional in 1836.

90. Mrs. C. L. Brown to Lydia Finney 12 June 1834; Mrs. C. G. Ingersoll to Lydia Finney, 10 February 1845; H. Norton to Charles G. Finney, 10 March 1832; Harriet Gillette to Lydia Finney, 28 February 1827. OCL, FP.

91. Amelia Ann Norton to Lydia Finney, March 1828, 8 March 1829, 11 March 1839; Mrs. C. O. Thompson to Lydia Finney, 12 October 1845; Susan P. Farnam to Lydia Finney, 6 April 1840; M. M. Anderson to Lydia Finney, 16 November 1829; Lydia M. Gilbert to Lydia Finney, February 1828; M. L. Mathews to Lydia Finney, 16 May 1831; William Green Jr. and Mrs. H. C. Green to Charles G. Finney, 9 July 1833; Mrs. C. L. Brown to Charles G. Finney, 26 June 1833, to Lydia Finney, 12 June 1834; Mrs. E. T. Ayer to Lydia Finney, 5 March 1846. OCL, FP.

92. "Statement of A. A. Weeks" (Finney's accountant), 3 March 1842, OCL, FP. The importance of ministers' wives' involvement in maternal associations is stressed by Catherine L. Adams, *Daily Duties, Inculcated in a Series of Letters, Addressed to the Wife of a Clergyman* (Boston: Crocker and Brewster, 1835), pp. 100–33.

93. Lucy Stone, "Workers for the Cause," undated. See also her speech "The Condition of Women" (ca. 1887), wherein she compares Oberlin to Bethlehem. The memorial to Finney was written on 21 August 1875. LC, BFP (Lucy Stone Papers).

94. William Lloyd Garrison to John Keep, 11 July 1868, LC, JKP.

95. Moral reform societies of the 1830s and 1840s should not be confused with the "moral societies" and "moral reform societies" that were formed in profusion from 1815 to 20 in New England for the suppression of vices like Sabbath breaking, swearing, and intemperance. Compare, for example, the labors encouraged by William Allen, *A Sermon, Preached before the Auxiliary Society for Promoting Good Morals, and the Female Charitable*

Society of Williamstown, June 7, 1815 (Pittsfield: Phinebas Allen, 1815), with "The Principles of the American Female Moral Reform Society," as reprinted in the *Oberlin Evangelist* 2 (9 September 1840): 152, and *The Constitution and Circular of the New York Female Moral Society, with the Address Delivered at Its Organization* (New York: J. N. Bolles, 1834). For the secondary literature see Carroll Smith-Rosenberg, *Religion and the Rise of the American City: The New York City Mission Movement, 1812–1870* (Ithaca: Cornell University Press, 1971), pp. 97–124; Cott, *Bonds of Womanhood,* pp. 151–54; Melder, "Ladies Bountiful," pp. 243–46; Ryan, "Power of Women's Networks," pp. 66–85; Barbara J. Berg, *The Remembered Gate: Origins of American Feminism* (New York: Oxford University Press, 1978); and Paul Boyer, *Urban Masses and Moral Order in America, 1820–1920* (Cambridge, Mass. Harvard University Press, 1978), pp. 54–66.

96. Melder, "Ladies Bountiful," p. 245; Cott, *Bonds of Womanhood,* p. 153.

97. Carroll Smith-Rosenberg appreciates the distinction in *Religion and Rise,* pp. 110–11.

98. Sarah R. Ingraham, *Walks of Usefulness among the Sinning and the Sorrowing; or, Reminiscences of the Life Work of Margaret Barritt Prior,* 17th ed. (New York: American Female Guardian Society, 1859), pp. 42, 52, 116.

99. Smith-Rosenberg, *Religion and Rise,* pp. 102–3.

100. *Emancipator: A Journal of Public Morals* 2 (2 December 1834). See also reprinted in the *Oberlin Evangelist* 2 (26 August 1840): 144, the "Appeal of the American Female Moral Reform Society, to Mothers and Clergymen."

101. Oberlin Female Moral Reform Society Minutes, p. 32, OCL.

102. *Advocate of Moral Reform* 1 (August 1835): 57–58. Typescript copy in OCL, RFP. Young men's moral reform societies were also formed in 1835 at Brown, Williams, Amherst, and Oneida Institute. See *Advocate of Moral Reform* 2 (January 1836): 7; Fletcher, *History of Oberlin College,* 1: 299.

103. *Advocate of Moral Reform and Family Guardian* 14 (1 February 1848): 19, notes Lydia's death and her contributions to the movement. Typescript in OCL, FP. Two of Finney's wealthy friends, William Green, Jr., and Lewis Tappan, underwrote the cost of $700 worth of home furnishings when Charles and Lydia set up housekeeping in New York City in 1832. Lewis Tappan to Charles G. Finney, 19 April, 28 June 1832, OCL, FP.

104. Elise Boulding, *The Underside of History: A View of Women through Time* (Boulder, Col.: Westview Press, 1976), p. 672.

105. Tucker, *Itinerant Preaching in the Early Days of Methodism,* p. 98.

106. Sarah R. Ingraham to Lydia Finney, 16 January 1847, OCL, FP.

107. Oberlin Female Moral Reform Society Minutes, Constitution, Article 4, pp. 2–3, OCL.

108. Keith Thomas, "The Double Standard," *Journal of the History of Ideas* 20 (1959): 195–216.

109. Oberlin women sponsored the removal to their village's ivy halls

and mud streets three reformed prostitutes from the nation's most notorious slum, New York City's Five Points, where according to one report, "nearly every house and cellar is a groggery below and a brothel above." The observation was that of George G. Foster, as quoted by Carol Groneman, "Working-Class Immigrant Women in Mid-Nineteenth-Century New York," *Journal of Urban History* 4 (1978): 261; Fletcher, *History of Oberlin College*, 1: 300.

110. Paul Boyer, *Urban Masses and Moral Order in America*, pp. 54–66; Stephen S. Foster, *The Brotherhood of Thieves; or, A True Picture of the American Church and Clergy: A Letter to Nathaniel Barney of Nantucket* (Concord, N.H.: Parker Pillsbury, 1886; reprint ed., New York: Arno Press and the New York Times, 1969), p. 43.

111. See the 23 September 1840 resolution in Oberlin Female Moral Reform Soceity Minutes, p. 21, OCL. See also Smith-Rosenberg, *Religion and Rise*, pp. 120–24 and Barbara Leslie Epstein, *The Politics of Domesticity: Women, Evangelism, and Temperance in Nineteenth-Century America* (Middletown, C.: Wesleyan University Press, 1981).

112. Oberlin Female Moral Reform Society Minutes, pp. 3, 14, 16, 17, 21, 34, 38, 44, 46, OCL.

113. Lewis Tappan to Charles G. Finney, 28 June 1832, OCL, FP; Finney's series of letters, "To Ministers of the Gospel of All Denominations," *Oberlin Evangelist* 2 (12 February 1840): 28, (26 February 1840): 25–26, (25 March 1840): 52–53; Ann C. Smith to Lydia Finney, 19 March 1839, OCL, FP; Samuel and Susan Andrews to Mr. and Mrs. Finney, 10 May 1840, OCL, FP.

114. After her graduation from Oberlin in 1847, Lucy Stone spoke before other female moral reform societies. See her 1850(?) address before the Female Moral Reform Society of Gardner, Massachusetts, entitled "Mission and Duties of Women," LC, BFP (Lucy Stone Papers).

115. *Evangelical Magazine and Gospel Advocate* 7 (1836). 208; Oberlin Female Moral Reform Society Minutes, pp. 30, 34, OCL.

116. Cott, *Bonds of Womanhood*, p. 153.

117. See especially Elizabeth Janeway, "On the Power of the Weak," *Signs* 1 (1975): 103–9.

118. Ibid., p. 103.

119. See for example the Yeopim (Yoppim?) Baptist Church Conference in North Carolina during the late eighteenth century, which functioned as a committee of the whole to conduct business and discipline and allowed women to vote. Henry S. Stroupe, "'Cite Them Both to Attend the Next Church Conference': Social Control by North Carolina Baptist Churches, 1772–1908," *North Carolina Historical Review* 52 (1975): 161–62. See also H. B. Blackwell, "Christianity and Women Suffrage," *Woman's Journal* 1 (1878): 268; William Lumpkin, "The Role of Women in Eighteenth-Century Virginia Baptist Life," *Baptist History and Heritage* 8 (1973): 161; Mary Summer Benson, *Women in Eighteenth-Century America: A Study of Opinion and Social Usage* (reprint ed., Port Washington, N.Y.: Kennikat Press, 1966), pp. 262–63. For a vigorous nineteenth-century Baptist defense of the franchise for church women, see George Keely, *The Nature and Order of a*

Gospel Church, and the Obligations of Its Members (Haverhill, M.: P. N. Green, 1819), pp. 22–27. A group of English Baptist women who signed a document testifying in 1706 to an investigation of a healing done by a pastor on a sixteen-year-old girl felt it necessary to explain why: "N.B. —The reason why we, the sisters, have signed this is, because we have more narrowly searched her as to the hip." Morgan Edwards, *Material towards a History of the American Baptists, in 12 Volumes* (Philadelphia: Joseph Cruikshank and Isaac Collins, 1777), 1: 121.

120. William G. McLoughlin, ed., *Diary of Isaac Backus*, 3 vols. (Providence, R.I.: Brown University Press, 1979), 2: 773.

121. The story of the fight over voting rights for women can be found in the church Minutes for 31 March 1743 and 4 May 1764, as quoted in William Williams Keen, ed., *The Bi-Centennial Celebration of the Founding of the First Baptist Church of the City of Philadelphia: 1698–1898* (Philadelphia: American Baptist Publication Society, 1899), pp. 151–54. The women evidently lost the battle, for on 2 June they were not allowed any part in the proceedings, and for the next three years they were conspicuous by their absence.

122. Ibid.

123. Emory Elliott, *Power and the Pulpit in Puritan New England* (Princeton, N.J.: Princeton University Press, 1975), pp. 57–58.

124. Benson, *Women in Eighteenth-Century America*, p. 259.

125. Penfield, "Women in the Presbyterian Church," p. 118.

126. Nathaniel Parker Willis, *The Rag-Bag: A Collection of Ephemera* (New York: Charles Scribner, 1855), p. 70.

127. For Elizabeth Wilson's radical affirmation of sexual equality, see *A Scriptural View of Women's Rights and Duties in All the Important Relations of Life* (Philadelphia: William S. Young, 1849), pp. 146–47. See also George Lewis, *Impressions of America and the American Churches . . .* (Edinburgh: W. P. Kennedy, 1845), p. 181.

128. The Methodists did so in 1868. Because of the autonomous nature of Baptist and Congregational church government, it is difficult to ascertain when their women received the vote. However, of the 252 New England Congregational churches that responded to a questionaire in the mid-1870s, 127 allowed women to vote, and 105 did not. See the *Ladies' Repository* 35 (1876): 555. The moderate debate over the institutional role of women in the church gradually moved on to more controversial levels, such as women's ordination and participation in national, juridical assemblies.

129. John J. Morrison, "Alexander Campbell: Freedom Fighter of the Middle Frontier," *West Virginia History* 37 (1976): 297. See *Ladies' Repository* (1875): 267; Saranne P. O'Donnell, "The Question of Eligibility of Women to the General Conference of the Methodist Episcopal Church—1888," in *"Women's Rightful Place": Women in United Methodist History*, ed. Donald G. Gorrell (Dayton: United Theological Seminary, 1980), 11–25; Barbara Brown Zikmund, "Women in Ministry: The Struggle for Official Sanction," paper delivered to the December 1979 meeting of the American Society of Church History.

130. James D. Thompson, *Organization in Action* (New York:

McGraw-Hill, 1967); James G. Houghland, Jr., and James R. Wood, "'Inner Circles' in Local Churches: An Application of Thompson's Theory," *Sociological Analysis* 40 (1979): 226–39.

131. Shirley M. Souther, comp., *A History of the Methodist Episcopal Church, Hingham, Massachusetts, 1828–1928* (n.p., 1928), last page.

132. Lumpkin, "The Role of Women," p. 161.

133. McLoughlin, *Diary of Isaac Backus*, 2: 1013.

134. Barbara Cunningham, "An Eighteenth-Century View of Femininity as Seen through the Journals of Henry Melchior Muhlenberg," *Pennsylvania History* 43 (1976): 211.

135. Lewis, *Impressions*, p. 181.

136. W. Emerson Wilson, *Diaries of Phoebe George Bradford, 1832–1839* (Wilmington, Del.: Historical Society of Delaware, 1976), pp. 22–23, 66.

137. Isabella Graham, *The Power of Faith, Exemplified in the Life and Writings of the Late Mrs. Isabella Graham*, ed. Joanna Bethune (New York: American Tract Society, 1843), pp. 117–18.

138. William C. Beecher and Samuel Scoville, assisted by Mrs. Henry Ward Beecher, *A Biography of Rev. Henry Ward Beecher* (New York: Charles L. Webster, 1888), 156.

139. David Benedict, *A General History of the Baptist Denomination in America and Other Parts of the World* (New York: Lewis Colby, 1848), p. 370; Isaac Backus, *A History of New England*, ed. David Weston, 2d ed., 2 vols. (Newton, Mass.: Backus Historical Society, 1871), 1: 96, 120, 122; William Cathcart, ed., *The Baptist Encyclopedia*, 2 vols. (Philadelphia: Louis H. Everts, 1883), 2: 811–12; William McLoughlin, *New England Dissent, 1630–1833: The Baptists and the Separation of Church and State* (Cambridge: Harvard University Press, 1971), p. 16. For Isaac Backus's elliptical reference to the woman who allegedly "stirred Mr. Williams up to this action," see *History*, 1: 87. See also John Winthrop, *Winthrop's Journal, "History of New England," 1630–1649*, ed. James Kendall Hosmer, 2 vols. (New York: Charles Scribner's Sons, 1908), 1: 297.

140. Benedict, *General History*, pp. 480, 481.

141. Lumpkin, "The Role of Women," p. 163.

142. Marion T. and Alva W. Plyler, *Men of the Burning Heart: Ivey—Dow—Doub* (Raleigh, N.C.: Commercial Printing Company, 1918), p. 100; George Coles, *Heroines of Methodism; or, Pen and Ink Sketches of the Mothers and Daughters of the Church* (New York: Carlton and Porter, 1857), pp. 132, 133; A. D. Field, *Worthies and Workers, Both Minister and Laymen of the Rock River Conference* (Cincinnati: Cranston and Curtis, 1896), p. 212; Carroll, *Moral and Religious Sketches*, 1: 44–45.

143. Lady Maxwell of Edinburgh appointed Wesley's preachers to her chapel in Hotwells, funded Wesley's Kingswood School, and corresponded with Wesley's preachers. Lady Huntington of London employed Wesley's preachers, entertained the Wesleyan Conference, and gave away a fortune to Methodist causes. See Stevens, *The Women of Methodism*, pp. 110, 144–74; Charles Wesley Buoy, *Representative Women of Methodism* (New York: Hunt and Eaton, 1893), pp. 91–103; Helen C. Knight, comp., *Lady Hunt-*

ington and Her Friends; or, The Revival of the Work of God in the Days of Wesley, Whitefield, Romaine, Venn, and Others in the Last Century (New York: American Tract Society, 1853). Other aristocratic women who patronized the Wesleyan revival in England were Anne and Frances Hastings, Lady Mary Hamilton, Lady Gertrude Hotham, Countess Delitz, and Lady Fanny Shirley.

144. Quoted in Edward Pessen, *Jacksonian America: Society, Personality, and Politics* (Homewood, Ill.: Dorsey Press, 1969), p. 76.

145. Buoy, *Representative Women of Methodism*, pp. 262–63.

146. Stevens, *Women of Methodism*, pp. 257–72; Buoy, *Representative Women of Methodism*, pp. 281–324; Julia M. Olin, "Mrs. Catherine Garretson," *Ladies' Repository* 24 (1864): 321–28.

147. Stevens, *Women of Methodism*, pp. 248–52; Coles, *Heroines of Methodism*, pp. 177–78.

148. Daniel Wise, *Sketches and Ancedotes of American Methodists of "The Days That Are No More"* (New York: Phillips and Hunt, 1883), pp. 79–82.

149. Buoy, *Representative Women of Methodism*, pp. 264–67, 275–78. For Richard Whatcoat's death on 5 July 1806 at Bassett's home, see *The Experiences of Several Eminent Methodist Preachers . . .* (Barrard, Vt.: Joseph Dix, 1837), p. 242.

150. Stevens says that "the constitutional organization of American Methodism may be said to have been constructed under its roof." Stevens, *Women of Methodism*, pp. 235, 236–38; Buoy, *Representative Women of Methodism*, pp. 267–73.

151. Stevens, *Women of Methodism*, p. 252; Douglas Summers Brown, "Elizabeth Henry Campbell Russell: Patroness of Early Methodism in the Highlands of Virginia," *Virginia Cavalcade*, 30 (1980), 110–17.

152. Francis Asbury to Rebecca Ridgely, 10 March 1807, MHS, R-PP.

153. Francis Asbury to Rebecca Ridgely, 24 May, 16 August 1804, 7 May 1810, MHS, R-PP.

154. Alexander, *Archibald Alexander*, p. 455.

155. For one example, see Judge R. C. Ewing, *Historical Memories, Containing a Brief History of the Cumberland Presbyterian Church in Missouri, and Biographical Sketches of a Number of Those Ministers Who Contributed to the Organization and the Establishment of That Church, in the Country West of the Mississippi River* (Nashville: Cumberland Presbyterian Board of Publication, 1874), p. 63

156. *American Baptist Magazine* 1 (1818): 465.

157. Five males deacons, and nineteen females, spearheaded the drive to persuade the presbytery to bring charges against their pastor, N. S. S. Beman, for bringing Finney to Troy. E. W. Gilbert to Charles G. Finney, 19 October 1827; J. P. Cushman to Charles G. Finney, 23 January 1827, OCL, FP; P. H. Fowler, *Historical Sketch of Presbyterianism within the Bounds of the Synod of Central New York* (Utica, N. Y.: Curtis and Childs, 1877), p. 729.

158. As quoted in Emory Elliott, "The Dove and the Serpent: The Clergy in the American Revolution," *American Quarterly* 31 (1979): 189.

159. For illustrations of women criticizing their pastors and registering displeasure with their sermons, see Sarah Brayton to Lydia Finney, 12 July 1827; Henrietta Platt to Lydia Finney, 5 January 1829; and Catherine Huntington to Lydia Finney, 19 November 1829. OCL, FP. See also Huntington, *Memoirs*, pp. 165–68.

160. On many printed sermons and addresses one finds the phrase "Published by request of the Society . . ." See as an example George L. Prentiss, *Address Delivered before the New Bedford Dorcas Society, Founded in 1831, On Sunday Evening, October 15, 1848* (New Bedford: Charles and Augustus Taber, 1848); and see also Ryan, "Power of Women's Networks," p. 78. It is not always clear whether the phrase meant that the women subsidized the address's publication or merely credentialized it. Either way, its very presence on the title page attests to the accountability clergymen felt toward women, which is also exemplified in the remarkable number of detailed memorials of female parishioners composed and published by pastors.

161. Miller, "Evolving Role of Women in the Presbyterian Church," pp. 54–58.

162. William Larkin Durden, *Top Sergeant of Pioneers: The Story of a Lifelong Battle for an Ideal* (Emory University, Ga.: Banner Press, 1930), p. 52.

163. Chauncey Hobart, *Recollections of My Life: Fifty Years of Itinerancy in the Northwest* (Red Wing: Red Wing Printing Company, 1885), p. 24.

164. Calvin Colton, *Thoughts on the State of the Country, with Reasons for Preferring Episcopacy*, 2d ed. (New York: Harper and Brother, 1836), p. 35.

165. Charles G. Finney, who took up one such collection at Third Presbyterian Church for the Rochester Female Charitable Society, brought in $78.03 along with "a gold ring, pen knife, etc." *Rochester Observer*, 10 February 1831, p. 3. See also Kihlstrom, "Morristown Female Charitable Society," p. 263. For the women's election of men, see Article VI of the Constitution, as printed in the *Circular of the Cincinnati Ladies' Home Missionary Society of the Methodist Episcopal Church . . .* (Cincinnati: Methodist Book Concern, 1854), p. 6.

166. *Ladies' Repository* 35 (1875): 76.

167. Quoted in J. D. Fulton, *The True Woman: A Series of Discourses by Rev. J. D. Fulton, (Tremont Temple, Boston) to Which Is Added Woman Vs. Ballot!* (Boston: Lee and Shepard, 1869), pp. 71–72.

168. These are the comments of Stephen R. Smith, corresponding editor of the *Evangelical Magazine and Gospel Advocate* 6 (1835): 350.

169. See Manross, *Episcopal Church in the United States*, p. 191; Lewis, *Impressions*, pp. 158, 222; Anstice, *Annals of St. Luke's Church*, p. 25, and passim.

170. Melder, "Ladies Bountiful," p. 236.

171. Hooker, *Memoir of Mrs. Sarah Lanman Smith*, pp. 118–20.

172. Wendell Phillips's speech, from which this quotation is taken,

was entitled "Woman's Rights and Duties" and was delivered in 1866. See his *Speeches on Rights of Woman* (Philadelphia: Alfred J. Ferris, 1898), p. 65.

Chapter Seven

1. Elizabeth Finney to Henrietta Bissell, 16 August 1850, OCL, FP.

2. Elizabeth Finney to James and Alice Barlow, 6 August 1860; Charles D. Cox to Charles G. Finney, 19 August 1850; C. E. Fisher to Charles G. Finney, 13 September 1850; L. D. Porter to Charles G. Finney, 1 March 1831. OCL, FP.

3. Vexed by the thought that her diseased lung, persistent cough, and inflamed throat might terminate her ministry, Elizabeth admitted, "I know God can work without me, but I love the work." Elizabeth Finney to Henrietta Bissell, 16 August 1850. OCL, FP.

4. Charles G. Finney, "Last Sickness and Death of Mrs. Finney, *Oberlin Evangelist* (5 January 1848): 3; Charles G. Finney to James and Alice Barlow, 11 December 1863. OCL, FP.

5. Phoebe Palmer, *Pioneer Experiences; or, The Gift of Power Received by Faith* (New York: W. C. Palmer, Jr., 1868), p. 68.

6. Oberlin Female Moral Reform Society Minutes, pp. 65, 66, 67, 71, 114, 110, OCL; Journal of Mary Louisa Cowles, 1851–1852, entry for 27 May 1851. Typescript in OCL, RFP. "One Reason for the Decline of Moral Reform Societies," *Advocate of Moral Reform* 7 (1841): 141.

7. "Antoinette L. Brown Blackwell's Reminiscences: Notes Taken by Alice Stone Blackwell, August 19, 1903." Typescript in OCL, RFP. Claude U. Gilson, ed., "Antoinette Brown Blackwell, the First Woman Minister," p. 15. Typescript in OCL, RFP.

8. For William Atkinson, see Ferdinand DeWilton Ward, *Churches of Rochester . . .* (Rochester: E. Darrow, 1891), pp. 80, 93; Vincent S. Jones, ed., *St. Paul's Episcopal Church, Rochester, New York* (n.p. 1977); *St. Paul's Episcopal Church, Rochester: A Brief History of the First One Hundred Years of Rochester's Second Episcopal Parish* (Rochester: Foss-Soule Press, 1927); and Paul E. Johnson, *A Shopkeeper's Millennium; Society and Revivals in Rochester, New York, 1815–1837* (New York: Hill and Wang, 1978), pp. 91–92.

9. Charles Pettit McIlvaine, *Rev. Mr. McIlvaine in Answer to the Rev. Henry U. Onderdonk* (Philadelphia: William Stavely, 1827), p. 4. Onderdonk was merely parroting the position of his bishop, William White, who condemned both excessive and extemporaneous preaching. See William White, *An Episcopal Charge on the Subject of Revivals, Delivered before the Forty-Eighth Convention of the Diocese of Pennsylvania, and Addressed to the Clerical Members of the Convention* (Philadelphia: Jesper Harding, 1832), p. 16.

10. Louis Chapin to George F. Wright, 10 February 1890, OCL, GWP.

11. *Lorain County News*, 13 January 1864; Blake McKelvey, *Rochester, the Water-Power City, 1812–54* (Cambridge: Harvard University Press, 1945), pp. 272, 278; *Rochester Daily Democrat*, 10 June 1841.

12. *Rochester Daily Democrat*, 7 April 1842.

13. "A Journal Kept by Mrs. Elizabeth Ford Atkinson Finney during a Visit to England, 1859–60," pp. 12, 18, OCL, FP. These promises came to her from Isaiah, and since one of her favorite metaphors to describe her mission was "light," it may be that she appropriated to herself the penitential promises in Isaiah 58, especially verses 5–8, where the righteous are promised an uncommon reflection of the light of God from their lives.

14. *Rochester Daily Democrat*, 21 November 1848, p. 3; Charles G. Finney to Brother and Sister Lawson, 19 January 1864, OCL, FP.

15. See the reminiscences of Mary R. Cochran to Eileen Thomas, 31. October 1961, OCL; Charles G. Finney to Julia Finney, 8 January 1855, OCL, FP.

16. Helen Jones to Helen M. Cowles, 4 December 1848, OCL, FP; Charles Penfield to Sister Helen, 24 November 1848. Typescript in OCL, RFP.

17. Charles G. Finney to F. J. Tytus, 16 January 1863, with a 20 January postscript, OCL, FP. For an example of Finney's excitement about his wife's leadership ability see Charles G. Finney to his family, 4 December 1849, OCL, CP.

18. Elizabeth Finney to Henrietta Bissell, 16 August 1850, OCL, FP.

19. Richard Carwardine, *Transatlantic Revivalism: Popular Evangelicalism in Britain and America, 1790–1865* (Westport, Conn.: Greenwood Press, 1978), pp. 134–35. The pastor of London Tabernacle, John Campbell, stated unequivocally that "no Protestant minister in Europe has, during the same period, put forth such a measure of intellectual and physical effort." *Oberlin Evanglist* 12 (23 October 1850): 170.

20. Charles G. Finney to his family, 4 December 1849, OCL, CP; *Memoirs of Rev. Charles G. Finney* (New York: A. S. Barnes, 1876), p. 412.

21. Charles D. Cox to Charles G. Finney, 19 August 1850, OCL, FP.

22. *Oberlin Evangelist* (22 May 1850): 83.

23. James F. Findlay, Jr., *Dwight L. Moody: American Evangelist, 1837–1899* (Chicago: University of Chicago Press, 1969), p. 184.

4. Elizabeth Finney to Henrietta Bissell, 16 August 1850, OCL, FP.

25. The *British Banner's* account of the tea meeting is reprinted in the *Oberlin Evangelist* 13 (21 May 1851): 82–83. The inscription read: "Presented to Mrs. C. G. Finney, as a token of respect and affection, by her friends in the Tabernacle, London, May 31, 1851, on her departure to her native land." For Finney's account of Elizabeth's London activities, see his *Memoirs*, p. 412.

26. John Campbell to Mr. and Mrs. Finney, 18 August 1851, OCL, FP.

27. John Campbell to Finney, 2 November 1853, OCL, FP. See also Robert Ferguson and A. Morton Brow, *Life and Labours of John Campbell* (London: Richard Bentley, 1867), pp. 416–24.

28. Henry Ward Beecher to Charles G. Finney, 30 August 1850, OCL, FP.

29. Charles G. Finney to daughters, 27 December 1852, 12 February 1853, OCL, FP; Finney, *Memoirs*, p. 421.

30. Finney, *Memoirs*, p. 419, 421, 438.

31. Ibid., p. 443.

32. Charles G. Finney to Julia Finney, 4 December 1857, 15 January 1857 [8?], 15 February 1858, OCL, FP.

33. *Lorain County News*, 13 January 1864. For Elizabeth's assessment of the Boston campaign for Christian perfection, see her "Journal," p. 12.

34. *Oberlin Evangelist* 19 (29 May 1857): 85.

35. Richard Carwardine is one of the few to have recognized the importance of Elizabeth Finney's work: "The work of both Elizabeth Finney and, less palatably, Phoebe Palmer demanded that the evangelical community reassess women's status and increase their active role in church life." *Transatlantic Revivalism*, p. 188. For a look at the careers of some forty women preachers during the 1860s, see Olive Anderson, "Women Preachers in Mid-Victorian Britain: Some Reflections on Feminism, Popular Religion and Social Change," *Historical Journal* 13 (1969): 467–84.

36. The paragraph, one of three in the recommendation, reads: "Mrs Finney, his wife, is a lady of genuine dignity and refinement. She fastens the respect of all who know her, laboring efficiently in spheres appropriate to Christian women and in the letters." Horace Bushnell to Charles G. Finney and To Whom It May Concern, 16 November 1858, OCL FP. Bushnell's wife, Mary Apthorp, and Elizabeth were fond of each other and tried to get the two aging warriors together for a chat during the spring 1857 revival in Boston. Horace Bushnell to Charles G. Finney, 3 April 1857, OCL, FP.

37. Catherine Mumford Booth, *Female Teaching; or, the Rev. A. A. Rees versus Mrs. Palmer, Being a Reply to a Pamphlet by the Above Gentleman on the Sunderland Revival*, 2d ed. (London: G. J. Stevenson, 1861), p. 30.

38. M. Foster to Charles G. Finney, 9 March 1859, OCL, FP.

39. Fergus Ferguson, Jr., to Charles G. Finney, 1, 13, 23 July, 6 December 1859; George Redford to Charles G. Finney, 22 February 1860; Joseph T. Cooke to Charles G. Finney, 17 September 1863.

40. Deacons of Angel Street Church to Charles G. Finney, 4 May 1850. See also J. Barbour to Finney, 4 September 1859, OCL, FP.

41. Charles G. Finney to Henry Cowles, 15 February 1859. Typescript in OCL, RFP.

42. *Oberlin Evangelist* 12 (23 October 1850): 170; Charles G. Finney to his family, 4 December 1849, OCL, CP.

43. Charles G. Finney to Henry Cowles, 15 February 1859. Typescript in OCL RFP. See also Charles G. Finney to Julia Finney, 24 March 1857 and 13 January 1858; John Campbell to Charles G. Finney, 28 July 1850, OCL, FP.

44. J. Hart to Charles G. Finney, 13 March 1859; Elizabeth Finney to Mr. and Mrs. Lawson, 12 January 1860. OCL, FP.

45. Charles G. Finney to Alice Barlow, 4 May 1861; Charles G. Finney to F. J. Tytus, 16 January 1863, OCL, FP.

46. *Life and Labours of John Ashworth* (London: A. J. Colman, 1873), pp. 68–69. For Elizabeth's health at this time, see Elizabeth Finney to Mr. and Mrs. Barlow, 9 April 1860, OCL, FP.

47. William G. McLoughlin, Jr., *Modern Revivalism: Charles Grandison Finney to Billy Graham* (New York: Ronald Press, 1959), p. 42.

48. Elizabeth Finney to Julia Finney, 27 April 1859. For other evidence of Elizabeth's great influence, see their letter to the Barlows, 26 October 1860, and Finney's letter to the same, 8 January 1868. OCL, FP. James Barlow had endowed two Oberlin scholarships for indigent students, over which Finney had sole control. Elizabeth wrote to Mr Barlow that the first award had been granted to an English girl who agreed to study summers and work as Elizabeth's cook during the winter.

49. Finney does make brief mention of Elizabeth's work in *Memoirs*, pp. 412–13.

50. Finney to Potto Brown, 1 October 1857, OCL, R. A. G. Dupuis Papers.

51. It is difficult to ascertain whether this "M. Clark" was Rev. George W. Clark, the Yale graduate, Lane rebel, evangelist, and Asa Mahan partisan who helped to found the ill-conceived "National University" in Cleveland but nevertheless was back in Oberlin in 1856 to deliver a commencement address. See Robert Fletcher, *A History of Oberlin College . . .* 2 vols. *Oberlin* (Oberlin: Oberlin College, 1943), 1:183, 250, 476, 482, 2: 838.

52. E. A. Finney, "Journal," p. 8, OCL, FP.

53. Some evidence suggests a long-standing strain in the relationship between Elizabeth and the college community. See for example the refusal of the Ladies' Board of Managers, of which she was a member, to grant permission on 2 June 1851 for a student to spend one evening a week at her home singing. Record of the Proceedings of the Ladies' Board, 1851–1862. Typescript in OCL, RFP.

54. E. A. Finney, "Journal," p. 13, OCL, FP.

55. My account of the contentious background to the Finneys' 1859 English trip is derived solely from Elizabeth's "Journal", pp. 1–16, OCL, FP, and should therefore be seen as biased in her favor.

56. John Kent exaggerates the failure of Finney's 1859–60 English revival because his observations are based on few sources; see *Holding the Fort: Studies in Victorian Revivalism* (London: Epworth Press, 1978), pp. 77–78.

57. E. A. Finney, "Journal," p. 56, OCL, FP.

58. Helen Kirk, *Women and Prayer; or, The History of the Ladies' Union Prayer Meeting, Held in Bristo Place Hall, Edinburgh* (London Thomas Ward, 1861), p. 28.

59. E. A. Finney, "Journal," p. 59, OCL, FP. For Finney's particular appreciation of the active role played by the wives of England's Wesleyan ministers, see John Moore to Charles G. Finney, 22 August 1862, and Charles G. Finney to James Barlow, 8 January 1863, OCL, FP.

60. Elizabeth Finney to Edwin and Mary Lawson, 1 April 1860, OCL, FP.

61. Carwardine, *Transatlantic Revivalism*, p. 144.

62. Kirk, *Women and Prayer*, p. 12.

63. Ibid., pp. 11, 223.

64. Ibid., p. 23.

65. Ibid., pp. 38–39.

66. Ibid., p. 26.

67. Ibid., p. 35.

68. For accounts of their Edinburgh labors, see E. A. Finney, "Journal," pp. 48, 50–532; Elizabeth Finney to Edwin and Mary Lawson, 1 January 1860, February 1861, OCL, FP; *Revival: A Weekly Record of Events Connected with the Present Revival of Religion*, 1 (26 November 1859): 139; and Kirk, *Women and Prayer*, pp. 1–39, 223, 262–64.

69. Kirk, *Women and Prayer*, pp. 34–35.

70. *Revival* (26 November 1859): 139; Kirk, *Women and Prayer*, pp. 36–37.

71. Kirk, *Women and Prayer*, pp. 38, 39.

72. Finney, *Memoirs*, p. 456.

73. Elizabeth Finney to James and Alice Barlow, 9 April 1860; John Kirk to Charles G. Finney, 19 December 1859, 2 January 1860, 5 February 1861; Elizabeth Finney to Edwin and Mary Lawson, 1 January 1860. OCL, FP.

74. Margaret M. Ferguson to Elizabeth Finney 10 January 1860, OCL, FP. If no one felt moved to speak at these meetings, Ferguson wrote, one or two passages from scripture were read, followed by singing and prayer. "We sometimes have as many as eight, and once I think we had ten prayers during the hour. Of course they were short." See also E. A. Finney, "Journal," p. 56.

75. *Revival* 3 (7 July 1860): 4 (14 July 1860): 13; Kirk, *Women and Prayer*, pp. 190–95.

76. E. A. Finney, "Journal," p. 68; John Kirk to Charles G. Finney, 19 December 1859, OCL, FP. See also Elizabeth to Edwin and Mary Lawson, 1 January 1860, OCL, FP, and *The Tea Meeting: Mrs. Finney and the Women of Bolton* (Manchester: William Bremner, 1860), p. 2.

77. Elizabeth Finney to Edwin and Mary Lawson, 1 January 1860, OCL, FP; Carwardine, *Transatlantic Revivalism*, p. 193; *Revival* 2 (17 March 1860): 83–84; *Revivalist* 6 (March 1860): 44.

78. For the Barlows, see Finney, "Journal," pp. 60, 62, 63; Elizabeth Finney to James and Alice Barlow, 6 August, 17 September, 19 November 1860, 5 January 1861; Charles G. Finney to Alice Barlow, 3 May 1875. OCL, FP.

79. Elizabeth Finney to James and Alice Barlow, 9 April 1860; Elizabeth Finney to Edwin and Mary Lawson, 1 January 1860; E. A. Finney, "Journal," p. 74; Finney, *Memoirs*, p. 459.

80. E. A. Finney, "Journal," pp. 63, 70, 72, FP, OCL; *Oberlin Evangelist* 22 (11 April 1860): 59.

81. Carwardine, *Transatlantic Revivalism*, p. 188; *Oberlin Evangelist* 22 (11 April 1860): 59, 64; Elizabeth Finney to Edwin and Mary Lawson, 1 January 1860, OCL, FP. For evidence of public prayer by women in England before Elizabeth's arrival and the hope of some Evangelicals that "in other meetings like liberty is enjoyed" to that of the women attending the Finney's Queen's Square meetings, see *Revival* 1 (8 October 1859): 84.

82. Elizabeth Finney to Edwin and Mary Lawson, 1 January 1860, OCL, FP.

83. John Kirk to Charles G. Finney, 2 January 1860, OCL, FP.

84. Charles G. Finney to Julia Finney, 20 July 1859; E. A. Finney, "Journal," p. 65. OCL, FP. James Barlow appears to have worked even more

closely with Elizabeth than with either Finney or Mrs. Barlow. He substituted for Elizabeth at an evening ladies' meeting when she was ill, and borrowed her idea for a tea meeting during the week of prayer for conversion of the world, closing his factory to allow time for his 1,000 employees to attend a tea meeting where he spoke to them. E. A. Finney, "Journal," pp. 65–66, 74, OCL, FP.

85. Quoted in *Oberlin Evangelist* 22 (11 April 1860): 59.

86. E. A. Finney, "Journal," p. 31; Elizabeth Finney to James and Alice Barlow, 23 November 1860, OCL, FP.

87. See, for example, Mary Whomell to Elizabeth Finney, 29 March 1860, OCL, FP.

88. Kent, *Holding the Fort*, p. 78.

89. *The Tea Meeting*, pp. 2–5; E. A. Finney, "Journal," pp. 52, 59, OCL, FP. For an account by Elizabeth of the testimonial tea, see her letter to Henrietta (Bissell?), 6 June 1860, OCL, FP.

90. E. A. Finney, "Journal," p. 78, OCL, FP.

91. *The Tea Meeting*, p. 7–8.

92. Ibid. Emphasis in original.

93. Ibid., p. 8 The text of Elizabeth's speech is in *The Tea Meeting*, pp. 6–8, and the text of her similar 8 March speech is in her "Journal," pp. 74–78, OCL, FP.

94. Elizabeth Finney to Barlows, 26 October 1860; also see Elizabeth Finney to Barlows, 17 September 1860, OCL, FP.

95. Elizabeth Finney to Barlows, 19 November 1860; 22 December 1860, OCL, FP; Kirk, *Women and Prayer*, pp. 195–97.

96. *Rochester Daily Union and Advertiser*, 27 November 1863, p. 2; Charles G. Finney to Barlows, 11 December 1863; Charles G. Finney to Lawsons, 10 December 1863, OCL, FP. For the state of Finney's nerves in late 1860 and early 1861, see Elizabeth Finney to the Barlows, 23 November 1860, 5 January 1861; Elizabeth Finney to Edwin and Mary Lawson, 12 January 1861; Angie to Mrs. Barlow, n.d. (but sometime in late 1860). OCL, FP.

97. Finney, *Memoirs*, p. 413.

98. Susan B. Anthony to Elizabeth Cady Stanton, 26 May 1856, Vassar College, Elizabeth Cady Stanton Papers. Quoted in Ellen Carol DuBois, *Feminism and Suffrage: The Emergence of an Independent Women's Movement in America, 1848–1869* (Ithaca: Cornell University Press, 1978), p. 50.

99. "Antoinette L. Brown Blackwell's Reminiscences." Finney genuinely liked the strong-minded Brown and Lucy Stone and teased them about their aggressiveness in a paternal way. President Finney "told me over twice to give his love when I wrote next," Alice Stone Blackwell wrote to Lucy sometime after her graduation from Oberlin in 1847. "President says tell Lucy to keep straight." See "Memoirs of Alice Stone Blackwell." Typescript copy in LC, BFP.

100. Finney, *Memoirs*, p. 413. The Princeton theologian Charles Hodge believed that Finney "had become very sweet and mellow in his later

years"; see Theodore Ledyard Cuyler, *Recollections of a Long Life: Auto-biography* (New York: Baker and Taylor, 1902), p. 219.

101. Frances J. Hosford, "Finney the Inscrutable," *Oberlin Alumni Magazine* 30 (May 1934): 234.

102. Mary Bushnell Cheney, *Life and Letters of Horace Bushnell* (New York: Harper and Brothers, 1880), p. 111; Lucy Drake Osborn, *Heavenly Pearls Set in a Life: A Record of Experiences and Labors in America, India and Australia* (New York: Fleming H. Revell, 1893), p. 131. For a contrasting appraisal of Mary Bushnell, see Ann Douglas, *The Feminization of American Culture* (New York: Alfred A. Knopf, 1977), pp. 53–54.

103. Henry Ward Beecher to Charles G. Finney, 30 August 1850, OCL, FP.

104. Mary A. Parker to Charles G. Finney, 7 June 1864, 8 May 1865, OCL, FP.

105. Lewis Tappan to Charles G. Finney, 15 October 1866, OCL, FP.

106. Mary A. Parker to Charles G. Finney, 22 May 1865, OCL, FP.

107. Mary A. Parker to Charles G. Finney, 9 May 1870, 27 June 1864, 22 May 1865, OCL, FP.

108. Katie C. Lloyd to Charles G. Finney, May 1860; Mary A. Parker to Charles G. Finney, 6 July 1869, OCL, FP.

109. *Oberlin News*, 17 September 1907.

110. Fredrick Norton Finney, *Letters from Across the Sea, 1907–1908* (Philadelphia: J. B. Lippincott, 1909), p. 245. Her own son, Thomas Rayl, apparently a member of the First Ohio Volunteer Infrantry, died in a Nashville hospital in late 1862 or early 1863.

111. Finney, *Letters from Across the Sea*, p. 246.

112. Osborn, *Heavenly Pearls*, pp. 88, 134–36, 138, 194, 196–204. Charles G. Finney to Mark Hopkins, 14 October 1874, OCL, FP.

113. Dorothy Ann Lipson, *Freemasonry in Federalist Connecticut, 1789–1835* (Princeton: Princeton University Press, 1977).

114. See the letters to Finney from Mrs. Hubert P. Main, 10 April 1968; Mary E. McPherson, 10, 29 April 1868; Ellen T. Beaumont, 13 April 1868; Mrs. M. E. J. Gage, 23 April 1868; Mrs. J. P. Foster, 29 April 1868; Lucia C. Cook, 8 July, 15, 27 August 1868, 12 May 1869; Mary L. Green, 27 July 1868; Mrs. A. W. Hall, 7 February 1869; Margaret M. Anthony, 19 March 1869; Olympia Brown, 1 April 1869; Harriet S. Miner, 24 January 1870; Harriet Newell Wood, 28 December 1870; Lizzie C. Augby, 13 January 1871; Miss A. M. Paul, 6 January 1871; Mrs. D. J. Babbit, 16 February 1871. OCL, FP.

115. Mrs. J. P. Foster to Charles G. Finney, 29 April 1868; Lucia C. Cook to Charles G. Finney, 8 July 1868, OCL, FP.

116. Charles G. Finney to Oliver Johnson, 25 April 1868; Charles G. Finney to Dolson Cox, 7 January, 2 September 1871. OCL, FP. Charles G. Finney, *The Character, Claims, and Practical Workings of Freemasonry* (Cincinnati: Western Tract and Book Society, 1869), p. 243.

117. Charles G. Finney to Oliver Johnson, 25 April 1868, OCL, FP.

118. Charles G. Finney to Mark Hopkins, 14 October 1874, OCL, FP.

119. Jennie F. Woodruff to Mr. Heydenbuck, 7 October 1941, OCL, WBP.

120. Rebecca A. Finney to George F. Wright, 22 October 1889, OCL, GWP.

121. See the series of Finney's letters "To Ministers of the Gospel of All Denominations," *Oberlin Evangelist* 2 (12 February 1840): 27–28; (26 February 1840): 35–36; (11 March 1840): 52–53; and (8 April 1840): 59–60.

122. Hosford, "Finney the Inscrutable," p. 234.

123. Rebecca to James Monroe, 4 February 1871, OCL, FP.

124. Whether or not the Corson's should be considered a partner ministry is difficult to determine, for while the son clearly thought of his parents as teammates, the husband eulogized his wife only for her "conscientious resolution never to be instrumental, in the least degree, in preventing him at any time, from fully discharging his arduous duties." John Carroll, ed., *"Father Corson"; or, The Old Style Canadian Itinerant . . .* (Toronto: Rev. Samuel Rose, D.D., at the Methodist Book Room, 1879), pp. 215, 22–23.

125. Hamline to Phoebe and Walter Palmer, 15 June, 17 July 1846, in *Life and Letters of Leonidas L. Hamline, D.D., Late One of the Bishops of the Methodist Episcopal Church*, ed. Walter C. Palmer (New York: Nelson and Phillips, 1877), pp. 224, 225.

126. *Life Sketches: Ancestry, Early Life, Christian Experience, and Extensive Labors of Elder James White and His Wife, Mrs. Ellen Gould White* (Battle Creek, Mich.: Seventh-Day Adventist Publishing Association, 1880), pp. 127–28, 202, 226, 238 (cf. 126), 255, 268.

127. Quoted in Julia Jones Beecher file, MS page, CCHS, BC.

128. [Thomas K. Beecher], *Eliza Steele Webster Jones* (n.p., n.d. [1888?]), pp. 1–7. Julia's father, Henry, a shy and uncertain man, left the ministry when she was two and became principal of a girls' school in Greenfield, Connecticut, In the late 1830 he founded a school for boys in Bridgeport, Connecticut.

129. Annis Ford Eastman, *A Flower of Puritanism: Julia Jones Beecher, 1826–1905* (Elmira, N.Y.: Snyder Brothers, n.d.), 28–29; *Centennial Album: Published during the One Hundreth Year of the Park Church in Elmira, New York* (n.p., 1946), p. 6.

130. Frances B. Myers, "Julia Jones Beecher—Elmira's Gay Rebel," *Chemung Historical Journal* 1 (1956): 120–24.

131. Ausburn Towner, "Rev. Thomas K. Beecher, and Wife, in 1870," Undocumented, undated newspaper clipping in CCHS, BC; W. Charles Barker, "The Fabulous Julia," *Sunday Telegram*, n.d. (1955), CCHS, BC; Eastman, *Flower of Puritanism*, pp. 8, 11.

132. Thomas K. Beecher to E. U. Van Aken, 25 December 1887, PCA. For Julia's public temperance speeches, see "Personal Interview with Mrs. William Martin by Carol W. Ivory, 16 December 1968," CCHS, BC. See also Bruce L. Bennett, "The Pool-Playing Preacher," *Journal for Physical Education and Recreation* 50 (1979): 57.

133. The 2 July 1895 "Stones to Mrs. Beecher" is quoted by Jervis

Langton in Julia Jones Beecher file, CCHS, BC. For the slightly different story told by Matthew Dorrin Richardson in "Round Town," an 8 March 1935 clipping from an unspecified newspaper, see the same file.

134. *Elmira Daily Advertiser*, 17 November 1905.

135. See for example Julia Jones Beecher to Cora A. Derby, 2 September 1890, CCHS, BC.

136. Minutes of the Park Church Missionary Society, December 1890, PCA.

137. *Elmira Advertiser*, 13 April 1895, as quoted in Eva Taylor, "Beecher Doll Club," *Chemung Historical Journal* 15 (1970): 104–5.

138. Ausburn Towner, "Beecher and Wife," CCHS, BC.

139. Quoted by Marie Caskey, *Chariot of Fire: Religion and the Beecher Family* (New Haven: Yale University Press, 1978), p. 280.

140. Annis Ford Eastman attended Oberlin, where she was influenced by Finney and met her husband, Samuel E. Eastman. A Civil War injury plagued her husband's ministry, and she stepped rather naturally from her role as a minister's wife into his personal duties at a Canandaigua church when his health failed. Her first solo pastorate was in Brooklyn, New York, to which she traveled on weekends; on weekdays she raised four children (Max Eastman was one of them) and assisted her husband in Canadaigua. Ordained by the Park Church's ministerial council, which Beecher led, she was called to West Bloomfield, New York, and from there Beecher called her and her husband in 1896 to be his assistants in Elmira. See Thomas E. Byrne, *Chemung County, 1890–1975* (Elmira, N.Y.: Chemung County Historical Society, 1976), pp. 412, 463, 502–3; Eva C. Taylor, *A History of the Park Church* (revised and enlarged ed., n.p., 1971), pp. 25–28.

Chapter Eight

1. William R. Leach, *True Love and Perfect Union: The Feminist Reform of Sex and Society* (New York: Basic Books, 1980).

2. For a parallel situation in England, see Olive Anderson, "Women Preachers in Mid-Victorian Britain: Some Reflections on Feminism, Popular Religion and Social Change," *Historical Journal* 12 (1969): 48.

3. My thanks to Winthrop S. Hudson and Evelyn Brooks Barnett for help in compiling this list.

4. Karen J. Blair, *The Clubwoman as Feminist: True Womanhood Redefined, 1868–1914* (New York: Holmes and Meier, 1980); Ruth Bordin, *Woman and Temperance: The Quest for Power and Liberty, 1873–1900* (Philadelphia: Temple University Press, 1981).

5. Reprinted as "The Minister's Wife" in *Presbyterian Banner* (11 June 1879): 3.

6. *A Useful Life: In Memory of Mrs. Annie C. F. Cunningham, Wife of Rev. David A. Cunningham, Pastor of First Presbyterian Church, Wheeling West Virginia, Who Died February 7, 1897* (Wheeling, W.Va.: Bullard, n.d.).

7. David J. Pivar, *Purity Crusade: Sexual Morality and Social Control, 1868–1900* (Westport, Conn.: Greenwood Press, 1973), p. 186.

8. Lois A. Boyd, "Presbyterian Ministers' Wives—A Nineteenth-Century Portrait," *Journal of Presbyterian History* 59 (1981): 17, n. 42.

9. Enoch Pond, *Lectures on Pastoral Theology* (Boston: Draper and Halliday, 1867), p. 314.

10. Lucretia A. Moody, "The Responsibilities of a Pastor's Wife," *Ladies' Repository* 31 (1871): 379–83; Laura Jones, *The Life and Sayings of Sam P. Jones* (Atlanta, Ga.: Franklin-Tarner, 1907).

11. "Ministers' Wives," *United Presbyterian* (28 April 1898): 6.

12. Margaret E. Blackburn, *Things a Pastor's Wife Can Do: By One of Them* (Philadelphia: American Baptist Publication Society, 1898), pp. 5–6, 10–27, 30, 31.

13. Ibid., pp. 70, 72, 73, 54, 39.

14. "Women's Record at Home," *Ladies' Repository* 36 (1876): 173.

15. "The Minister's Wife," *Presbyterian Journal* 24 (14 September 1899): 8.

16. "The Minister's Wife," *Southwest Presbyterian* (10 September 1903): 7.

17. N. D. Williamson," The Perquisites of Preachers' Wives," *Christian Intelligencer*, 66 (1895): 5.

18. "The Ministers' Wives," *United Presbyterian*, 6.

19. "The Minister's Wife," *Presbyterian* 70 (14 February 1900): 10.

20. Marion Harland, "Ministers' Wives," *North American Review* 149 (1889): 375, 371–72, 373.

21. Alice Kessler-Harris, "American Women and the American Character: A Feminist Perspective," in *American Character and Culture in a Changing World*, ed. John A. Hague (Westport, Conn.: Greenwood Press, 1979), p. 232.

22. Catharine Beecher and Harriet Beecher Stowe, *The American Women's Home* (New York: Ford, 1869), p. 19; W. H. Felix, *The Work and Sphere of True Womanhood* (Louisville: Caperton and Cotes, 1877), p. 38.

23. William D. Jenkins, "Housewifery and Motherhood: The Question of Role Change in the Progressive Era," in *Woman's Being, Woman's Place: Female Identity and Vocation in American History*, ed. Mary Kelley (Boston: G. K. Hall, 1979), 142–53.

24. Daniel T. Rodgers, *The Work Ethic in Industrial America, 1850–1920* (Chicago: University of Chicago Press, 1978), p. 185.

25. According to the census of 1870, 6 percent of women were working, and 54 percent of the working women were employed as domestics. *Woman's Journal* 11 (1878): 220.

26. Beverly Wildung Harrison, "The Early Feminists and the Clergy: A Case Study in the Dynamics of Secularization," *Review and Expositor* 72 (1975): 42, n. 3.

27. Elizabeth Cady Stanton, *The Woman's Bible: The Original Feminist Attack on the Bible*, reprint ed. (New York: Arno Press, 1974).

28. Donna A. Behnke, "Forgotten Images: Women in American Methodism," *Explor* 5 (1979): 29.

29. Anne M. Boylan's excellent study "Evangelical Womanhood in

the Nineteenth Century: The Role of Women in Sunday Schools," *Feminist Studies* 4 (1978): 62–80, errs in claiming that "the Superintendent and other officers were always male" (p. 72). See also Boylan's "Sunday Schools and Changing Evangelical Views of Children in the 1820s," *Church History* 48 (1979): 320–33. For examples of women serving as superintendents, see P. H. Fowler, *Historical Sketch of Presbyterianism within the Bounds of the Synod of Central New York* (Utica, N.Y.: Curtiss and Childs, 1877), p. 722; Lot Jones, *Memoirs of Mrs. Sarah Louisa Taylor; or, An Illustration of the Work of the Holy Spirit, in Awakening, Renewing, and Sanctifying the Heart*, 4th ed. (New York: John S. Taylor, 1843), pp. 107–8, 112–13; Harriet E. Bishop, *Floral Home; or, First Years in Minnesota* (New York: Sheldon, Blakeman, 1857; micropublished ed., New Haven: Research Publications, 1975), pp. 85–87, 112; Mary B. Allen King, *Looking Backward; or, Memories of the Past* (New York: Anson D. F. Randolph, 1870), p. 117; William Wilson Manross, *The Episcopal Church in the United States, 1800–1840: A Study in Church Life* (New York: Columbia University Press, 1938), p. 190; Catherine DeKossett Kennedy to Elizabeth DeKossett, 10 November 1837, DeKossett Family Papers, SHC.

30. Helen Barrett Montgomery, *Western Women in Eastern Lands. . .* (New York: Macmillan, 1913), pp. 68–69.

31. Rosemary Skinner Keller, "The Deaconess: 'New Woman' of Late Nineteenth Century Methodism," *Explor* 5 (1979): 40; Richard V. Pierard, "The Bedfellows of Revival and Social Concern," *Christianity Today* 24 (4 April 1980): 25.

32. For women city missionaries, whom I have not discussed, see the career of "America's Florence Nightingale," Lizzie Aiken, as given by Mrs. Galusha Anderson, *The Story of Aunt Lizzie Aiken* (Chicago: Jansen, McClurg, 1880).

33. Pierard, "Bedfellows of Revival and Social Concern," p. 24. The order of deaconess was not unknown to the early settlers of America. Governor William Bradford wrote of a Puritan experiment in Amsterdam with a "deaconess" who visited the sick and needy and on Sunday "sat in a convenient place in the congregation, with a little birchen rod in her hand, and kept little children in great awe from disturbing the congregation." Quoted in John Malcolm Ludlow, *Woman's Work in the Church: Historical Notes on Deaconesses and Sisterhoods* (New York: A. Strahan, 1886; reprint ed., Washington, D.C.: Zenger, 1978), p. 199. In the eighteenth century, William Muhlenberg supported the establishment of religious sisterhoods for unmarried women. See Alvin W. Skardon, *Church Leader in the Cities: William Augustus Muhlenberg* (Philadelphia: University of Pennsylvania Press, 1971).

34. Robert Leonard Tucker, "The Place of Woman in the Church," *Biblical World* 54 (1920): 585; *The Bishop Potter Memorial House: A History of Its Origin, Design, and Operation, Illustrating Woman's Spiritual Mission in the Christian Church* (Philadelphia: King and Baird, 1868); *Ladies' Repository* 35 (1875): 267; Fredrick S. Weiser, *Love's Response: A Story of Lutheran Deaconesses in America* (Philadelphia: Board of Publication of the United Lutheran Church in America, 1962).

35. Jane Marsh Parker, "Scrap Book of Early Writings," p. 96, RPL.

36. Lucy Ryder Meyer, "Deaconesses and Their Work," in Elwood Morris Wherry, comp., *Woman in Missions: Papers and Addresses Presented at the Woman's Congress of Missions, October 2–4, 1893, in the Hall of Columbus, Chicago* (New York: American Tract Society, 1894), pp. 182–97. For an intimate account of a deaconess home, see Margaret E. Todd, "The Providence Deaconess Home," in *Souvenir History of the New England Southern Conference* ed. and comp. Bennetts C. Miller (Nantucket, Mass.: Bennetts C. Miller, 1897), pp. xxxi–xxxviii. The General Conference of the Methodist Episcopal Church, South, created the office of deaconess in 1902.

37. See B. T. Roberts's penetrating chapter on "Deaconesses" in *Ordaining Women* (Rochester, N.Y.: "Earnest Christian" Publishing Office, 1891), pp. 105–110. Rosemary Skinner Keller, though a celebrator of the deaconess movement, is nevertheless sensitive to the conservative rhetoric of some of its supporters. See "The Deaconess," p. 38.

38. Appropriately, the first Methodist parsonage in America was furnished in 1770 by eighteen women who made up the first Ladies' Aid Society in Methodism.

39. J. B. Simmons, *Women's Bible Bands . . .* (Philadelphia: American Baptist Publication Society, 1888), p. 11.

40. For other criticism of the practice of saddling women with the economic cares of the congregation, see Fredrick A. Agar, *"Help Those Women": A Manual for Women Church Workers* (New York: Fleming H. Revell, 1917), pp. 24, 53, 65, 79.

41. See the lament of Thomas Wentworth Higginson, *Women and the Alphabet: A Series of Essays* (1881; reprint ed., Boston and New York: Houghton Mifflin, 1900) p. 179.

42. JBFD 1876–1880, MHS.

43. For Dodge see James H. Smylie, "Notable Presbyterian Women," *Journal of Presbyterian History* 52 (1974): 106–7. For sketches of the seven black women pioneers, see Sadie Iola Daniel, *Women Builders* (Washington, D.C.: Associated Publishers, 1931).

44. An example of such a woman can be found in Emily Faithfull, *Three Visits to America* (New York: Fowler and Wells, 1884), pp. 55–56.

45. Barbara Welter, "She Hath Done What She Could: Protestant Women's Missionary Careers in Nineteenth-Century America," *American Quarterly* 30 (1978): 638.

46. Frances E. Willard, *Women in the Pulpit* (Boston: D. Lothrop, 1888), pp. 62, 55–57. For Willard's career see Ida Tetreault Miller, "Frances E. Willard: Religious Leader and Social Reformer" (Ph.D. diss., Boston University, 1978).

47. An editorial on Gardner appears in the *Ladies' Repository* 31 (1871): 394–95. For Torrey see Roland H. Bainton, "The Office of the Minister's Wife in New England," in *Christian Unity and Religion in New England* (Boston: Beacon Press, 1964), pp. 277–82.

48. Anna J. Copper, *The Life and Writings of Charlotte Forten Grimke*, 2 vols. (n.p., 1951), 1: 37–44, 2: 20–26.

49. Charlotte Forten Grimke: Diary Number Five, November 1885 to July 1892, 21 November, 29 November, 10 December, 29 December 1885; 7 January 1886. M-SRC, CFGD.

50. Prentiss defined the role of a minister's wife thus: "to feel the *right* to sympathize with those who mourn, to fly to them at once, and join them in their prayers and tears." George L. Prentiss, *The Life and Letters of Elizabeth Prentiss* (New York: A. D. F. Randolph, 1882), p. 295, and George L. Prentiss, *The Life of Elizabeth Prentiss: Author of Stepping Heavenward*, rev. ed., 2 vols. (New York: A. D. F. Randolph, 1989), 1: chap. 8, "The Pastor's Wife and Daughter of Consolation"; Edward Smith Parsons, "Lyman Abbot," *Religion in Life* 47 (1978): 313; Rosena Rowe Anderson, *In Memoriam* (n.p., n.d.), pp. 6–9, 13, 24, 28; Lucy Drake Osborn, *Heavenly Pearls Set in a Life: A Record of Experiences and Labors in America, India and Australia* (New York: Fleming H. Revell, 1893), pp. 251, 269, 276–90. For other authors see Lucy Scaman Bainbridge, *Round the World Letters* (Boston: D. Lothrop, 1882), and Marion Harland Terhune, as mentioned in *Ladies' Repository* 35 (1875): 363.

51. Howard Allen Bridgman, "Have We a Religion for Men?" *Andover Review* 13 (1890): 388–96. See also the very slipshod study by the Committee on the War and the Religious Outlook, *Religion among American Men: As Revealed by a Study of Conditions in the Army* (New York: Association Press, 1920).

52. Bari Watkins, "Woman's World in Nineteenth-Century America," *American Quarterly* 31 (1979): 127.

53. James R. McGovern, "David Graham Phillips and the Virility Impulse of Progressives," *New England Quarterly* 39 (1966): 334–55; Jack Dubbert, "Progressivism and the Masculinity Crisis," *Psychoanalytic Review* 61 (1974): 443–55.

54. Ann Douglas, *The Feminization of American Culture* (New York: Alfred A. Knopf, 1977), pp. 124–30; I. W. Willey, "The Contemplation of Christ," *Ladies' Repository* 26 (1866): 9.

55. Don Harrison Doyle, *The Social Order of a Frontier Community: Jacksonville, Illinois, 1825–70* (Urbana: University of Illinois Press, 1978), p. 177.

56. "Phillips Brooks the Preacher," in Mary Clemmer Ames, *Men, Women, and Things* (Boston: Ticknor, 1886), pp. 69–70; Thomas Hughes, *The Manliness of Christ* (Boston: Houghton, Osgood, 1880); E. P. Roe, *Rose Barriers Burned Away* (New York: Dodd and Mead, 1872); Lew Wallace, *Ben-Hur, a Tale of Christ* (New York: Harper, 1880); Carl Delos Case, *The Masculine in Religion* (Philadelphia: American Baptist Publication Society, 1906); Harry Emerson Fosdick, *The Manhood of the Master* (1913; reprint ed., New York: Association Press, 1958).

57. As quoted by William T. Doherty, Jr., "Nineteenth Century Businessmen and Religion," *North Dakota Quarterly* 46 (1978): 7.

58. The quotation is from the University of Chicago president William Rainey Harper, *Trends in Higher Education* (Chicago: University of Chicago Press, 1905), pp. 67–67. The American sermon on the bicycle is

excerpted in Clyde Binfield, "Congregationalism's Baptist Grandmothers and Methodist Great Aunts: The Place of Family in a Felt Religion," *United Reform Church History Society Journal* 2 (April 1978): 8.

59. Department of Commerce, Bureau of the Census, *Religious Bodies: 1916* (Washington, D.C.: Government Printing Office, 1919), part 1, p. 41.

60. Howard Grimes, "The United States, 1800–1962," in *The Layman in Christian History: A Project of the Department of the World Council of Churches,* ed. Stephen Charles Neil and Hans-Rueli Weber (London: SCM Press, 1963), p. 248. Earlier efforts at men's religious societies never got off the ground. For examples of efforts that failed, see Rufus Babcock, Jr., "The Claims of Education Societies; Especially on the Young Men of Our Country," *Baptist Preacher* 3 (1830): 53–70; Orlo J. Price, *The Significance of the Early Religious History of Rochester,* Publication Fund Series, vol. 3 (Rochester: Rochester Historical Society, 1924), p. 4.

61. Reverdy C. Ransom, *The Pilgrimage of Harriet Ransom's Son* (Nashville: Sunday School Union, n.d.), pp. 82–83.

62. Ames, *Men, Women, and Things,* p. 298. For an early attack on the husband's abnegation of authority in the home, see the volume by the Vermont diocese's bishop of the Protestant Episcopal church, John Henry Hopkins, *The American Citizen* (n.p., 1857), p. 280.

63. Harrison, "Early Feminists and the Clergy," 42, n. 3.

64. This is especially evident in Pond's *Lectures on Pastoral Theology.*

65. See as an example D. F. Bonner's *The Educational Position and Work of Woman* (Philadelphia: George S. Ferguson, 1878), pp. 37–40.

66. *Journal of the General Conference of the Methodist Episcopal Church: 1840, 1844,* 2 vols. (New York: Carlton and Phillips, 1856), 2: 52–53; *Ladies' Repository* 36 (1876): 180–86.

67. James M. Hoppin, *The Office and Work of the Christian Ministry* (New York: Sheldon, 1869), pp. 341, 460–61.

68. Ibid., p. 460.

Index

Note: Asterisk indicates status as a minister's wife.